D0078615

MANNING THE NEW NAVY

Recent Titles in
Contributions in American History
SERIES EDITOR: Jon L. Wakelyn

Henry Highland Garnet: A Voice of Black Radicalism in the Nineteenth Century
Joel Schor

Blacks in the American Revolution
Philip S. Foner

The Prophet's Army: Trotskyists in America, 1928-1941
Constance Ashton Myers

American Revolutionary: A Biography of General Alexander McDougall
William L. MacDougall

Working Dress in Colonial and Revolutionary America
Peter F. Copeland

In the Almost Promised Land: American Jews and Blacks, 1915-1935
Hasia R. Diner

Essays in Nineteenth-Century American Legal History
Wythe Holt, editor

A Right to the Land: Essays on the Freedmen's Community
Edward Magdol

Essays on American Music
Garry E. Clarke

Culture and Diplomacy: The American Experience
Morrell Heald and Lawrence S. Kaplan

Voting in Provincial America: A Study of Elections in the Thirteen Colonies, 1689-1776
Robert J. Dinkin

The French Forces in America, 1780-1783
Lee Kennett

Cold War Political Justice: The Smith Act, the Communist Party, and American Civil Liberties
Michal R. Belknap

The Many-Faceted Jacksonian Era: New Interpretations
Edward Pessen, editor

Manning the New Navy

THE DEVELOPMENT OF A MODERN NAVAL ENLISTED FORCE, 1899-1940

Frederick S. Harrod

Contributions in American History, Number 68

GREENWOOD PRESS
westport, connecticut . london, england

Library of Congress Cataloging in Publication Data

Harrod, Frederick S.
Manning the new Navy.

(Contributions in American history; no. 68
ISSN 0084-9219)
Based on the author's thesis, Northwestern University.
Bibliography: p.
Includes index.
1. United States. Navy—Recruiting, enlistment, etc.
—History. 2. Seamen—United States—History. I. Title.
VB263.H37 359.2 77-82697
ISBN 0-8371-9759-7

Library of Congress Catalog Number: 77-82697
ISBN: 0-8371-9759-7
ISSN: 0084-9219

First published in 1978

Greenwood Press, Inc.
51 Riverside Avenue, Westport, Connecticut 06880

Printed in the United States of America

Acknowledgment

"The Navy Marriage Ceremony as It Could Be" is reprinted with permission from *Our Navy*, vol. 31 (May 1, 1937).

10 9 8 7 6 5 4 3 2 1

To Kathleen

Contents

Preface

Enlisted personnel are the forgotten men of naval history. Historians write of tactics and technology but ignore the people who compose the service. This omission leads to accounts that are not so much incorrect as incomplete. It is obvious that the ability and character of the enlisted force affect the performance of a navy; yet the consistency with which this fact is disregarded makes repetition necessary.

Because enlisted men have been studied so little, there are many more aspects of the subject that deserve attention than can possibly be included in a single monograph. I have chosen to concentrate on the first part of the twentieth century, since those were the crucial years in which the navy was building a modern enlisted force to man the new ships coming into commission. Even within this period, not every topic can be considered. I feel that the best place to start is with those policies that determined the basic personnel structure. I therefore have focused primarily on the measures the Navy Department adopted as it strove to create an enlisted force that met its twentieth-century manpower needs. For perspective, I have also briefly examined the personnel practices of the old navy in the years following the Civil War.

Writing about enlisted men presents several difficulties. First is the question of continuity. Change occurred neither suddenly nor completely. Reforms were often suggested years before they were implemented, and old ways sometimes persisted after a new policy had been officially adopted. Changes in the kind of men recruited thus did not mean that the older type of sailor immediately disappeared. As a consequence, a study of this nature reveals trends rather than abrupt transformations, and dates often serve as convenient markers rather than as precise turning points.

Closely related to the problem of continuity is that of size. However convenient it is stylistically to write of the enlisted "man," he is not one man but many men. The enlisted force consists of nonrated men, petty officers, and chief petty officers. It includes recruits just a few days removed from first enlistment and veterans with years of duty at sea. Each person, in addition, experiences the navy in a different way. Such diversity naturally produces contradictions to every generalization; nevertheless, changes were taking place, and it is possible to discuss trends in matters relating to the enlisted force.

Another difficulty in studying enlisted men arises from the nature of the sources. There are no personnel files for men who served before 1885. The files of those who served after 1885 are stored in the National Personnel Records Center in St. Louis, Missouri. Unfortunately, these folders are not yet open for general research but are available only to the individuals whose records they are, their next of kin, or agencies of the government. Although it might be possible to obtain access to some records, any useful study would require a sample of all men and not just of those men who could be located today and who would give permission for their files to be used.

The unavailability of personnel folders presents a serious but not insurmountable obstacle to studying the history of enlisted personnel. For the twentieth century, other sources supply some of the information that might be obtained from personnel files. Nineteenth-century records such as enlistment returns sometimes make it possible to compile comparable data for the enlisted force of the old navy. Many questions, however, must remain unanswered. The twentieth-century navy, for example, believed that its best men came from small towns in mid-America. This judgment could be tested by correlating place of birth and residence at enlistment with such indices of success in the navy as length of service, advancement, and number of infractions against discipline. Without the personnel jackets, these comparisons cannot be made.

Of the records available, the files of the Navy Department in the National Archives are the most valuable. Within the naval collections, the Records of the Bureau of Naval Personnel, Record Group 24, have been the most useful for this study because they delineate policies on a broad range of enlisted matters.

Other sources supplement official records. A few enlisted men wrote autobiographies, and I have corresponded with and interviewed some former bluejackets. Several magazines also catered to sailors and provided a forum for their opinions. The most important of these was *Our Navy*, which was published from 1909 to 1972. The private papers and memoirs of officers sometimes mention the men and thus provide yet another view. The *United States Naval Institute Proceedings* carried articles giving officers' views on enlisted topics. In addition, items relating to enlisted personnel occasionally appeared in other publications—from reports of congressional hearings to popular magazines. There is, however, almost a total lack of secondary material concerning enlisted personnel for the years covered by this study.

The subject is ignored even in a journal such as *American Neptune,* which attempts to cover a broad range of naval and maritime history.

During the course of my study I have received assistance from many people. I wish first to thank Richard W. Leopold of Northwestern University, who provided guidance, advice, and encouragement while I was writing the dissertation on which this book is based. Charles C. Moskos, Jr., and Sterling Stuckey of Northwestern University, Dean C. Allard and Vice Admiral Edwin B. Hooper of the Navy Department, Naval History Division, Neville T. Kirk of the United States Naval Academy, and Jon L. Wakelyn of Catholic University read the manuscript at various stages and made many helpful suggestions. Robert L. Clarke of the National Archives offered valuable comments on the sections dealing with blacks. I have also benefited from frequent conversations on naval history with David Healy of the University of Wisconsin-Milwaukee. Responsibility for errors and omissions, of course, remains with me.

Others have helped in the course of my research. Staff members of the National Archives directed me through the often confusing navy files; in particular, I extend my gratitude to Harry Schwartz, Peter N. Laugesen, Elaine C. Everly, Cary Conn, and Gibson Smith. Archivists of the Southern Historical Collection, the Manuscript Division of the Library of Congress, and the Naval History Division facilitated my use of the papers in their care. Walter B. Greenwood and Fred S. Meigs of the Navy Department Library also aided my search for material. In addition, I wish to thank the former enlisted men who added to my understanding of navy life: Orlie L. Bennett, Myrln F. Fischer, Charles A. Herget, Arnold S. Lott, Clarence O'C. McDonagh, Sr., Donald M. McPherson, Mitchell Nykiel, George Sutton, Earl Wanton, and Van Watts. The editors of *Our Navy* helped in locating many of these men by publishing my letter seeking information from bluejackets who had served before 1940.

The Graduate School of the University of Wisconsin-Milwaukee funded both a summer of research and a computer study of nineteenth-century muster rolls and enlistment returns. The Social Science Research Facility of the same university lent technical assistance for that project. Gladys Shimasaki and Sharon Lannon typed drafts of the manuscript with speed and accuracy. Finally, I wish to thank my wife, Kathleen A. Mach, who provided invaluable criticism and editorial assistance throughout the project.

Frederick S. Harrod

MANNING THE NEW NAVY

chapter 1

Introduction

In 1906 the United States Navy published a pamphlet called *The Making of a Man-o'-Warsman,* its first illustrated recruiting brochure prepared by a professional advertising agency.[1] The title evoked romantic images of deep-water sailors on high-masted frigates; yet, ironically, the booklet was issued when the traditional "man-of-warsman" was rapidly becoming a part of the past and was giving way to a new breed of sailor-technician.

This revolution in enlisted personnel stemmed from a transformation of the fleet itself. During most of the nineteenth century, the navy had been a relatively stable institution. Until the 1880s and 1890s, it had relied on wooden vessels whose primary means of propulsion was wind power.[2] Although the Navy Department was aware of the new naval technology that was being developed during the nineteenth century, it clung to tradition and adopted innovations so slowly that the changes that were made did not require major alterations in its personnel system. Steam warships, for example, entered the fleet with the launching of the *Mississippi* and *Missouri* in 1842, but these vessels also carried sails and were primarily wind driven, with steam available in case of need.[3] During the Civil War, the demands of blockade duty and river warfare increased the use of steam. With the return of peace, however, the service retreated to an older sense of priorities and emphasized maneuvering under sail whenever possible, even though most ships were equipped with steam engines.

The navy resisted a full commitment to new technology in other areas as well. Rather than adopt shell-firing guns that were available from midcentury on, for example, the American force retained the old solid shot for another thirty years. Similarly, the service was unenthusiastic about developing an oceangoing armored ship. The shallow-draft monitors that it had used during the Civil War were in many ways the most modern ships in the world. Yet, at the end of that conflict, most of these vessels were laid up or sold off, and the navy abandoned further development of armored ships.

The naval personnel system reflected this essentially static technology. The number of enlisted men that the service required remained relatively constant, fluctuating between 6,500 and 10,000 from the mid-1830s until the eve of the Spanish-American War, except for a temporary surge to 50,000 during the Civil War.[4] Furthermore, since the technology the service employed changed so little, the skills that the men needed also remained virtually unaltered. Most of the crew were sailors in the literal sense of the word—individuals who handled the canvas of the ship. Criteria for these seamen were not stringent. Men were prized "more for their strength than intelligence," and needed only "to be able to reef, furl, and steer."[5] Persons possessing these skills were enlisted for naval service from the pool of professional mariners readily available in the ports of the world.[6]

While the American fleet retained time-honored equipment and practices in the years after the Civil War, other navies were embracing radically new technology. They reduced the area of sail, added armor, and installed more deadly armament. Compared to the ships of the British and French navies, American vessels resembled floating museums rather than warships; they evoked nostalgia from visiting officers, but certainly not awe. So strong was the American commitment to the traditional warship that in 1873, when Congress authorized the first new naval vessels since the Civil War, these ships resembed the vessels the American navy already possessed rather than ships being developed abroad.

The obsolescence of the American ships produced increasing demands for modernization of the fleet. In addition, evidence of corruption or mismanagement in the maintenance of the vessels focused attention on the state of the navy. Spurred by charges of waste and weakness in the service, in 1876 Congress began an investigation of the Navy Department. Although this action was partly a Democratic effort to embarrass the Republican administration, the evidence demonstrated that the American navy was a poorly managed institution. These revelations strengthened critics inside and outside the service who were demanding reform. As a first step in changing the navy, in 1882 Congress limited ship repairs to 30 percent of the cost of a new vessel of the same size and class; the next year it reduced the amount to 20 percent of replacement cost. The measure was adopted to prevent the navy from undertaking expensive repairs to unsound and increasingly antiquated ships.

This limitation on repairs assured the retirement of increasing numbers of ships. As a consequence, Congress also turned to the question of providing new vessels. For guidance it had not only the results of its own investigation but also the report of the First Naval Advisory Board, which Secretary of the Navy William H. Hunt had appointed to consider the number and types of ships the service needed. In November 1881 the board recommended construction of sixty-eight vessels at an estimated total cost of $29,607,000.

Congress rejected such grandiose suggestions. Instead, in 1883 it authorized four steel vessels—the cruisers *Atlanta, Boston,* and *Chicago* and the dispatch boat *Dolphin.* Because these four ships possessed many modern features, they mark the beginning of the so-called new navy. Congress continued to add other ships, until by 1889 it had approved thirty-four vessels of different classes—including the battleships *Maine* and *Texas.*

These new ships, and the worldwide naval race of which they were a part, thrust the service into the limelight in a way that it had not been before. From the time of its founding the navy had been ignored by most Americans; even newspapers in coastal cities paid little attention to the doings of the fleet. The gleaming white vessels of the new navy changed that. They became national status symbols, and interest in and knowledge of the navy spread across the continent. At Chicago's Columbian Exposition of 1893, for example, the navy exhibited a brick replica of a modern battleship; thousands of eager citizens toured the "ship" during the fair. Coincident with the exposition, the service hosted a naval review on the East Coast to which other major naval powers sent vessels. Proud American editors compared United States men-of-war to those of other nations.[7]

The new ships were soon to require basic changes in personnel matters. In the past the navy had largely disregarded its enlisted personnel system since it had been able to secure enough men without major innovations. As the new ships reached completion, however, the service found itself struggling to recruit the number of sailors needed to man them. As shown in table 1 of the Appendix, the authorized enlisted force had been stabilized at 8,250 through the 1880s and the first few years of the 1890s. By 1897 it had reached 10,000 men and boys. Dramatic growth began to occur after the Spanish-American War, when new ships were commissioned at a rapid rate. Authorized strength doubled between 1899 and 1903, growing from 13,750 to 28,000. By 1908 it had nearly tripled, increasing to 38,900. The numbers continued to climb until 1913, when it leveled off at 51,500 until American entry into World War I.

Recruiting large numbers of men was not the navy's only manpower problem. Crews on modern warships needed skills far different from those of their predecessors of just a few years before. With the abandonment of sail, many ratings became unnecessary. At the same time, the introduction of such varied innovations as electric motors, gyrocompasses, and self-propelled torpedoes required men trained to operate and maintain this sophisticated equipment. Yet the department's previous policies had not been designed to develop such skills.

Recognizing the inadequacy of its personnel policies, in the early twentieth century the navy undertook important changes to secure the men it needed. To meet the sheer numerical demands of the new ships, it turned its attention away from the nation's ports, which could no longer fill their traditional role as the main supplier of sailors to the fleet, and carried its recruiting into inland areas. Enlisting men throughout the country forced the department to develop a larger, more efficient recruiting service and to advertise on an unprecedented scale. Since it could no longer be assumed that most young men entering the service had previous sea experience, training stations had to be established to initiate recruits in their duties before assigning them to cruising vessels. Additional instruction prepared men to care for the various components of modern warships. Because these new recruiting and training ventures involved considerable effort and expense, the department also sought to encourage men to remain in the navy by adopting new measures to improve service life and the benefits of service.

The shift to securing men from inland areas was greatly facilitated by existing pronavy sentiment across the country. The favorable publicity of rebuilding during the nineties had been followed by the stunning victories of the Spanish-American War, which in turn had given way to the presidency of naval enthusiast Theodore Roosevelt. The tasks of securing relatively large numbers of men and of covering increasingly large areas strained the recruiting service, but the navy was assured a sympathetic hearing wherever it went.

Inland recruiting, furthermore, changed the character of the navy in a way that pleased both the service and the nation. During the nineteenth century the navy had been a multinational force. As the fleet became a symbol of national power, it became increasingly important to officers that bluejackets embody what was felt to be the best youth in the nation. The twentieth-century navy boasted that its personnel represented respectable families from the heartland of America rather than what it considered disreputable elements from the waterfronts. The new sailors, it claimed, sought recreation in museums rather than in barrooms. These changes, furthermore, increased the identification of landlocked areas with the navy, and this fact reinforced any existing attitude favorable to the service.

The measures that the navy adopted fundamentally altered its personnel system and formed the basis for the recruiting and training of today's navy. Yet, as revolutionary as they were, they were undertaken surprisingly rapidly—virtually all were begun within a decade after the Spanish-American War. The remainder of the period until the Second World War produced refinements of the basic structure created earlier, but at no time would the navy undergo such basic personnel changes as it had between 1899 and 1910.

If anything could have jarred the new personnel system, it would have been the chaos of the First World War. From 1917 through 1921 the enlisted force was in constant flux. On March 25, 1917, Secretary of the Navy Josephus Daniels dispatched an urgent telegram to over a thousand newspapers announcing that the president had authorized a large increase in the navy.[8] Once the United States entered the conflict on April 6, 1917, the service grew even larger, experiencing more than a sixfold increase during the war, from 86,000 in April 1917 to almost 532,000 in November 1918.[9] With the signing of the armistice, the service contracted with equal suddenness as the rush to join became a scramble to get out. Compounding the difficulties of postwar reductions was an almost complete turnover of personnel. During the months after the war, the navy lost many of its experienced men. On June 30, 1920, for example, 91,390 men of a force of 108,950 had served less than four years; worse still, 43,381 had enlisted in the previous twelve months.[10]

During these hectic four years, the navy passed hurriedly from crisis to crisis in dealing with its manpower problems. Yet, in spite of the stress, existing personnel methods remained essentially intact. At the beginning of the war, facilities for recruiting and training were expanded, but the methods employed remained the same. An increasingly formal bureaucratic structure was adopted to deal with the larger number of enlisted men, but few new functions were undertaken. The policies developed in the first years of the century had proved adequate to handle even the extraordinary problems of the war and the postwar adjustment.

By late 1921 the navy had largely recovered from the turmoil that had characterized it since 1917. A convenient date for the service's "return to normalcy" is October 1921, when the Great Lakes and Newport Naval Training Stations temporarily stopped receiving recruits. The postwar crush had ended, and by 1923 the service had acquired an enlisted force of the size it would maintain until World War II—between 80,000 and 90,000 men.[11]

Having survived the demands of the war years, the personnel system was easily adapted to peacetime. In the twenties the enlisted force maintained a stable size with an increasing number of experienced men. Reenlistment, desertion, and court-martial rates improved steadily. The depression, a watershed in many areas, had only a slight impact on the enlisted force—most noticeably contributing to increased reenlistment. The thirties, in fact, merely followed the pattern established in the twenties, and the entire interwar period has a unity that discourages division.

After two decades of relative calm, the navy experienced another period of upheaval during World War II. As the demands of war accelerated the reliance of the services on sophisticated technology, the enlisted man became even more of a specialist.[12] Yet the navy had instituted wide-ranging reforms in enlisted policy earlier in the century; by World War II it already had devised a basic system for recruiting, training, and holding the skilled manpower on which it could build to meet the new emergency.

chapter 2

The Old Navy, 1865-98

In the early twentieth century, veteran enlisted men fondly reminisced about the days of "wooden ships and iron men." Although their boast of the superiority of the old navy to the new is debatable, the differences in ships and men were real enough. During the first century of its existence, the navy had sought professional seamen to fill enlisted ranks; its policies of recruiting, training, and treatment of sailors assumed that such men would dominate the crews. These policies were as different from those of the twentieth century as frigates were from battleships.

The men the nineteenth-century navy usually enlisted belonged to an easily identifiable international seafaring population. Work at sea isolated mariners from other groups, and even when sailors went ashore, they remained near waterfront areas. These habits greatly simplified recruiting. When advertising was needed, the navy merely placed posters in areas "most frequented by *sailor men*."[1] Nor was it necessary to send agents inland to fill enlisted ranks. In fact, permanent recruiting stations—or rendezvous—were maintained only in the few coastal cities that possessed navy yards—Boston, New York, Philadelphia, Norfolk, San Francisco, Portsmouth, New Hampshire, and Washington, D.C. As an alternative method of recruiting, captains of vessels were permitted to enlist men to fill vacancies in their complements while their ships were in port anywhere in the world. Shipboard enlistment was an important source of manpower—between one-third and one-half of the men serving in the latter part of the nineteenth century were enlisted directly by captains rather than through rendezvous.[2]

The navy encountered greater difficulties in recruiting on the West Coast than along the eastern seaboard. Labor was relatively scarce in the West, and adequate numbers of men were difficult to obtain. In 1875, for example, the commanding officer of the *Portsmouth* complained that "in consequence of the high rate of pay in gold and the inducements offered to sober and reliable men on this coast" he was unable to recruit the kind of men he desired.[3] To attract men on the Pacific Coast, the navy at one time offered a ten-dollar bounty to men who enlisted, but apparently it did not maintain this practice.[4] Without any clear solution to the manpower shortage, officers in that region frequently could recruit only those individuals who were having trouble earning a living as civilians.[5]

Obtaining mariners on the Pacific Coast plagued the merchant marine as well as the navy. Indeed, securing crews was sometimes so difficult that skippers resorted to shanghaiing to fill their rosters. Occasionally navy men fell victim to this practice, as did George Williams, who while on liberty in San Francisco in 1867 was "shanghaied or drugged" and sent aboard the merchantman *Lizzie Oakford*.[6] A year later a similar fate befell Jonathan Simon, who was shanghaied onto a ship fittingly named the *Blue Jacket* and taken to Liverpool as an able seaman.[7] Shanghaiing affected few sailors, but the fact that some merchant captains felt compelled to use such methods underscores the manpower problems in the West. Yet even in this area where the old system was being strained, the navy made no significant innovations in recruiting. Instead, traditional practices prevailed until almost the end of the nineteenth century.

The old recruiting system persisted because, despite its shortcomings, it met the overall manpower needs of the service during the late nineteenth century. The navy desired enlistees who were already familiar with their duties and who therefore required little or no training for their jobs. Such men dominated the force. A sample of muster rolls from the years 1870, 1880, and 1890 supports this fact. Approximately two-thirds of all enlisted men reported previous occupations that were employable aboard ships. Of these, over a third listed "mariner" as their previous occupation; about 10 percent recorded engine-room skills, with fireman and machinist most common among these; and another 20 percent listed occupations immediately useful aboard ship—approximately half of the 20 percent were cooks, stewards, and waiters, and the remainder followed such trades as carpenter, painter, sailmaker, and musician.[8]

Not every sailor had pursued a skill directly transferable to the service before enlistment. Some listed a variety of previous occupations—cigar-maker, shoemaker, salesman, and puddler, to name just a few. A sizable number (from 6 to 8 percent) also recorded "laborer," and an even larger group (from 11 to 17 percent) entered "none." Those who listed no previous occupation on the muster rolls included many apprentices, who composed 20.2 percent of the enlisted force in 1880 and 17.2 percent in 1890 and who were often too young to have had a job before enlistment. In 1870, when no apprentices were enlisted, and to a lesser degree in later years, "none" seems to have been used as a synonym for "laborer" since many of the men were of an age that they had undoubtedly earned a living in some way.

Because most enlistees were familiar with shipboard routine, the sailing navy offered little special preparation even to men who had never been to sea. After 1826 the service did begin placing receiving ships in major ports to house men who were waiting transfer to cruising vessels. On these ships recruits learned the handling of masts, yards, and sails, as time permitted.[9] Over the years, some additions to the instruction were made, but the course remained brief, and upon enlistment most men went almost immediately to sea to fare as best they could.[10]

Although preferring to enlist experienced men, the nineteenth-century navy placed few other restrictions on the type of recruit it sought. In sharp contrast to the policies it would adopt in the early twentieth century, the service did not practice official racial discrimination in accepting applicants. In 1870, for example, the Bureau of Equipment and Recruiting, the unit responsible for enlisted personnel, replied to an officer's query about "what portion or percentage of the recruits are to be colored men" by stating that they "may be enlisted without other limits" than those governing general recruitment.[11] The level of black enlistment reflects this policy: blacks constituted 10 percent of all enlistees in 1870, 14 percent in 1880, and 9.5 percent in 1890.[12] Once aboard navy ships, they served as seamen, firemen, jacks-of-the-dust (storekeepers), carpenters, water tenders, oilers, and in other specialized billets. Since men ate and slept in the company of shipmates performing similar functions, this integration of work assignments produced integrated messing and berthing. In addition, blacks were permitted to enlist as naval apprentices. Because the navy selected apprentices with the hope that these young men would form the core of its future enlisted force, the existence of blacks in this rating demonstrates that the service was willing to incorporate at least a small number of blacks as permanent members of all parts of the enlisted force.[13]

Even though the navy was a comparatively open institution in the late nineteenth century, it did not escape the prejudice of the era. For example, only a handful of blacks served as second- or third-class petty officers, and none was listed as a first-class petty officer in the second quarter of 1870, 1880, or 1890. Furthermore, blacks were much more likely than whites to have served as cooks, stewards, and landsmen.[14] Although landsmen performed a variety of unskilled tasks aboard ship, it is likely that many blacks holding that rating acted as messmen—a category not created until 1893. In fact, one former black sailor defined "landsman" as "the service designation for domestics."[15]

There is correspondence during the late nineteenth century that also suggests that, although blacks were not rejected automatically, neither were they always interchangeable with white applicants. In December 1874, for example, an officer at the Norfolk navy yard reported: "Regarding the probability of enlisting the requisite number of men to fill up the crew of the 'Brooklyn,' I would state that there are no men offering here for enlistment except a few colored men."[16]

Other evidence also indicates a worsening status for black sailors after the Civil War. Although the level of their enlistment remained relatively stable, the type of blacks entering the service seems to have changed. Enlistment returns reveal that at the same time the proportion of blacks who listed mariner as their previous occupation decreased from 13.1 percent in 1870 to 5.9 percent in 1890, the percentage of blacks who had been cooks and waiters increased from 28.9 percent to 49.3 percent. The place of birth of black enlistees also indicates the shifting character of black sailors. In the period from 1870 to 1890 the importance of northern states declined, and the proportion of men from the Upper South—especially from Virginia and Maryland—grew.[17] In part the preponderance of men from these two states reflects the convergence of naval installations and black populations; nevertheless, few of the applicants from these states had had previous sea experience, and the navy thus seems to have been losing interest in blacks who could serve as seamen and preferring those who could be employed as domestic servants.

Despite such evidence of the inequality of black sailors, the status of blacks in the late nineteenth-century navy was better than it would be later. The department had not yet institutionalized racial discrimination, as it would do in the twentieth century. Instead, it allowed individual officers to advance or restrict blacks on the basis of their personnel needs or their own prejudices. The result was a confusing pattern in which blacks were neither equal to white seamen nor yet the victims of complete and systematic discrimination.

Although generally able to obtain the relatively small number of men it needed, the old navy was never totally satisfied with the personnel it attracted. The service was often thought of as the last refuge of the drunken or incompetent.[18] Even the Bureau of Equipment and Recruiting admitted that "some of our best men in the Navy suffer from alcoholism."[19] The sailors' love of alcohol was so strong that liquor sometimes proved a more effective incentive than money. When the *Monadnock* needed extra men to serve in the fireroom in 1865, for example, an initial call for volunteers that offered the inducement of an extra forty cents per day produced only three men. The same offer to which had been appended an additional incentive of half a gill of whiskey per day quickly elicited seventeen responses.[20] Since the grog ration had ceased in 1862, this payment provided a rare opportunity for legal liquor aboard ship.[21]

Nineteenth-century sailors were in general a rough and coarse lot. Working the ship required hard physical labor, and even on vessels that had steam engines, most tasks were performed without motorized help. When not at work, the men endured living conditions that were damp, crowded, and cramped. In the vessels of the old navy, "human beings are crowded together . . . breathing a scanty supply of air vitiated by the retention of their own excretions."[22]

A wide variety of factors contributed to the unpleasant nature of shipboard living. Because bilges on many ships were too small to clean easily, they were often simply ignored. As a result, dirt, grease, and water collected and the bilges became "fecund generators of noxious vapors."[23] The unprotected outside location of the head at the side of the deck on many ships compounded discomforts. Surgeon J. B. Parker of the *Wachusett* protested that the resulting "exposure of the men during severe weather and gales, especially at night when in a partly nude condition and on leaving the fire-room, cannot fail to increase the sick list and cause invaliding."[24]

The most frequently voiced complaints, however, dealt with overcrowding and poor ventilation. Even though hammock hooks were only fourteen inches apart, many vessels could not accommodate both watches at once, as they had to do when a ship was in port.[25] Because the only ventilation came through hatches, the air below decks was usually stagnant. On the *Minnesota*, there was "an almost sickening odor prevailing [on the berth deck] at night, after the men have gone to their hammocks."[26] Poor ventilation also prevented rapid drying of areas between decks; as a consequence, the men often lived in continual dampness. Water seeped in around caulking in the hull, fell through hatches in stormy weather, and was brought in with wet clothing. In addition, some captains had their crews wet down the decks every day in pursuit of cleanliness. Medical officers almost uniformly argued that the dampness inside ships was more dangerous to sailors than the sea itself. Yet efforts to develop forced-air ventilation systems in the nineteenth century never advanced beyond the experimental stage.[27]

Although many officers in the old navy recognized that conditions aboard ship needed improvement, little was done. Indeed, in 1876 Captain Robert W. Shufeldt, chief of the Bureau of Equipment and Recruiting, charged that "it is a rare thing to see anything in the outfit of a man-of-war intended to enhance the comfort or even protect the health of the enlisted men." Shufeldt also protested that there was a "constantly-increasing tendency of the officers' accommodations on board of a ship in our service to encroach upon the space allotted to the crew."[28] These complaints, though, did not achieve any significant results, and shipboard habitability did not improve noticeably until the construction of the modern fleet.

The navy was not totally unaware of the lot of its men. Secretary of the Navy Gideon Welles wrote that "measures should be taken to ameliorate and improve their condition."[29] Officers often recommended new enlisted personnel policies during the nineteenth century, but little came of these ideas. When the commanding officer of the receiving ship at Mare Island proposed erecting a gymnasium for enlisted men at the yard, for example, the department quickly rejected his suggestion, though it did offer dumbbells and boxing gloves for use on the ship.[30] The most frequently made suggestion was to give a clothing allowance to men at enlistment and thus to eliminate the necessity of recruits' going into debt to satisfy uniform regulations. Almost as common were recommendations to create a savings program that permitted sailors to deposit money with paymasters.[31]

A few reforms were adopted. After 1855 a sailor could receive a slight increase in pay plus a bonus of three months' wages if he enlisted within three months of receiving an honorable discharge. This policy had great potential impact. The three months' pay upon reenlistment in effect provided a paid vacation between cruises. Before this time many sailors had shipped out again almost immediately; under such circumstances family life was impossible. With time ashore between enlistments, a sailor could remain with his family for a reasonable period. The presence of such benefits, if they had reached a larger number of men, would have greatly increased the attractiveness of the service. Few men, however, enlisted with continuous service.[32]

Naval life also offered some provisions for old age. Although there was no retirement for men in the navy until 1899, old sailors were not totally neglected before that time. A man incapacitated by injury or age could either seek admission to the Naval Home in Philadelphia or apply for relief from the naval pension fund, to which all personnel contributed monthly. Older sailors also frequently secured assignment to receiving ships, where duties were lighter than on cruising vessels.[33]

These few benefits of naval life did little to improve the stability or change the character of the enlisted force. In fact, officers' complaints about the men continued throughout the century. Most of their grievances centered on the high level of desertion and the large number of foreigners in the navy.

Desertion had plagued the navy throughout its history. Although there were fluctuations in numbers, approximately a thousand men from a total authorized strength of about eight thousand deserted each year in the post-Civil War era.[34] At times desertion almost amounted to mass flight. Captain William G. Temple of the *Tennessee* reported in 1871 that fifty-one of his crew had deserted during just two weeks at the New York navy yard. In another incident, Commander Francis A. Roe complained that his ship's boats "would go ashore and men would leap out and run. If the officer followed, the whole Boat's crew would likely desert."[35]

Although the navy recognized the extent of desertion, the causes usually baffled the service. In a few cases it claimed that civilians lured sailors away. In one incident reported in 1874 the chief officer of a merchant steamer persuaded at least one navy man to jump ship at Panama.[36] More often, reports involved agents to whom merchant skippers offered rewards for securing men at difficult times. The navy was never able, however, to attribute more than a handful of desertions to such actions of third parties.

Examining the question further, many officers condemned the advance wages that were given to encourage enlistment. For over a decade after the Civil War the navy followed the practice of prepaying wages to recruits; the amounts varied, but they were never more than three months' pay.[37] Sailors often used advances to meet obligations they had incurred to boardinghouse proprietors. As a consequence, these landlords acquired unwelcome influence in the recruiting process.

Coming ashore at the end of a cruise on either a merchant or naval vessel, mariners frequently lodged in rooming houses that catered to the seafaring trade. When it was time to ship out again, many sailors found themselves indebted to the owners of the boardinghouses, and they readily permitted the landlords to serve as agents to secure new positions for them. After the men signed on to a vessel, they received their advances, and the landlords then received the money owed them. This relationship gave the agents control over many mariners. Landlords thus had "great power to advance or retard the enlistment of Seamen for the Navy."[38] The navy, in fact, frequently found itself unable to act independently of them.[39]

The service's dislike of this unsolicited civilian participation in recruiting was compounded by evidence of fraud in the conduct of many landlords who desired "to get the *whole*" of the sailor's advance.[40] These men inflated legitimate bills and duped the seamen of yet additional sums. Sometimes they told sailors that the navy recruiting officer demanded a bribe before he would accept them. The seamen usually paid the agents without knowing that the officer had neither required nor received the bribe. At other times, agents took money from the men with a promise of delivering liquor or other items but never returned to the ship.[41] Officers believed that men victimized in this way at enlistment frequently became discouraged by the thought of repaying an advance that had slipped through their fingers so rapidly and therefore deserted.[42]

Many officers associated desertion with the advance-wage system per se, regardless of whether sailors were cheated. They argued that even though the men wanted the money when they enlisted, the prospect of their working up to three months to repay the advance produced discontent. They also contended that the navy's practice of forbidding or limiting liberty to men who owed the government money helped foster an unhappiness that led to desertion.[43]

Despite the fact that many officers considered the advance-wage system a major cause of desertion, evidence indicates no direct correlation between advances and the desertion rate. Indeed, a decline in the practice of granting advances had no noticeable effect on desertion. In 1870, 63 percent of the men joining received advances, which averaged $36.07; only 10 percent of the enlistees in 1880 were paid advances, which in that year averaged only $10.14; no advances at all were given in 1890.[44] Yet, instead of following this downward trend, the rate of desertion fluctuated from 12 percent in 1870, to 8 percent in 1880 and 12 percent in 1890.[45]

If advances were not themselves a major cause of desertion, they do focus attention on the first months of an individual's service, during which most desertions occurred.[46] The problems of adapting to navy life and discipline, compounded with other difficulties the men might have been having and the lack of incentives to remain, undoubtedly produced the decision to desert. In addition, the navy's screening system was unable to eliminate those men who signed on warships only to secure transportation to another port. Since the system of advances was relatively easy to change without fundamentally altering personnel policy, however, it is not surprising that officers attributed desertion primarily to this single cause.

The navy had no clear response to desertion, aside from guarding recruits to prevent their escape, as did Commander John Watters, commanding officer of the *Czane*. After receiving seventy-five enlistees through the help of a civilian agent, Watters

> instituted the most vigorous watch and guard to be kept on them to prevent escape; anticipating all the maneuvers that sailors adopt to deceive an unwary officer, and particularly directing great attention to the boats; having a sentry at post on the forecastle to watch those at the swinging booms which were only to be there between color hoisting & sunset and that all the boats should be hoisted at that hour except the dingy, which was reserved for use at 10 o'clock, with some of the old crew. [He] ordered the oars removed from the dingy at sunset.[47]

Such precautions vividly demonstrate that nineteenth-century officers often had to serve as wardens over newly enlisted men. And in spite of Watters' efforts, four men managed to steal a boat and escape.[48]

Officers decried desertion because of the immediate loss of efficiency on a short-handed vessel. The detrimental effects of enlisting foreigners, on the other hand, were less obvious. Yet, if anything, the service was even more displeased with what Secretary Benjamin F. Tracy called its "mongrel crews" than it was with the level of desertion—an attitude reflecting the widespread anti-foreign sentiment in the country at the time. One officer expressed an opinion common in the navy when he characterized the enlisted force as "the dregs of all countries."[49]

A cosmopolitan force might present difficulties. Even issuing orders could become a problem on a ship that lacked a common language. A popular anecdote concerned a vessel in the harbor of Villefranche whose muster roll contained nineteen nationalities; communication became so frustrating that someone placed a sign on the gangway, *Ici on parle Anglais* ("English spoken here"), in the manner of French shopkeepers.[50] How, critics demanded, could a crew respond in times of danger if orders were not properly understood?

Beyond possible complications in giving commands, the navy feared that non-Americans might prove disloyal in war. Officers also contended that alien crews detracted from the patriotic glory of the navy, reflecting on the country or, at least, on naval officers. As one lieutenant complained in 1890: "What pride can an officer feel in his vain attempts to arouse some national spirit and esprit in such crews?"[51] Almost two decades earlier Commander Stephen B. Luce, who was to be instrumental in establishing a naval apprentice program and in founding the Naval War College, had included a similar lament in a letter to the secretary of the navy:

> Our ships go to sea manned by heterogeneous crews, representing nearly every country on the face of the Globe; men, many of them utterly destitute of any feeling of attachment for, or interest in, the navy; whose only care it is to earn a present subsistence till something better can be found. The majority are ignorant of the navy & its traditions; indifferent to its honor & reputation; impatient under its discipline, & who go through with their military duties, under protest, as it were.[52]

Many observers felt that Americans were almost totally absent from navy crews. Admiral of the Navy David D. Porter remarked in 1873 that "frequently on the return of a United States vessel from a cruise, about the only nationality she has is in her officers and the flag flying at her peak."[53] This type of evaluation of the ethnic composition of the enlisted force was reinforced by incidents such as the sinking of the *Ashuelot* in the China Sea in 1883; news reports of the disaster stated that only 19 of the 111-man crew were native-born Americans.[54]

A single ship, especially one stationed in the Far East, was hardly representative of the entire enlisted personnel, and contemporary critics who relied on such evidence as the crewmen of the ill-fated *Ashuelot* formulated a distorted impression of the overall composition of the enlisted force. An examination of enlistment returns and muster rolls from the late nineteenth century reveals that in reality approximately one-half of the enlisted force was foreign-born.[55] Luce came close to this figure when he calculated that 46.6 percent of the men in the Mediterranean Squadron in 1872 were Americans.[56] Luce and other critics of the makeup of the enlisted force, however, often used "noncitizen" and "foreign-born" interchangeably. In an era of extensive immigration, many citizens may have been born abroad. It thus seems likely that a sizable number of the men were naturalized citizens of the United States.

Information on this subject is scarce. Enlistment returns and muster rolls do not indicate citizenship status, but enlistment returns do contain some evidence that most of the foreign-born regarded the United States as home. Virtually all of the men who gave a place of usual residence when they enlisted in 1870, 1880, and 1890 named a city in the United States.[57]

When the Bureau of Navigation finally published citizenship information in 1890, it listed 58 percent of the force as citizens (and 47 percent as native-born).[58] The proportion of citizens rose during the ensuing years. By 1897 the chief of the Bureau of Navigation reported that of the entire service 54 percent of the men were native-born, 74 percent were citizens, and another 12 percent had declared their intention of becoming citizens.[59]

This increase was probably caused by a combination of factors. First, the new steel ships enhanced the prestige of the navy and undoubtedly encouraged some Americans to enlist. At the same time, the depression of the 1890s most likely made naval service more attractive to American citizens. Finally, an 1894 act of Congress permitted sailors with five years' service and an honorable discharge to become citizens.[60] It is thus likely that many enlisted men earlier in the nineteenth century also would have become citizens had it been easier for them to meet residency requirements.

Regardless of the actual level of foreign-born enlisted men, officers continued to express concern over the presence of these men in the fleet. Although they recorded no incidents of operational problems, the distress that officers felt over the situation led to efforts to limit the number of foreign sailors. In 1869 the department instructed recruiters to give preference to applicants of American birth.[61] In the same year, the navy created the rating of seaman gunner, to be open only to citizens.[62] This encouragement, however, had little impact on the composition of the force.

In the final analysis, reducing the proportion of foreign-born sailors could be accomplished only by increasing the number of Americans in the pool from which men were recruited. The most obvious way to expand this source of manpower was to recruit from the interior of the country as well as from the seacoast. This idea surfaced intermittently throughout the nineteenth century. In 1825, for example, Secretary Samuel Southard called for increasing the number of American seamen in both the merchant marine and navy and excluding foreign-born men from the service. Southard hoped to accomplish his goal both by developing a naval and merchant marine apprentice program and by enlisting "robust and healthy landsmen in the interior."[63] In 1828 the navy sent a recruiting party to Carlisle and Chambersburg, Pennsylvania, and during the Civil War the department tried to enlist fishermen from the Great Lakes area.[64]

The idea of enlisting landsmen emerged again in 1879 when Secretary Richard W. Thompson proposed recruiting young men from the South and

Midwest.[65] A decade later Commander Francis J. Higginson, commandant of the Newport training station, argued:

> What we want must come from the country, from the other side of the Alleghanies and south of the Ohio. We want boys who have never seen, and do not know, any other flag than the American, who have good American backgrounds, and who have no old world allegiance or affiliations. We want the brawn of Montana, the fire of the South, and the daring of the Pacific slope.[66]

Commander Higginson's statement not only reflects a widespread displeasure with foreigners in the navy but also implies a desire to avoid the type of enlistee secured from major ports, regardless of national origin. Certainly, native-born sailors of the nineteenth-century enlisted force came almost entirely from a few coastal areas. The hosts of the seven permanent rendezvous—California, the District of Columbia, Massachusetts, New Hampshire, New York, Pennsylvania, and Virginia—provided almost two-thirds of enlistees born in the United States; if Connecticut and Maryland are added, the number reaches three-fourths.[67] Officers such as Higginson felt that recruits from waterfront classes represented undesirable elements of the national population and argued that the proportion of these men in the service should be reduced. Turning inland, they claimed, would bring a more respectable type of individual into the navy.

Regardless of its potential, the idea of moving away from traditional recruiting areas seemed expensive and unnecessary to the sailing navy, and the few brief experiments never survived for more than a short time. In fact, the navy instituted only one program in the nineteenth century aimed at an extensive alteration of the enlisted force: the enlistment of young boys to serve as apprentices. It hoped that such an undertaking would free it from the traditional reliance on professional mariners and create a native-born enlisted force composed of men who would make naval service a career. Apprenticeship failed to attain these lofty goals, but it was the most important reform in personnel attempted in the old navy. Even when the program was abandoned, the experience proved valuable as a precedent for training programs of the twentieth century.

When the navy began apprentice training in 1875, the idea was not new. The department had inaugurated the use of apprentices in 1837, but the program failed because the boys dropped out when they did not obtain the commissions they had hoped for and because the navy received unfavorable publicity after an alleged mutiny aboard the apprentice training ship *Somers* in 1842. In 1855 Secretary of the Navy James C. Dobbin revived the system, but the outbreak of the Civil War ended training. The service tried once more in 1863, and was again unsuccessful.[68]

In 1866 the navy for yet another time turned to enlisting apprentices. The secretary of the navy wrote that the program "promises encouraging results. Having been imperfectly understood and not judiciously carried into effect at its origin, nearly thirty years ago, and compelled to encounter not only indifference and prejudice, but opposition, the execution of the law [establishing the apprentice program] had been neglected and fallen into disuse."[69] The promise the secretary wrote of, however, once again went unfulfilled because a congressional reduction in the enlisted force compelled the navy to cut the size of the apprentice program in 1868 and to abandon it entirely in 1869. Even after these several reincarnations, apprentice training still contained serious shortcomings. One officer declared in 1869 that he had "yet to find a commanding officer who approves of the present Apprentice System." He charged that it was expensive and that the desirable boys left the navy at their first opportunity.[70]

In spite of this disappointing record, apprentice training nevertheless seemed the most obvious way to change the type of men that composed the enlisted force, and as such it maintained a number of advocates. In 1871 Admiral Porter called for its revival; Captain Luce argued for an apprentice system at the first meeting of the United States Naval Institute, an organization established in 1873 to foster professional discussion among officers.[71] By 1875 the navy was ready to try again. Citing "the great want of intelligent native-born seamen," it began enlisting boys sixteen to eighteen years of age to serve as apprentices until age twenty-one.[72] More successful than previous attempts, this last apprentice training system was to continue until 1904.

In reinstituting the instruction of boys, the service tried to avoid what seemed to be obvious mistakes of the earlier efforts. No longer did the department permit a small number of apprentices to receive appointments as midshipmen at the Naval Academy, since the disappointment of those who did not become officers weakened the program. This time the secretary of the navy stressed that "the object of the system adopted is solely to make the boys good and intelligent sailors for the Navy, without attempting to prepare them for any higher grade."[73] Apprentices were to "receive an elementary English education"; more importantly, they were to be "initiated in all the duties of sailors on a man-of-war." By June 30, 1875, 260 boys were in training, and the chief of the Bureau of Equipment and Recruiting recommended expanding the program.[74] In 1879 it was given an authorized strength of 750.[75]

As had been the earlier practice, apprentices were assigned to ships devoted solely to training. Starting in 1875 with a single vessel, the *Minnesota*, the training system grew to five ships by 1882, only to decline to three in 1886 and to one in 1889. By 1898 the force had returned to five.

Regardless of the number, the training ships were usually older sailing vessels in various states of disrepair. Typical of the ships assigned to this duty was the sloop-of-war *Jamestown,* which was first commissioned in 1844 and which by 1884 needed repairs "not only for the health and comfort of her people, but for preservation of the ship."[76]

In December 1877 Captain Luce, who had argued for the renewed enlistment of apprentices, joined the program.[77] Scattered in eastern ports and housed in obsolete vessels, the apprentice training service was not impressive, but Luce refused to be discouraged. He wrote that the "training 'system', in its present state, may be compared to an infant suffering from retarded development. Its capabilities are yet unsuspected by those who have not made the subject a study."[78] Committed to the idea of the apprentice program, Luce set to work, and until his reassignment in 1884 he remained a major force in shaping the venture.[79]

Luce believed that the program's potential would most quickly be reached by uniting the several elements of training in one place, under one man.[80] In November 1880, therefore, the navy appointed a board, of which Luce was a member, to select a location for the headquarters of the training squadron. After examining New London, Connecticut, and Narragansett Bay at Newport, Rhode Island, the board chose Coaster's Harbor Island in the bay. Ceded by Rhode Island to the United States on March 2, 1881, the island was to remain the only home of the apprentice program for over fifteen years.[81]

The selection of a site on the northeastern coast of the country reflected the area from which most boys were recruited. Occasionally the bureau did attempt to attract populations from beyond the North Atlantic coastal area, enlisting boys in southern or midwestern ports, but the results were never good enough to warrant permanent efforts in those regions.[82]

Originally the navy had intended to instruct boys on both coasts.[83] The booming California economy, however, hampered recruiting for all positions in the navy, and the apprentice program proved unable to enlist enough boys to justify establishing facilities in that region. In the absence of a West Coast training squadron, boys from that area who wished to join the program sometimes were placed aboard vessels of the apprentice training service that happened to be in the Pacific.[84] By 1892 the bureau that oversaw the program was again willing to try "the experiment of enlisting Apprentices on the Pacific Coast" but soon discontinued the attempt, "as it was found impracticable to give them the necessary training, prior to transferring them to cruising vessels."[85] Not until 1896 did the navy successfully begin enlisting and training boys at the Mare Island, California, navy yard.[86]

Renewed training in California coincided with efforts by United States Senator George C. Perkins to secure an apprentice training station on the West Coast that offered facilities similar to those at Newport. In support of his measure, Perkins noted the value of encouraging American boys to join the service; he also voiced the desire of his constituents, who faced unemployment from the economic depression of the 1890s, to have an apprentice station. With the help of such pronavy senators as Henry Cabot Lodge of Massachusetts and Eugene Hale of Maine, in 1896 Perkins secured authorization for a training station on Yerba Buena Island, north of San Francisco, which was opened in March 1899. Thus, after nearly a quarter of a century since the apprentice training was renewed, the West Coast finally became a continuing part of the program.[87]

Despite the acquisition of training stations at Newport and later at Yerba Buena, the navy decided to keep instruction afloat rather than transfer it to land. On board the training ships, the program was to instruct the apprentices in "the elements of English education, alternating with practical seamanship and other professional occupations designed to prepare them for sailors in the Navy."[88] In practice, the academic subjects were subordinated to more purely naval skills. As it evolved, training consisted of three stages—initial instruction at a station ship, a cruise on vessels of the training squadron, and then service on a cruising man-of-war until the apprentice reached age twenty-one. The total time necessary to complete the first two phases of training was reduced from a minimum of twenty months in 1881 to from twelve to fifteen months later in the century. The third phase thus lasted between two and five years, depending on the age of enlistment.[89]

The navy anticipated great rewards from the apprentice system, envisioning the creation of a new type of personnel. The department wanted the program to attract youths who were American citizens, who came from what the navy considered to be good homes, and who resided outside major metropolitan areas. Most importantly, it was hoped that apprentices would reenlist so that the program would produce a career enlisted force composed of American citizens of good character.

The service soon modified its expectations since the boys it desired rarely wished to enlist. Many officers, in fact, began arguing that the department should not seek young men from rural districts in preference to those from the large cities of the eastern seaboard, because, they said:

> Boys from the large towns are accustomed to the confinement of houses, and have not the range of country to roam over, that the country boy has, and consequently would feel the constraint of ship life less: besides he would come from a class, to whom the abundant food and good clothing of the Navy would be a much longed for and unexpected boon. He has already known of some of the vices that tempt the sailor, and by the benefits received of good food and clothing, would be constrained from further indulgence in them. The country boy, well fed and clothed at home, would not realize to the same degree the benefits conferred by the care received, and would be the more apt to indulge in vices to which he had heretofore been a stranger, and would require coercion and punishment to keep him from yielding to temptation, and be more likely to become dissatisfied, and either desert or leave the Service after his enlistment had expired.[90]

In a similar vein, a chief of the bureau in charge of enlisted personnel noted the unsuitability for service of boys "who come from good and comfortable homes in the West" and expressed the opinion that the best apprentices were "boys who have no homes."[91] Obviously, officers themselves maintained no illusions about the comforts of naval life.

Although forced to accept boys who came to the service because they had no suitable alternative, the navy resisted becoming a dumping ground for incorrigibles. As a result, it vigorously rejected any suggestion that it should take boys from reform schools or who were thought to be in need of discipline.[92]

Relying on the urban poor was only one disappointment the navy faced in its efforts to maintain the apprentice system. Perhaps more disturbing, a strong current of dissatisfaction arose almost immediately within the program. Luce noted the "large numbers of desertions among the boys; the unpopularity of the training service among the men; and the general feeling among the officers" against the program, and he recommended modifications.[93] Furthermore, the boys' parents complained, with justification, that their sons were not receiving the academic instruction they had been promised.[94]

Apparently the navy never succeeded in increasing the attractiveness of service to the boys. Almost two decades after Luce had described apprentice dissatisfaction, the department refused a mother's request to discharge her unhappy son because it said that it was "in daily receipt of letters of the same tenor as your own, and if each request for discharge was granted, there would be but few apprentices left in the Navy"—certainly a startling confession.[95]

Apprentice discontent, in turn, contributed to the most serious failing of the program—few of the boys reenlisted after reaching age twenty-one. In 1890 one lieutenant estimated that only 10 percent chose to remain in the navy. A study of muster rolls for that year shows that former apprentices composed only 2.3 percent of the force—about 170 out of approximately 7,500 men.[96] An officer familiar with the apprentice service ruefully noted that "the best and brightest boys do not come back for a second enlistment." Secretary of the Navy Benjamin F. Tracy concluded that the navy "derives little benefit" from the apprentices because the "Government educates them as boys to lose their services as men."[97]

Apprenticeship marked the major effort of the nineteenth-century navy to deal with a variety of manpower problems. Yet the program did not represent any radical departure in the recruitment and training of the enlisted force. Although the boys rarely had had previous experience at sea, they were nevertheless drawn from the large coastal cities that traditionally supplied the majority of men for the service. Furthermore, because the program was plagued by dissatisfaction among the boys and a low reenlistment rate at age twenty-one, it never became a major source of sailors. It was not these shortcomings, however, that ultimately forced the service to abandon the idea. The navy was to find that the apprentice system was incapable of providing the numbers of men that the ships of the new navy would require. In addition, apprenticeship was geared to producing sailors skilled in handling wind-powered vessels at a time that the naval revolution was ending the need for such men. Thus, although the mere existence of a training program was in itself a modification of manpower policy, the apprentice program remained tied to traditional practices. For that reason, it had to be altered and finally discarded in the early twentieth century when the navy began undergoing changes that compelled it to develop a new enlisted personnel system.

chapter 3

Enlisted Men and the Government

Before an examination of how the enlisted force of the old navy was transformed to meet the needs of a modern fleet, it is necessary to consider briefly the units of government that affected the men. Governments, and particularly their military institutions, were among the first organizations to develop bureaucratic structures. The existence of a bureaucracy in the navy determined much of the treatment the enlisted men received, and bureaucracy was always a part of the sailors' lives.

Within the Navy Department, primary responsibility for enlisted personnel rested with the secretary of the navy until 1862, when the Bureau of Equipment and Recruiting was established to handle enlisted matters. After Secretary Benjamin F. Tracy reorganized the department in 1889, the Bureau of Equipment and Recruiting lost authority over bluejackets and "Recruiting" from its name. At the same time, the Bureau of Navigation, which had been the navy's scientific division since its creation in 1862, assumed control of commissioned and enlisted personnel and relinquished its scientific functions.[1]

At first the Bureau of Navigation managed matters pertaining to the enlisted force apparently without creating a special enlisted men's division. One writer dates the appearance of a formal enlisted division from 1906, the year in which supervision of training stations was placed under one officer in the bureau.[2] The Enlisted Personnel Division grew from this modest beginning; by 1913 it was the busiest unit in the bureau.[3]

American participation in World War I produced an irrevocable expansion of the bureaucracy that dealt with enlisted men. During the war, divisions were formed within the Bureau of Navigation to handle training, recreation, and matters relating to chaplains. These functions continued to receive separate recognition after the armistice, even though there was some renaming and shuffling of units during bureau reorganizations.[4]

Since the Bureau of Navigation had little to do with navigation after 1889, the old title was obviously inappropriate. The chiefs of the bureau sought a more fitting designation, but their repeated efforts to change the name failed. It was not until 1942 that it was renamed the Bureau of Naval Personnel.[5]

Although major responsibility for the enlisted force rested with the Bureau of Navigation after 1889, other parts of the navy also affected enlisted men's lives. The Bureau of Medicine and Surgery participated in recruiting and caring for the men. The Bureau of Supplies and Accounts was responsible for pay and for ordering stores. The Office of the Judge Advocate General rendered opinions affecting personnel and assisted the Bureau of Navigation in trying and punishing offenders against naval discipline. The judge advocate general also managed naval prisons and disciplinary barracks. None of these organizations, however, possessed the type of comprehensive interest in the men that the Bureau of Navigation had.

In 1915 Congress created the post of chief of naval operations, "charged with the operation of the fleet, and with the preparation and readiness of plans for its use in war."[6] Although this broad authority encompassed enlisted matters, the chief of naval operations had but an indirect impact on the men. Generally, he considered only the total force the navy required and its distribution among the ships and stations, leaving matters of recruiting, training, and treatment to the Bureau of Navigation.[7]

Agencies of the government outside the Navy Department can be dismissed quickly. Although the State, Interior, Justice, and Treasury Departments all might have had dealings with men in the service, their contacts were with individual citizens and not with enlisted men of the navy per se. In Congress, both the House and Senate committees on naval affairs and appropriations largely ignored the men. Their hearings revolved around either new construction or officers' problems. Because the men moved in a different social stratum from officers and thus generally had no acquaintances in Congress, Congress seldom concerned itself with them. Apparently the only time enlisted men organized lobbying activity was after World War I when a petty officers' organization sent representatives to Washington in support of a pay bill.[8] Although their testimony was well received, this activity did not continue. The only other contact Congress and enlisted men had was when congressmen handled sailors' correspondence. This function consisted largely of forwarding the sailors' letters to the Bureau of Navigation for response. Congressional staffs seem to have been more concerned with receiving any answer, whether favorable or not, than with fulfilling the bluejackets' requests.[9] The official world with which enlisted men had significant and continuing dealings, therefore, was composed almost solely of the Navy Department; within the department, that world was dominated by the Bureau of Navigation.

Any description of governmental responsibility for the enlisted force is incomplete without considering the personalities of the individuals who had primary jurisdiction over the men—the secretaries of the navy and the chiefs of the Bureau of Navigation. The people who held these posts occupied positions that carried tremendous potential for influencing the lives of enlisted personnel.

THE SECRETARIES OF THE NAVY

In exercising authority over the service, the secretary of the navy was second only to the president. As a civilian, an appointee normally assumed office unfettered by friendships or jealousies within the service. These facts might have made it possible for the secretary to carry out reforms, but they often had the opposite result—they limited his actions. As an outsider in a specialized world, the secretary could become captive of bureau staffs and of Navy Department officers who interpreted the ways of the service to him. He could also have his authority undermined by a president who wished to be his own secretary of the navy, as did both Roosevelts. Furthermore, every secretary had to devote much of his time to persuading Congress to approve various naval projects; consequently, secretaries had little time left for enlisted personnel.

Despite the limitations inherent in the post, the personalities and backgrounds of the men who occupied the position to a large degree explain why the secretaries rarely gave firm direction to personnel matters. The individuals appointed to the office brought a diverse set of credentials.[10] One had served as a prosecutor of accused murderess Lizzie Borden; another had published children's stories. Of the twelve who assumed the office from 1897 to 1939, only Paul Morton had not attended college. Of the eleven collegians, five had studied at Harvard and two at Yale. Four of the men had served in other cabinet posts, two had been in the Senate, and three had served in the House. Although two secretaries—Paul Morton and Josephus Daniels—stemmed from modest backgrounds, men from prominent families were usually chosen, including one descendant of Napoleon and another of John Adams.[11]

Most secretaries performed their duties competently, but there were exceptions. Edwin Denby, who served from 1921 to 1924, had not provided strong direction to his office even before he was tarnished by association with the Teapot Dome oil-lease scandal. Curtis Dwight Wilbur (1924-29) replaced Denby. As the former chief justice of the California Supreme Court, Wilbur brought to his new post the prestige it needed. His previous interest, however, concerned juvenile law and not naval administration. One contemporary critic went so far as to dismiss Wilbur as a "Benevolent Blunderer":

A well-meaning gentleman of unquestioned integrity, Mr. Wilbur no sooner opens his mouth than something occurs to demonstrate that he is speaking without adequate knowledge, too hastily, upon misinformation, or contrary to the policies of his chief, Calvin Coolidge.[12]

John D. Long, who served from 1897 to 1902, also failed to bring strong leadership to the office. One historian has characterized the secretary as a man who "labored with patience and tact to maintain the *status quo* in an organization that needed change."[13] Long, furthermore, was determined not to tax himself in running the navy. He wrote in his journal:

I make [it] a point not to trouble myself overmuch to acquire a thorough knowledge of the details pertaining to any branch of the service. Such a knowledge would undoubtedly be a very valuable equipment, but the range is so enormous I could make little progress, and that at great expense of health and time, in mastering it. . . . What is the need of my making a dropsical tub of any lobe of my brain, when I have right at hand a man possessed with more knowledge than I could acquire, and have him constantly on tap?[14]

Even though ineptness in office was not typical, the more competent secretaries, too, generally had little impact on policy relating to the enlisted men. Their annual reports delivered ritual praises of sailors, but generally nothing more about enlisted matters emanated from the office of the secretary. In part the secretaries' lack of interest in the enlisted force may have resulted from their limited familiarity with naval affairs. Most of the twelve appointees entered office with no previous knowledge of the navy, served a short term, and moved on to other pursuits. For many the cabinet post was but a steppingstone in their careers. Charles J. Bonaparte (1905-6), for example, became secretary of the navy while waiting for an appointment as attorney general.[15] Assuming office under these circumstances, the secretaries were overwhelmed by the new naval world, and they were probably content to leave enlisted matters to the Bureau of Navigation.

Ignorance alone, however, does not completely explain secretarial neglect because even those better prepared did not influence the enlisted force. Truman H. Newberry (1908-9) had helped organize the Michigan Naval Brigade in 1895 and subsequently served in the Spanish-American War as a lieutenant, junior grade, on the *Yosemite*. After his term in the cabinet, Newberry returned to the navy in World War I as a lieutenant commander in the Fleet Reserve and was the assistant to the commander of the Third Naval District. Edwin Denby had served in the navy as an enlisted man during the Spanish-American War. Curtis D. Wilbur had graduated from the Naval Academy in 1888. Although third in his class, Wilbur decided that the navy offered few opportunities to an ambitious man and resigned his commission.

These naval backgrounds, including Denby's service as an enlisted man, produced no noticeable interest in the enlisted force.

Unlike the others, two secretaries did manifest a concern for enlisted personnel. They were George von Lengerke Meyer, secretary from 1909 to 1913 under William Howard Taft, and Josephus Daniels, secretary from 1913 to 1921 under Woodrow Wilson. Called by Elting Morison "one of the ablest men ever to hold the position," Meyer attempted to introduce a number of reforms aimed primarily at limiting the independence of the bureaus and at exerting the secretary's control over the department.[16] To this end, in 1911 he created four aides to oversee different parts of the naval establishment and to report directly to the secretary. The aide for personnel was responsible for the Bureau of Navigation, the Bureau of Medicine and Surgery, the Marine Corps, the Office of the Judge Advocate General, and the Naval Examining and Retiring Boards.[17] In an experiment of more immediate value to enlisted men, Meyer extended the use of the probation system. He also urged the American navy to adopt the British system of disciplinary barracks, which permitted men to be reinstated after court-martial for some offenses, thereby avoiding dishonorable discharges.[18]

Although Meyer did more for the enlisted force than most other secretaries, his overall interest was nevertheless slight, and he devoted just a small portion of his efforts to enlisted policy. In the years between the Spanish-American War and World War II, only Josephus Daniels demonstrated an active and continuing interest in sailors. Forceful and controversial, Daniels deserves and even demands special consideration.[19]

At the time of his appointment, there was little in Daniels' background to suggest the impact his secretaryship would have on the men. His credentials for the post consisted of loyal support of Wilson, ownership of an influential Raleigh, North Carolina, newspaper, and only a slight familiarity with the navy. Despite this last deficiency, Daniels was determined to control the navy himself, and he did so to a surprising degree. As one historian has written, "The Navy is still undecided whether Daniels was an asset or liability; but no one could call him a rubber stamp."[20]

Among the idiosyncrasies of the new secretary was an unprecedented and abiding concern for the men. On his third day in office, Daniels expressed a desire to meet one of the sailors. Chief Gunner's Mate Peter F. Sokolowski, a fifteen-year veteran, was ushered in to shake the secretary's hand.[21] Shortly after that incident, Daniels wrote: "I will say it gives me the greatest pleasure to meet men of the navy and it will always be my endeavor to do everything which will increase their happiness."[22] His interest was so clear that magazines serving enlisted men reacted to him with unusual enthusiasm, and Daniels received far more space and acclaim in those publications than any of the other eleven secretaries who served from the Spanish-American War to World War II.

To insure control over enlisted policy, Daniels appointed Victor Blue, a fellow Carolinian, chief of the Bureau of Navigation.[23] Daniels also removed the aide for personnel who he felt was not amenable to new ways.[24]

Daniels proved active in matters concerning enlisted men, but it is often difficult to assess his accomplishments. A former editor, he used his annual reports adroitly to extol his own achievements. The secretary was not modest, and historians who rely too heavily on these reports often give him excessive credit for innovation. The reports, in fact, leave the impression that Daniels must have invented enlisted men. To evaluate Daniels, one must place his work in the perspective of general trends.

Donald W. Mitchell praises Daniels for reversing an unsatisfactory personnel situation and for reducing desertion through the use of experts in sociology, law, and penology.[25] A fair analysis, though, should acknowledge the improvements in recruiting and training before Daniels. Because of those developments, Daniels inherited a better force to work with than his predecessors had enjoyed. Also, while Daniels' reforms might have had some effect in reducing desertions, it is well to note that the desertion rate had dropped dramatically in 1909 (from 9 percent the previous year to 5 percent) and had continued to decline during Meyer's secretaryship. In addition, unemployment had increased sharply in 1914, and desertion generally decreased in response to economic trouble.[26]

One of Daniels' most publicized and discussed reforms was General Order 63 of December 16, 1913, which provided mandatory shipboard instruction for all men. Daniels proclaimed "every ship a school," and the new policy received widespread attention and applause. As a result, Daniels' son asserted:

> It was in fact a revolutionary procedure. Daniels' foresight in an increasingly technical Navy was that a revolution was required. The much romanticized old-time sailor . . . was often illiterate and sometimes disreputable at sea and ashore. Daniels envisaged the educational program for both the Navy and the men. There was a disciplinary advantage in using the men's spare time in training which would let them leave the Navy with knowledge and skills. The opportunity at training would attract better men and the Secretary understood apparently almost alone that Navy enlisted personnel would more and more have to be a group of trained technicians using intricate equipment and requiring education and knowledge. . . . In the face of such change Daniels' educational program was not only essential then; it was also the precursor of the elaborate training courses which became so important a part of the work of the armed services in World War II.[27]

In the face of such assertions, it is necessary to examine both how singular and how permanent Daniels' actions were. As will be discussed in greater detail in a later chapter, the navy had initiated training programs well before Daniels became secretary. By 1913 it had four recruit training stations and a growing number of advanced courses. These courses did not expand dramatically under the Daniels administration until the war began. In addition, the experiment in basic education Daniels had envisaged under General Order 63 met with mixed success and support, and it was discontinued without much regret during World War I. After the armistice, even Daniels did not try to reinstate universal education. Instead, he transferred his support to Naval Training Courses. These were voluntary, correspondence-type endeavors, not mandatory for all enlisted men, and they represent no radical departure from the pre-Daniels era. It is probable that pressures for more skilled men at a time when the service was reluctant to transfer men from the fleet for training ashore would have produced something like the Naval Training Courses without General Order 63.[28]

In other areas, too, Daniels altered an existing system but did not introduce any dramatic innovations. During World War I, in a much-publicized experiment, Daniels began returning prisoners to duty. But this program was not new; the navy had been using probation since at least 1901, and Daniels had inherited two disciplinary barracks from Secretary Meyer.[29]

Even if both admirers and detractors exaggerate Daniels' uniqueness, it would be equally wrong to dismiss the secretary's impact. Daniels displayed a strong concern for the "boys" in the navy that deserves recognition. Enlisted men received attention they had never before experienced. Daniels' interest, however, proved to be a mixed blessing for the men because it was a paternalistic concern stemming from Daniels' confidence in his own moral perceptions. In many ways Daniels tried to improve the sailor's life, but at the same time he demanded conformity to his own standards. He felt:

> I am the father of more than 50,000 young men . . . and there is nothing more upon my heart than to see them men of strong Christian character, living clean lives for home and kindred and country.[30]

Though the father of his boys, in the opinion of one seaman, Daniels "was not a sailor, not a Navy man" but rather "more of a southern Preacher trying to make men and officers see things his way."[31] Solicitude from the moralistic, prohibitionist Daniels did not always prove popular with the men. His efforts to implement his convictions against liquor or premarital sexual relations, in particular, failed to meet with universal approbation from his boys.

Daniels' many controversial actions have produced a number of critics. Because his detractors have been vehement, his defenders have tended to overcompensate by bestowing on him superhuman attributes. Attempts to counterbalance the paeans and to restore perspective on Daniels' accomplishments have the unintended effect of seeming to belittle his achievements. Yet the character of the navy did circumscribe the range of his innovation. Daniels was most successful when advocating policies well within existing trends in personnel policy, as, for example, his experiments with probation. But he did, nevertheless, pursue matters of enlisted policy far more actively than did the other secretaries; he championed the men and experimented to improve their lot. Throughout his term, Daniels focused attention on the sailors, whom other appointees had hardly noticed. His significance lay not in establishing dramatically new programs but in emphasizing and publicizing concern for the enlisted force.

The limitation of the secretary's power is suggested in Daniels' failure to rebuild the service in his own image. One man, even a determined and strong-willed person, could not wrench the navy from a course that it held with the momentum of tradition and the backing of bureaucracy. He could at most encourage minor innovations and accelerate the pace of development. Similarly, lethargic leaders such as Denby or Wilbur did not spell an end to change. Life for the men continued, whether or not the current secretary was interested.

THE CHIEFS OF THE BUREAU OF NAVIGATION AND OTHER OFFICERS

The secretary of the navy devoted large portions of his time to matters unrelated to personnel. The chief of the Bureau of Navigation, on the other hand, had a continuing responsibility for military manpower. In this office, too, an individual might have had extensive power over the lives of the men. Yet as close as this office was to enlisted matters, there do not appear to have been any discernible differences in bureau policy that might be ascribed to the character of the chiefs.

Eighteen men served as chief of the bureau during the forty years between the Spanish-American War and the Second World War.[32] All had seen long periods of service before being named chief—ranging from a low of twenty-four years for Leigh C. Palmer to a high of forty-six years for Willard H. Brownson, and with an average of almost thirty-nine years.[33] Their records attest that they were men of ability and standing within the naval profession. Ten assumed their duties with previous experience in the Bureau of Navigation. Five had served at training stations or on training ships. Five had served in other bureaus, including George A. Converse, who had been chief of the Bureau of Equipment, and William D. Leahy, who had been chief of the Bureau of Ordnance and later became chief of naval operations. Nine of the men went on to become commanders of a multiship unit.[34]

In spite of the clear competence of the chiefs of the Bureau of Navigation, not one left a distinctive mark of his personality. Perhaps their previous careers had eliminated individual differences. At any rate, it is difficult to relate changes in enlisted policy to any of these individuals. Indeed, it is hard to find any officer who manifested a continuing interest in enlisted personnel.

All officers, of course, had daily contact with enlisted men. Most had opinions about how sailors should be treated, but few pursued careers that can be considered connected closely with enlisted affairs.

There were three officers who showed a deeper-than-average involvement in matters relating to the men, although none of the three became chief of the Bureau of Navigation. During the second half of the nineteenth century, Stephen B. Luce dominated naval training for both officers and men.[35] His interest in the instruction of officers led him to publish a text on seamanship in 1863 and, more significantly, to press for the creation of the Naval War College in 1883. Similarly, the education of bluejackets remained a concern for Luce throughout his career. As early as 1864 he proposed a system of training for sailors. Nothing came of this suggestion, but Luce was later to find a new opportunity to work for reform in personnel policy. In 1872 he was appointed equipment officer of the Boston navy yard, a position with few duties. Luce used his leisure to publish his recommendations for an apprentice system. The inauguration of apprentice training in 1875 was partly due to his efforts, as has been seen; consequently, in 1877 he was assigned to a billet in the training service. Even after his career took him elsewhere, Luce maintained an interest in enlisted personnel into the twentieth century.[36]

Neither Albert C. Dillingham nor William F. Fullam attained the stature that Luce enjoyed, but both were deeply involved in formulating enlisted policy.[37] Dillingham began his military career at age fifteen as a member of the Seventh Pennsylvania Infantry during the Civil War. Changing services, he entered the navy in 1865, graduated from Annapolis, and rose slowly in rank during the nineteenth century. Finally, in 1899 he was made lieutenant commander for gallantry in the Spanish-American War. In the new century, promotions came more rapidly, and Dillingham achieved the rank of rear admiral before his retirement in 1910. His slow advancement was not unusual in the navy of the nineteenth century, but his involvement in enlisted affairs was exceptional. Dillingham's first formal assignment dealing with the education of new men came in 1893 when he began service on the training ship *Portsmouth*. In 1904 he returned to the training service as the commanding officer of the receiving ship *Franklin* in Norfolk, a major site for the instruction of landsmen. He remained in this billet until 1909, retiring a year later. Dillingham thus occupied important positions during the development of land-based training for recruits. His influence was also increased through the articles he wrote, two of which were entitled "Methods Employed at Training Stations for Training Apprentice Seamen for the Fleet" and "How Shall We Induce Our Men to Continue in the Navy?"[38] In his correspondence with the Bureau of Navigation, he demonstrated the same interest both in the question of initial instruction of recruits and in the problem of retaining men in the service.

Like Luce, Fullam was active in the instruction of both officers and men. He graduated at the top of his class at Annapolis in 1877, returning seven years later for the first of five tours of duty at the academy and ultimately becoming superintendent in 1914. Fullam also very early displayed an interest in the education of enlisted men. In 1890 he published an article entitled "The System of Naval Training and Discipline Required to Promote Efficiency and Attract Americans."[39] Other articles followed. In the first years of the twentieth century he also compiled several drill manuals for enlisted men.[40] Fullam, too, spent an unusual amount of his career on assignments relating to training. He served on the training ship *Lancaster* from 1899 to 1902 and became the commanding officer at the Newport Naval Training Station from 1907 to 1909 and at the Great Lakes Naval Training Station from 1911 to 1913. And he was the aide for personnel in 1913 and 1914.

Even in the cases of these three officers, however, the formation of enlisted policy was a secondary part of their careers. Individuals generally left no strong imprint on enlisted matters. Luce, in fact, is better remembered as the founder of the Naval War College. Fullam's more limited fame rests on the aviation articles he wrote under the pseudonym "Quarterdeck" for the *New York Tribune* after he retired in 1919. The new enlisted personnel practices that were developed in the twentieth century are therefore best understood if they are considered to have derived from the demands of the service rather than from the thrust of assertive leaders. Innovations resulted from the contribution of many persons, usually over many years. For this reason, the history of change in the recruiting, training, and treatment of the enlisted force is best presented in terms of policies of organizational units rather than in terms of the exploits of prominent individuals.

chapter 4

Recruiting for the New Navy

Supporters of the new navy in the late nineteenth century recognized that the construction of modern steel warships doomed the familiar wooden vessels that had previously composed the fleet. It was less apparent, however, that this action also threatened the existing personnel system. Although the chiefs of the Bureau of Navigation and the secretaries of the navy during the 1890s occasionally warned of the need for crews for these ships, little heed was paid them. In 1891, for example, the Bureau of Navigation estimated that the navy needed 13,746 men and boys, but the authorized strength for that year was only 8,250 and did not reach the 13,000 level until 1899. As late as 1897 the *Chicago Tribune* lamented that "Congress has authorized one big battleship after another, but has utterly failed to supply the men to man them."[1]

The personnel needs of the new ships could not be ignored forever. After years of little change, the authorized enlisted strength doubled between 1897 and 1900—from 10,000 men and boys to 20,000. By 1909 it had doubled again to 44,500.[2] The navy very early found that such large numbers of men could not be recruited through traditional procedures. There were simply too few trained mariners to supply the number of sailors the service needed. As a part of its recruiting effort, therefore, the department undertook programs to seek men in areas of the nation it had never before tapped, to enlarge its recruiting service, and to develop recruiting and advertising techniques to appeal to this new and larger population. The new system of recruiting was a fundamental ingredient in transforming the enlisted force.

When the coastal areas that had supplied sailors for the enlisted force could no longer meet the demand, recruiting throughout the nation began to be considered as a means of expanding the source of manpower. Even though the navy had attempted nationwide recruiting occasionally during the nineteenth century, it had never shown any sustained interest in the idea. Inland recruiting had seemed too expensive; it required that the service maintain rendezvous far from any other naval activity and transport enlistees hundreds of miles to the coast. As late as 1895, Secretary of the Navy Hilary A. Herbert rebuffed a suggestion from Illinois Senator Shelby M. Cullom that a rendezvous be opened in Chicago because, Herbert said, the additional cost of recruiting there was not justified at a time when the department faced "no difficulty in enlisting upon the sea coast all the men and boys needed for the Navy."[3]

Even as Herbert wrote, however, coastal rendezvous were proving incapable of satisfying navy requirements. In just two years the department would begin recruiting in the Midwest, motivated not only by the need to increase the number of enlistees but also by the desire to reduce the proportion of aliens in the service. In June 1897 the *Chicago Tribune* reported that Secretary John D. Long and Assistant Secretary Theodore Roosevelt wished "to reman the navy on American lines" and that as a part of the plan men would be sought in the Great Lakes area and perhaps along the Mississippi River.[4] At the same time, the chief of the Bureau of Navigation asked the Branch Hydrographic Offices in Cleveland and Chicago about the prospects of enlisting seamen in their cities. Both offices responded favorably, but Lieutenant George H. Stafford in Cleveland suggested Chicago or Milwaukee as better rendezvous sites than Cleveland because the sailing ships of the lumber trade called at these ports. He felt that the men from these ships would be the most suitable for the navy. W. J. Wilson of Chicago also reported that from ten to twelve men inquired weekly at his office about naval service and that many of these men had both salt- and fresh-water experience.[5]

After these encouraging reports, the Bureau of Navigation decided to begin developing the Midwest as a source of manpower. Selecting Duluth, Chicago, Milwaukee, and Detroit as the most promising cities, it sent Lieutenant Commander John M. Hawley to open recruiting rendezvous in each. Hawley rented office space and announced the rendezvous through local newspapers, proclaiming that the navy "desired to give Western men a chance to enlist in the Navy upon an equal footing with men in the Eastern coast cities" without their having to travel east at their own expense. When the recruiting office opened in Chicago, it was swamped by a large crowd of applicants. At the end of his three-week stay Hawley boasted that he had "been particularly successful in getting good material." This success was repeated in the other cities. In a total of thirty-four days of recruiting, Hawley had enlisted 224 men and boys: 20 seamen, 51 ordinary seamen, 67 apprentices, 19 landsmen, 13 shipwrights, 12 painters, 25 machinists, 6 firemen, 6 coal passers, 4 landsmen for yeomen, and 1 bayman. He reported happily that all were citizens and that most had been born in the United States.[6]

Hawley returned to Washington pleased with his success. He suggested that the navy continue such recruiting and recommended winter as the best time because ice prevented shipping on the Great Lakes and idled seamen. He also proposed establishing a permanent recruiting station in Chicago. Although encouraged by this report, the department responded cautiously. In the fall of 1897 it stated that it did not intend to open a recruiting station at Chicago. Instead, it merely authorized the Branch Hydrographic Office there to hand out recruiting information to people who inquired at the office.[7] By the following spring, however, when war with Spain seemed imminent, Hawley was sent back to Chicago to resume recruiting there.[8]

During 1897 and 1898 the navy accepted the idea of recruiting in areas away from the seacoast. Yet, because it still was seeking men knowledgeable in the duties they would perform aboard a warship, it extended its recruiting only to the Great Lakes region, where such men might be available.

After the Spanish-American War the department experienced increasing difficulty in enlisting trained sailors.[9] With traditional sources rapidly proving inadequate, in 1899 the navy initiated a program of enlisting "landsmen for training"—young men with no previous experience at sea who would be instructed in their duties before assignment to cruising vessels. Having made this commitment to turn landsmen into seamen, the navy no longer needed to confine its recruiting to maritime areas. It energetically expanded into the interior of the country, soon reaching such previously untouched areas as Kansas, Nebraska, and Colorado.[10] In 1901 the chief of the Bureau of Navigation reported that the service was regularly sending recruiting parties into the Mississippi Valley with uniform success.[11] By 1907 interior stations were enlisting 73 percent of the 15,500 first enlistments and coastal cities about 27 percent, a sharp contrast to earlier years; in 1890, for example, stations and ships in the cities of the seven permanent rendezvous had signed on 77 percent of men entering the navy, with New York and San Francisco alone contributing half.[12]

THE RECRUITING SERVICE

With more men needed for its enlarged fleet and more territory to canvass for enlistees, the navy began to expand its recruiting organization. The system grew from seven permanent stations and eight traveling parties in 1903 to fourteen permanent stations in 1906 with only two traveling parties.[13] By June 30, 1919, there were forty-nine main recruiting stations and 267 substations.[14] Furthermore, the service remained larger than it had been at the turn of the century, even when the wartime need for recruits declined. The depression saw the number of first enlistees fall to the lowest number since the navy began publishing statistics on first enlistments—4,572 in 1933 compared to 9,306 in 1905 and over 20,000 throughout the late 1920s. Even in 1933, however, thirty-one main recruiting stations and seventy-nine substations remained—a network far larger than anything known thirty years before—demonstrating both the increased importance of the recruiting function and the inertia of an entrenched bureaucracy.[15]

In 1918 the Recruiting Service, renamed the Navy Mobilization Service, also supervised the navy's brief experience with the draft. During the war the navy continued to secure enough voluntary enlistments, even though the army had had to rely on the draft from June 1917. The army charged that it was hampered in meeting its manpower needs because the navy preempted the best men; it therefore demanded that the navy also participate in the draft. Finally, after resisting the use of conscription, the navy relinquished voluntary recruiting and turned to the draft under terms of an act of Congress approved August 31, 1918. Because the navy did not receive men inducted under selective service until November 1918, however, the war ended before draftees could make any impact on naval personnel. With the armistice, the Mobilization Service quickly reverted to its old name and function.[16]

The growth of the recruiting network during the early twentieth century led to moves to standardize station procedures. Many were trivial. One directive, for example, required that all names on shipping articles be typed. Another supplied uniform letterheads to recruiting offices.[17] More important were steps to provide effective supervision of the nationwide organization, as the navy made the new system a permanent part of the Bureau of Navigation.

As the recruiting system spread into all parts of the country, it became too large to operate as one unit directly under the Bureau of Navigation in Washington. In 1916, therefore, the country was divided into an Eastern and Western District.[18] Although the number of divisions varied, the navy maintained a district organization after 1916 except between 1922 and 1926 when it returned recruiting officers to the direct supervision of the Bureau of Navigation.[19]

The Recruiting Service had been developed to produce enlistments at a time when the navy was chronically in need of men. On those occasions the service reached its authorized size, first enlistments were merely stopped until men were needed again, as had been the practice in the nineteenth century. In 1917 the department turned to another method: the use of quotas to distribute openings throughout the country during periods when the navy had a high applicant/vacancy ratio. This measure was adopted to cope with the initial wartime flood of applicants who offered their services faster than the department could absorb them. Quotas were unnecessary in the postwar personnel turnover, but as the demand for new enlistees slackened, the system was reinstated. By 1927 all stations had a weekly quota they were not allowed to exceed. During periods of stability and relatively low numbers of enlistments as in the 1930s, quotas could be used both to distribute enlistments geographically and to regulate the recruiting workload.[20]

Most officers and men were eager to become recruiters since it provided a chance for shore duty and an opportunity to return to home areas. Selection of recruiters from among the many volunteers was difficult, however, because the billet was not directly associated with any other assignment. Early standards for enlisted men required only that a person have at least one previous enlistment and at least two years remaining in the service. Although the Bureau of Navigation realized that these criteria alone would not insure good recruiters, efforts to judge potential recruiting ability were of limited success, and the navy continued to face the problem of choosing individuals for a duty unrelated to their shipboard tasks.[21]

In the hectic efforts to maintain full enlisted strength after World War I, the navy supplemented its regular number of recruiters by transferring men with only a short time remaining in the service from receiving ships, where they were awaiting discharge, to stations near their homes. There, after a brief indoctrination, they were to assist in recruiting by canvassing among their friends and neighbors.[22] This practice was only an expedient, apparently motivated as much by a desire to increase morale on receiving ships as to secure enlistments. The irony of men who were leaving the service trying to persuade others to join could not have been lost on potential recruits.

A more successful spur to recruiting was a competitive program instituted among the stations. Faced with a projected need for 38,000 first enlistments in fiscal year 1923, the bureau inaugurated recruitment contests and set criteria for performances of stations. The department was to publish the names of the leading recruiters; in addition, those who failed to meet a minimum standard were to be replaced. When the demand for recruits tapered off, this competition was suspended.[23] In addition to this special drive, from 1922 to 1931 the bureau permitted enlisted men excelling in recruiting to extend their tour of shore duty an additional year.[24]

Another measure the department adopted to improve the performance of volunteers for this duty was the establishment of schools for recruiters at Hampton Roads and San Diego. Here both officers and men received one month's training before going into the field. Instruction, however, was not begun until 1926—after the big enlistment drives of the postwar years—because the creation of the schools had to be postponed until the navy could spare recruiters long enough to attend them.[25]

Even before the navy developed schools for recruiters, many recruiting officers had sought to improve their efforts with techniques borrowed from the civilian world, including psychological testing and the concept of salesmanship. Salesmanship was a particularly popular idea, and it formed the core of several articles in the *Proceedings*. In 1922—when the navy was still suffering from the effects of the postwar turnover in personnel—the Bureau of Navigation reprinted an essay entitled "Recruiting Salesmanship" by Lieutenant Commander J. Ogden Hoffman for distribution to the Recruiting Service. In that article, Hoffman argued that the navy should adopt modern techniques of selling to enlist the men it needed. He also maintained that if the Recruiting Service followed the lead of private industry, it would be more successful.[26] Not all officers were enthusiastic about becoming salesmen. Some felt that the service should be able to select the best men from waiting lists; they regretted that the recruiter was "forced into the salesman's attitude by the lack of voluntary applicants."[27]

Other recruiters advocated the use of psychological testing for screening applicants. In 1921, for example, an officer complained that the navy, unlike industry or educational institutions, had not been in the lead in embracing the new science of psychology. If the service applied the discipline correctly, he felt, individuals prone to disciplinary infractions or desertion could be detected before enlistment, and the character of recruits would be improved. Such suggestions did not meet with universal approbation. One officer dismissed psychology as a new catchword like the "scientific management" vogue of previous years, which, he claimed, merely tried to make the procedures that had been in use for some time seem mysterious.[28] In the end, the service did not institute the use of psychological testing, though it did make increasing use of aptitude tests.[29]

ENLISTMENT ABOARD SHIP

Although the enlarged Recruiting Service supplied most personnel in the twentieth century, men continued to be enlisted in other ways. Enrolling seamen directly aboard cruising vessels remained a source of manpower for part of the new century. Nineteenth-century commanding officers had routinely signed on men for their own ships. In the twentieth century this practice was progressively restricted; indeed, the degree to which the department encouraged shipboard enlistment provides an index of the service's manpower needs.

When the navy was short-handed, cruising vessels were exhorted to find men for their own use and for the service at large. In 1907, for example, the newly constructed battleship *Nebraska* had to raise her own crew. Working from the Seattle navy yard, recruiting parties scoured the states of Washington and Oregon. One particularly successful group in Portland "almost denuded the sailor boarding houses of firemen and seamen."[30] In the same year the Bureau of Navigation instructed the entire Pacific Fleet to enlist men in the ports it visited. The bureau directed the captains to transfer apprentice seamen and landsmen to the naval training station in San Francisco and to retain others on board, though no promise could be given that the ship assignments would be permanent. Again, in 1913 vessels in home waters were authorized to accept men for all ratings except printers and sailmaker's mates and to keep all recruits on board ship.[31]

When the war years strained the Recruiting Service, shipboard enlistment was also used extensively. In January 1917, as the likelihood of American involvement in the conflict increased, the bureau instructed all ships to designate a recruiting officer and to form at least one recruiting party to operate continually in home ports.[32] After the armistice, naval manpower requirements remained high, and personnel from seagoing ships continued to aid in the search for enlistees. To enhance the appeal of service, in 1919 the navy permitted men to remain on the ship which enlisted them. During a special fleet visit to New York City, over five hundred recruits joined the service, many attracted by the possibility of choosing their ship and thus ending any uncertainty about assignment after enlistment. In September of the same year, all vessels in home waters cooperated in a special recruiting drive.[33]

During the early 1920s, the Bureau of Navigation continued to permit recruiting by the captains of cruising vessels. The major campaigns of former years, however, were over, and men were enlisted only to fill vacancies in ship complements. The commanding officer usually was only too happy to exchange his recruits for men who had been enlisted by the Recruiting Service and who had completed instruction at training stations. By 1925 shipboard enlistments had been discontinued entirely; regulations for that year directed that "first enlistments are authorized to be made only at regular recruiting stations and at naval training stations."[34]

OTHER RECRUITING AGENTS

Although the establishment of the new recruiting system freed the navy from its former reliance on landlords or their agents, the department did make occasional use of outside help. Sometimes it had shipping agents secure skilled men for the engine-room force from the merchant marine—as it did in 1903 when it offered them two dollars for each acceptable machinist, water tender, oiler, or fireman, third class, they recruited.[35] Employment of agents was not extensive, and these men never regained the dominant position over naval recruiting they had enjoyed in some ports in the nineteenth century. In any event, the practice seems to have been discontinued early in the twentieth century as navy recruiting improved.

More commonly, the Bureau of Navigation received unsolicited offers of assistance from civilian volunteers. The service usually politely rebuffed the aid; in World War I, however, when the raising of the armed forces became a national concern, the navy tolerated and even welcomed outside help in recruiting. Enthusiastic citizens extolled the glory of service, and young girls donned middy blouses to exhort youths not to be slackers.[36] Some naysayers protested the use of high-school girls "in soliciting men promiscuously to join the navy" because "permitting these unsophisticated, emotional young women to accost men on the streets or to appeal to them from the sex standpoint, not only breaks down the first barrier of defense which every woman should be taught to guard most carefully, but also lowers the standard or ideal of patriotic service in the eyes of the men recruited."[37] Most, however, felt that the call of national service excused such techniques. After the war, the navy returned to recruiting without civilian assistance.

In addition to sometimes employing civilians in the recruiting process, the navy also conducted two experiments in having other parts of the government cooperate in raising its force. Because the marines were under the secretary of the navy's authority, it was occasionally suggested that navy and marine recruiting be combined. In 1912 the secretary directed that each represent the other in cities where one had no recruiting office. Under that system, an applicant was to receive information on the service of his choice regardless of the recruiter's affiliation.[38] This recommendation, however, proved unpopular and was soon abandoned. Later proposals—even if only for sharing clerical forces—were rejected as harmful to competition between the services.[39]

The idea of using the Post Office Department in the recruitment process, on the other hand, was highly successful. Local postmasters offered a convenient auxiliary already established in most cities and towns of the country. In 1902 the postmaster general instructed his employees "to cooperate with the recruiting officers of the Army and Navy by displaying the posters in a conspicuous place" and by preventing posters from being concealed or destroyed. The 1908 *Postal Guide* also directed postmasters to distribute material to interested young men.[40]

At the same time that postmasters began distributing navy literature, a more comprehensive proposal was made to permit them to serve as recruiting agents. That suggestion received no support from the Bureau of Navigation, and until 1916 postmasters did little more than display advertisements in their offices.[41] The Naval Appropriation Act of August 29, 1916, significantly increased their role by allotting postmasters five dollars for every person they recruited who was accepted for enlistment. On July 2, 1918, however, this provision was repealed because the postmaster general felt that postal employees should cooperate without payment. Although the navy was never able to reinstate the gratuity, it continued to display material in post offices.[42]

ADVERTISING

An important function of recruiting was advertising to attract men to the service. As with many other aspects of personnel policy, the use of advertising had roots in the nineteenth century; Herman Melville, for example, observed in *White Jacket* that the frigate navy always had signs posted along the waterfront proclaiming Men Wanted![43] When the navy turned to seeking enlistment throughout the nation, the traditional posters no longer reached the areas in which the navy wished to recruit or the men that the service desired to attract. The Bureau of Navigation therefore began experimenting with alternative methods of carrying its message.

Newspapers constituted the mainstay of advertising for the new navy; the most efficient use of this vehicle, though, was subject to debate. The typical practice early in the twentieth century was to insert small announcements in the Help Wanted sections of local papers. One such advertisement read:

> WHAT THE NAVY OFFERS YOUNG MEN. For the young man between 17 and 25 years of age, who has a good character and sound body, not afraid to leave home, the United States Navy offers excellent opportunity for steady employment; work is not severe, and plenty of time for recreation; athletics of all kinds encouraged. Pay $16 to $70 a month, according to ratings, with no expense for food, lodging, doctor's attendance and medicine. A complete outfit of clothing furnished gratis on first enlistment.[44]

Such placements in classified sections remained a favorite form of advertising, though the results were often mixed. In 1908, for example, the Philadelphia recruiting station tried this medium and received seventy-three requests for circulars. Yet only three men actually visited the office—a cook and two bakers; the cook was overage, and the bakers were aliens and thus could not be enlisted.[45]

Because not all officers were satisfied with the small announcements, some tried to initiate different methods. As early as 1903 Lieutenant Commander William H. Webb, the officer in charge of the Philadelphia recruiting station, suggested a full page in a Sunday edition. Webb, who considered newspapers far superior to posters, argued that full-page advertisements would allow a description of the "Moral surroundings" of the navy "as compared with the average of the city life," the financial advantage of the navy, and the "Democratic character of the service."[46]

Newspaper advertising on as large a scale as Webb desired was not used before World War II. At least part of the reason was that the navy discovered that it could obtain other kinds of space without payment and that free publicity could also be an effective recruiting tool. Recruiting officers therefore tried to induce editors to run stories about the navy—both of a general nature and on the service activities of local boys. The department often found articles of this nature so effective that it did not have to buy advertising.[47] In addition to helping attract young men to the navy, the stories also enhanced the reputation of the service among the general public. As a consequence, these features also became the navy's first systematic public relations efforts on a nationwide scale.

Although magazine advertising was similar in format to newspaper announcements, the use of that medium developed more slowly. The Bureau of Navigation received a suggestion to include periodicals in recruiting campaigns as early as 1904, but the secretary of the navy did not approve magazine advertising until 1906. Thereafter, the department employed magazines frequently, but they never rivaled newspapers for the department's advertising dollars.[48]

At the beginning of the century, the navy had allowed newspaper advertising only where it lacked a permanent recruiting station. These advertisements announced the arrival of a traveling recruiting party and the location of the office the party would use during its stay. By 1905 the department reconsidered its policy and soon permitted permanent stations to advertise as they needed.[49]

Posters constituted another major medium of advertising, and, like newspapers, they were first employed to announce the coming of a recruiting party.[50] The permanent recruiting stations only gradually began placing posters around town. In 1904, for example, the Chicago recruiting officer rejected the idea, feeling that displays in post offices were sufficient. He added, though, that more newspaper advertising might be helpful.[51]

In addition to experimenting with the use of posters, the navy tried to improve content and format. In the early years of the twentieth century, the bureau began reducing the amount of text and increasing reliance on eye-catching pictures. In the nineteenth century, placards had supplied extensive information about the terms of enlistment; in the early twentieth century, they became more and more a means of attracting attention and directing applicants to the recruiter. By 1903 recruiting stations expressed a preference for colored picture posters because color was more likely to arouse interest than the older black-and-white printed forms. At this time, though, recruiters still wished to give the applicant as much information as possible and often flanked a picture poster with descriptive ones. This trend toward simplification continued, and by 1917 navy posters contained little besides a picture and a slogan.[52]

Although newspapers and posters were the main forms of advertising, the navy gradually adopted other methods—booklets, direct mail, and films. Until the early twentieth century, the navy had no attractive literature to give potential recruits. Circulars containing the necessary enlistment information did exist, but they merely described navy requirements and benefits and were not designed to promote service life. In 1905 the Bureau of Navigation considered publishing an illustrated booklet and arranged for Street and Finney, a New York advertising agency, to produce it. The bureau wanted a pamphlet for widespread distribution that presented an interesting account of the training and opportunities the navy offered. After overcoming some difficulties in developing the leaflet and selecting a title, the bureau published *The Making of a Man-o'-Warsman* in 1906. This thirty-two-page pamphlet became a mainstay of the recruiting effort, rapidly going through several editions.[53]

Direct-mail advertising was also a new feature of recruiting. A poll of applicants in 1908 indicated that approximately half had received or seen one of these recruiting letters, which were sent unsolicited to young men who were of the proper age for naval service. The system grew from a modest beginning in which the personnel of each station handled the mailing in their spare time to a highly centralized operation. In 1910 the Bureau of Navigation created six district publicity offices to mail the literature. The next year the system was consolidated into two districts operating from New York and Indianapolis.[54] The bureau developed mailing lists by obtaining names from rural mail carriers, catalogs of educational institutions, teachers, and the space on the application form requesting the names of "others who might be interested." Although only about 2 percent of the addressees requested further information, recruiting officers felt that the men who did respond were of good character and that the method was particularly beneficial because it reached the rural population and youths with permanent addresses.[55]

Although successful for the navy, direct mailings produced some adverse reaction. Most came from parents who were displeased that their sons had received the material. James McIntosh, for example, complained of a letter sent to his son at Phillips Exeter Academy that seemed to be aimed at "decoying boys away from their present pursuits into a navy career." Shortly thereafter, in response to complaints relayed through members of Congress, the bureau advised its recruiters to avoid mailings to schoolboys.[56]

Motion pictures offered the twentieth-century navy a novel advertising tool, and the department soon put the medium to use. Unlike the circular letter, which was directed solely to young men of proper age, movies reached the whole community. In this respect they were both a public relations venture and a recruiting tool—just as were the newspaper articles that recruiters tried to have published. For the modern navy, recruiting and public relations were closely allied functions. Attracting good applicants from noncoastal regions required that the public hold the navy in a favorable light. Yet little information about the service had formerly penetrated inland areas. By providing favorable accounts of naval activity, the department hoped to create a climate of opinion that would encourage enlistment.

The films themselves found a ready showing for reasons unrelated to the intent of the Bureau of Navigation. The public was hungry for any motion picture, and theater owners welcomed a free program. At first the films were on short subjects depicting everyday scenes in the navy. In 1908, for example, such titles as *Distributing Mail, Fleet at Sea, Battalion of Infantry and Section of Artillery at Training Stations*, and *Submarine "Porpoise" Diving* were available. After American entry into World War I, the navy expanded its filmmaking; by 1920 it had fifteen films in circulation and four more in preparation.[57]

To meet the wartime demand for men, the department increased its advertising and developed several new approaches to promoting the service, including extensive use of athletic team events, naval band concerts, and special displays. Since most of these projects reached a broad range of citizens rather than just men of service age, they also reflected the navy's greatly enlarged public relations activity. Among the special promotions during the war was a large wooden "battleship" built in New York City's Union Square Park by the Mayor's Committee on National Defense. Christened the *Recruit* on Memorial Day 1917, it served double duty as a super billboard and a recruiting station. The structure remained in the park until 1920, when it was pronounced an "eyesore to the public" and removed.[58]

Because recruiting problems were even more severe after the war than during the conflict, the Bureau of Navigation maintained and intensified the special activities it had developed. Athletic teams and displays of naval life continued to tour the country. Training stations were urged to have their teams compete against as many high schools as possible and to offer the visitors an opportunity to examine the stations.[59] In addition, the navy either used or devised special events to draw crowds and to publicize the service. The seaplane *NC-4*, fresh from its transatlantic flight, went on tour in New York City, along the Atlantic coast, and up the Mississippi Valley. The presence of the plane in New York helped increase weekly enlistments from about 75 to 100—although other factors, such as the introduction of a two-year enlistment instead of the usual four-year term, make it hard to determine the exact effect of the aircraft.[60] In 1919 the navy also sent an antisubmarine flotilla consisting of a destroyer, a submarine, three submarine chasers, and three flying boats up the Mississippi. The flotilla carried a baseball team from the Atlantic Fleet, a glee club from the Hampton Roads training station, a movie outfit and recruiting films, two navy bands, and a recruiting party. Indeed, the entourage included so much equipment that a Rock Island freight car had to be hired to transport the paraphernalia.[61]

Just as the war and the immediate postwar years produced heavy demands for enlistment and consequently for large-scale advertising, when the need for recruits decreased during the twenties, advertising also declined. In 1926, for example, William R. Shoemaker, chief of the Bureau of Navigation, reminded recruiting stations that every newspaper advertisement required the permission of the secretary of the navy. He added that, since enough recruits were enlisting without publicity, newspaper advertising had not been used for a number of years.[62]

Because applicants came in the late twenties and in the thirties in sufficient or even excessive numbers, the department could graciously yield to criticism of its promotional methods. When the Highway Department in Pennsylvania complained of improperly placed or objectionable billboards, the navy replied that because of the "present state of Navy recruiting, that is, the large excess of applicants over enlistments, the Navy Department is willing, upon request, to cooperate in the discontinuance of recruiting signs along State highways."[63]

THE RECRUITER'S MESSAGE

When the navy embraced nationwide recruiting in the first years of the twentieth century, it found that it not only had to alter its techniques of advertising but also had to change the content of its publicity. Advertising now strove to present an image of the navy so pleasing that it would stimulate the enlistment of young men who had not had any previous experience as sailors, rather than merely encourage seamen to sign on with the navy instead of the merchant marine. The service quickly discovered the best themes to accomplish this purpose; once developed, the basic nature of naval advertising remained essentially unchanged between the Spanish-American War and World War II.

A convenient summary of the motifs was given by Lieutenant Commander J. Ogden Hoffman in 1921. Hoffman offered nine items in his recruiter's "Bags of Tricks." The inducements that he recommended using included travel, education, athletics, free room, board, and medical care, good opportunities for promotion, and no layoffs in bad times—in short, all a young man could desire.[64]

Because the recruiting process naturally emphasized the benefits of naval life—adventure, pay, and security—there was always the possibility that the department might misrepresent duties involved in service. Hoffman wrote of "travel in a way only the very rich in civil life can afford," neglecting to mention that the wealthy seldom clean their own yachts. Indeed, the subject of work was often ignored; recruiting slides focused more on sailors' viewing pyramids than on their swabbing decks. In striving for some balance, *The Making of a Man-o'-Warsman* included a section called the "Hardships of the Man-o'-Warsman's Life," but even there the authors could not find unmitigated privations: quarters are cramped, but the sailor "has more room than he who dwells in a city apartment"; the bluejacket is subject to discipline, but discipline is good for character; he cannot quit his job, but the obligation teaches him "stick-to-it-iveness." In any case, the writers were primarily concerned with presenting the positive side of naval life and in countering slurs about the navy made by what they called "disgruntled and discharged bluejackets" or found in "uncomplimentary reports."[65]

Although the Recruiting Service was lavish in its praise of naval life, the department nevertheless sought to avoid making promises it could not keep. The Bureau of Navigation constantly tried to eliminate statements which could be construed as guaranteeing a specific cruise or assignment. In 1910, for example, it criticized the New York publicity office for a proposed direct-mail advertisement because of what it considered almost an official promise of assignment to a planned Mediterranean cruise. It explained:

> The Bureau's experience has been that any such promises are very embarrassing; also, it should be made plain that the proposed cruise was for practice, and not conveying

the impression that the principle [*sic*] purpose was to give enlisted men liberty in foreign ports.[66]

Again in 1914, the bureau admonished the New York office about seeming to promise recruits assignment to vessels attending the opening of the Panama Canal.[67] The bureau was even reluctant to use slogans similar to "Join the Navy and See the World," which ultimately became a part of popular culture. As early as 1903 a poster had included the inducement of "An Opportunity to See the World," but in 1905 the bureau ordered a recruiting party to remove "a chance to see the world" from a handbill. Again, in 1909 the bureau removed "See the World" from a flier. Although the bureau gave no reason for the deletions, it is probable that it wished to avoid promising travel that might not materialize.[68]

In spite of this care, Secretary Daniels felt that at the time he took office recruiters still were promising travel that was not produced. After this situation was brought home to him in a conversation with a disgruntled Kansas youth who had spent the first two years of his enlistment at the Norfolk navy yard, Daniels ordered the navy either to increase travel or to end the promises. It chose the former rather than lose the one advantage that few other employers could offer young men.[69]

The war temporarily eliminated problems of advertising content because an appeal to patriotism could replace an appeal to self-interest. During 1917 and 1918 posters simply dramatized the navy in action and promised nothing beyond national service. With the return of peace, such methods failed to be productive, and the service reverted to stressing travel and adventure as it had before the war.

As the Bureau of Navigation honed the rough edges from its advertising, it completed the creation of a modern recruiting system. Because the navy had found that it could no longer enlist enough men for the new ships in waterfront areas, it began for the first time to create an organization to attract young men from across the nation for naval service. From a small network of rendezvous operating in conjunction with receiving ships in seven port cities, the Recruiting Service grew to a nationwide complex of stations divided into districts for easier administration and staffed with graduates of special recruiting schools.

At times in the twentieth century the need for men was so great that the navy had to supplement its new recruiting system by using shipping agents and by encouraging captains to enlist recruits aboard cruising vessels. Both methods had been staples of nineteenth-century recruiting. The curtailment and eventual ending of reliance on these techniques from the past attested to the success of the Recruiting Service.

The most widespread evidence of the new recruiting was the advertising that carried the navy's message to the public. No longer did the department merely place recruiting posters in waterfront areas, as it had in the nineteenth century. The modern navy spread its message across the nation through newspapers, posters, magazines, films, and other media. As an outgrowth of this effort, the navy discovered that its publicity efforts served the dual purpose of attracting recruits and developing favorable opinion of the service among all segments of the population. Indeed, the public relations function—which doubtlessly had the added effect of helping gain public support for naval appropriations—became an integral part of the recruiting process.

The new advertising sought to do more than merely inform professional mariners of openings on ships. Its goal was to sell navy life to men from the interior who were unfamiliar with the sea. Although the ease of recruiting varied, the new advertising methods and the recruiting system of which they were a part attracted large numbers of such applicants to the service. Ultimately, these men would radically alter the composition of the enlisted force and change the character of the sailors who manned the navy.

chapter 5

Men of the New Navy

Creating interest in a seafaring life and obtaining applicants were only first steps in the recruiting efforts of the new navy. The service next had to cull suitable men from among those offering themselves. This process was more complex than it had been in the sailing navy when the department's main objective had been merely to recruit men with sea experience and in relatively good health. Not only was the twentieth-century navy recruiting and judging men without maritime experience, but it also hoped to recruit men who it believed would elevate the character of enlisted personnel and enhance the prestige of the service. Although it sometimes had to take anyone available, the department always maintained a clear idea of whom it wanted.

NAVY REQUIREMENTS

The department selected through elimination—examining for reasons to reject individuals and enlisting from the survivors. Generally around one-third to one-fourth of the applicants met all criteria; only during the period from 1920 to 1923, when the navy was still recovering from the postwar turnover of enlisted personnel, were more than half accepted.[1]

Age provided a quick test for initial screening. The navy in the late nineteenth century had enlisted apprentices as young as fourteen and "boys" younger still. When the apprentice program ended in 1904, the minimum age at which a boy could enlist was raised to seventeen with his parents' consent or eighteen without it. As a maximum age limit, the sailing navy had allowed first enlistments for all but apprentices up to age thirty-three or thirty-eight, depending on the rating. In contrast, the new navy lowered the maximum age at which it permitted first enlistment to twenty-five or thirty-five, depending on the rating. This tightening of age allowances reflected the fact that the new navy was recruiting young men and training them itself rather than primarily seeking individuals who already possessed the skills needed aboard ship.[2]

Implementation of age standards presented problems for the new navy because determining age was often difficult. Underage applicants were a far more common problem than overage ones. If an underage boy decided that he did not like the navy or if his parents discovered he had enlisted without their permission, the youth had only to present evidence of his true years to compel the navy to discharge him. To prevent these occurrences, the appropriation act for the fiscal year ending June 30, 1907, required a birth certificate or other written evidence of age the recruiter deemed satisfactory. Incomplete birth records and overly eager recruiters, however, weakened the effectiveness of this provision.[3]

In the twenties, the navy made further refinements in the age requirements. In 1924 it demanded consent papers from the parents of all applicants under twenty-one. Also during this decade, Congress enacted provisions permitting the discharge of any youth joining under an assumed name within sixty (later ninety) days of the time his parents discovered that he had enlisted. Most significant in reducing this problem, however, was the declining number of first enlistments. Because recruiters had time to investigate ages more fully, during the 1930s there were several years in which there were no underage discharges at all.[4]

In addition to improper age, the fact that an applicant was married sometimes prevented first enlistment. The navy sought men who would be able to stay the full term. Although one would think that the enlistment of married men would tend to increase the stability of the enlisted force, in some cases it had the opposite effect. Many sailors found it impossible to support their families on beginning naval pay, and such men often had to be given "special-order discharges" for financial hardship. As a result, the Bureau of Navigation discouraged the enlistment of married men whenever there were enough single recruits. It was not until the thirties, however, that the navy's preference for the unmarried became policy. In February 1929 the Bureau of Navigation ordered that no married man be accepted for first enlistment without the bureau's permission; consent would be given only to those who would be unlikely to make a later request for hardship discharge. By 1932 the recruiting situation was so favorable that the bureau refused first enlistment of all married men and also of divorced men who paid alimony or had dependents.[5] Furthermore, by this time the lowest three pay grades could re-enlist only with permission of the bureau. The navy could thereby reject men who had acquired obligations beyond the income of these grades.[6]

Having passed the initial screening, the applicant next received a physical examination. The examination, which had not changed much from the nineteenth century, consisted of a check for acceptable height, weight, and eyesight, twenty sound teeth, and physical ailments which could prevent enlistment—such as venereal disease or bad hearing. The most frequent causes for rejection in the early twentieth century were inadequate vision, flat feet, and defective teeth.[7] Doctors also watched for signs of alcoholism and drug addiction. Even though the latter problem was negligible, the navy continually feared enlisting narcotic users and issued periodic warnings to its medical officers. Those warnings urged special care in the cases of men enlisting for the hospital service, because these men would have access to drugs.[8]

Although medical standards were theoretically uniform, the quality of the examination varied considerably. In times of intense recruiting, unqualified men slipped through, only to be rejected later at training stations. Sometimes a sympathetic doctor passed eager but unfit youths.[9] At other times inadequate facilities or the rush of applicants prevented a proper physical inspection. The Bureau of Medicine and Surgery naturally attributed errors to situations beyond its control. It complained that "poorly lighted, badly located examining offices at so many recruiting stations" invited mistakes. A man whose heart was later discovered to be hypertrophied had passed in New York City because the "examinations are conducted in the front room, overlooking the street, and that the incessant noise from the traffic below is so deafening that the ring of the telephone bell frequently becomes inaudible."[10]

After the physical examination, which constituted the main cause for rejecting applicants, the recruiter had to determine that the man was not a felon, not a deserter, not dishonorably discharged, able to read and write, and in possession of sufficient evidence of good character to be enlisted. To an even greater degree than other requirements, the extent of this investigation depended on the need for men and the time available to the recruiter. During hectic enlistment drives, a recruiter might accept an illiterate or try to help him through in spite of regulations barring such men.[11] During the 1930s, on the other hand, recruiters had time to apply the navy's standards more stringently, and the service received enough fully qualified applicants to more than fill its limited needs.[12]

Character references were designed largely to avoid enlisting individuals who wished only to obtain transport to another city, where they would then desert. Fraudulent enlistments of this type continually plagued the services, and efforts at control were never totally successful. One man enlisted in the armed forces forty-five times between 1908 and 1927: ten times in the navy, eleven in the marines, and twenty-four in the army.[13]

To avoid being victimized in this way, the navy adopted a series of measures to detect former servicemen who applied for enlistment. By the end of the nineteenth century the service was issuing physical descriptions of deserters, but it was difficult for a recruiter to recognize a man from these fliers. A surer, though often cumbersome, method was fingerprinting all applicants, which the recruiting system began on January 1, 1907. Though improved, detection was still imperfect.[14]

In spite of experimentation with various methods of screening applicants to reduce the number of fraudulent enlistments, the twentieth-century navy still relied most heavily on the judgment of the recruiter. Before an investigation was made, the applicant had to arouse suspicion. In many cases there were clear signs of previous service even if the man claimed not to have had any. Overfamiliarity with the enlistment process indicated that the applicant might have undergone the procedure before—possibly several times. Similarly, the medical officer carefully noted any tattoos that were common among servicemen.[15]

After passing all examinations, the applicant was either sworn in immediately or his name was placed on a waiting list until a vacancy arose. It seems that the navy first used a waiting list, "something unique to the Service," in 1910. Even though recruiting in that year was restricted to a few ratings, the Bureau of Navigation instructed recruiters to keep a file of names of qualified individuals because it believed that Congress would authorize an additional 2,000 men for the next fiscal year.[16] Generally, though, before the 1920s the navy made few attempts to maintain contact with interested men when recruiting was temporarily suspended in a particular rating.

Once an applicant was accepted, he was required to sign the shipping articles and to take the following oath:

> I [name] do solemnly swear (or affirm) that I will bear true faith and allegiance to the United States of America, and that I will serve them honestly and faithfully against all their enemies whomsoever; and that I will obey the orders of the President of the United States, and the orders of the officers appointed over me, according to the Rules and Articles for the Government of the Navy.[17]

By taking this oath, the civilian formally became a part of the navy, placing himself under service regulations for the period of his enlistment. Usually a recruit obligated himself for a term of four years, but even the length of service fluctuated in response to the recruiting market. The late nineteenth-century navy had generally used a three-year enlistment, though one-year and cruise enlistments were also common. The four-year enlistment contract was adopted in 1899 and remained standard until World War I.[18] At the outbreak of the war men flocked to serve, undeterred by the length of the obligation. Later wartime applicants, on the other hand, grew cautious and were reluctant to commit themselves to service after the war, should the conflict end in less than four years. They wished to enlist only until the end of the war. After initially resisting suggestions for duration-of-the-war enlistments, the navy finally yielded to the demand.[19]

In the postwar scramble for recruits, four years again proved too long an obligation, and the department offered a choice of two-, three-, or four-year enlistments. About 95 percent chose the two-year contract. Many who selected the three-year enlistment did so because it was required for assignment to a trade school.[20] By the end of 1921, the navy had enough men in service to revert to the four-year enlistment period. In 1923 it also imposed limitations on reenlistment by ending one-year extensions.[21]

The department obviously preferred the longest enlistment possible since an extended enlistment period reduced the burden of recruiting and training and provided a more experienced force. Four years survived as the most the market would bear, but attention sometimes turned to extending the time. Noting that Britain required a twelve-year obligation, some officers hoped that the American navy could increase its term to at least six years. In 1923 the Bureau of Navigation polled recruiting officers about such a proposal. Twenty-one felt that six-year enlistments would not secure enough recruits, contending that men seldom enlisted with the idea of a career and that American youth was too restless to commit itself that long. Fourteen other officers supported the idea, arguing that the navy could enlist enough men by lowering the minimum age to sixteen. It would then be possible to attract boys and to train them for a career in the navy.[22] Although the service decided not to lengthen the obligation at that time, in 1939 the Bureau of Navigation again sought recruiting officers' opinions about a six-year enlistment, and they replied favorably. Consequently, in July 1939 the navy began accepting only six-year enlistments.[23] Even though in 1923 recruiters had believed that a longer period demanded a lowered age requirement, in 1939 the navy felt confident enough about securing the necessary manpower to raise the age limit from seventeen to eighteen.

Whenever possible the navy enlisted men for general service—that is, for assignment at the navy's convenience. It rarely allowed recruits entering the service for the first time to select a ship or station, as it frequently had in the nineteenth century. Sometimes, however, it was compelled to permit such choices. After the armistice, in desperate need of enlisted personnel, the navy tried a number of ideas to make service more attractive. One inducement it tried was allowing men enlisting on a ship to remain on that ship for training and initial service. Going even further, it designated special ships for certain classes of men; for example, only ex-soldiers were accepted for the *Champlin*, a new destroyer.[24] Another destroyer, the *Rizal*, was manned by Filipinos, and there was even some unofficial talk of permitting a similar ship for blacks. A more ambitious program begun in 1920 was to enlist only men from Tennessee for the new battleship *Tennessee* and from California for the *California*. The bureau had received a similar suggestion as early as 1904 and again in 1916, but each time it had rejected the proposal as attractive but not worth the trouble. After initially recruiting most of the crews from those states, in the 1920s the navy found it was inconvenient to maintain the special nature of the ships and abandoned the effort.[25]

THE RECRUIT

Successful recruiting was determined not only by the number of men enlisted but also by the type of men who served. As has been seen, many in the navy believed that the ideal sailor was native-born, young, educated, white, from a small town or rural area, and from what the navy considered a "good family." The department thought that such a person would be most able to learn the skills a modern navy needed, would most probably stay for the full term of enlistment, and would reflect most favorably on the service.

Inland recruiting proved to be a significant step in attracting the men the navy desired. Although a few officers in the twentieth century might have felt that the men were still being recruited "principally from seaboard cities,"[26] this view was not true. The recruits came from the interior in increasing numbers, and they were being deliberately sought there. As Rear Admiral Reginald F. Nicholson explained to a House subcommittee in 1911:

> It has been our endeavor to enlist men throughout the whole country rather than to take them from the water front. We get a better class of men when we get them from the interior. They stay; they do not run away; they are not transients; they have homes, and they are people who respect the obligations of oaths more than the class of people who enlist along the water front.[27]

The Bureau of Navigation urged recruiting officers to "go after the country boys of their Districts rather than the city boys, who are less desirable material." It thought that "raw recruits from Ohio, Indiana, Illinois, Wisconsin, Minnesota, Iowa, and Missouri make the best material, and the rural districts should be carefully combed for recruits."[28] The converse of this feeling that rural areas and small towns offered the best manpower pool was the navy's belief that the cities supplied riffraff. Some officers even felt that the New York City and Philadelphia recruiting stations should be closed.[29] The department never went to that extreme, but it did remain hostile to suggestions that the urban dweller, especially the poor, foreign element, would be best suited to the navy.[30]

Having determined where to find the men it wanted, the department made strong efforts to get them. Table 3 of the Appendix demonstrates that the navy enjoyed considerable success in securing recruits from the areas it had come to prize. The number of sailors born in the midwestern states of Ohio, Indiana, Wisconsin, Minnesota, Iowa, and Missouri, which the Bureau of Navigation had recommended, grew from 1.8 percent of the force in 1890 to

20.6 percent in 1915. The navy's new inland recruiting efforts also extended into the South. In the twentieth century, the number of sailors born in such states as North Carolina, Georgia, Kentucky, Louisiana, and Texas increased significantly—from 1.1 percent in 1890 to 9.9 percent in 1915. At the same time, the proportion of men born in Maryland and Virginia, two southern states that had been important in the nineteenth century, declined; since these states had supplied many of the black enlisted men, the decline probably resulted from a decrease in the number of blacks in the service.

The increased proportion of men coming from the Midwest and South did not mean that the populous East Coast ceased supplying men to the twentieth-century service. Indeed, the proportion of enlisted personnel born in such states as New York or Massachusetts remained approximately the same in the nineteenth and twentieth centuries—about 12 percent for New York and 7 percent for Massachusetts.[31] The difference was that the navy was enlisting increasing numbers of recruits from outside the major urban areas; in 1916, for example, the Recruiting Service operated offices in twelve cities in New York State and seven in Massachusetts, whereas in the nineteenth century, rendezvous in these states were located only in New York City and Boston.[32]

The navy had adopted its new recruiting system partly as a means of increasing the proportion of citizens—and particularly of native-born citizens—in the enlisted force. Although nineteenth-century officers had exaggerated the numbers of aliens in naval crews, the service came to feel that the modern warships should be manned completely by Americans. As the new policy of seeking men without maritime experience increased the number of citizens available for enlistment, noncitizens were steadily eliminated. As has been seen, in 1897, 54 percent of the men in the navy were native-born and 74 percent were citizens; table 4 of the Appendix shows that, by 1907, 84 percent were native-born, 94.3 percent were citizens, and another 1.6 percent were from the islands which the United States had acquired during the Spanish-American War. Since the supply of American enlisted men seemed assured, on January 5, 1907, the navy limited first enlistments to citizens of the United States and its insular possessions. The number of noncitizens continued to decline until by 1917 only 0.2 percent of the men were not citizens.[33]

In addition to being citizens, twentieth-century recruits tended to be young; most men seem to have entered the service near the bottom of the permitted age limit. In 1907, for example, the average new enlistee in training at Norfolk was twenty-one years of age, at San Francisco nineteen years, ten months, and at Newport nineteen years.[34] In general, the navy preferred younger recruits since it was thought they usually adapted to naval discipline more readily than older men. The service also realized, though, that a young force presented its drawbacks:

It is true that youth presents the advantage of alertness and a readier susceptibility to training, but it presents the great disadvantage of lightness in weight, immaturity of mind, the lack of power to endure hardship or exposure, and it is doubtful if their physical and mental powers would coordinate in time of some trying emergency.[35]

Recruits became even younger when the demand for men increased. After the armistice the navy was deluged with youthful applicants, a large number of whom it had to enlist to compensate for the postwar exodus. As one veteran observed of the recruits boarding the battleship *Texas* in 1919, there was not "a razor in the lot. They were the boys . . . too young for the war, and were out for adventure now, full of yearning for excitement."[36]

Although recruits' ages remained relatively low, their educational level gradually improved over the years. The twentieth-century navy could insist that its men know how to read and write as a qualification for enlistment. No longer did men sign shipping articles with an "X," as 33.2 percent had done in 1870.[37] A partial high-school education became increasingly common for enlisted men. In 1923, for example, 46.5 percent of recruits had completed one or more years of high school, 42.8 percent had completed the seventh or eighth grades, and only 10.7 percent had less than a seventh-grade education.[38] This improvement reflected both the navy's growing ability to attract better-educated men and the increase in school attendance among the American population in general.

In spite of the navy's literacy requirement in the twentieth century, illiterates did enlist. In 1904 the training ship *Prairie* received nine landsmen for training who could not read. The commander in chief of the Atlantic Training Squadron complained to the Bureau of Navigation: "As the instructions for enlisting men specifically require that they shall be able to read and write, gross carelessness on the part of the enlisting officers must be apparent in the above cases."[39] The problem arose again in the confusion following World War I. The *Tennessee*, commissioned in 1920, established a special class for its sailors, some of whom could not read or write and others of whom had had only a year or so of schooling and desired more instruction. Even in the thirties, the cooks school at Hampton Roads reported receiving illiterates as trainees.[40]

The profile of enlisted men can be drawn more sharply by examining the kinds of men the navy excluded. In addition to aliens and illiterates, the navy wished to prevent the enlistment of criminals. Accepting felons had been forbidden in the nineteenth century, but the ban was not actively enforced both because criminal records were difficult to uncover and because the fleet needed men. Although the department was better able to implement this prohibition in the twentieth century, the public image of the seafaring forces as a home for fugitives and brigands continued. The navy remained sensitive to that image; it denounced any suggestion that it should accept a man with even a minor infraction on his record. The service zealously ferreted out cases of judges who offered youthful offenders a choice between jail and enlistment. Rebuking the judges, the navy reminded them that it did not enlist criminals.[41]

Even when the navy was experimenting with placing its own prisoners on probation during World War I, Secretary Daniels rejected a proposal by the warden of Michigan State Prison to release certain inmates for service in the armed forces. Although Daniels felt that the suggestion raised interesting sociological questions, he could not agree because, he said,

> the Navy is filled with young men from the best walks of life and the parents of these boys feel that the Navy Department had taken somewhat of a parental obligation in looking after their welfare, and if it should become known, which of course it would, that their sons were being thrown in close daily associations with men who have been through prison, it would have a most disastrous effect upon the enlisted personnel and particularly upon recruiting.[42]

Black applicants were almost as unwelcome as convicts in the modern navy. As has been seen, after the Civil War the navy enlisted blacks in relatively large numbers, allowed them to serve in a variety of ratings, and maintained integrated messing and berthing. Although there is ample evidence that the old navy was not without prejudice and probably enlisted blacks primarily because it needed the manpower, nevertheless it did not establish official policies of discrimination. In the twentieth century such was not the case. As the department found that it could raise enough men without blacks through inland recruiting, it officially enunciated a policy that limited black enlistees to the messmen and lower fireroom ratings. Because the men ate and slept in the company of sailors performing similar duties, this new policy effectively led to segregated messing and berthing. Ultimately, the navy was to stop the enlistment of blacks altogether.

One of the first signs of increasing restrictions on blacks was the service's decree that blacks should not be admitted to the new rating it had created for recruits without maritime experience. As early as 1901 the navy declared that it did "not consider negroes desirable persons for landsmen for training."[43] This policy supported the preference for a white force expressed by many recruiting officers. In 1904 a New Orleans recruiter, for example, refused to enlist blacks because he claimed that accepting Negroes would have made it impossible to enlist whites. Since instructions from the Bureau of Navigation called for enlisting only qualified and desirable men, the recruiting officer reasoned that he could reject blacks because his "experience with colored men on board ship places them in my mind as less desirable than white men."[44]

Although the navy was taking definite measures in the early twentieth century to curtail black enlistments, it was still reluctant to publicize this fact.

When in 1908 H. C. Smith, editor of the Cleveland *Gazette*, requested an official response to a report that the service sought to employ only white men as cooks and servants—and thus to exclude blacks from even the messmen branch, where the majority of them had traditionally served—the secretary of the navy replied that the "circulars and instructions for recruiting officers . . .contain no provision whatsoever for discrimination between colored and white men."[45] Only four days before this letter, however, the Bureau of Navigation had informed recruiting stations that it preferred white men as officers' cooks and stewards.[46]

Those blacks still accepted in the early twentieth century were placed in the less desirable engine-room ratings and in the messmen branch. Though statistics on distribution among ratings by race are not generally available for this period, a 1913 letter vividly reflects the opportunities open for blacks: only 152 blacks were serving on the ships scheduled to send sailors to march in the inaugural parade. Twenty-one of the 152 were in the engine-room force, six served in the commissary branch, three were gunner's mates, and the remaining 122 were messmen. None of the men detailed to march was black.[47]

Segregation aboard ship also becomes increasingly evident in the early years of the twentieth century. In 1900, in one of the first indications of a desire to separate the races, Captain Willard H. Brownson requested that since it would not be possible for the soon-to-be-commissioned *Alabama* "to fill the complement of Ward Room Messmen with white men, as intended," the three whites already accepted "be discharged, so that colored men may be enlisted in their places."[48] In 1905 a black sailor complained to Theodore Roosevelt that separate tables were being used aboard the receiving ships in the navy yard at Norfolk.[49] Four years later, the Constitution League protested the formation of segregated eating aboard the battleship *Mississippi*. In this case, the Bureau of Navigation investigated and reported that an all-Negro mess had been formed among the engine-room force as a result of charges by black personnel that they "were not receiving proper and fair service at meals" when they were seated with whites. This step was taken in the interests of the men, and "since that time there have been no further complaints." Four black men who belonged to other divisions aboard the ship continued to sit with white sailors, and twenty-five black messmen ate with nine messmen of other races.[50]

When the entire federal government reduced job opportunities for blacks during Woodrow Wilson's presidency, the navy joined a trend that fit its own course.[51] World War I also failed to reverse navy policy. During the hostilities, the department rejected suggestions that it increase its enlistment of blacks. Shortly after the declaration of war, for example, a Minnesota congressman forwarded a letter from a member of the black community who offered to aid in recruiting. The Bureau of Navigation declined the help, with the explanation:

The Bureau appreciates the patriotism of the negroes, but, as you can readily understand, it is not good policy for negroes to be enlisted as apprentice seamen and be required to live under the congested conditions which frequently prevail on board ship and at training stations. . . . In view of the fact that the Navy is obtaining enlistments in gratifying numbers, it is suggested that Mr. Smith direct his attention to the enlistment of men for the colored regiments in the Army.[52]

At about this same time, Secretary Daniels wrote to Senator Joseph S. Frelinghuysen of New Jersey:

You are informed that there is no legal discrimination shown against colored men in the Navy. As a matter of policy, however, and to avoid friction between the two races, it has been customary to enlist colored men in the various ratings of the messmen branch; that is, cooks, stewards and mess attendants, and in the lower ratings of the fireroom; thus permitting colored men to sleep and eat by themselves.[53]

The standard monograph on blacks in the navy suggests that the department continued "its policy of enlisting Negroes into the ranks on a fully integrated basis" after the Spanish-American War and that segregation dates from World War I.[54] Yet the evidence refutes this interpretation. Indeed, Daniels' assertion that limited opportunities for blacks were "customary" in 1917 clearly demonstrates that by World War I segregation was already well established in the navy.

Daniels wrote in his letter to Frelinghuysen that blacks were allowed in the lower engine-room ratings. The record suggests, however, that the navy did not wish them even in that position. Nonservant billets for blacks were steadily reduced, and blacks were increasingly confined to the messmen branch. For example, in 1916 the department suggested renaming the "coal passer" rating "fireman, third class," because it thought the designation "coal passer" hampered recruiting for the billet. Rear Admiral Victor Blue, chief of the Bureau of Navigation, was particularly concerned that midwesterners were not enlisting as coal passers; it therefore is clear that the service wished to man the engine-room force with whites.[55]

The prime motive for this policy seems to have been that the department did not wish blacks to achieve positions of authority over whites. This practice of restricting blacks succeeded until in the postwar navy black petty officers in ratings outside the messmen branch were considered relics of an earlier era. The navy felt that such black petty officers remaining from former years did "not fit in anywhere"; consequently, it had trouble finding assignments for them in which "their services can be used with satisfaction to all concerned."[56]

As restrictive as the department's policy toward the employment of blacks was, it still fails completely to describe the plight of the Negro in the twentieth-century navy. For if the navy decreed that blacks could enlist only as messmen, it also preferred messmen to be of another race. Because a long-established tradition in the service held that Chinese recruited in Asia made the best servants, the navy sometimes waived its 1907 citizenship requirement to permit continued enlistment of a small number of these men for service in the Far East. More importantly, since regulations allowed recruitment from United States insular possessions, the Philippines offered a new and acceptable supply of Asiatic servants—a source the navy quickly tapped. As shown in the Appendix, table 5, "Color of the Enlisted Force, 1906-40," the number of Filipinos rose rapidly and by 1914 had surpassed the number of blacks. Finally, on August 4, 1919, the navy halted first enlistments of Negroes altogether; as blacks retired or left the service, their numbers declined, reaching a low of 441 in 1932 out of a total enlisted force of 81,120 men—or 0.55 percent of the total.[57]

Entry of nonwhites into the navy ceased completely in December 1930 when the Bureau of Navigation suspended first enlistments of Filipinos because no new messmen were needed. In late 1932, however, the bureau decided to reopen the rating. Reversing a navy policy that had been in effect since 1919, the director of enlisted personnel recommended that the new enlistments be made within the "Continental United States from men of negro blood." He argued that in case of war, especially conflict in the Pacific, it would be difficult to maintain lines of communication to the Philippines for new messmen; furthermore, Congress seemed likely to grant the islands independence.[58]

In the discussion within the bureau that followed, some officers asserted that Filipinos were superior servants and that returning to recruiting blacks would "be a distinct step backwards."[59] Most officers, though, concurred with the proposal to enlist blacks but urged careful selectivity in enlistment. They felt that blacks in northern urban areas were undesirable since, as one wrote, they were "apt to be independent, insolent, and over-educated."[60] On the other hand, "by training and environment the Southern colored man has inherited a servant's point of view and is usually contented and happy in that position."[61] Thus the consensus favored concentrating recruiting in the South to secure the "unspoiled young negro."[62]

Following these recommendations, the Bureau of Navigation resumed enlistment of blacks on January 4, 1933, and opened a school at Hampton Roads, Virginia, to train the new recruits in the duties of mess attendant, third class.[63] In order to insure the enlistment of the proper type of blacks, the bureau limited the stations that were given quotas for Negro mess attendants. At first, enlistments were carefully confined to a few southern cities.[64] Later, the bureau assigned quotas to other areas but continued to give the South a disproportionate share. When recruiting was allowed only in the South, an applicant from another area was permitted to take a preliminary examination at a station near his home, but he had to travel at his own expense to a station authorized to accept enlistments in the rating, usually located in a city near the mess attendant school.[65] This practice, though adopted partially to reduce transportation costs for the navy, shows clearly that northern blacks were unwelcome in the service.

Although naval policy during the 1930s limited blacks to the messmen branch, this restriction was apparently not explained to many black applicants before they enlisted. The National Association for the Advancement of Colored People received complaints from men that recruiting officers had said any specialty was open to them and that training was available, but that upon reporting to training stations "we found that we were segregated into one branch."[66]

Many officers in the thirties were still not pleased with the performance of blacks. The executive officer of the *Wyoming*, to which some graduates of the messmen school were sent, reported:

> I believe that any negro who is a good servant is the exception and that he compares only favorably with the average oriental servant. Generally, the negro is lazy, slow thinking, and slow acting. He is dirty about his person. He does his work in a slovenly fashion and requires constant supervision for even routine matters. He has a distorted idea of truthfulness and honesty. He has an abnormal appetite and eats whenever he can lay his hands on food. . . . He is more easily susceptible to colds, influenza and other respiratory diseases than other members of the crew.[67]

The average size of blacks compared to Filipinos also drew much adverse comment. One officer noted the "great number of large mess attendants reaching the Fleet," the amount of food they consumed, and "the unmilitary appearance generally presented." He felt that, everything else being equal, a man of average or less than average height and build was "better suited for the duties of an officer's servant than one six feet or over."[68]

Dissatisfaction with black mess attendants produced a desire to return to the more acceptable Asians. Since it seemed impossible at the time to resume the enlistment of Filipinos, after much discussion the navy began enlisting Chamorros, natives of Guam. On July 1, 1937, it assigned Guam a monthly quota of ten mess attendants, third class, and later increased the number to fifteen. Officers in the service responded enthusiastically to the Chamorros.[69]

During the late 1930s suggestions to resume the use of Filipinos continued. Captain Jesse B. Oldendorf, later to achieve fame in the Battle for Leyte Gulf, recommended a distribution in the messmen branch of 60 percent Filipinos, 15 percent Chamorros, and 25 percent Negroes, but because the islands were scheduled for independence, the question of the legality of enlisting Filipinos prevented the navy from adopting such a policy. The department had to wait until after World War II for a special agreement permitting the enlistment of Philippine citizens as messmen.[70]

The renewed acceptance of blacks in the messmen branch failed to affect the navy's determination to exclude Negroes from other parts of the service. To the occasional inquiries concerning this practice, the navy replied:

After many years of experience the policy of not enlisting men of the colored race for the seaman and other branches of the Naval Service, except the messman branch, was adopted to meet the best interest of general ship efficiency. Experience in former years has shown clearly that men of the colored race, if enlisted in the seaman branch and promoted to the position of petty officers, cannot maintain discipline among the men of the white race over whom they may be placed by reason of their rating, and that as a result team work, harmony, and ship efficiency are seriously handicapped.[71]

This passage is from a letter to A. C. MacNeal, president of the Chicago Branch of the National Association for the Advancement of Colored People, but the responses to all correspondents during the thirties remained virtually the same. The navy justified its action by the existence of white prejudice, assuming that the correctness of its policy was apparent to all.

The racial attitudes that led the navy to limit the enlistment of blacks also affected the enlistment of other minorities. Only Filipinos were enlisted in large numbers. Yet if Filipinos were preferred to blacks, they still were offered only limited opportunities. They were restricted largely to the messmen branch, although some served as musicians.[72]

During World War I there was a brief experiment in the more extensive employment of Filipinos. In the early days of the war, the Philippine legislature offered to pay for a destroyer and a submarine provided that the crews be composed of Filipinos. The navy accepted the vessels, agreed to follow the stipulation, and on May 20, 1919, commissioned the destroyer *Rizal*, named for a Philippine patriot shot by the Spanish in 1896. The use of Filipinos in all ratings, however, did not work well. Edmund S. Root, their commanding officer and an American, reported that the men were severely handicapped by lack of training and unfamiliarity with English. He also believed that they lacked the character to show leadership and initiative and that an all-Filipino crew would be feasible only after a long period of training. At the time of the commissioning Root thought that the crew was incapable of operating the vessel without endangering the ship and their own lives and therefore requested that the number of American petty officers be increased.[73]

The navy soon abandoned its attempts to establish a nonwhite crew. Until the Second World War it cited the failure of the *Rizal* in rejecting suggestions for an all-black ship (an idea perhaps inspired by the black units in the army).[74] No one in the bureau seems to have mentioned the fact that Filipinos had operated vessels of the Insular Forces since 1901; thus the *Rizal*'s failure undoubtedly can be attributed less to the crew's racial characteristics than to the problems of training and language.[75]

Other races were generally too small a proportion of the enlisted force to receive much attention. American Indians never numbered more than a few men in any one year. The main issue in enlisting Indians was the question of their citizenship. Once enlisted, they were not restricted as were blacks.

Puerto Ricans and other Caribbean peoples were usually lumped in a category with American Negroes.[76]

Jewish sailors did not suffer the same kind of discrimination as other minorities. The navy apparently accepted Jewish applicants without hesitation. Because they were classified as "white" and the Bureau of Navigation kept no statistics on the religions of enlisted men, their exact number cannot be determined. It is certain, nevertheless, that they formed only a small part of the total personnel. In 1917 the navy's first Jewish chaplain reported that on his ship, the transport *Grant*, he found only five coreligionists in the crew of six hundred. He later estimated that no more than 2 percent of the navy's total enlisted force was Jewish.[77]

If numbers are hard to discover, the treatment Jews were accorded aboard ship is even more difficult to determine. The novel *Delilah*, generally accurate on enlisted matters, tells of one crewman who was ostracized, in part because he was Jewish.[78] A Jewish veteran of eleven years of naval service declared in a 1931 *Our Navy* article that "nowhere else in the world can tolerance be found to equal the degree of its practice as existing in one of the finest institutions in the world—THE UNITED STATES NAVY." The author admitted, however, that before the First World War the situation was not as happy as the one he was describing; in that earlier time, "the Jew was usually singled out in the service and woe to him unless he was more than able to take care of himself. He was the target for all sorts of jibes and insults."[79]

Although it is difficult to be sure how Jews were received aboard ship, official policy did at least recognize the presence of Jewish bluejackets. In 1917 the Bureau of Navigation appointed David Goldberg as the first Jewish chaplain. Goldberg served until 1919, when he resigned rather than face the anomaly of a Jewish chaplain's ministering to a predominantly Christian crew. Twelve years later in 1931, Herbert C. Straus became the second Jewish chaplain in naval history, and he remained in the navy until 1946.[80]

A single chaplain obviously could only partially meet the religious needs of the scattered Jewish seamen. Of more value to all Jewish personnel was the policy the Bureau of Navigation adopted in 1921 of ordering commanding officers to grant as much leave as possible during major Jewish holidays.[81]

Because of the lack of statistics on religious affiliation of the enlisted force, it is also impossible to determine the number of Catholics among the men. It seems, however, that there was probably a sizable number. In his history of the Chaplain Corps, Clifford Drury suggests that the 1862 act of Congress freeing sailors from required attendance at religious services on board ship was brought about by the growing number of Catholics in the navy. Certainly the ethnic composition of the nineteenth-century enlisted force indicates that there may have been large numbers of Catholics in the service. In 1870, for example, 16.7 percent of the men had been born in Ireland and another 1.3 percent in Italy. Not all of these men were necessarily Catholic, but undoubtedly many were. Reflecting the needs of Catholic sailors, the navy appointed its first Catholic chaplain in 1888, and three more were commissioned during the remainder of the nineteenth century. By 1913 there were six Catholic priests out of a total of twenty-three chaplains.[82]

Although there was anti-Catholic sentiment in the nation, there is little evidence of it in the navy. It is possible that a component of officers' dislike of aliens and men from port cities stemmed from anti-Catholicism, but such a feeling was not made explicit. Similarly, some members of the force probably did harbor prejudice against Catholics; yet only one episode involving that bias appears in the records. In that case a sailor wrote his friends that officers "dressed in big robes of white" had compelled the crew of the *Oregon* to attend a Catholic service aboard ship and to salute the priest. This story was published in the August 28, 1897, *Herald and Presbyter* of Cincinnati, Ohio. Captain A. H. Barker of the *Oregon* reported to the secretary of the navy that the man had deserted shortly after writing the letter and that apparently "knowing of his intention to desert, he wrote to his friends appealing to their religious prejudices, in order that they might not judge him too harshly for doing a dishonorable act."[83]

Navy recruiting not only culled out unwanted racial minorities but also avoided the enlistment of political dissidents. It is difficult to find even a hint of radicalism among the enlisted force between the Spanish-American War and World War II. An incident tenuously connected with extremism did occur in 1921 during the Red Scare. Discovering a "Ship's Morale Committee" aboard the battleship *Michigan* that had been formed to "assist the ship's morale officer or commanding officer in his work," alarmists raised the cry of "sovietism" in the navy. A front-page story in the *New York Times* linked this body to an article that had appeared in *Our Navy* urging bluejackets to send representatives to Washington to safeguard their interests. On closer examination, this threat of bolshevism vanished. Formed under Daniels' secretaryship, the committee had been designed to improve morale, not to share the captain's responsibilities. And the sailors in the *Our Navy* article who were considering lobbying sought a modest pay raise rather than revolution. The episode quickly slipped from the news, and no other case arose to take its place.[84]

Before 1942 the enlisted force was entirely male, except during World War I when the naval reserve enrolled over eleven thousand women. In his own account of the war, Secretary Daniels related that he asked the admiral in charge of the legal bureau whether there was anything to prevent women from serving in the reserve; when told there was not, he ordered their enlistment. Although it is not clear from the official records whether Daniels did indeed initiate the idea, he certainly supported it, and the acceptance of women required his sanction.[85]

When women joined the navy in 1917, they became part of the Naval Coast Defense Reserve. In explaining its authority to accept women, the department cited the legislation creating the reserve, which had provided for the enrollment of "persons" for service in connection with the coastal defense, including work with "coast-defense vessels, torpedo craft, mining vessels, patrol vessels or as radio operators."[86] On March 19, 1917, the Bureau of Navigation authorized commandants of naval districts to enroll women for shore duty "in the ratings of yeoman, electrician (radio) or in such other ratings" as the commandant regarded as essential.[87] Two days later, Loretto Perfectus Walsh, the first female sailor, enrolled as a chief yeoman at the naval home in Philadelphia. During the war, women served in a variety of capacities—from cook to electrician—but most enlisted in the yeoman rating, performing clerical duties; indeed, the popular term for all women in the navy became "yeomanette." Because women were not assigned to sea duty, the department created the yeoman (F) designation to distinguish women from men in the yeoman rating.[88]

As reservists, women received the same pay and allowances as men, and they functioned essentially as any other reservist on active duty. Members of the Navy Nurse Corps (Female), which had been formed in 1908, on the other hand, were civilian employees and thus were not part of the enlisted force. Nurses were under the authority of the Surgeon General, not of the Bureau of Navigation, worked under a separate pay scale, and served only in naval hospitals.[89]

Because virtually no planning had preceded the 1917 decision to enroll women in the navy, female recruits found the service unprepared for them. At first there were not even regulations for a physicial examination—a fact which caused some embarrassment and confusion for both the doctors and the women.[90] Nor was there a uniform for women; the enlistees devised their own from such navy items as seemed appropriate, supplemented with their own clothing. The absence of an official uniform also raised the question in paymasters' minds of whether women were eligible for the clothing allowance given to all male recruits. The department held that they were entitled to it. The adoption of an official uniform finally settled the matter.[91]

The yeomanettes were generally well received, especially by officers, for they provided the navy with office help when it was greatly needed. For example, Rear Admiral Samuel McGowan, paymaster general of the navy, claimed that the "efficiency of the Navy's entire supply system would have been impaired had it not been for the women Reservists."[92]

Most complaints about the enlistment of women seem to have originated with male yeomen who objected to sharing their rating with women. An *Our Navy* editorial noted the resentment over "the fact that the girls were allowed to wear the yeoman's rating badge and carry a yeoman's rating" and suggested that the "proper thing to do would have been to provide a special name for female clerks on shore duty" because "the yeoman branch, like all other branches of the Navy, is and always was a MAN's branch—a *seagoing* man's branch."[93] Not all sailors felt this way, and there is no evidence of the protests' going beyond off-duty grumbling.

Although the department enrolled women in the reserve on the same basis as men, it seems to have regarded the women as essentially civilians. This nonmilitary status was most apparent in disciplinary action. Secretary Daniels, for example, established a policy of limiting the use of courts-martial to punish female offenders. In December 1917 he recorded in his diary that he had overturned a court-martial decision involving a female because he felt the navy "cannot deal with women as with men."[94] In the same month, Captain William Watts, the judge advocate general, testified before Congress that female yeomen would be disciplined under civil service rules rather than by deck court-martial. A general exemption from deck courts-martial, which handled minor offenses, eased life somewhat for the women.[95] Yet, the navy's protective attitude and the fact that women could not serve at sea suggests that the department never viewed women as full-fledged members of the enlisted force.

After the war many of the women reservists wished to remain in the service, and apparently some of the men also hoped they would stay. One magazine which catered to enlisted men begged for their continued presence:

Don't fire 'em, Josephus;
To our plea don't be deaf.
The Navy won't be any fun
Without the Yeomen (F.).[96]

Congress, however, quickly eliminated the possibility of women's serving in the peacetime navy by passing the Naval Appropriation Act of July 11, 1919, with the requirement that all women be discharged.[97]

Because women were barred from future service, some officers thought that females should not be given "honorable" discharges because these discharges always carried a recommendation for reenlistment. The yeomanettes protested; they argued that since the type of discharge reflected the quality of service, issuing a woman a lesser discharge than earned would imply that she had not performed her duties satisfactorily. They were particularly concerned because the type of discharge would affect their chances for civilian employment. The women appealed to sympathetic officers—including Rear Admiral Charles B. McVay, Jr., the chief of the Bureau of Ordnance—who carried their case to the secretary of the navy. Ultimately, they secured the right to receive the type of discharge that each individual's record warranted.[98]

After the war, women at first received the rewards of service without trouble; they were issued the Victory Medal and paid the sixty-dollar gratuity for wartime service along with male enlisted men. In 1924, however, Congress tried to exclude women from the adjusted compensation bill (later called the Bonus Act). Only strong protests secured an amended bill which included female reservists.[99]

After discharging the women as required by law, the navy seemingly forgot many officers' past enthusiasm for female reservists. With the advent of World War II, the department resisted the drive to enlist women. Indeed, as late as February 1942—just five months before the creation of the WAVES (Women Accepted for Voluntary Emergency Service) the chief of the Bureau of Navigation wrote that the department "did not intend" to seek legislation permitting the acceptance of women in the navy or the naval reserve.[100] Soon, of course, women were once again accepted into the navy and became a permanent (albeit still limited) part of the enlisted force.

WHY MEN JOINED

Determining the types of men the navy wanted is fairly straightforward, but analyzing what the recruits expected from the navy is not as simple. Aspirations of recruits were diverse. Charles Blackford had longed to serve on torpedo boats from the time he was five. Murry Wolffe formed a "secret ambition" to enlist from playing around the Brooklyn navy yard as a boy. One of Blackford's shipmates from North Carolina, on the other hand, had thought he was taking a regular job when he enlisted to escape the relatives of a girl he was in trouble over.[101] Yet, even though every applicant had his own reasons for enlisting and many applicants would have had problems explaining fully why they joined, certain common themes do emerge. These motives, furthermore, remain generally constant during the forty years from the Spanish-American War to World War II. The only major exception was the period from 1917 to 1918, when more men than usual enlisted from a sense of patriotism.

The lure of travel and adventure was stronger than any other attraction of naval life. Few men who became sailors would have been able to tour the world as civilians. Seamen eagerly investigated every port their ships visited, and in later years many former seamen remembered more of their journeys than they did of their shipmates. Some recruits were so eager to get to sea that they declined the opportunity to take leave at the end of training because they wanted to begin the adventure of naval life as soon as possible. In a sense, the navy served a function similar to that of college; it offered young men a chance to get away from home, to see new things, and to have a socially acceptable break between adolescence and adulthood.

As has been seen, navy recruiting emphasized the romantic conception of a sailor's life. Throughout the period, travel remained a mainstay of advertising efforts. It was also the formula to which the service reverted in times of extreme need. Furthermore, the publicity accompanying a particularly exciting event—such as the 1908 cruise of the White Fleet or the occupation of Veracruz in 1914—stimulated enlistments.[102] Travel, possibly spiced with a brief amphibious operation, was a prime motive for signing on with the navy.

Although the Bureau of Navigation stressed career opportunities in its advertising almost as much as it did travel, this consideration remained a secondary attraction for most men enlisting for the first time. Only 5 percent of the recruits in 1923 chose an enlistment period of longer than two years, even though a three-year obligation was required for assignment to trade school.[103] Despite this fact, enlistees knew about the instruction the navy offered, and many no doubt felt that they might acquire a worthwhile skill. Recruits who wrote articles for training station newspapers under the rubric "Why I Joined the Navy" asserted the importance of a career and steady employment, though they may have been stressing the arguments they felt their officers wished to hear. The prospect of a career or training might well have reinforced a decision made for other reasons and might also have helped sway a reluctant parent. Given the youth of most first enlistees, however, long-range career goals probably never outranked a short-run desire for adventure.

Desire for adventure or for a career can be taken as more or less constant factors in motivating youth to join the navy; they do not in themselves, however, explain the fluctuations in the number of applicants for service. In addition to these factors, the state of the economy must be considered in analyzing the pattern of enlistments, for the lure of the sea proved strongest when civilian jobs were scarce. Not every applicant who visited the recruiter during a business slump came because of economic hard times; yet the ratio of applications for enlistment in relation to places available usually rose during periods of increased unemployment.[104] While an occasional officer might have claimed that "'labor' conditions have no effect or influence whatever on the number of applicants,"[105] most knew otherwise. The surgeon general, perhaps more candid than the Bureau of Navigation might have been, wrote in 1908:

> While credit must be given and due allowance made for the new methods adopted to stimulate enlistments, and the improved system of recruiting inaugurated by the Bureau of Navigation, it is to be observed that the striking increase in the naval force corresponded in time with the recent financial crisis and the resulting far reaching depression of industrial activity and business operations in general. The government services felt the effects of those unsettled and trying conditions, and the navy in

particular experienced a popularity among the unemployed of the country, who, in addition to their quest for occupation under the impelling influences of short rations, were attracted by the widely discussed cruise of the Atlantic Fleet around South America.[106]

Aware of the influence of economic conditions, the bureau encouraged recruiters to watch local situations. A strike or layoff, for example, might force desirable workers into the labor market.[107] The depression in the thirties, of course, made recruiting the easiest it had ever been.

Just as bad times made obtaining men easier, good times made recruiting more difficult. George A. Converse, chief of the Bureau of Navigation, testified to Congress in 1907 that he foresaw an improvement in recruiting because he believed that the good crops and the railroads' heavy demand for labor could not continue.[108] The economic boom that occurred just before the United States entered the war in 1917 also slowed recruiting. Leigh C. Palmer, then chief of the bureau, lamented that Detroit was no longer a good recruiting station because the European war was stimulating production. At that time, in fact, the demand for men in the private sector was so strong that employers were seeking aid from navy recruiters.[109]

Noting the influence of the economy on enlistments, Peter Karsten has suggested that the navy may have served as a minor "safety valve" for urban discontent, especially for skilled craftsmen.[110] This theory, however, cannot be supported by the mere fact that recruiting became easier in hard times. The navy could employ some men, but the numbers were so small that the service could hardly have been much of an outlet for urban unrest—especially given the navy's preference for nonurban applicants. In 1908, for example, when unemployment was 8.5 percent of the work force and about 3 million people were without jobs, the navy enlisted 17,852 men, or 0.6 percent of the unemployed. During the thirties the navy became even less important as a potential employer; when unemployment reached an all-time high in 1933, the navy accepted only 4,572 men at a time when about 12.8 million were out of work—a mere 0.03 percent. It is difficult to imagine that the number of men taken into the navy provided noticeable relief in either case.[111] Furthermore, the navy not only accepted a limited number of men, but it also carefully screened applicants and took only the best qualified—those men most employable in any market.

REENLISTMENT

A successful naval personnel policy demands not only attracting recruits but encouraging desirable men to remain beyond their first enlistment. Because trained and experienced veterans provide the core of an effective force, persuading them to stay in the service should have been a major part of the navy's policy. Yet, while the Bureau of Navigation experimented with new methods of inducing civilians to join, it devoted surprisingly little attention directly to encouraging men to reenlist.

The basic incentive to reenlistment was the continuous-service bonus, inaugurated by a general order of April 7, 1855. As discussed in chapter 2, the order provided three months' pay to a man who had earned an honorable discharge and who rejoined the navy within three months after his previous enlistment expired. In 1899 the bonus was increased to four months' pay for reenlistment within four months.[112] Each reenlistment under continuous service was also accompanied by an increase in base pay, but the new enlistment had to be for a full term. The navy did not further liberalize the provisions for reenlistment until 1912. The appropriation act passed that year permitted extensions of one, two, three, or four years, allowing a sailor to remain in the service without committing himself to another four years. The continuous-service bonus was then paid when the extensions totaled four years.[113]

Despite the navy's neglect of the problem of encouraging men to remain in the service, the reenlistment rate generally improved from 1905 (the year reenlistment data was first published) until the eve of World War II, even though there were sometimes fluctuations from year to year. Reenlistment responded to a variety of forces. The overall upward trend probably resulted from the new selection process, which helped avoid men too restless to adapt to naval discipline, and from improving conditions of shipboard life. Specific yearly fluctuations, on the other hand, are best explained through factors external to the service, such as the level of employment opportunities in the civilian world or the exigencies of wartime.

Table 6 of the Appendix demonstrates the general increase in reenlistment—the rate rose from 54 percent in 1905 to 72 percent by 1915, remained around 70 percent through most of the twenties, and climbed to over 90 percent in the thirties. Even before the exceptionally high rates of reenlistment and unemployment during the Great Depression, however, large numbers of men had decided to remain in the service. Information on length of service, as shown in table 7 of the Appendix, reveals that, by 1926, 42.5 percent of the enlisted force had served four years or more—almost double the level of 1907, the year the navy started publishing these statistics.[114]

In spite of the general improvement, one can also discern from table 6 the strong relationship between external factors and the reenlistment rate. The drop from 54 percent in 1905 to 32.2 percent in 1907 closely follows the declining rate of unemployment. Along the same lines, the upward swing in reenlistment rates beginning in 1908 parallels a worsening situation in civilian employment.

During 1917 and 1918 reenlistment rates were high—reaching 83.4 percent in 1918. Patriotism and the national commitment to the war encouraged men to remain in the service, just as they spurred enlistments from civilians. So strong were these incentives to military service that the reenlistment rate increased at the same time that unemployment was falling. After the armistice, reenlistments fell dramatically, and the rate dropped to 36 percent in 1919 and 1920. The general desire of men who had volunteered for the duration of the war to return to civilian life probably swept up some sailors who ordinarily would have remained with the service. Others left because they saw that opportunities out of the service were more attractive than in it; the economy seemed to be entering a prolonged prosperity in 1919 and 1920, and unemployment was declining. Charles Blackford was only one of many who transferred to better-paying civilian jobs—in his case to the merchant marine.[115]

When the reenlistment rate plummeted suddenly after the war to its lowest level since 1907, the navy adopted a number of temporary incentives. In 1920 it allowed a man to reenlist up to a year after his discharge and still receive the continuous-service benefits if he reenlisted within six months after the passage of the offer. The Bureau of Navigation also granted thirty days' leave in addition to continuous-service benefits to men who reenlisted on their ships.[116]

By 1921 the reenlistment rate had risen to a more normal level, aided by a postwar recession. It then declined once more in 1923—paralleling a drop in unemployment. In reaction to this situation, the bureau again gave special attention to retaining veterans. As it had done immediately after the war for some new enlistees, it permitted men who reenlisted to choose the ship on which they wished to serve, including the new scout cruisers about to be commissioned. In 1923 the bureau also had each command appoint an officer who was "warm-hearted, popular and sincere" to encourage reenlistment.[117]

The belated assignment of personnel to the task of encouraging reenlistments indicates that the navy's approach was more casual to reenlistment than it was to promoting first enlistments. In effect, officers with other primary duties attended the problem as the need warranted. The bureau apparently did not even produce an informational leaflet on reenlistment for the men until 1926.[118]

Reenlistment rates remained relatively high after 1923. Service-wide statistics, however, concealed the fact that some branches had significantly higher return rates than average. In 1928, when 68.5 percent of the men eligible to reenlist did so, the rates by branches varied from 82.9 percent for the aviation branch to 64.9 for the artificer.[119] The retention of certain highly skilled ratings, as in aviation, greatly aided the navy in maintaining an efficient force.

With the coming of the depression, reenlistment boomed, and the rate soared to a previously unequaled 93.25 percent in 1933. The percentage dropped the next year, but it remained high during the remainder of the thirties. Naval service provided a refuge from the depression economy, and men were glad to have the shelter. *Our Navy*, for example, warned its readers:

It is all right for you to get a calendar and a huge blue pencil and mark off days as the date of your discharge approaches, or to swear in stentorian tones, very much to the amusement of your incredulous shipmates, that you will never ship over. Indulge in such harmless buffoonery if you wish but be very careful that you mark on that same calendar with an even larger blue pencil the final date of grace allowed before your opportunity for reenlistment expires. After you're out a few months and have lost the chance to return, no more will you say, "All shipmates went down with the Maine!"[120]

The ease the navy enjoyed in retaining men during the 1930s was obviously due to the state of the economy rather than to actions of the Bureau of Navigation. In fact, Congress suspended the reenlistment bonus from 1933 to 1938, without deterring men from shipping over.[121]

Although economic trouble invariably boosted both reenlistments and applications for first enlistment, even in times of prosperity the twentieth-century navy increasingly secured the numbers and type of men it desired. Inland recruiting expanded the pool of potential applicants; with more men to choose from, the service could experiment with its requirements for enlistment and refine its system of selection. Thus the navy was able to take such measures as instituting a literacy requirement and decreasing the age span for first enlistees.

More significant than such changes, inland recruiting permitted the navy to alter the character of the enlisted force in ways officers perceived as an improvement. With its enlarged source of manpower, the department was able to end its reliance on waterfront populations and to bring into the service men who were American citizens and who fit more fully the cultural and racial biases of the naval hierarchy—and of a good portion of the public. The navy prohibited first enlistment of aliens in 1907. It also steadily reduced the proportion of blacks in the navy, segregated black enlistees into servant billets, and eventually ended the first enlistment of blacks altogether. To a large degree, the aliens and blacks who had formed a significant part of the old navy were easily replaced by recruits from the Midwest and parts of the South—areas virtually unrepresented in the nineteenth-century force. If Secretary Daniels' boast that in the navy "we have the soberest, cleanest young fellows in all the land" contained considerable hyperbole, it nevertheless expressed the department's newly discovered pride in its men.[122]

Although the service was generally pleased with the type of personnel the recruiting system secured, the new man-of-warsman enlisted as a landsman, not as a trained mariner, and needed instruction before he could be sent to sea. Furthermore, the ships of the modern navy demanded a large number of technically schooled men. Because of these two requirements, the department found in the twentieth century that it had to develop a comprehensive system of training for the enlisted force.

chapter 6

Training the Men

The success of the Recruiting Service in bringing into the navy young men without previous service at sea presented the department with a new challenge: assimilating a large number of green hands. In adopting its new recruiting system, the department had also committed itself to the task of teaching virtually all enlistees basic seamanship before assigning them to cruising vessels. At the same time that new sailors required this elementary instruction, other forces were producing the need for advanced training. Even if the old man-of-warsmen had been available in adequate numbers for the new navy, many of their skills would have been obsolete aboard a twentieth-century warship. The new navy thus found that, in addition to establishing a system of basic training for landsmen, it also had to create special schools and courses to supply the skilled manpower the fleet required.

The first step in absorbing large numbers of inexperienced recruits into the service was the establishment in 1899 of a new designation—"landsman for training." The "landsman" rating had been created in 1838 for men not qualified for enlistment as ordinary seamen (the lowest rating for experienced mariners). The old-style landsman served as a laborer or domestic servant aboard ship and was clearly at the bottom of the naval hierarchy. Even the Bureau of Navigation admitted that "the position, though honorable, is not a desirable one. It affords but a poor chance for a young man of any ability or ambition."[1] Thus, it often was a dead-end rating, with little opportunity for on-the-job training or advancement. The new 1899 category, in contrast, indicated men enlisted for instruction in seamanship. The navy anticipated that landsmen for training would advance rapidly within the enlisted ranks. It was also common to accept men for preparation in specialized ratings—e.g., landsman for electrician, landsman for machinist, or landsman for yeoman.

Although committing itself to teaching inexperienced hands the duties of sailors, the Bureau of Navigation recruited landsmen for training before it had any clear idea of what the training should be. At first the recruits were simply sent directly to cruising vessels. Their position on board was untenable, however, and officers, seamen, and even apprentices scorned them as hopeless landlubbers.[2] The bureau quickly realized its mistake and designated the *Hartford, Lancaster, Buffalo, Dixie,* and *Topeka* as training ships for landsmen.[3] At the same time, some of these novices were also trained on receiving ships. Others were sent to the training stations that had been established in the nineteenth century for apprentices. In 1901, for example, the San Francisco Naval Training Station drilled landsmen for training on board its station ship, the *Pensacola*. The commandant there considered the experiment a success and suggested expanding the program.[4]

With the new century and the creation of the landsman for training designation, the older apprentice system appeared increasingly indefensible. The boys' youth and immaturity limited their usefulness aboard ship, and the length of the instruction made apprenticeship more expensive than training landsmen. Furthermore, as has been seen, the low reenlistment rate at the end of the program meant that it failed to produce enough men who made the navy a career. Reform raised the minimum age of apprentices from fourteen to sixteen, but this was only a temporary solution.[5] Finally, the department decided to end the training of young boys altogether and to restructure the landsman for training program. To accomplish this goal, in 1904 it created the new rating of apprentice seaman, with a minimum age requirement of seventeen, to replace the four previous categories of apprentice first, second, and third classes and landsman for training.[6]

THE ERA OF SHIPBOARD TRAINING

Both the apprentice and landsman for training systems had relied on shipboard training. To make training more uniform and thorough for both ratings, in 1902 the navy formed the Atlantic Training Squadron composed of the *Minneapolis, Hartford, Topeka, Essex, Buffalo, Dixie, Prairie, Yankee,* and *Columbia*. Even as the training squadron was being created, however, there raged a debate about whether training should be at sea or on shore.

The proponents of instruction afloat argued that the recruit should be placed immediately in the natural environment of a sailor. Luce, a retired rear admiral on special duty at the Naval War College, continued to support training at sea, which he had helped develop for the apprentice system. Even after the navy had ceased using training vessels, he maintained that land-based teaching failed because it did "not recognize the prime necessity of reconciling the recruit to ship life from the very beginning."[7] Luce felt that shipboard instruction produced a man who was more valuable when he was transferred to the fleet:

Which of the two seamen-apprentices gives most promise of usefulness on board ship—the one who has spent four months in barracks or under a tent, or the one who has spent the same time on board a school ship. . . ? There is nothing taught in barracks, or in a camp, that cannot be taught just as well, or even better, on board a school ship, with the additional advantage that every day spent on board ship tends to reconcile the recruit to his novel surroundings afloat.[8]

Supporters of shipboard training for the modern navy had to contend with the problem of finance because shipboard instruction was more expensive and required more officers and men than did training ashore. In the expansion of the early twentieth century, the navy did not have the resources to spare and thus came to prefer instruction on land. The Bureau of Navigation argued in 1902 that the main purpose of the initial indoctrination was to instill the proper military discipline in landsmen, that military drill was the best way to do this, and that this type of training was most easily given on land. After being introduced to military life ashore, the sailor could then be transferred to the regular vessels of the navy. Here he would receive a continuing training throughout his career to prepare him for a specialized rating.

It is a necessity to have the first training of these men on shore until they learn how to look after themselves and their clothing and gain the required military bearing and preliminary instruction to fit them for further training on board ship, and to allow the weeding out of those who are not suitable and cannot take advantage of said instruction.[9]

In spite of the sentiment of the bureau for land training, the advocates of ship training had sufficient support to gain congressional approval in 1903 of three new training vessels—the *Cumberland, Intrepid,* and *Boxer*.[10] This triumph, however, proved to be the last, for in 1905 the training squadron ceased to exist. As the chief of the Bureau of Navigation explained:

Owing to the great scarcity of officers and the necessity for their services on vessels of large cruising and battle efficiency, it was deemed best to retire the vessels that had been employed exclusively in training service and give the necessary preliminary training to the recruits at the three stations equipped for that purpose at Newport, Norfolk, and San Francisco.[11]

Abolishing the training squadron, though, did not mean an end to some training at sea before a recruit was assigned to a regular service vessel. The training stations put men on tenders, tugs, or other small vessels attached to the stations. The voyage could last a week or two or just a day at a time, with the men returning to the station for dinner and sleep.[12] But even this practice soon died out, apparently from the need to reduce the time in training.

The creation of a reserve fleet in 1912 revived pressure to send recruits to sea. In the same year, the Bureau of Navigation received a proposal to use ships in the reserve to instruct recruits for two of the four months of training.[13] Although the navy found the idea attractive, it was not adopted until 1916, and then it seems to have been a part of limited efforts to prepare for entry into the war. Rear Admiral William F. Fullam, commander in chief of the Pacific Reserve Fleet, twice suggested using recruits on reserve ships before the Bureau of Navigation finally agreed.[14] But shipboard instruction as a normal part of recruit training did not survive the war.

At the same time that officers debated whether or not to use training vessels, proponents of shipboard training contended among themselves over whether such ships should be sail, steam, or sail with auxiliary steam. This debate continued long after warships had abandoned sail. In the final analysis, it was a question of developing character versus developing skill. The advocates of sail stressed the "qualities of courage, resourcefulness, activity, strength," which they felt were best instilled by handling sail.[15] Purists like Luce rejected even auxiliary steam because, they said, crews generally used steam to enter or leave harbors and to avoid storms, thereby missing the best training opportunities.[16]

An important component of the argument for sail amounted to an almost mystical communion with the sea. The sailing ship put a person in direct contact and combat with the ocean, wind, and weather. Because some officers thought a technician on a large ship did not develop a sense of dependence on the sea, they feared that he would become estranged from the very elements of his home. These men wished to have the recruit first grasp the mood and spirit of the sea. Only then would it be time to worry about developing mechanical skills.[17]

Advocates of steam countered that training on sailing ships wasted precious time teaching skills that would never be used again. Contending that the "day of seamanship as represented by the Portsmouth, Saratoga, and Jamestown is passed and can never be revived," they felt that the recruit should be trained on the type of ship on which he would serve.[18] As Captain Charles D. Sigsbee, later skipper of the ill-fated *Maine*, observed:

> If we want a sailor, or to use a better term, a "seaman," who is seven-tenths soldier and mechanic, then the best place to make him is not on board a sailing ship. . . . It would not be thought necessary on shore in hay-making to keep a man at the old-fashioned scythe for six months in order to educate him up to a seat on the mowing machine.[19]

A future chief of naval operations who had served on a battleship in the training squadron also considered the use of sailing ships obsolete, saying:

> We would better face the new conditions now than later on, and boldly break away from the square-rigged vessels for training, and adopt a system in keeping with the naval advancement of the day.[20]

In spite of the navy's increasing dependence on technology, the prosail faction remained strong and possibly dominant. The three new training vessels Congress authorized in 1903 represented a major victory for that side—all were propelled by sail alone.[21] Ironically, as has been seen, the high cost of shipboard training undercut both the sail and steam factions, and the abolition of the training squadron in 1905 effectively ended the debate.

TRAINING STATIONS

The navy had first created training stations for instructing apprentices before sending them to sea in training ships. By 1905, when the disbanding of the training squadron had the effect of transferring the entire apprentice seaman instructional program to land, stations already existed at Newport, San Francisco, and Norfolk.[22] The Bureau of Navigation opened another at Great Lakes, Illinois, in 1911 and in 1923 transferred the facilities at San Francisco to San Diego. As with so much concerning the enlisted force, all these training stations grew slowly and haphazardly—more from the pressure of the moment than from any long-range plan.

Newport and San Francisco had been developed as a part of the apprentice program. Norfolk, on the other hand, became a training station almost by accident and apparently without design. Because Norfolk was a major naval base with a central location, a good climate, and good transportation facilities, it seemed natural to send apprentices to the receiving ship there for training whenever Newport became overcrowded or was placed under quarantine. As the navy began enlisting landsmen for training in 1899, many of them were also sent to the receiving ship at Norfolk. The training station at Norfolk was about the same size as the one at Newport, but at times it became so crowded that messing had to be done in three shifts.[23]

Despite the fact that Norfolk was used as a training station, it was not officially recognized as such and had to operate with material left over from the navy yard there. Such a policy was clearly contrary to the importance of the training facility. Captain Albert C. Dillingham, the commanding officer of the receiving ship *Franklin*, reminded the Bureau of Navigation in 1907 that "the training station at Norfolk seems to be still without an official status" and that as a result "there are not the proper facilities for caring for the command that should exist."[24] The bureau, however, had already recognized the problem and at least as early as 1902 had sought an appropriation for the "maintenance of a Training Station" at Norfolk, but Congress did not fund the station until 1914.[25]

Training stations assumed greater importance as the navy increased its reliance on landsmen. When additional facilities were needed, the Bureau of Navigation turned to the questions of size and location of the installations with a new concern. At first it decided to establish several small facilities of from 1,000 to 1,500 recruits. It rejected the alternative of one central complex to handle from 5,000 to 6,000 men because the British experience with a station of 9,000 taught that "it is impracticable to handle and instruct such a large body of green and undisciplined young men at one station."[26]

The expanding enlistment of landsmen required an increase in the number of training stations. In 1902 the bureau suggested New London, Connecticut, and Port Royal, South Carolina, as sites.[27] Apparently little came of the suggestion to use New London for recruit training, but the navy did utilize briefly the base at Port Royal because it was abandoning the shipyard there and needed another use for the property. A board appointed to investigate the area had reported in April 1901:

> The Board is of unanimous opinion that the Port Royal Station is a most suitable one for the purpose of training landsmen, owing to its mild and healthful climate, to the opportunities furnished by the commodious buildings for quarters, drill and instruction rooms, to the quiet and spacious waters adjoining for boat drill, gunnery practice and exercise afloat, to the extensive level ground that can be made available for drill and parade, to its remoteness from large cities with their accompanying distractions, and to its ready access by rail and water, and believes that if a sufficient quantity of fresh water could be furnished to allow a liberal supply for the purposes of cooking, washing, bathing and scrubbing clothes, hammocks etc., the site would fulfill every requirement.[28]

After this report, the Bureau of Navigation ordered the commandant at Port Royal to prepare plans and estimates for a training station for 1,000 landsmen and a school for fifty petty officers.[29] Although a few landsmen went to Port Royal for training, the training station never received an appropriation and was eventually abandoned.[30] The bureau first held it in reserve in case of sickness at Newport or Norfolk and then employed it as a disciplinary barracks from 1912 to 1915, when it finally turned it over to the Marine Corps, which developed its Parris Island facility there.[31]

At least part of the reason for not developing Port Royal was the rival claim of a proposed station on the Great Lakes. The Naval Appropriation Act for fiscal year 1903, passed July 1, 1902, provided $5,000 for a board to survey possible sites for a training station in the Midwest. With the development of inland recruiting, the navy wished to establish a training station near the homes of the new enlistees, and the natural location for such a station seemed to be on the Great Lakes.[32] In its choice of locations, the board considered access from settled areas, transportation to the Atlantic coast, and harbor accommodations. It hoped to find a parcel of high land of at least 100 acres, with good water, and with a waterfront of not less than a half mile in length. The site also had to be close enough to a large city that could provide both entertainment for men on leave and a manpower pool for recruiting.[33]

(The navy was above all flexible—it had liked Port Royal because it was away from city "distractions.")

After considering numerous areas that various cities and individuals proposed, the board ranked Lake Bluff, Illinois, as its first choice over Racine and Milwaukee, Wisconsin, Muskegon, Michigan, and Michigan City, Indiana.[34] The cost of the land played an important role in the final decision. Ultimately, the Commercial Club of North Chicago enabled the department to obtain its first preference by purchasing the property the navy wanted and donating it to the service.[35]

On July 1, 1905, Captain Albert Ross, the commandant of the new station, took possession of the property for the government. Even before the navy received title to the land, it had hired an architect to plan a station that would accommodate 400 men in receiving barracks and 1,000 in the main barracks.[36] Work on the station proceeded slowly, and the completion date was steadily pushed back. In 1909 the secretary of the navy expressed his hope that the station would open about July 1, 1910, but it did not begin operations until July 1, 1911.[37]

Criticism of the Lake Bluff location soon arose. While the facilities were under construction, a board of inspection suggested that no plans for expansion be considered until "the utility and value of this station may be demonstrated." The board felt that the station could do little to accustom boys to the seafaring life and urged that recruits be sent to the coast and to sea as quickly as possible.[38] Even after the station had been completed, Rear Admiral A. C. Dillingham, an officer with considerable experience in the training program, wrote, "I can find no sanitary or service reason whatever, for having located a training station at Chicago, a thousand miles from the coast, with a climate in no way suitable for training purposes."[39]

Despite the criticism, the Great Lakes Naval Training Station was completed—the last such facility developed before World War I. Located far from the ocean, it demonstrated the navy's commitment to both inland recruiting and training ashore. More than any of the other three stations, Great Lakes was developed solely for instructing landsmen; because of that fact it symbolized the new importance of training to the navy.

With America's entry into World War I, thousands of young men joined the service. This horde of eager enlistees soon overwhelmed the training stations. Although in 1916 the Bureau of Navigation had estimated that its four sites together could accommodate a maximum of 6,850 recruits—2,500 at Great Lakes, 2,200 at Newport, 1,200 at Norfolk, and 950 at San Francisco—by the end of June 1917 there were 40,000 men in training at these four locations.[40] All stations suffered a shortage of housing. When even a tremendous enlargement of the four permanent stations proved inadequate, the navy had to establish thirteen temporary camps. On October 31, 1918, the department had a total of 124,531 recruits in training.[41]

During this wartime expansion, Newport, Norfolk, and Great Lakes acquired more land. Great Lakes added 878.87 acres; Newport purchased 151 acres of hard land and seven acres of land under water at Coddington Point, directly opposite Coaster's Harbor Island and connected to it by a causeway; and Norfolk bought the site of the 1907 Jamestown Exposition at Hampton Roads.[42] The training station at San Francisco, on the other hand, could not expand because it was limited by the size of the island on which it was located. Surplus recruits were temporarily housed in a camp on Mare Island. This problem at Yerba Buena Island during the war helped revive suggestions to build a new West Coast training station.

The Bureau of Navigation had been unhappy with the San Francisco site since 1912 and had sought a larger location, preferably in San Diego. During the war only a training camp was established there. After 1918 interest continued, and the navy finally acquired 278 acres from the San Diego Chamber of Commerce and the city of San Diego.[43] On July 31, 1923, the department closed its station at Yerba Buena Island at San Francisco and moved all Pacific Coast training to San Diego, which had been commissioned on June 1.[44]

In the immediate postwar years, the turnover in enlisted personnel placed continued burdens on these stations. As recruiting subsided, however, the number of men in training also declined, and the large wartime capacity became unnecessary. A period of uncertainty about the future of individual stations followed. A letter from Captain Archibald H. Scales, who had served briefly as the commandant of the Great Lakes station in December 1918 and January 1919, to the executive officer of Great Lakes suggests the problems facing that facility:

> I can understand your almost paternal feeling in regard to it and I hope that it may always retain its importance and virility. You must not be surprised, however, if now that the war is over, great difficulty should be found in keeping it in its present important place. Other stations will be clamoring for a share of the business and, candidly, I am afraid that there will not be enough training in the Navy, or rather money for enough training, to keep four tremendous training stations in operation at one time.[45]

Scales was correct in his fear that money would limit the immediate future of the training stations. An economy-minded administration compelled the navy to reduce its facilities, and the training stations were prime targets.

Suggestions for economizing included combining training stations. At first the navy resisted the idea. It argued, for example, against closing Newport on the grounds that it would be unhealthy for New England boys to train at Norfolk.[46] As the pressure continued, the department increasingly allowed the burden of defense to be carried by sympathetic congressmen while it stood in the background and expressed its willingness to do whatever Congress and the Bureau of the Budget wished.[47] Finally, in October 1921 the navy halted recruit training at Newport and Great Lakes, although the aviation school that had been opened at Great Lakes during the war remained in operation. The Bureau of Navigation reached this decision slowly, though, for as late as March 1921 it had written that the "Department intends to maintain the Newport Training Station" and "has no intention of cutting down the number at Newport any more than at any other station."[48] By July, though, the bureau had obtained an estimate of the money that would be saved; in October it issued orders to close the two facilities. Newport reopened July 1, 1922, but Great Lakes did not resume recruit training until July 1, 1923.[49]

Although all four training stations operated at reduced capacity for the rest of the decade, the threat of closing one or more continued. In 1925, for example, the department considered shutting down both Great Lakes and Hampton Roads.[50] Another suggestion to halt training at Hampton Roads came from the Board on Shore Establishments, known as the Rodman Board. Richard Leigh, assistant chief of the Bureau of Navigation, emphasized that the navy was considering the recommendation only at the insistence of the Bureau of the Budget.[51]

During the depression, the threat of closing surfaced once more. As was the case a decade earlier, decreased enlistment and increased economy-mindedness made four recruit training stations a luxury the navy could not justify. Consequently, it discontinued the use of Newport and Great Lakes from July 1, 1933, to July 1, 1935. The department selected these stations instead of San Diego or Norfolk because their equipment was older than San Diego's and because they were not, as was Norfolk, part of a large naval base that would continue in operation. In 1935 the Bureau of Navigation at first planned to reopen only Newport and to hold Great Lakes in reserve, but congressional pressure easily persuaded it to recommission both stations.[52]

Although an undercurrent of concern about the excess capacity of the training station existed through most of the interwar years, there apparently was never any serious discussion of abandoning any station permanently. A single installation operating at full capacity could easily have accommodated the recruits entering the service at any one time during this period. The navy, however, remained committed to a policy of maintaining several small stations. A major reason was that it wished to have a readily available reserve capacity in case of war. It also wished to simplify transportation of recruits to and from training and possibly to preserve desirable shore billets. In addition, the unwillingness of the navy to reconsider its use of the training stations also reflects a satisfaction with the network of recruit training facilities that had been developed and a reluctance to alter that system.

RECRUIT TRAINING

Creation of training stations obviously solved only part of the problem that the new policy of recruiting landsmen posed; the instruction itself also had to be developed. With only the limited experience of the apprentice program as a guide, the department entered a period of experimentation, marked by troublesome diversity.

The navy recognized the desirability of uniform recruit training, but that goal was not quickly achieved. As early as 1900 the Bureau of Navigation had asked the vessels of the training squadron to exchange drills and instructions so that all ships could employ the best methods. In 1907 the superintendent of the training service ordered all stations to follow the same course of instruction and suggested the formation of a board to coordinate station training programs.[53] Such a board apparently did not materialize until 1920, when the training station commandants met to consider the problem. The members were pleased with the results of their first meeting and suggested holding other sessions in the future.[54]

A second means of standardization was the publication of drill books. While there always had been handbooks for young sailors, the twentieth century saw a new interest in and official status for such volumes. In 1902 the *Bluejacket's Manual* by Lieutenant Ridley McLean and the *Recruit's Handy Book* by Lieutenant Commander William F. Fullam appeared, and both went through many editions. The *Recruit's Handy Book*, with changes in title, survived into the twenties; the *Bluejacket's Manual* is currently in its nineteenth edition. By General Order 114 of November 17, 1902, the Navy Department required every recruit to know the contents of the *Recruit's Handy Book* and issued a copy to each. In addition to supplying enlistees with information about the navy, the new series of publications also helped assure that petty officers in the service operated in a uniform manner. In 1902, for example, Fullam published the *Petty Officer's Drill Book*. This upsurge in the publication of handbooks attests to the fact that oral instruction was no longer sufficient for an enlarged force. In addition, of course, it demonstrates that the twentieth-century navy assumed that its sailors could read—and could read English.

Another important step toward uniformity was the placement of all newly enlisted men, except messmen, in training station programs. At the beginning of the century, only apprentices and landsmen for training attended such schools. Two major groups that were not included in the new training program were members of the engineer's force, who went directly to assignments, and members of the hospital corps, who attended a special school operated by the Bureau of Medicine and Surgery. Gradually, however, the navy came to believe in the value of training station instruction for these men, and all recruits eventually shared a common indoctrination to the service.

Traditionally men in the engineer's force had enlisted as coal passers and were sent immediately to cruising vessels. Without training or an introduction to naval life, they found themselves in the most physically demanding job in the navy. Not surprisingly, coal passers led all other ratings in desertion.[55] It was thought that providing coal passers with some training before assigning them to the fleet might help solve this problem. As early as 1877 the navy had enlisted apprentices for the engineer's force, but that experiment soon ended.[56] Finally, in 1904 it assigned a ship of the Atlantic Training Squadron, the *Columbia*, to train men for the engineer's force. The commander in chief of the Atlantic squadron further recommended that the course be designed so that men could eventually qualify for higher engine-room ratings.[57] The abolition of shipboard training in 1905 ended such instruction, but the navy did not relinquish its desire to train members of the engine-room force. As one means of insuring that coal passers understood the nature of the job, in 1907 the department began to enlist new men as apprentice seamen and only then to permit the choice of engine room after some experience in naval life. In this way, coal passers had an idea of what lay ahead of them as well as a familiarity with military drill.[58]

When the new rating of hospital apprentice was created in 1898, the Bureau of Medicine and Surgery took charge of the instruction. Although at first the men received no more than a casual training at naval hospitals before assignment to the fleet, the bureau tried to improve training, and by 1905 it had established a four-month course at Norfolk. A similar course at Mare Island was undermined by the demand for hospital corpsmen for the fleet.[59]

In 1910 the Bureau of Medicine and Surgery concluded that its system of training was unsatisfactory. It therefore began sending all hospital apprentices to training stations for the regular course, except that first-aid drill was substituted for gunnery. At the end of training, hospital apprentices went to sea with apprentice seamen but served in the medical departments. After one year, they might be assigned to naval hospitals for further training.[60]

The transfer of hospital recruits and recruits for the engine-room force to the training stations completed the consolidation of all recruit training. Standardization, however, involved more than just centralizing initial training. Even a simple question like the length of instruction received no single answer. Because the training stations competed with the fleet for men, the Bureau of Navigation had to balance its desire to give a man thorough preparation against the desire of a ship's captain to have a full complement. As a result, the length of training varied widely.

Even though the bureau might have wished to maximize the period of training, the trend was to shorten the officially prescribed time. In 1881 the apprentice program had required a minimum of twenty months; by 1900 an apprentice received just twelve months' training before he was transferred to the fleet. With the introduction of the training of landsmen, the bureau projected a minimum period of about six months.[61] The manpower needs of the service, however, often frustrated even this hope. Thus in 1903 the Bureau of Navigation reduced training to three months, but increased it to four in 1906, and extended it to six in 1915.[62] After World War I, four months were allowed for training, although commandants were permitted to transfer promising recruits to the fleet with as little as three weeks of training. A course of nine weeks was introduced in 1930, and then finally it was set at twelve weeks on July 1, 1931.[63]

The amount of time the department established as the official training period does not necessarily reflect the time a recruit actually spent in the courses because the navy frequently raided training stations to supply the fleet with men. Norfolk, located within a major naval base, offered an especially tempting pool of manpower; in 1907, for example, it was able to train men only an average of one month, ten days, although the official training period was four months.[64] As long as the demand for men remained high, the time officially allocated remained an optimum often not reached. In 1912 Rear Admiral Philip Andrews, chief of the Bureau of Navigation, testified that, though the training period was set at four months, it sometimes lasted only two. Again, in 1914 the Bureau of Navigation had to reassert that instruction should run four months.[65]

American entry into World War I temporarily destroyed any standard training period. With the commissioning of reserve ships and the assignment of a full wartime complement to every ship, the navy literally transported boys directly from the recruiting station to the fleet. One officer complained:

> On Thursday evening we received a draft of about 100 boys from the Great Lakes Training Station. They had been under training only about one week, were only partially fitted out with clothing and that was in gunny sacks. They not only did not know anything about the Navy but they had never even been told about it. . . . Poor boys, I felt sorry for them. Strangers in strange surroundings, uninstructed, untrained and unprepared. It is not fair to them or to the service that they should be sent out in such conditions. We now seem to be trying to see how many men (or boys for most of our recruits are 17 or 20) we can get in regardless of their value.[66]

The chaos of the opening months of the war soon passed, however, and the navy was able to return to a longer training period.

The difficulty the department encountered in setting the duration of training is one indication of its trial-and-error approach to handling its new type of recruit. Another problem the navy had to face was its lack of public health measures. Traditionally, new men awaiting assignments were quartered on receiving ships—old vessels tied to docks and often aground on garbage and silt. At the urging of medical officers, recruits were moved from these ships and placed in barracks, but the stations still suffered epidemics.[67]

A board that was established in 1908 to investigate sanitation at Norfolk found that contagious diseases such as measles, mumps, and scarlet fever were often contracted at the training station. Each new draft of recruits introduced diseases which spread throughout the base. The board recommended that the Norfolk station temporarily stop receiving new recruits and that it transfer to the fleet only those men who had been at the station two months or more and could thus be assumed to be free of disease. To prevent future epidemics, it suggested a thorough examination of each incoming recruit, the cleaning and disinfecting of all buildings, and the establishment of a detention camp.[68]

Finally, in 1908 the navy adopted a system of detention camps in which companies of new recruits were quarantined for their first three weeks in the service. At Norfolk the camp was set up on the ground that formerly had been occupied by the Reserve Torpedo Flotilla. The camp also served as a receiving barracks to examine new recruits and to issue clothing.[69] The value of detention camps was demonstrated in 1917 when men were rushed to the fleet without spending time in such camps and spinal meningitis spread to the battleships.[70]

A training curriculum was developed perhaps even more hesitantly than were health practices. Because the navy had never before dealt with such large numbers of men, it was uncertain what the content and method of instruction should consist of. As previously discussed, the century opened with a debate on whether indoctrination should be on ship or on land. Operations afloat had an attractive logic, but they required a heavier commitment of officers, men, and ships than did shore-based training. For this reason, the navy abolished the training squadron in 1905 and confined its schooling to shore. But although economics dictated the location of training, the nature of such training still had to be developed through experimentation.

The main trend was to reduce the breadth of coverage. At first the navy had hoped to transform the recruit into a fully trained sailor. Such thoroughness, however, required a long time, and efforts to compress the necessary material into the available time proved futile. As Lieutenant Commander Fullam observed in 1902: "The routine and course of instruction may be very exhaustive and impressive on paper; but the graduate may not impress us to the same extent except perhaps in the matter of exhaustion."[71]

Because the navy found itself unable to produce a thoroughly trained seaman in its initial course of instruction, it modified its goal to merely introducing the recruit to naval life. In 1903, the chief of the Bureau of Navigation described the training as consisting of:

> Care of person, clothing and bedding, handling of boats, contents of Recruit Manual, Infantry Drill, Small Arms Firing, Compass, Helm and Lead, and [drilling] in loading 4-inch or 5-inch B.L. rifle, dummy charged and pointing.[72]

At this time the navy defined the objectives of instruction primarily in terms of several specific skills. Gradually, however, the main purpose of training shifted to a greater emphasis on forming what the navy considered the proper attitudes in the recruit toward the navy. In 1916, for example, Commander William F. Moffett, commandant of the new Great Lakes Naval Training Station, wrote that, in addition to acquiring basic military and naval skills, the recruit was required "to show in his bearing, actions and words a sincere amenability to discipline, to demonstrate special aptitude for his work and to maintain a conduct standard of the highest order."[73]

This trend toward simplification continued. By 1930 the *Yearbook of Enlisted Training* stated that "the mission of the training stations is to bridge the gap from civilian to military life, introducing the recruits to discipline, naval duties, and esprit de corps." In fulfilling this objective, the station concentrated on "six fundamental subjects": taking care of one's person, pulling a whaleboat, swimming fifty yards, learning the manual of arms, using small arms, and establishing a classification for future training.[74]

Since recruits in the nineteenth century usually went quickly to sea, they did not participate in a common and uniform introduction to naval life. In the twentieth century, on the other hand, all new enlistees underwent much the same routine, even though the content of instruction may have varied over the years.[75] Upon arriving at the training station, a recruit received a medical examination, took a bath, had his hair cut, and sent his civilian clothes home. He then deposited valuables with the paymaster and surrendered such contraband articles as cigarettes, chewing tobacco, drugs, liquor, playing cards, and obscene literature, which were destroyed in his presence. The recruit next received a hammock, bedding, and part of his clothing allowance. (The navy preferred not to burden the recruit with too much clothing, lest he lose it during the hectic training period.) He then learned how to mark his clothing and how to roll it for wrinkle-free storage in a seabag. As the youth went through the reception center, he was encouraged to draw money for stamps and stationery and to write home. Commandants were aware that parents would be anxious about their sons and that the sons would probably not write. As an added precaution, the commandant sent a form letter to parents confirming a recruit's arrival and explaining the nature of the training he would receive—a procedure unheard of in the old navy.[76]

The basic goal of recruit training was insuring an "amenability to discipline," a phrase that frequently occurs in officers' writings. Receiving a recruit from an environment under the "influence of our democratic institutions," the training station had to mold him to the "military character of the business he is undertaking."[77] Upon arrival, each boy was assigned to a squad and given drill instruction under a petty officer. Although a sailor had some need for competency in marching when in parades or landing parties, the main purpose of close-order drill was actually to introduce the novice to military life.[78]

The key to initial training was the petty officer in charge of the squad. To the young recruit, the petty officer was the navy. He translated the directives from above into a program. As the recruits' immediate contact with their new life, the petty officer was also often an irritant, and complaints from the new men usually involved the conduct of the squad leaders.[79]

While petty officers looked after the military side of training, chaplains assumed moral instruction. Traditionally undertaking odd jobs not clearly belonging to anyone else, chaplains had participated in some kind of training throughout the navy's history. In the nineteenth century they frequently taught reading to illiterate seamen and tried to guide bluejackets to temperate and moral paths. As training grew more formal, the chaplain's role became more routine. Their participation in the 1931 course at San Diego indicates the duties they performed. In detention camp a junior chaplain met the recruits to obtain information on next of kin and religious preference and to send a joint letter with the enlistee to his family explaining the navy. Shortly before the recruits left detention, a chaplain spoke to them about government insurance. Before their first liberty, the senior chaplain addressed them concerning "worthwhile places to see, etc." At the end of training, the senior chaplain discussed shipboard life.[80]

In 1925 the Bureau of Navigation incorporated intelligence and aptitude tests into the procedures. The navy had been interested in intelligence examinations as an aid to recruiting since before World War I, but it did not adopt them at that time, feeling that they provided little information that would not be apparent to trained recruiters. After the war, there was renewed interest. As before, there were objections that the tests measured education rather than intelligence or motivation.[81] The navy nevertheless instituted an experimental program of using such examinations to select candidates for trade schools. In December 1924 the bureau instructed all training stations to test every recruit and to keep a record of the results.[82] By 1929 the bureau had found this data supported the contention that men with better scores advanced more rapidly and were less likely to be delinquent than men with low scores. It also established that some ratings required higher scores than others.[83] In 1931 the Bureau of Navigation therefore began administering a general intelligence test to all applicants at the recruiting stations, rejecting those who could not score above a set level. When the recruits reached the training station, they repeated the general test and also took mechanical aptitude and arithmetic tests that determined eligibility for specialized training. Men at sea who wished to be sent to trade schools were given these same examinations.[84]

Since boot camp could serve as no more than an introduction to naval life, training had to continue on the ships. Those connected with the problem early realized that "it is evident that the fleet is part of the training system, and unless the preliminary training at the training stations is perpetuated in the fleet, on board the fighting ships, the desired results . . . will not be obtained."[85] Although many ships took special notice of newly arrived recruits, the navy did not adopt an official shipboard policy until 1924, when it established two months of training aboard ship to follow the two months on shore. Advancement from the rate of apprentice seaman required a minimum of four months' total instruction.[86]

ADVANCED SCHOOLS

Training stations, at best, supplied sailors of limited experience and skill. To fill specialized ratings the navy had traditionally relied on "strikers"—seamen who learned from others on the job—and on the enlistment of trained individuals from civilian life. The old system of on-the-job training proved too slow to meet the needs of the rapidly expanding navy. On the other hand, attempting to enlist trained civilians not only failed to secure the number of men the navy required but also often meant that the service was accepting what it felt were the discards of the merchant marine or factories—persons who possessed only mediocre skills or whose habits interfered with their usefulness.[87]

The navy obtained some skilled manpower through sailors' taking further training on their own initiative to qualify for promotion. In the late nineteenth century, correspondence courses and self-help books were sold throughout the nation, and some sailors made use of this type of instruction. Many bluejackets, for example, enrolled in courses from the International Correspondence School, which advertised extensively in naval magazines.[88] In 1906 that firm reported that several thousand enlisted men were taking its courses and that, of the twenty white hats who had received commissions, thirteen were its graduates.[89] These courses, however, proved inadequate for the modern fleet. Enrollment, course content, and the quality of instruction all lay outside the navy's control. The department thus could not choose which men received training, could not be assured that courses would be offered for the specialties the service required, and could not gear the content of instruction to specific navy needs. Although such courses may have helped improve the general educational level of some enlisted men, the service found that it had to institute its own advanced training to fill skilled ratings.

The department had made a modest beginning to that end in 1883 when it set up a gunnery class at the Washington navy yard. A similar school opened at Newport in 1885. The bureau further expanded that training in 1897 with a class for gun captains aboard the training ship *Amphitrite*.[90] Gunnery remained the only subject the department considered worthy of a special school until electricity schools were established at Boston and New York in 1899.[91]

When the dramatic increase in the size of the enlisted force in the first years of the twentieth century produced a demand for large numbers of men in all advanced ratings, the navy embarked on the creation of an extensive system of advanced schools. Many of its courses—such as the electricity schools—were obviously geared to the new technology. Yet even billets which were only indirectly affected by changes in the equipment of a man-of-war could no longer be filled satisfactorily without formal advanced training. In 1901, therefore, the Bureau of Navigation inaugurated a petty officers' school at the Newport Naval Training Station to secure more boatswain's mates, quartermasters, and coxswains. Locating the new school at Newport meant not only that facilities were available for instruction but also that there were apprentices available who would provide "suitable material for the school to use in furnishing practical instruction."[92] To make the school attractive to eligible men, the navy issued General Order 70 on December 3, 1901, which provided two dollars per month in addition to the pay for the rating to petty officers who had successfully completed the course.

Because the navy no longer was able to enlist adequate numbers of skilled craftsmen, in November 1902 the Bureau of Navigation expanded its training program by creating an artificers' school in Norfolk that provided three months of instruction for woodworkers, plumbers, blacksmiths, painters, and shipfitters. Since the school sought to prepare men for the specific needs of the navy, its curriculum was narrower than civilian trade schools. In its first decade the school graduated 600 woodworkers, 247 plumbers and fitters, 278 painters, 132 blacksmiths, and 125 shipfitters—some 1,382 craftsmen in all.[93]

After this initial success, the navy steadily added to its trade school program both by establishing new courses in subjects it had not previously offered and by offering existing courses at additional facilities. Thus the department created a curriculum for machinists at New York and Newport in 1903, one for cooks, bakers, and commissary stewards at Newport in 1907, and one in aviation at Pensacola in 1913. New schools begun at additional navy installations included a school for electricians at San Francisco and a machinist school at Charleston, South Carolina. By 1916 the department had instituted about forty schools to prepare men for advanced ratings.[94]

World War I saw a proliferation of these training courses. In 1917 the service needed skilled men rapidly; the only way it could meet its needs was to train recruits after they had joined the navy. Consequently, it enlarged existing schools, opened new ones, and used the facilities of a number of private institutions or factories. Among the many courses the navy itself established were several on aviation at Great Lakes and one on mining and minesweeping at Hampton Roads. In addition, the Dunwoody Institute in Minneapolis prepared men to be petty officers before they had even seen the ocean; the Ford Motor Company, the Curtis Flying Boat Company, and other manufacturers instructed men in caring for equipment the businesses produced. Reflecting the urgency of wartime, training was accelerated and concentrated on teaching the performance of a narrow task rather than skills of general application.[95]

During the period of high personnel turnover in the immediate postwar years, the navy continued its expanded training efforts. Because the fleet was reduced in size, however, it no longer required the same level of training once the rapid turnover abated. Furthermore, attempts to reduce the shore establishment increased the emphasis on advanced training aboard ship.

From modest beginnings, the number of courses offered ashore had increased dramatically. In 1925, the Bureau of Navigation divided the schools it operated into four classes by type of instruction: Class A—designed to prepare nonrated men for a specialty; Class B—advanced training for petty officers; Class C—training for special-duty assignments (e.g., submarine school); and Class D (added in 1927)—schools of temporary or special nature not subsumed under other categories (e.g., gas mask school, submarine periscope school).[96]

When first enlistments returned to normal levels, the number of men in attendance declined. As was the case with recruit training stations, by the late twenties many advanced schools were closed or operating at greatly reduced capacities; with the depression, others also ended instruction. This contraction, however, reflected the existence of a veteran enlisted force that had less need for shore training. It did not represent an abandonment of the well-entrenched training program.

As soon as the navy initiated advanced training, it faced the problem of selecting students. The goal was to obtain men who were capable of instruction and who would be of most use to the navy when trained. Mistakes were perhaps most common early in the century when training was new. At that time gunnery training ships complained of receiving men who could not see the targets or who were too old or illiterate. The petty officers' school also reported that many of the twenty-four men in its first class required preliminary instruction before proceeding to the advanced work.[97] The poor selection process meant a low rate of completion for the early schools. In fiscal 1903, of the 136 men who had received instruction at the petty officers' school, seventy-five earned certificates of graduation, fifty-three returned to the fleet without graduating, five were discharged because their enlistments had expired, one deserted, and two were discharged from the service for other reasons.[98]

Experience helped eliminate many of these early problems. Rapid expansion in World War I, however, also produced complaints about the type of men sent for training. The haste to transform civilians into rated men meant that the navy had to rely on a man's own statement of his qualifications and that the applicant had to accept a harried recruiter's description of training or a hurried decision in recruit training camp.[99] The introduction of aptitude testing in 1924 offered the navy a better indication of the men most likely to succeed. By requiring all recruits and all men who wanted to transfer from ships to trade schools to take the examinations, it could eliminate many of those incapable of doing the work.

Measuring aptitude was not the sole problem involved in selection. Officers were often unwilling to assign personnel to undergo training because the men most likely to benefit from the courses were also those most valuable on board ship.[100] Another difficulty was finding men who were interested in the course and who had not merely been sent to it by their commanding officers.[101]

By the 1920s, trade schools were firmly established, and the navy could concentrate on experimenting with training methods. In 1923, for example, the ground school of the naval air station at Pensacola tried, with some success, sleep learning to teach code.[102] More significant was the beginning of the use of training films. Before the war it had been suggested that recruits be shown films of life at sea to help prepare them for the transition, but that suggestion was not implemented.[103] In 1926, however, the navy finally prepared a training course on film—a fifteen-reel motion picture on the care of oil-burning boilers. A film course on electricity was also being prepared in that year. By 1930 the yearbook on training listed ten titles for use in training courses, including *World Struggle for Oil, Turbine Engines, Radiotelephone and Audion*, and *Principles of Electricity*.[104]

In addition to motion pictures, the department also began using slide films as a training aid. The slide film offered certain advantages over motion pictures: it was easier to show, cost less to produce, could be shown in a room that was not completely dark, and permitted a frame to be kept on the screen as long as the instructor desired.[105] The navy first produced slide films in 1930. In that year it made eighteen films and distributed 105 slide projectors. By 1933 the Bureau of Navigation had issued 1,860 copies of slide films to the service. Nine new titles for 1933 included *Machine Tools*, part IV; *The Foundry*; *Submarine Salvage*, part II; *Compartmentation of Ships*; and *Boat Handling under Oars*.[106]

These pioneering efforts in the production of visual aids declined in the late thirties. By 1940, in fact, the use of films had ended; officers who requested copies of films listed in the *Yearbook of Enlisted Training* were informed that they were no longer available. In April 1941, when the Training Division of the Bureau of Navigation decided to make instructional films again, copies of the earlier works were difficult to obtain.[107]

"EVERY SHIP A SCHOOL"

The educational program that the navy developed in the early twentieth century stressed orientation to naval life and instruction in advanced skills. The major exception to this pattern was Secretary Josephus Daniels' attempt to introduce compulsory general education for enlisted personnel.

Daniels came to the navy committed to education and to uplifting the bluejacket. In his first annual report, he stated:

It is my ambition to make the Navy a great university, with college extensions afloat and ashore. Every ship should be a school, and every enlisted man, and petty and warrant officer should be given the opportunity to improve his mind, better his position and fit himself for promotion.[108]

Moving rapidly to implement his program, in June 1913 Daniels asked for a survey of educational societies on naval vessels. Of the twenty-six battleships, fourteen cruisers, and sixty-five other ships that reported, only four vessels had such societies, and these were all battleships.[109]

While the survey was being conducted, Daniels instituted a program of general education at the naval training stations and on the cruiser *Des Moines*.[110] In October he circulated General Order 53 announcing that the department wished "to put into effective operation an education and vocational training system for the benefit of the enlisted man of the Navy, both ashore and afloat." This training, he continued, was already in operation at the training stations and soon would be begun on all vessels.

On December 16, 1913, Daniels issued General Order 63 requiring compulsory education for every bluejacket in the first two years of his enlistment. The order directed that every ship and station set aside two hours daily for that purpose. The course was to begin with the basics every seaman should know and then proceed to instruction in mathematics, history, and technical skills. A year later, the order was modified to permit the suspension of classes during docking, overhaul, and target practice, including a two-week period before the practice.[111]

Daniels was greatly pleased with his experiment, feeling that it did much to increase the enthusiasm of the enlisted men for the service. In 1916 he asserted:

I have seen no sufficient evidence . . . that American youth enters the Navy for a four-year bluejacket truancy afloat. The school system in the Navy has, I believe, appealed strongly to American parents, and almost as strongly to American youth itself.[112]

The secretary devoted large portions of his annual report each year to describing the favorable reaction to General Order 63. The program did, indeed, capture the attention of the popular press and receive a great deal of public acclaim.[113] Within the navy, though, reaction among both officers and men was mixed. Some sailors who had joined the service to escape school were unhappy; others saw in Daniels a rare and true friend and interpreted any defects in the program as efforts by the naval establishment to undermine the instruction by making it as dull as possible.[114]

Officers tended to be more hostile to the order than the men, though there were some who endorsed it. Rear Admiral Victor Blue, Daniels' chief of the Bureau of Navigation and protégé, was optimistic about the benefits of the training and felt that the men would eventually appreciate it no matter what their immediate reaction was. Admiral Blue did not believe the officers objected to it since "our officers do not object to orders." Blue did admit that some officers might feel that they could do a better job teaching if the classes were voluntary.[115] Other officers, though willing to undertake the instruction, found it difficult to teach men of widely different backgrounds and interests and soon abandoned the attempt. Their sessions degenerated into telling anecdotes that they hoped conveyed a lesson about proper conduct.[116]

A number of officers felt that Daniels' program was an unmitigated disaster for the navy. These same men, however, were almost certain to oppose any suggestion Daniels made because they thought that he was coddling enlisted men. Captain Lyman Cotten, for example, attributed much of the navy's lack of preparedness in 1917 to the secretary's concern for education. "The attempt to make the navy an instrument of reform and educational and industrial uplift," he wrote, "has of course reacted on the military character of its personnel."[117] Six months later Cotten still complained that what he saw as the men's lack of dedication to the service was "the logical result of the policy of the last four years (fathered by Daniels) that the Navy is merely a training institution for such things as will aid a man *when he gets back into civil life*. It is all 'what can *I get* out of the government' and none of 'what can *I give* the service.'"[118]

NAVY TRAINING COURSES

An assessment of the compulsory education program is difficult to make, for each side claimed wide support in and out of the service. In the end, the opponents carried the day. The courses were suspended during World War I, and after the war the navy did not reinstate education along the lines of General Order 63. Instead, it instituted Navy Training Courses, also known as Navy Education Courses. These were voluntary, correspondence-type courses, which required only minimal assistance from officers. Explaining the advantages of this new program, Captain David F. Sellers of the Bureau of Navigation explicitly rejected the prewar compulsory general education idea:

> It is entirely voluntary on the part of the men and they do it in spare time. In other words, instead of turning a ship into a school we have fitted the school into the ship.... There is no desire or intention to turn it into a university.[119]

Even Secretary Daniels supported the new program and apparently did not try to resurrect his old system. He did, however, continue to stress the benefits of education in the "production of better citizens for civil life."[120]

To establish the Navy Training Courses the Bureau of Navigation hired Dr. Lewis R. Alderman of Portland, Oregon, as a consultant for six months beginning in August 1919. With Alderman's help, the bureau reviewed correspondence courses from thirty-three institutions and selected those that it thought would benefit enlisted men most and require the least supervision. The new system was inaugurated on the U.S.S. *Rochester* on June 1, 1920; by January 1921 courses were offered on the *Dixie, Oklahoma, Tennessee, Nevada, Florida,* and eighteen destroyers. The experiment's success led to its implementation throughout the service.[121]

Although the courses were voluntary, the bureau applied some pressure on officers to use them. It did not "desire to insist upon the adoption of its educational system" but stressed that it "would look with favor on the promotion of educational activities which would make use of the courses prepared by the Bureau."[122]

With such urging by the bureau, relayed to the men by officers who suggested the value of the courses in obtaining promotion, the courses began to be widely used, especially as shore school training was curtailed for economy reasons.[123] The number of unit courses issued soared from 23,000 in 1923 to 72,126 in 1925, although it slipped to 57,632 in 1926. As the program gained in importance, the department replaced privately developed technical courses with ones prepared by the navy and aimed directly at the requirements for a rating. Thus, in 1922 there were no navy rating courses; by 1926 forty-two were available. During the same period, the number of privately prepared technical courses dropped from thirty to one. The service, however, continued to offer in 1926 twenty-three privately developed, nontechnical courses in subjects such as mathematics—only one less than in 1922.[124]

The Navy Training Courses received extensive support from some ships. In January 1926 the battleship *New Mexico* reported that 57.5 percent of the crew were taking them, and the *Oklahoma* listed 35.3 percent.[125] In 1930 the Bureau of Navigation happily noted that the *New Mexico*, which stood first in gunnery, also ranked first in the number of men in the gunnery ratings who had completed training courses. Furthermore, the ship with the lowest number of men who had completed the course stood last; with only one exception the two rankings correlated for all other ships.[126]

By the thirties the Navy Training Courses were well established. When the depression led to the closing or limiting of many shore schools, these correspondence courses enabled men eager for promotion to develop the skills they needed.

With the creation of Navy Training Courses, the department's system of education reached its final stage of development before World War II. That system now included recruit training, shore schools for advance ratings, and correspondence courses for use aboard ship. This range of offerings was in sharp contrast to the nineteenth century, when the service's only major educational effort was the apprentice program—and that had failed to become a major source of manpower. The modern navy had become an educational institution that affected a sailor throughout his naval career.

The physical facilities housing much of the training program symbolized this transformation of the naval personnel system. Trade schools and recruit training stations flourished at navy installations on both coasts. In addition, the opening of the Great Lakes Naval Training Station in the Midwest reflected not only the fact that the navy was committed to training recruits but also that it was securing many of its men from the interior of the nation. The idea of a training station so far from the sea would have been unthinkable in the nineteenth century, but it was almost a necessity in the twentieth.

As the navy developed its training stations, it also experimented with the content of instruction. The service was forced to examine as it never had to before what it expected a sailor to know and at what stage of his career he was to know it. Considerations of time and money, for example, led the department to rule that training need not include the handling of sails and that initial instruction could be carried out more easily on land than at sea. These decisions represented a major psychological break of the new navy from the old and were an assertion that instruction would emphasize subjects immediately useful to the sailor in his job. This utilitarian direction of training was reaffirmed when Secretary Daniels' effort to institute compulsory general education and thus to make "every ship a school" faltered.

In addition to questions of content, the new training system raised the problem of selecting which men would benefit from the instruction. To help choose the most suitable men, the navy adopted an aptitude-testing program. The selection process was not to be taken lightly, since training opened the way to promotion and thus influenced a man's position within the navy. Training also had far-reaching consequences for the navy. First, the navy training system was the only way the department could secure men for advanced ratings. In addition, the effort and expense of instructing men increased the department's estimation of the value of its sailors. The expansion of the training program thus helped increase concern for the treatment and welfare of the enlisted force. One such area of concern was the terms under which men served.

chapter 7

Ratings and Terms of Service

The basic conditions of service—pay, promotion, discharge, and retirement—constitute significant factors in the development of a personnel system. Recruiting might find the men the service wanted and training might increase their usefulness to the fleet, but an individual often weighed the merits of a naval career in terms of the rewards offered. The terms of service could provide a direct incentive for men to remain in the navy or a reason to follow better opportunities elsewhere. Although innovations in these areas were often delayed while the navy faced more pressing difficulties, some conditions of service were improved as the department sought to solve its manpower problems.

RATINGS

Closely connected to any discussion of the conditions of service is the rating structure. Before World War II the term "rating" referred to both occupation (such as seaman, oiler, or fireman) and pay level. Because of this usage, the rating structure reflected the pay a sailor received and set the bounds of his line of promotion. Considered in the sense of occupation, the type of ratings that existed at any one time also mirrored the skills the navy employed and thus the nature of the service itself.

The old navy possessed a comparatively simple rating system. In 1801 there were only twenty-one ratings. Because the enlisted force numbered only about 2,500 men, an extensive subdivision of sailors into classes was unnecessary.[1] In addition, the technology was simple and there was little reason for highly specialized occupational categories. Of the twenty-one ratings, ten concerned the sailing of the ship and the operation of weapons (for example, seaman, boatswain's mate, and gunner's mate) and thus composed what was later called the seaman branch. Four involved the care of the vessel or its armament (for example, armorer and carpenter's mate), a function later subsumed under the artificer branch. A few clerks, a cook, and a steward rounded out the complement.[2]

This basic scheme prevailed until the late 1830s. At that time, perhaps because of the growth of the enlisted force from 3,691 in 1831 to 7,651 in 1837, the navy recognized some new specialties among those who worked the ship; for example, captain of the mizzentop, a new petty officer rating for seamen in the rigging, was created in 1838. By 1840 the service had twenty-nine ratings. The new ratings, however, reflected more an increase in the size of the force and a resulting specialization rather than a change in the type of men aboard ship; in 1840 approximately half of the ratings still directly concerned the sailing of the ship.[3]

When steam power came into use, the rating structure had to be adapted to this new technology. The navy, though, was slow to recognize the new field. In 1842 the coal heaver and fireman ratings were established; five years later fireman was divided into first and second classes. Yet the engine-room force would have to be content with just these three ratings for another nineteen years until after the Civil War, even though during that period new ratings were being created in other areas.[4]

Although the post-Civil war navy emphasized the use of sail as much as possible, new ratings eventually were created for the mechanical trades. As shown in table 9 of the Appendix, machinist was established in 1866, followed by boilermaker in 1869, blacksmith in 1879, and oiler and water tender, both in 1884. Some of the reasons for this slowness in creating new engine-room ratings may have been a need for time to determine what specialties were most needed to care for the new machinery. Much of the delay, however, was most likely caused by the navy's emphasis on sail and reluctance to give too much status to engine-room personnel.[5]

As the overall number of ratings grew, it was necessary to develop a system of classification. The first such formal classification was adopted in 1885. The existing ratings were placed in the seaman, artificer, or special branches and into one of six hierarchical grades—from seaman, third class, to petty officer, first class.[6] The artificer branch included the engine-room force and other craftsmen; the special branch comprised such miscellaneous ratings as yeoman, musician, and tailor. Although the categories undoubtedly reflected existing usage, the new system indicated more clearly the lines of promotion and the equivalency of ratings in different areas of the ship.

When the prosail forces finally lost influence at the end of the nineteenth century, the men who cared for the machinery found it increasingly easy to obtain specialized ratings. In addition, with the unequivocal commitment to steam, numerous specialties required on wind-powered men-of-war became obsolete. The service abolished such unneeded assignments as captain of the maintop and captain of the mizzentop, both of which were disestablished in 1893.[7] Although some ships still carried canvas, sails were no longer important to the navy; thus it was no longer necessary to give special recognition to the men skilled in handling them.

The increasing size of the enlisted force also produced an expansion of the number of ratings. Starting with seventy-one ratings in 1897 and an enlisted strength of 10,327, the number reached eighty-eight in 1910 when the force was 45,076 and 108 in 1930 with 84,938 men.[8] This steady increase in specialties reflected both the subdivision of ratings into two or more pay grades and the recognition of new specialties. Printer, a rating created as ship's printer in 1869, for example, was subdivided into printer, first class, and chief printer in 1918; then in 1921 second- and third-class pay grades were added. New specialties created after 1890 included electrician (1898), turret captain (1903), patternmaker (1917), torpedoman (1921), and aviation carpenter's mate (1921).[9]

The distribution of ratings among branches reveals that growth was taking place primarily among the skilled trades and in the engine room—as would be expected in a structure adapting to the technology of the new warships. The number of ratings assigned the engine-room force of the artificer branch rose from eight in 1890 to twelve in 1910 and to eighteen in 1930; the number of nonengine-room artificers grew from eight in 1890 to seventeen in 1910 and to twenty-nine in 1930. Altogether, the artificer branch had increased from 22 percent of all ratings in 1890 to 43 percent in 1930. After World War I, aviation ratings became a separate branch; by 1930 that branch had ten ratings, or 9 percent of all ratings. At the same time as those branches were growing, the number of ratings in the seaman branch declined from twenty-three in 1890 to twenty in 1910, and to nineteen in 1930—or from 32 percent of the total in 1890 to 17 percent in 1930.[10]

As was the case with the engine-room force, the date a specialty was created did not necessarily represent the beginning of the navy's use of that skill. For example, the department used electricity over a decade before it established the electrician rating.[11] Delay in creation of a rating, moreover, was usually the rule because it took time to assess fully the value of new technology to the fleet and to decide that it required individual recognition instead of being included as a duty under an existing rating. Thus, when wireless communication entered the navy early in the twentieth century, electricians added the new equipment to their other assignments until the rating of radioman was created in 1921.[12]

The addition of new ratings alone does not fully describe the changed nature of the force; to an extent, some of the need for new ratings was met by altering the duties of existing ones. Thus not every old rating disappeared when its original reason for existence vanished. Seamen no longer reefed and furled canvas in the rigging, but the rating remained. Men holding the seaman rating constituted the main body of the deck force and performed a wide range of duties in the new navy. In other cases, the nominal duties stayed the same, but the skills required changed. Gunner's mates continued their concern with armament, but found their smoothbore muzzle-loaders replaced by breechloading rifled guns. Even the sailmaker's mate remained until 1939, surviving by applying his needle to the manufacture of boat covers and awnings rather than sails.

PAY

Whenever the navy decided a new rating was needed, it asked the president to issue an executive order creating the position and setting the pay. The president had had this authority since 1794. He could also change the pay of existing ratings with a similar proclamation. The pay table produced by these orders resulted in discrepancies in pay for men with different specialties but holding the same rank. In 1900, for example, a chief boatswain's mate received fifty dollars per month, but a chief machinist was paid seventy dollars. Although some of this inequality can be regarded as quirks inherent in the process of setting remuneration piecemeal, there was a clear pattern of offering greater amounts to certain nonnautical, skilled occupations—such as machinist, pharmacist, and boilermaker—and less to seafaring ratings.[13]

By 1900 the navy was having difficulty obtaining manpower for all ratings. Pay may have been a part of the problem. Comparisons between navy and civilian salaries are difficult since by that time the service offered such benefits as free medical care, a clothing allowance at first enlistment, and a reenlistment bonus that supplemented the pay a man received. Nevertheless, navy wages were apparently below those offered by civilian employers. In 1903 an officer reported civilian wages on the Pacific coast for fireman of fifty dollars and for coal passers of forty dollars; at this time the navy paid thirty-five dollars and twenty-two dollars, respectively. The same officer reported civilian seamen earned twenty-five to forty dollars, at a time that the navy paid twenty-four.[14]

Navy pay became somewhat more competitive in 1908 when Congress granted a 10 percent increase to all men. At the same time, Congress took over the function of establishing ratings and setting pay. It did not, however, attempt to end the varying incomes received by different specialties of the same grade.[15]

Congress added ratings as they were needed after 1908, but it did not raise wages again until 1917, and then only as a war measure. Shortly after the declaration of war, it voted additional compensation for all enlisted men. The amount varied from fifteen dollars a month for men whose prewar base pay was under twenty-one dollars a month to six dollars for sailors making over forty-five dollars.[16] Although the bonus was to expire six months after the termination of the war, on July 11, 1919, it was extended until the end of the enlistment of those men already in the service and for the terms of men enlisting or reenlisting before July 1, 1920.[17]

Despite this wartime bonus, navy salaries were not competitive with those of civilian workers because the average earnings of all industries had more than doubled between 1909 and 1919.[18] During 1919 there was substantial pressure to improve the pay of enlisted men, especially of petty officers. Supporters argued that attracting good men depended on the compensation offered:

If Congress is not willing to give a living wage to the members of our Navy as a matter of justice, perhaps it will be swayed by arguments of expediency. At present rates we shall soon have in the Navy only men who could not earn a living wage anywhere, with a few men of means who do not have to.[19]

Responding to such arguments, on May 18, 1920, Congress adopted a new schedule that set uniform remuneration for all specialties within each grade—all first-class petty officers, for example, now received the same pay. This new schedule was to last only until a joint committee had investigated pay for all services.[20]

The continuing examination of military pay produced another pay bill on June 10, 1922. This act for the first time established parity between the army, navy, and marines; in the case of the navy, the new table meant the same level of enlisted pay as granted in 1920, except that the lowest grades were raised. In this statute Congress also delegated to the secretary of the navy the authority to establish new ratings, but it retained the power to make changes in the amount the various grades received.[21]

The 1922 law was to be the last change before World War II, even though a strong movement for another increase arose in the late twenties. At an unofficial level, letters to *Our Navy* complained of the inability of a sailor to support a family on existing wages.[22] In addition, the Interdepartment Pay Board, reporting in July 1929, detailed both the rising cost of living and the decreasing purchasing power of the dollar. The board recommended a pay schedule which would have increased salaries by up to 20 percent.[23]

Black Friday and the depression destroyed chances for any increase; instead, in 1933 Congress cut the pay of all federal personnel by 15 percent.[24] Not surprisingly, the reduction was unpopular. *Our Navy*, which at this time rarely criticized official policy, complained bitterly:

Can the President justify the recruiting of a quarter million young men as forestry workers, paying them $30 a month and sustenance, while there are thousands of men in the Army and Marine Corps with long and honorable service who draw only $21 per month (less 15%) and thousands in the Navy whose $30 a month has been cut to $24.50? [*sic*] It takes a long time in any branch of the service for a man to pass the $30 mark.[25]

The Navy Department also protested the measure and argued that the armed services had not shared in the previous prosperity.[26] And, of course, the men directly affected by the pay cut questioned whether the savings were worth the hardship they caused.[27] Whether because of such complaints or because of a general improvement in the economy, 10 percent of the reduction was restored in 1934 and the remaining 5 percent on April 1, 1935.[28]

In addition to base pay, the enlisted man could receive a variety of temporary and permanent allowances. The navy used these incentives to shape the enlisted force in the way it desired. It rewarded long service, encouraged proficiency in special fields, and recognized the hazardous nature of submarine and aviation duty.[29] The act of June 10, 1922, greatly simplified the allowance structure by eliminating all permanent additions to pay, except increments for medals and reenlistment. It also changed the computation of the reenlistment bonus and reduced the number of temporary additions.[30]

Beyond these additions to his regular income, a sailor or his family could collect several types of special payments. The most significant was the bonus for reenlisting under continuous service. A death benefit paid the sailor's heirs a sum equal to his salary for six months if his death occurred in the line of duty.[31]

World War I produced not only a postwar pay raise but also special bonuses. After the armistice, Congress granted sixty dollars to all men who had served during the war.[32] This act, strangely enough, provided for payment only on discharge, tempting men to leave the service just as the Bureau of Navigation was encouraging them to stay in. Once discharged, a man could reenlist, but many did not. In addition to this federal payment, some states provided a bonus for their residents who had served during the war.[33]

Each seaman also received a clothing allotment upon his initial enlistment. As has been seen, the granting of this allotment had been widely advocated in the nineteenth century. The navy first adopted a "bounty for outfits" of forty-five dollars for naval apprentices in June 1890; in 1900 in extended the bonus to landsmen for training.[34] This allowance was intended to supply the recruit with the necessary regulation garments, without his becoming indebted to acquire the clothing.

Although the navy required each new man to have a minimum amount of clothing, the allowance remained a fixed sum. As rising prices drove the cost over the authorized amount, recruits had to pay the difference between the cost and the allowance. Many went into debt, despite the advertised promise of free clothing. By 1906, for example, the outfit cost $58.60, while the allowance was still $45. In 1907 Congress increased the allotment to $60, but prices continued upward. By 1917 the required apparel cost $65.97 for an apprentice seaman and $69.47 for a fireman, third class.[35] With the war, the figure jumped to $95 for all ratings; Congress finally raised the allowance to $100.[36] During the twenties, prices moved steadily higher, until in 1929 the price of the outfit reached $126.71. This amount was the maximum for the years before World War II because the depression reduced the cost to a low of $88.40 in 1933. Possibly because the cost was below the allowance, in 1932 Congress finally permitted the secretary of the navy to determine the clothing allowance and to adjust the allotment to meet new prices.[37]

The extra charge for clothing was a major deduction from a new man's salary during training, but not the only one. After having been told that navy pay was "clear" with no charge for room, board, or medical care, the sailor was often shocked to end the first month in debt to the government. In 1926, for example, a recruit received an allowance of $100 for clothing, but he had to spend $113. In addition, he typically encountered charges for razors, haircuts, movies, tailoring, and other small items amounting to about $5. If he wanted pictures, a dozen cost him $4. His expenditures therefore reached $22 at the end of his first month of service, to be deducted from his $21 per month salary. Receiving no pay, the sailor often reconsidered the wisdom of enlisting.[38]

After his first allotment of clothing, the bluejacket had to replace and maintain the contents of his seabag from his regular pay. Since the army and marines both offered an allowance to replace worn articles, the Interdepartment Pay Board recommended that the navy allot each sailor five dollars per month for that purpose. This suggestion, though, died with the depression.[39]

PROMOTION

Within the established pay tables, the amount of money a sailor received depended on the rating that he held; his chances for a raise were tied to the possibilities for advancement to the next rating. If promotion was of obvious concern to the men, it was also a subject the navy regarded as important. Not only did it contribute to the morale of the enlisted force, but it was also a means of insuring the proper distribution of men among the different ratings.

Regardless of rating, a commanding officer promoted men in accordance with regulations. In general, he advanced men to fill vacancies in the complement of his ship, though in some cases the Bureau of Navigation permitted him to promote in ratings with shortages regardless of authorized complement. At other times, if there was a service-wide excess in a particular specialty, the bureau transferred men to the ship rather than fill a vacancy from the crew. The commanding officer could also reduce without court-martial any rate he had given. Only petty officers holding permanent appointments were exempt from this power to disrate. Petty officers first received acting appointments from their captains; at the end of a year the bureau gave them permanent appointments that could be reduced only by a general or summary court-martial or by a deck court. After 1929 only chief petty officers received permanent appointments.[40]

Advancement depended on a combination of the sailor's qualifications, his time in rate, and the needs of the service. The Bureau of Navigation established general requirements, but within these guidelines there was considerable variation. A future commander in chief of the Asiatic Fleet wrote that on some ships it seemed "the ability to keep paint work or bright work clean is given greater consideration than professional ability."[41] The bureau gradually extended its control over promotion by setting minimum levels of performance for quarterly proficiency and conduct marks and by administering technical examinations before advancement to the petty officer rates.[42] By the 1920s, at least part of the examination was written. In addition to meeting the requirements for promotion, the support of either an officer or a petty officer in the rating helped, though it is difficult to tell just how much.[43]

By requiring a certain amount of time in one rate before promotion to the next, the navy provided a rough assurance that the bluejacket had mastered the techniques of his grade before he moved upward. At the lower ranks, time in grade was the only requirement for promotion, such as from apprentice seaman to seaman. For petty officers, the navy early in the century expressed its preference for continuous-service men. As its need for men declined, it formulated as requirements for promotion definite minimum lengths of service in addition to other professional qualifications.

Minimum periods of service necessary for advancement are little help in determining the actual time most men remained in a rate. Without personnel records, this information cannot be ascertained. It can only be said that a man could rise rapidly in times of expansion or languish with little hope of promotion in times of stability.[44]

The needs of the service constituted perhaps the most important factor in promotion policy. To operate smoothly the navy required not only the proper number of enlisted men but also the right distribution of the personnel among grades and specialties. A navy of all apprentice seamen or all chief petty officers was clearly unsatisfactory. As in any organization, any imbalance in distribution affected speed of advancement. When there was an excess of men in the lower ratings and a deficiency in the higher, promotion could take place rapidly as the navy sought the petty officers it needed. When there were too many petty officers, promotion might virtually cease until vacancies occurred.

During its expansion at the beginning of the century, the navy suffered from a shortage of advanced rates. Petty officers made up 30.1 percent of the enlisted force in 1899; by 1902 that proportion had dropped to 24.7 percent.[45] As a result, men were promoted rapidly; John W. Swift enlisted as a landsman in 1898 and rose to chief yeoman in just eighteen months.[46] Still, the supply of skilled men was not enough. As a further measure, the Bureau of Navigation opened the petty officers' school in 1901 to qualify individuals for more rapid advancement. In 1903 it also urged that commanding officers promote men as quickly as possible, regardless of vacancies on board. These measures, coupled with a stabilization of size, decreased the shortages by the time Daniels became secretary. In 1913 petty officers comprised 35.8 percent of the enlisted force, and promotions slowed from their former pace.[47]

When American entry into World War I produced a sudden upsurge in enlisted personnel, the opportunities for promotion improved. As the navy accepted thousands of untrained recruits, it needed officers to supervise their work. Men already in the service rose swiftly, and newcomers with special skills entered at much higher levels than before.[48] Immediately after the war, the turnover of personnel produced a chaotic situation in which speedy promotions continued.

Declining enlisted strength and reduced recruiting in the mid-1920s eased the wartime and postwar personnel crisis. The navy was no longer desperate for men in advanced ratings; it now had more than it needed. It therefore began establishing waiting lists for promotion. When openings occurred, the bureau filled them from men known to be qualified. The bureau was also able to require a sailor to spend a minimum of one year in one petty officer grade before he was eligible for the next.[49]

During the twenties, and in any time of slow turnover at the top and lack of growth, the nature of the bluejacket's specialty influenced his chance for advancement. At the end of January 1924 there was a deficiency of 3,585 petty officers in the service (reduced from a shortage of 6,158 at the end of the previous August), but 88 percent of the vacancies were for pharmacist's mates, enginemen, electrician's mates, machinist's mates, radiomen, motor machinist's mates, torpedomen, and signalmen. Since sailors in other ratings faced a wait of months or even years before advancement was possible, the bureau recommended that men be encouraged to train in areas where openings existed.[50] Because after 1929 the service needed few new petty officers at all, the rate of promotion was consequently very slow for all ratings.

Upward movement for enlisted men usually ceased at chief petty officer. A few men with excellent quarterly marks, strong letters of recommendation, and satisfactory scores on examinations could become warrant officers. Beyond that, promotion was rare. Although it was theoretically possible for an enlisted man to win a commission, his chances were slight.

Service as a warrant officer became one avenue to a commission. An act of March 3, 1899, provided that a sailor who had been a warrant officer for ten years could become a chief warrant officer. As such he was said to rank "with but after ensign," implying that an enlisted man in his third or fourth enlistment was almost but not quite equal to an officer just graduating from Annapolis.[51]

In 1901 additional legislation permitted a chief warrant officer, after passing an examination, to become an ensign. This provision, though, hardly deluged the officer ranks with former enlisted men. Between 1901 and 1906 only twenty-three warrant officers were commissioned.[52] Not only was the route to a commission difficult, but some officers were hostile to such promotions. Rear Admiral William T. Sampson, commander of the North Atlantic Squadron during the Spanish-American War, for example, reportedly refused to recommend one admittedly qualified man because he feared the effect on discipline and morale if such promotions were allowed.[53]

It was not until Josephus Daniels became secretary that impetus was given to the policy of promoting from the enlisted force. In the four years preceding Daniels' secretaryship, only three enlisted men passed the examination for ensign; in the first three years of his tenure, thirteen did.[54] Daniels, furthermore, opened Annapolis to at least a few bluejackets by persuading Congress in 1914 to grant the secretary of the navy 15 appointments to the Naval Academy to be made from enlisted ranks. This number was later increased to 25 in 1917 and finally to 100 in 1918.[55]

To be eligible for a place at the academy, a sailor had to have served at least one year in the navy, to have been under twenty years of age on the date of admission to the academy, and to have passed the regular entrance examination.[56] By 1919 it was found that the quotas were not being filled because men had trouble studying for the entrance examination on board ship. To overcome the problem, the navy opened preparatory schools at Norfolk and San Diego. Statistics testify to the schools' success: in 1936 only 15.7 percent of the men taking the examination at sea, without attending the school, qualified for admission, while 91 percent of those who had completed the preparatory course passed. Over a period of several years, only 11 percent of those who took the examination without coaching qualified; 59 percent with special instruction at the school passed.[57]

The expansion of wartime, however, created the best opportunities for commissions. Needing men familiar with naval duties at the officer level, during World War I the Bureau of Navigation elevated petty officers and warrant officers to temporary commissions. After the war, some of these appointees reverted to their former status, but 202 enlisted men received permanent officer rank—194 as lieutenant, 7 as lieutenant, junior grade, and 1 as ensign.[58]

DISCHARGE

When a sailor left the navy, he received a discharge. During his service he had been evaluated in quarterly reports, and the marks and recommendations on these reports determined his type of discharge. The nature of a seaman's release from service affected not only any possible future for him in the navy but also his civilian employment and civil rights.

An honorable discharge was the best issued, and the navy stressed its importance to the bluejacket from the time he enlisted. Attesting to the sailor's "fidelity, obedience, and ability," the honorable discharge was necessary to obtain the benefits of reenlistment under continuous service, which had been established in 1855. By 1922 the Bureau of Navigation had standardized the requirements through a system of minimum average quarterly marks for an honorable discharge.[59] Men terminating their service before the end of their enlistment because of injury incurred in the line of duty were eligible for an honorable discharge if their records permitted it, though not of course for reenlistment.

An ordinary, later called a good, discharge was given to men whose records neither merited an honorable nor demanded a disciplinary discharge. The commanding officer noted on the discharge whether or not the sailor was eligible for further service. A recommendation for reenlistment did not require quarterly marks as high as those required for an honorable discharge.[60]

When a court-martial sentenced an enlisted man to dismissal, he received either a bad-conduct or, in extreme cases, a dishonorable discharge. Both precluded further enlistment. The dishonorable discharge could also cause loss of citizenship and could prejudice claims to the Veterans' Bureau. Because some states deprived a man who received a dishonorable discharge of his civil rights, the Bureau of Navigation discouraged the use of this type of discharge except for desertion or for cases that constituted felonies in civil courts.[61]

The navy also dismissed men before the expiration of their first enlistment on grounds of undesirability, inaptitude, or unfitness. These classifications were designed to avoid attaching the stigma of a disciplinary discharge to the men but at the same time to rid the navy of men it considered unsuitable.[62] Until 1932 commanding officers on their own authority could discharge up to 1 percent per year of the seamen under their command for undesirability or inaptitude.[63] Although the sailor had the right to appeal, the bureau usually upheld the officer. When in 1932 the Bureau of Navigation revoked their authority to issue these discharges, officers felt a loss of power over their crews. They complained that to remove an obviously unfit man from the service it was now necessary to wait until he committed an infraction serious enough to go to court-martial.[64]

In addition to these disciplinary or conduct-related discharges, a sailor sometimes could get a discharge before his enlistment expired by purchase or by special order. After 1893 the department allowed discharges to be purchased for a stipulated sum to reimburse the navy for some of the expense it had incurred; the amount was determined by a sliding scale of percentage of yearly pay.[65] The department granted this discharge at its own discretion and only during the first enlistment.[66]

Personal hardship—usually financial—constituted the grounds for special-order discharges granted by the president, the secretary of the navy, or the chief of the Bureau of Navigation without cost to the sailor. Generally the navy limited these discharges to cases of hardship which arose after enlistment and which could not have been foreseen. Consequently, discharges for inability to support a wife and family were seldom allowed.[67] Enlisted men receiving appointments to one of the service academies also were granted special-order discharges to free them from the obligations of their enlistment contract.

Before World War I and for a brief time thereafter, the navy experimented with granting furloughs without pay. Authorized by an act of August 29, 1916, this furlough permitted a man to return to civilian life without purchasing a discharge but with an obligation to return to active service should a national emergency occur before the end of his enlistment.[68] Because a man with sufficient reason to receive a furlough was not the individual most suited for an emergency call-up, the idea did not work well. By 1925 the bureau had discontinued the practice.[69]

The distinctions between types of discharge were of necessity somewhat vague, and practices in issuing discharges varied from officer to officer. The Bureau of Navigation reviewed discharges and attempted to correct injustices, although any benefit of doubt went to the commanding officer. In some cases in which the man's record had been disregarded, however, the bureau did set aside unfavorable discharges and grant better ones.[70]

Not only did officers' standards in issuing discharges differ, but the department's policy varied to suit its changing need for men. The Bureau of Navigation, for example, discouraged the use of undesirable discharges when there was a personnel shortage.[71] On the other hand, when enlisted strength was satisfactory, the navy was not interested in redeeming every marginal case. Because he was secretary in a period when recruiting was generally easy, Daniels adopted a policy of discharging unsuitable men and permitting dissatisfied sailors to buy their discharges.[72] As a result, the number of discharges purchased soared from 451 in the fiscal year ending June 30, 1914, to 2,303 for fiscal 1915.[73] Daniels' action received a mixed reception. *Our Navy* hailed the order as "the emancipation of the American sailor."[74] Others were distressed by the number of bluejackets leaving. The commandants of both the Great Lakes and Newport Naval Training Stations urged tempering the liberal policy so that recruits would not buy discharges before they gave the navy a chance or before they had considered what they would do after returning to civilian life.[75]

In the interwar period of the 1920s and 1930s, the department never again adopted Daniels' generous policy of discharge. Although the favorable recruiting market permitted such a course, low turnover gave the navy a veteran force that made the service a career and that did not seek early release. The number of discharges issued before the end of enlistment steadily decreased.[76]

RETIREMENT

Unlike other terms of service, which could have a direct impact on all sailors, the effects of retirement were not immediate. Benefits offered after active duty, however, could provide sailors with an incentive to remain in the navy; thus they could help induce men to reenlist and to behave in a way that avoided expulsion from the service. Yet, despite the possible value of such a program in building a career force, it was not until after the Spanish-American War—fourteen years behind the army—that the navy began offering retirement benefits.

Although a pension fund had cared for men disabled in the line of duty in the nineteenth century, such a pension was obviously not as satisfactory a benefit as retirement pay given in recognition of long service. In 1885 Congress passed the first armed services retirement act, but only for the army and marines. It was hoped that provisions for old age would make soldiers "more likely to support the monotonous life of the service" and reduce the number of desertions.[77] Almost immediately, the chief of the Bureau of Equipment and Recruiting recommended "some legislation looking to the retirement of enlisted men of the Navy after thirty years of service."[78] During the next fifteen years a number of naval retirement bills were introduced into both houses of Congress, but without success. In spite of the occasional recommendations the navy made to Congress, retirement benefits for enlisted men remained a low priority for the Bureau of Navigation.

During the early 1890s, veteran groups assumed the crusade, and petitions from local garrisons inundated Capitol Hill.[79] Finally, Congress amended an 1899 personnel bill to include enlisted retirement.[80] This amendment permitted a sailor fifty years or older to retire after thirty years of service, with rank and three-fourths pay and allowances. A period of service in the Spanish-American or Civil War was multiplied by two in determining length of service.[81]

The retirement act was passed in the hope that it would "induce a desirable class of men to enlist" and "tend to discourage desertion and other offenses which result in debarring those guilty of them from the benefits of continuous service."[82] The navy soon discovered, however, that retirement benefits were of little help in achieving these goals. Thirty years was too long for a young man to plan ahead; indeed, it was often too long to expect men in some ratings to survive.

Because earlier retirement seemed to be the solution to making retirement benefits more effective in improving the enlisted force, various proposals in that direction soon were made. One suggestion was to reduce the required service to twenty-five years. Truman Newberry, secretary of the navy under Theodore Roosevelt, recommended this plan on the grounds that the army and marines could allow time overseas to count double, making it possible for a soldier or marine to retire after as little as fifteen years of service. The shorter time for retirement in the navy would recognize the fact that after twenty-five years a man was often not suitable for duty and had to be either discharged or carried until retirement, even though he was no longer fully capable. Navy regulations, in fact, gave men with more than twenty-five years' service first choice in assignment to receiving ships.[83]

A more common proposal was for a graded retirement. Though the suggestions varied, they all permitted earlier retirement at a lower percentage of pay. Secretary Meyer in 1911 suggested retirement after sixteen, twenty, or twenty-five years with two-fifths, three-fifths, or three-fourths pay, respectively.[84]

In spite of official support, graded retirement never became law. The Naval Reserve, created in 1915, however, served much the same purpose. Enlisted men could be transferred to the reserve from the regular navy and receive a retainer pay until they completed thirty years of service, at which time they retired. Until July 1, 1925, men could transfer to the reserve after either sixteen or twenty years service, but men enlisting after July 1, 1925, could transfer only after twenty years.[85] Since the reserve included provisions for recall in case of a national emergency, it was not the same as graded retirement, but for most men it served that end.

Retirement, even a form of graded retirement, was but one part of the terms of service. The adoption of this new feature, of course, did not mean that the navy completely restructured its personnel policies; in fact, the department retained many practices inherited from the nineteenth century. Yet modifications did occur as the navy developed a system capable of handling a large, technically skilled enlisted force and sought ways to make life more appealing to the young men the modern navy wished to attract and hold. The rating structure underwent a continuous process of change, reflecting the increased importance of machine-oriented skills. In addition, the method of creating and establishing ratings and pay was simplified to permit the secretary of the navy to decide what ratings were required, thus enhancing the service's ability to respond to its manpower needs. At the same time, the pay table was streamlined by the elimination of different wages for ratings of the same relative rank.

New policies were adopted in other areas as well. The navy took a major step toward standardizing its system of promotion when it included written examinations as part of the criteria for advancement. In addition, it raised the ceiling for promotion and after 1914 began appointing a few men from the fleet to the Naval Academy. For new men, the department eliminated what had been a major grievance in the nineteenth century by extending the clothing allowance from apprentices to all recruits. Yet not all conditions of service encouraged men to prefer the navy to other employment. Navy pay, for example, never became totally competitive with civilian wages, despite repeated complaints from both the men and the department.

Ratings, pay, promotion, discharge, and retirement were not the only areas of service life that were affected by the emergence of the modern navy. As the type of men who enlisted altered, relations between officers and sailors also began to change, and the department began to manifest a new interest in the force through experiments with its system of justice.

chapter 8

Officers and Naval Justice

An enlisted man's life was subject to rigid control. The traditions of military service and the demands of running a ship required a smooth flow of orders from top to bottom of the naval hierarchy and a prompt obedience to superiors. Because of these requirements, a sailor's conduct was carefully regulated, with his officers standing watch to insure compliance.

The basic forms of the relations between officers and men and of the system of naval justice had been inherited from the eighteenth-century British navy and maintained in the age of sail. During the nineteenth century, the service was able to achieve only a mixed success in governing the rough group of men that composed the enlisted force. In the twentieth century, as the size of the force grew and as the old ways proved cumbersome and inflexible, reform in the treatment of the men became necessary. Alterations in the relationships between officers and men and in the legal system, however, were not as dramatic as changes in the methods of recruiting and training sailors. Indeed, the new recruiting and training programs lessened the need for reform in other areas of naval policy because they helped produce an enlisted force that was more carefully selected and better indoctrinated into naval ways than had been the case in the old navy.

Officers were a sailor's direct contact with the naval establishment; naval law devoted much of its attention to defining the relationship between officers and the men. Yet, because officers had considerable latitude in exercising the powers of their command, they determined much about the kind of treatment bluejackets received within the range of possibilities under the formal legal structure. A consideration of the navy's system of justice, therefore, requires first an examination of the relation between officers and men.

OFFICERS

Officers and enlisted men were united by their common membership in the navy. They shared the confines of the same ship; they worked together; they faced danger together. In spite of these bonds of service, the two groups remained distinct, with each constituting something of an unknown quantity to the other. To the men, the officers loomed "as a kind of golden incomprehensible cloud ever on their horizons."[1] To the officers, the men were equally mystifying.

Basic in understanding relations between officers and men is recognition of the barriers between them. Each group entered the service in a different way, received different training, and pursued a different career pattern. In the nineteenth century boys nominated to places in the Naval Academy came from families prominent enough to have some political influence. Even in the twentieth century, when congressmen and senators generally used competitive examinations to select nominees, incoming midshipmen belonged to families which were more urban and professional than was a representative sample from the entire population. Once in the academy, four years of indoctrination obscured any differences that might have existed among entering midshipmen to produce a "naval aristocracy."[2] In contrast, seamen were generally of a lower class and never attained as high a level of education.

In addition to differences in background and status, the weight of tradition and regulations buttressed the hierarchy of the naval establishment. Enlisted men, for example, saluted officers, used different ladders, and responded differently from officers to a sentry's hail.[3] Regulations prescribed imprisonment and dishonorable discharge for enlisted men convicted of some infractions for which an officer incurred only dismissal from the service.[4]

Although the relationships between officers and men were deeply rooted in tradition, they were not unchanging. In the twentieth century, the pride that officers felt in the service slowly extended to include the enlisted force. Peter Karsten notes that at roughly the time of the Spanish-American War a new crop of senior officers assumed command. These officers had long advocated a variety of reforms in the naval establishment—including upgrading the enlisted force.[5] Although these "Young Turks" of the turn of the century eventually became the old guard of the 1930s, their concern for the enlisted force continued. Young officers were reminded that the bluejacket was "representative of the young, vigorous, intelligent, and self-respecting class of young American manhood that is to be found in every part of the country" and that "he wants his intelligence and abilities to be appreciated."[6]

Earlier, officers usually had been content to let the men suffer slander or ill-treatment at the hands of civilian populations. Even as late as the 1890s, some sailors believed that their superiors did not discourage poor treatment ashore because it made the men happy to return to the ships.[7] Officers of the new navy, on the other hand, increasingly defended the men, even when their values conflicted with those of local establishments. In 1906, for example, Rear Admiral Robley D. Evans threatened to move the entire Atlantic Fleet in order to pressure the council of Provincetown, Massachusetts, to rescind a ban on Sunday baseball playing. To Evans, the men's welfare justified creating a major incident.[8]

Undoubtedly the fact that the character of the enlisted force was changing helped alter officers' attitudes and motivated them to improve the men's lot. The old cosmopolitan enlisted force had been an alien entity to officers, both literally and figuratively. Sailors in the modern navy, in contrast, were culturally similar to their officers, though from a lower social position. Officers' opinions of the enlisted force rose; the former "dregs of all countries" became young Americans who compared "favorably with [their] brother entering college or even the Naval Academy."[9] These were men who, in naval parlance, would be "amenable to discipline." An important facet of the improvements that many officers discussed was that enlisted men seemed to accept legitimate authority over them cheerfully when it was exercised well.[10]

Although in the twentieth century the men generally received more consideration from their officers than they had previously, nevertheless, if an enlisted man felt he had been treated unjustly, he had little practical recourse. Naval law prescribed that grievances be submitted upward through normal channels. The sailor was thus often compelled to go to the very man about whom he was complaining. Fear of reprisal discouraged him from this course. In addition, regulations warned that the man who lodged a complaint "will be held accountable if his representations are found to be vexatious, frivolous, or false." Clearly the navy did not encourage action against superiors.[11]

To avoid the possible repercussions of an official protest, sailors sometimes sought outside assistance. The opportunities for such aid, however, were limited. There is little evidence about how frequently outside help was requested. *Our Navy* and other enlisted men's magazines claimed they stood ready to champion justified grievances. Because the publications guaranteed the complainant anonymity, the danger to a sailor's subsequent career was reduced. Nevertheless, the successful intervention of a magazine was doubtlessly rare.[12]

Sometimes enlisted men turned to congressmen for aid. Inquiries were transmitted from congressional offices to the Navy Department, which in turn referred them to the officer involved. Investigations initiated in this manner had no better chance of favorable action that complaints through channels; possibly they had less since the navy frowned upon the use of congressional influence.[13] In any case, few specific grievances could be considered without the complainant's name, and the protection of anonymity was therefore impossible.

An incident in 1920 demonstrates the navy's hostility to grievance procedures outside the chain of command. During a congressional hearing it was suggested that an office be established in the Bureau of Navigation to receive charges against superiors. Admiral Henry B. Wilson, then commander in chief of the Atlantic Fleet, rejected the proposal, arguing that the existing machinery was satisfactory. Furthermore, he said, "to permit anyone to voice a fancied grievance and criticize his superior officers and receive consideration would result in a tearing down of the fundamentals of discipline."[14] Though speaking for himself, Wilson undoubtedly reflected a consensus. The idea, needless to say, was not pursued.

Here the limits in the officers' relations with the men stand out clearly. Officers readily adapted in some ways to the changed nature of the enlisted force, but they also expected inferior members of the naval establishment to accept acts of their superiors with childlike faith. A training station newspaper, for example, told recruits that "if we have a grievance we can go to our officers like to a good father and tell our troubles, and they will be righted and like a good father the Navy rewards us when we prove to be good sons."[15] Because of this attitude, officers had difficulty comprehending that sailors often felt constrained by even the most benign paternalism.

NAVAL JUSTICE

Discipline

When officers discussed the attributes they desired in the enlisted force, the most frequently used word was "discipline." Indeed, the concept of discipline lies at the heart of any discussion of naval customs and laws. Discipline was considered the fundamental quality of an efficient military force, and the entire legal structure strove to develop and maintain it. The navy equated discipline with obedience. Discipline was "the *habit of obedience* by which a man obeys an order naturally and without question, without stopping to consider whether he wants to obey or not."[16] This obedience was vital to a man's success in the service:

> Absolute obedience is all that the government asks of you in order to let you partake of all the benefits it offers. If you are not so efficient as you should be, it simply results in your not being promoted so rapidly; but if you are not obedient, you are not promoted at all, and, sooner or later, you will be discharged.[17]

Discipline constitutes the keystone of naval law, which receives more concrete expression in the *Articles for the Government of the Navy* and in the

Regulations for the Government of the Navy. The *Articles*, whose essence has remained virtually unchanged since the navy's founding, are older and shorter than the *Regulations*. The *Articles* are incorporated in the federal statutes and form a "constitution" of the navy. Outlining the "character of the rights, the duties, the obligations and the privileges of the officers and men," they were deemed important enough to be read to the crew once a month. The *Regulations*, on the other hand, have been expanded and altered to meet the changing needs of the navy. They both amplify the *Articles* and govern such administrative matters as enlistment, pay, discharge, and accounts.[18]

At one level, discipline means submission to the *Articles* and *Regulations*; the threat of punishment contributed to the sailor's compliance. But the concept of discipline involves more than mere pro-forma obedience. Discipline "is a prompt, ready, zealous, and complete compliance with orders given. A slow, unwilling, partial compliance with orders is as bad as flat disobedience."[19]

Determining the spirit motivating obedience presented a particularly complex problem. Because attitude is elusive and difficult to measure, officers desired visible indicators of discipline to reflect the degree of submission to authority. Most officers felt as did the lieutenant who wrote in the *Great Lakes Bulletin* that the "failure to salute reflects upon the discipline of the entire service and indicates a slackness which . . . will not be tolerated."[20] The lieutenant argued that the purpose of the rituals of military etiquette was not to boost officers' egos but to preserve the discipline—and hence, he felt, the efficiency—of the navy.

In the days before war-crime trials, obedience was expected in all cases. Recruits were admonished that they were "*never justified* in deciding upon the legality or the propriety of an order."[21] The only problem the authors of such passages foresaw was the possibility of conflicting orders. In such a case, the enlisted man discharged his responsibility by citing the conflicting instructions and by then letting the officer decide which he should follow. Nothing in the bluejacket's training raised the possibility that a naval officer would issue immoral or illegal orders, the execution of which would violate an individual's conscience and be tantamount to a violation of law.

Offenses

Naval law recognized two types of infractions: criminal and military. Criminal offenders included men "guilty of acts of moral turpitude which would be punishable by a term in prison if the offender were a civilian." Such men committed the usual range of felonies—e.g., assault, theft, and murder.[22] Upon conviction on a criminal charge, the bluejacket might be imprisoned either in a naval prison or in a state or federal penitentiary. Military infractions, on the other hand, often either had no counterpart in civilian jurisprudence or, if they did, the offenses were treated far more lightly outside the service. Military offenses included disobedience to orders, inattention to duty, and desertion.[23]

Military offenses were more common than criminal infractions. Of the cases reaching general courts-martial between the years 1904 and 1939, those involving unauthorized absence composed by far the greatest number, amounting to over two-thirds of the total in each year (see table 10 of the Appendix). Drunkenness and scandalous conduct were also major items, though they accounted for far fewer cases. Prosecutions involving homosexuality were negligible.

Unauthorized absence, the most common of all violations, involved three offenses: absence without leave, absence over leave, and desertion. Desertion required a "manifest intention not to return."[24] To prove such an intent, the commanding officer could rely on a sailor's statements to other crew members before his disappearance or the fact that he took unusual amounts of money or clothing when he left for liberty. Regardless of other circumstances, any man absent without permission over ten days was declared a deserter.[25] The practice in most cases seems to have been to wait the full period before so classifying a sailor.

Desertion was not, of course, a new problem in the twentieth century; it had been a common complaint among officers in the nineteenth century and was one of the continuing personnel problems the navy hoped to solve through implementation of its new policies.[26] The department especially hoped that better selection and training of men entering the service would eliminate potential deserters. Finally, around the beginning of the new century, the rate of desertion began to show a marked improvement. After hovering around 15 percent of the enlisted force from 1899 to 1908—roughly the same level as in the late nineteenth century—the rate dropped to 8.8 percent in 1909 and continued downward (see table 11 of the Appendix). During World War I, the rate of desertion fell to less than 1 percent in 1918. In the immediate postwar period, desertion jumped to 9.5 percent in 1920. With the development of a stable enlisted force during the midtwenties, however, the rate declined once more—to 4.9 percent in 1925, and then to 2.4 percent in 1929. During the depression it dropped lower still and remained under 1 percent after 1932.

Although the desertion rate improved, the service continued to regard unauthorized absences as its most serious disciplinary problem. Concern was so strong that the navy took elaborate steps to dissuade men from attempting desertion. Recruits were impressed with the enormity of the crime, the likelihood of punishment, and the permanent stain it made upon a man's record. It was also the only infraction of regulations for which the navy routinely offered a reward for the capture and return of the individual involved.[27]

To gain further understanding of this vexing problem, the Bureau of Navigation periodically studied deserters and desertion. These investigations in the first decades of the twentieth century all revealed essentially the same pattern. Most desertions occurred in the first year of enlistment (as had been true in the nineteenth century). Sailors in ratings of low prestige or unpleasant duties—messmen or coal passers, for example—deserted most often. Battleships, which received most of the recruits from the training stations, suffered a higher rate than did submarines or destroyers, which were manned by volunteers for the particular type of duty. Reflecting the fact that sailors needed a suitable site for desertion, ships in home waters sustained more absentees than those in Asiatic areas.[28]

In addition to collecting statistics, the navy questioned deserters who had been apprehended and solicited officers' opinions on the subject. These studies concluded that desertion could be attributed to various factors, grouped broadly as the personal life of deserters, the demands of the navy, and the state of the economy.[29]

Most apprehended deserters ascribed their action to personal factors—family problems, women and drinking, or an inability to adapt to naval discipline. Naval authorities, not unexpectedly, favored such explanations since they indicted the character of the men rather than the nature of the service. In explaining desertion by this interpretation, officers contradicted the high opinions of enlisted men they expressed in other public statements. Especially in times when the demand for recruits was great, officers attributed desertion to the low quality of men in the service. In 1903, for example, Captain Eugene H. C. Leutze lamented:

> In my opinion, in a great number of cases, we do not get the best elements of the male population of the communities in which enlistments occur. In fact, we get rather the poorer and men of roving and adventurous dispositions. These have never known restraint, so that the discipline and routine work of the Navy is irksome to them.[30]

After World War I, one officer wrote to the Bureau of Navigation that the "poor class of men enlisted since the Armistice accounts for the large numbers of instances of leave breaking."[31] Such reasoning, of course, contains an element of tautology: since only undesirable men desert, deserters must be undesirable.

Other common explanations of desertion concerned conditions in the navy. Enlisted men cited unfair officers, poor food, and injustices in promotion or punishment as causes of desertion. The service so circumscribed the men's lives that often flight provided the only escape from real or imagined inequities.[32] Most officers were unsympathetic to these grievances. Others charged that eager recruiters presented an overly sanguine picture of naval life. Applicants listened to exciting tales of the glamour and adventure of being a sailor but heard little about the discipline the navy expected from its men.[33]

The navy preferred to reject explanations that stressed internal conditions of the service, even though that was the most easily correctable cause of desertion. To some extent, however, it did take remedial action. During periods of plentiful applicants, careful and honest recruiting prevented enlisting youths under a false impression of the nature of service life. Furthermore, the continued improvement in the habitability of naval vessels in the twentieth century no doubt helped to reduce some of the irritations producing desertion.

Although it was possible to alleviate some causes of desertion, one important factor remained beyond the navy's control—the state of the economy. Many officers responding to a 1920 survey, for example, cited the lure of high-paying civilian jobs as the reason for desertion.[34] On the other hand, high unemployment in 1908 (8.5 percent of the work force) no doubt contributed to the significant drop in desertion during the fiscal year ending June 30, 1909.[35] Similarly, the exceptionally low desertion rates during the thirties reflected the fact that there was little outside the service to entice the men. A total explanation, of course, is more complex. Trouble in the nation's economy encouraged reenlistments, which produced an experienced enlisted force that, in turn, would be less likely to desert. Similarly, hard times increased the number of applicants for enlistment and permitted the service to exercise greater selectivity in choosing recruits. On the other hand, it is also true that the overall rate of desertion followed a downward trend from 1908, as has been seen. Thus, other factors not related to the national economy—such as improved recruiting and better living conditions aboard ships—undoubtedly helped reduce the desertion rate.

Courts

Whatever his offense, an accused enlisted man faced trial by a naval court. Naval law not only defined the nature of offenses but also established the judicial machinery to try alleged violations. Except for certain avenues of appeal, naval courts were independent of the civilian judiciary and operated under procedures that were often quite different. In 1929 the Board to Examine into the General Nature of the Laws Affecting Naval Discipline and Punishment spoke for the service when it expressed doubts that

> Congress intended or that it is at all necessary in safe-guarding the rights of the accused for the Navy to follow all the rules of civil criminal procedure, especially when the offense charged concerns merely misfeasance or nonfeasance in office.[36]

Disregard of civilian court practices resulted in complaints that the navy neglected enlisted men's rights, but officers dismissed the protests as uninformed or unfair.[37]

Depending upon the severity of the offense, an enlisted man could be tried in a general court-martial, a summary court-martial, a deck court, or at the captain's mast. In this order, the courts handled offenses of decreasing seriousness and could assess punishments of lessening severity.[38]

Major infractions (such as desertion, flagrant disobedience, and felonies) and all cases against officers were referred to general courts-martial. Consisting of from five to thirteen officers, a general court-martial could be convened by the president, the secretary of the navy, the commander in chief of a fleet or squadron, or the commanding officer of any naval station outside the continental United States. Only a general court-martial could dispense capital punishment or sentences involving lengthy imprisonment.

The summary court-martial, composed of three officers, considered cases less serious than those handled by a general court-martial and could be convened by the commanding officer of any vessel or by the commandants of naval yards, naval stations, or marine barracks. As implied by its name, the summary court-martial was designed to deal quickly with offenses too minor to justify a general court-martial. It could sentence an enlisted man to a bad-conduct discharge, solitary confinement not exceeding thirty days, solitary confinement on bread and water or on reduced rations for a period not exceeding thirty days, confinement not exceeding two months, reduction to the next inferior rate, deprivation of liberty on foreign station, or extra duties and loss of pay for a period not exceeding three months.

The general and summary courts-martial had proved adequate for the volume of trials in the relatively small sailing navy. Early in the twentieth century, however, the increase in the size of the navy meant both more men and more violations; a proliferation of court-martial cases threatened to cripple the existing judicial system. At first the department urged commanding officers to handle more cases on their own authority instead of referring them to summary courts-martial.[39] When this appeal failed to reduce the number of summary court-martial cases, the navy sought relief in the creation of a new judicial mechanism—the deck court. Authorized in 1909, the deck court consisted of only one officer, who was usually appointed by the commanding officer of the ship.[40] A sailor had the right to demand a summary court-martial instead of a deck court, but in doing so he made himself liable for greater punishment.[41] As demonstrated in table 12 of the Appendix, deck courts did not reduce the number of summary court-martial cases, but they did help curtail further rapid increase.

Officers welcomed the deck court as a means of reducing the burden of court-martial duty, but the men questioned the advantage of the new court. As *Our Navy* complained editorially, the deck court permitted just one officer to disrate a petty officer holding a permanent appointment—a power that not even the commanding officer had formerly possessed. The magazine charged that this

> shows how the Navy Department can reach around the President, the Secretary of the Navy, and the Congress, and land a strong-arm jab in the ribs of the enlisted man, when and where he is least expecting it, and make him say he likes it.[42]

The editorial also expressed the sailor's fear that demanding a summary court-martial marked a person as a troublemaker in officers' eyes and thereby reduced chances for acquittal.

The deck court enjoyed considerable vogue immediately after its introduction. At first a high proportion of the enlisted force—about 20 percent in 1910—appeared before the court. By 1912 the rate had fallen to 11.05 percent. After 1912, however, the rates for all three courts followed a similar downward trend, except for a brief increase in the postwar period. In 1937, the proportion of men tried before each court reached its lowest level—0.24 percent and 3.25 percent for general and summary courts-martial, and 2.13 percent for deck courts.[43]

Whatever the number of cases, an enlisted man's chances of acquittal were slight. Courts seldom exonerated defendants, particularly enlisted men; only 2.9 percent of the bluejackets who were tried before general courts-martial between 1904 and 1939 were acquitted. Sixteen percent of the officers were found not guilty.[44] In part, the conviction rates were the result of a thorough pretrial investigation, which insured that only those cases in which convictions were likely went to trial.[45] Yet, since officers stood a better chance of acquittal than did enlisted men and since it seems unlikely that an officer's case would have received a less thorough investigation than an enlisted man's, other factors must have been involved.

A major reason for the high conviction rate of enlisted men certainly was that many of the infractions the men committed were desertion or absence without leave. In these cases the evidence was clear—a man either was absent or was not. On the other hand, officers were more likely than the men to be charged with offenses in which guilt was more difficult to determine, such as "conduct unbecoming an officer" or "negligence." Another factor working in favor of officers and against enlisted men might have been an unconscious bias of court members. Court-martial judges, after all, were officers, familiar with and probably sympathetic toward officers' problems. They might therefore have tended to see extenuating circumstances in an officer's case; the enlisted man they might have perceived under a cloud of guilt since he had been charged by a fellow officer after a thorough investigation.

Most infractions did not require a court-martial or deck court but were handled by commanding officers at the mast. Throughout the navy's history, the captain had possessed wide latitude in disciplining his crew. The modern navy continued to rely on the commanding officer as the foundation of its disciplinary system. Although the captain no longer held court at the base of the mast, he did confront offenders as the situation demanded. He tried and punished minor infractions or ordered a court-martial for serious violations. On his own authority a commanding officer could reduce any rate he himself had established. He could also sentence a man to confinement for not more than ten days, solitary confinement for not more than seven days, solitary confinement on bread and water for not more than five days, deprivation of liberty, or extra duty.

The mast was also intended to serve as a forum for praise and commendation, but this aspect never received extensive use. After World War I, the Bureau of Navigation campaigned for routine employment of the meritorious mast. Finally on March 10, 1924, it issued a circular letter establishing officially the commendatory mast. Even after this endorsement, however, commendations formed a minor part of the normal conduct of the mast.[46]

Although the captain's mast in many ways constituted the core of the naval system of justice because of its initial and often sole jurisdiction, little comprehensive information about it exists. The judge advocate general did not collect statistics on it as he did on the deck court and on summary and general courts-martial. Captains did, however, record all decisions in the ship's log and in individual personnel jackets; an indication of the character of the mast can be gleaned from these logs. An examination of logs from 1900, 1910, 1920, and 1930 permits some generalization. Types of misdeeds and types of punishments do not seem to have varied in the different periods. The most common problem was unauthorized absence, usually absence over leave for less than a day. Various lapses of conduct—disobeying orders, shirking duty, and using profanity—followed. Drunkenness and failure to care for clothing and equipment also accounted for a large number of violations.[47]

A man's chances for receiving only a warning from the mast were slim, and punishment was almost inevitable. The most common punishments were restriction of liberty and imposition of extra duty. A captain usually had his favorite remedy and relied on one punishment more than any other. Solitary confinement was imposed less frequently than was restriction of liberty or extra duty, but it was not uncommon. Although it was not possible to determine from the logs which men were repeat offenders, it is reasonable to assume that punishment grew more severe the more a man appeared before the mast.

Another question about the mast concerns incidence; i.e., a sailor's chances of appearing before it. Although, again, the judge advocate general compiled no statistics on how many times men appeared before the mast, it is possible to gain a rough indication by examining conduct books that officers of vessels kept. These books contain information on each sailor's enlistment, a listing of next of kin, the sailor's rating, the marks a seaman was given each quarter for obedience, proficiency, and sobriety, and remarks on disciplinary action or special recognition.

Examination of a sample of the records of 185 names listed in conduct books from 1900 to 1905 shows that only 72 men (39 percent) maintained a clear record.[48] Despite its obvious inperfections, this statistic does indicate that minor infractions were fairly common. As a consequence, they were probably not taken too seriously by either officers or men. Though it is difficult to prove with the available data, it also seems likely that as the number of courts-martial declined in the late twenties and in the thirties, the number of infractions at the mast also decreased.

The mast gave the captain wide latitude in the administration of the ship—a discretion that permitted him to be either understanding and lenient or petty and tyrannical. In the mast at its best the captain took extra pains to discover the truth and to uncover extenuating circumstances that might allow clemency.[49] At its worst the mast was held in an arbitary manner, as in the following example related by an officer urging greater care in its conduct.

> The captain of a certain vessel was holding mast and as usual had a line of more or less repentant sinners in front of him. A young seaman, in turn, stepped up, saluted, and jerked off his hat.
>
> "You are charged with being absent over leave. What have you to say for yourself?" snarled the captain.
>
> "Why, sir, I—a—"
>
> "Shut up! Shut up! I'll get you for lying," bellowed the captain. "Five days solitary confinement. Next!"[50]

In practice, most captains were neither wholly enlightened nor totally despotic. What the two extremes do suggest is the uneven conduct of the mast and the helplessness of the enlisted man before it.

Punishment and Probation

Once convicted—and most trials of enlisted men led to conviction—a sailor might receive a sentence involving imprisonment, loss of pay, restriction of liberty, reduction in rate, or discharge from the service. Until 1909 he also faced the possibility of confinement in double or single irons. In that year, although many officers favored irons and in spite of the Navy Department's efforts to prevent their abolition, Congress forbade their use "except for the purposes of safe custody or when part of the sentence imposed by a general court-martial."[51]

Although the *Regulations* set limits on punishment, within those boundaries they left the sentences to a court's judgment. Consequently, a wide spectrum of treatment of similar offenses existed. This variation and the charges of injustices arising from it encouraged repeated efforts toward standardizing sentences. Such proposals were most common before World War I, coinciding with the navy's attempts to develop uniformity in the training and recruiting of its enlarged force.

Opponents of the navy's attempts to standardize sentences contended that commanding officers needed to use discretion in considering individual cases. Rear Admiral Robley D. Evans, who led the battle fleet on the first leg of its world cruise in 1907-8, argued:

> Uniform restrictions and punishments will never arrive at the end sought as the men themselves differ so much in characteristics that personalities must be considered. What would be a corrective influence for one would at times be without any effect at all on another.[52]

Because of this need for flexibility, a completely uniform code was never adopted, but moves toward consistency were made at various levels. A commanding officer, for example, might publish a schedule of punishments for his ship. The schedule helped insure equal treatment of the men in his command, and other officers reading it might adopt a similar list for their own ships. At a higher level, the commander in chief of a fleet might circulate his opinion on the use of certain types of punishments. Although his suggestions might be labeled "for information only," the fact that they were issued by the commander in chief undoubtedly produced some compliance.[53]

The community of opinion within the service also created an informal but nevertheless powerful force toward uniformity. Both officers and men, for example, believed that restricting liberty for long periods was self-defeating because confining a sailor to ship increased his frustration and dissatisfaction with the service, causing rather than preventing desertion.[54] Occasionally an officer adopted a policy of never denying men liberty.[55] Generally, however, denial of liberty was too handy a penalty and could not be resisted completely, although most captains tried to limit its use.

The review process provided another strong check in assigning punishment. Every court-martial conviction was submitted to a higher authority for approval before sentence could be imposed.[56] The records of all cases were also sent to the Office of the Judge Advocate General for review to determine if any impropriety had been committed in the proceedings. Additionally, by an act of February 16, 1909, the secretary of the navy was given the power to remit or mitigate sentences that courts-martial imposed.[57] Although decisions were rarely overturned, the knowledge that there would be a subsequent review no doubt influenced court-martial boards to tailor their decisions to the norms. Review by the judge advocate general permitted the Navy Department to discover unwise or undesirable practices and to admonish the service about them. In 1933, for example, the *Bureau of Navigation Bulletin* noted an excessive use of disrating and emphasized that this punishment should be used only in cases relating to the individual's ability to perform at the rate he held.[58] At best, the review system merely set bounds of penalties assigned throughout the navy. A definitive formula for all cases was impossible to devise. Yet the fact that the modern navy expressed such concern reveals an interest in fair and uniform treatment of the men that appears to be unique to the twentieth century. Correspondence of this type is not found in Navy Department files for the nineteenth century. Although it is possible that no situation arose that required admonishment, it seems likelier that the nineteenth-century navy was less interested in exercising such supervision over officers and the judicial system.

More successful than efforts toward standardized sentencing was the encouragement of leniency for new recruits and first offenders. Because these men often violated rules from ignorance rather than from malice, the navy gained little by inflicting the maximum punishment the *Regulations* allowed. In 1922, for example, the Bureau of Navigation instructed that all offenders under eighteen years of age on trial for unauthorized absence be tried only by summary courts-martial and only for absence without leave or absence over leave, regardless of the duration of the absence.[59] At that time the navy was experiencing extreme difficulty in securing recruits, and it was willing to use extraordinary measures to keep the men it had. When the manpower situation was less desperate, it was not as generous, but it nevertheless always showed some clemency to new men.

Concern for young offenders was but a part of the new navy's interest in restoring convicted men to duty. The department also sought a more formal rehabilitation program for convicted sailors. Although these efforts paralleled reforms in civilian penal practices, the navy's acceptance of them reflects a new interest in all aspects of enlisted personnel policy.

Early in the twentieth century, the navy began experimenting with probation. In September 1900 Captain Samuel C. Lemly, judge advocate general, attended a convention of the National Prison Association. Lemly credited this meeting with arousing his interest in probation and suspended sentences. In 1901 he began testing the idea in the navy; pleased with the results, he recommended that the program be continued.[60]

Probation continued to be granted on a small scale until 1911, when it was combined with the use of disciplinary barracks. In June 1911 a board composed of the judge advocate general, the assistant chief of the Bureau of Navigation, and the commanding officer of the naval prison at Boston suggested that men convicted of military crimes who "may be developed into desirable members of the service" be placed in disciplinary barracks instead of in naval prisons.[61] In August of the same year, George Meyer, secretary of the navy, visited an English detention camp and returned enthusiastically espousing a similar program for the American navy.[62] As a result of this high-level support, the navy opened its first camp at the abandoned naval station at Port Royal. On June 1, 1912, another barracks opened at the naval yard at Puget Sound in Washington State.[63]

At the disciplinary barracks the navy strove to reclaim an offender for future service rather than to punish him for past misconduct. He wore the regular naval uniform instead of prison garb and performed drill rather than hard labor. After satisfactorily serving two-thirds of his sentence, the offender could return to regular duty with a new opportunity to earn an honorable discharge or promotion.[64]

Although the disciplinary barracks returned about two-thirds of their inmates to regular service, Josephus Daniels decided to close both the Port Royal and Puget Sound barracks in 1914.[65] That act did not mean that Daniels rejected the idea of probation and restoration to duty; rather, he wished to change the conditions under which reinstatement took place. Daniels replaced the disciplinary barracks with General Order 110 of July 27, 1914, which encouraged disciplinary discharges for many offenders who formerly would have received prison sentences. It also permitted probation at large on reduced pay for men deserving clemency. If the probationer maintained a clear record until the end of his enlistment, he received the pay that had been withheld. If his behavior was unsatisfactory, he was discharged, and the pay was forfeited.[66]

In supporting the new policy, the judge advocate general argued that the "expense of the detention system was out of all proportion to its results."[67] The department claimed a higher rate of success for the new system than disciplinary barracks had achieved, and Daniels extolled the savings gained from closing the barracks and from reducing the number of men in confinement.[68] By adopting General Order 110, however, the navy in effect abandoned all efforts to deal with many classes of offenders and simply discharged troublesome cases. In taking this step, the service asserted that "the theory of reclaiming and rehabilitating offenders is not of the same importance in the naval service as in civil life."[69]

Only men who were deemed worthy of rehabilitation or who were convicted of relatively minor offenses received probation or discharge instead of imprisonment. Most men who did face confinement received short sentences and were incarcerated in the ship's brig, a cell required to be at least 6 feet long, 3½ feet wide, and the full height between decks. Longer sentences required transfer to either a state or federal penitentiary or, more commonly, one of the prisons maintained at several naval installations.

In the naval prisons, the sailor was given a short haircut and clothed in a special uniform. He was not allowed to salute his superiors; his mail was censored; and the number of visitors he could receive and the times he could see them were limited. Prison food was designed to be healthful but plain. Such regulations and the imposition of hard labor insured that prison life was an unpleasant alternative to service.[70]

Even naval prisons experienced the impact of the enlarged enlisted force. Shortly after the Spanish-American War, the proliferation of court-martial cases caused by the increasing number of men in service overcrowded existing prisons. To provide adequate facilities, the navy constructed a new prison at Portsmouth, New Hampshire, for the Atlantic coast area. Work began on March 11, 1904, and the first inmates arrived on April 11, 1908. Although Portsmouth never replaced all other naval prisons, it quickly became the home of the majority of naval prisoners.[71]

Because prisons generally housed men that the navy considered unworthy of retention, there was not the same incentive to improve the treatment of these men as there was for the rest of the enlisted force. As a result, only one significant experiment in prison reform was undertaken in the years between 1898 and 1939. Significantly, that experiment took place during World War I and the influx of large numbers of civilians into temporary naval service. At Secretary Daniels' suggestion, Thomas Mott Osborne, warden of Sing Sing, examined the naval prison system and early in 1917 made recommendations for change. He suggested eliminating special prison clothes, abolishing the cropped hair, and improving a prisoner's chance of returning to the service. Daniels was so impressed by these proposals that on August 1, 1917, he appointed Osborne a lieutenant commander in the naval reserve and placed him in charge of the Portsmouth prison. Osborne wrote Daniels:

> The purpose of my going to Portsmouth, as I understand it, is to work out a fundamental change in the purpose of the prison. It has been a prison; you wish me to make it a school. It has been a scrap heap; you wish me to make it one of humanity's repair shops.[72]

Osborne immediately instituted changes. When he arrived, he found 190 marines guarding 180 prisoners. Dismissing the marines, Osborne began using inmates as guards. This policy met with such success that during the war the prison handled approximately 6,000 prisoners without guards in the prison enclosure. Osborne also formed an honor system, eliminated physical punishment, and repealed what were considered demeaning regulations. Portsmouth prison during Osborne's tenure sent 4,000 men back to the service, men who ordinarily would have been lost to the war effort.[73]

After Osborne left the service in March 1921, the old ways returned. Lieutenant Colonel Hampton South of the marines became the next commandant; upon assuming his post, South immediately installed 150 marine guards over the 500 prisoners.[74] During the twenties and thirties both prison and probation retained the character that had been established before the war. Probation followed the principles of Daniels' General Order 110; prison officials, rejecting Osborne's reforms, reverted to the earlier system.

Overall both the prison and judicial systems of the navy escaped major restructuring as the new American navy was being created. Some modifications, however, were made to meet the needs of the twentieth-century force. The inauguration of the deck court and the construction of Portsmouth prison, for example, reflected pressures from the sheer increase in the number of offenders that the larger force produced.

Although the absolute number of offenders was greater than in the nineteenth century, the desertion rate and the proportion of enlisted men appearing before naval courts declined through most of the first forty years of the twentieth century. As an index of enlisted behavior, the lowered desertion and court-martial rates support the argument that a change occurred in the type of individuals serving in the navy; modern man-of-warsmen displayed a greater "amenability to discipline" than their nineteenth-century counterparts.

The less troublesome conduct of the enlisted force reinforced the navy's belief that it had a new—and better—type of sailor who deserved a kind of treatment not offered before. For their part, many officials displayed a new concern for improving the conditions of the service. A consequence of this attitude for the legal system was a willingness to give many offenders a second chance through some kind of probation. Although probation underwent several transformations—from Lemly's initial experiments, to Meyer's use of disciplinary barracks, to Daniels' General Order 110—the basic idea of granting clemency for certain types of offenses and restoring men to duty became a permanent feature of the modern navy.

Concern for improving the treatment of the enlisted force was not confined to the judicial system. Other aspects of enlisted life received much greater attention. In particular, the navy began to provide recreational programs as a means of increasing morale and enhancing the attractiveness of service and turned its attention to other aspects of welfare. These interests did not come suddenly and did not embrace every area of enlisted life; rather, they were worked out gradually as the navy began its first steps in building its modern personnel system.

Josephus Daniels, Secretary of the Navy from 1913 to 1921. NH-2336, Naval History Division, Navy Department.

Rear Admiral Stephen B. Luce, ca. 1888. NH-002323, Naval History Division, Navy Department.

Rear Admiral Albert C. Dillingham. NH-50406, Naval History Division, Navy Department.

Rear Admiral William F. Fullam, 1915. NH-49447, Naval History Division, Navy Department.

Hoisting in the Steam Cutter aboard the U.S.S. Pensacola. *Even with steam propulsion, the old navy depended upon the muscle of large portions of the crew—including marines—to perform many tasks. NRBL(0)-6231, Naval History Division, Navy Department.*

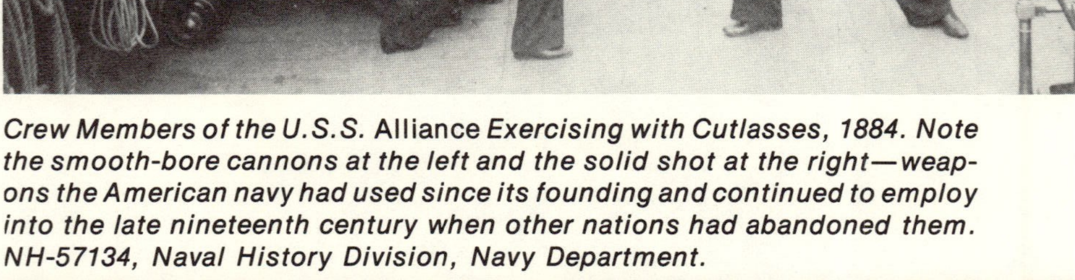

Crew Members of the U.S.S. Alliance *Exercising with Cutlasses, 1884. Note the smooth-bore cannons at the left and the solid shot at the right—weapons the American navy had used since its founding and continued to employ into the late nineteenth century when other nations had abandoned them. NH-57134, Naval History Division, Navy Department.*

Recruiting Poster, 1909. Early advertising efforts of the new navy sought to give specific information on the benefits of service in addition to providing an eye-catching color picture and slogan. NH-65452 KN, Naval History Division, Navy Department.

Recruiting Poster, World War I. During the war, posters simply appealed to a sense of patriotism and urgency. NH-81544 KN, Naval History Division, Navy Department.

HAILING YOU

for

U.S.
NAVY

Service, Travel, Trade-

Instruction

NAVY PAY RAISED

Bonus for former Navy Men

APPLY NAVY RECRUITING STATION

Recruiting Poster, ca. 1919. With the coming of peace, navy recruiting returned to emphasizing travel and material benefits. NH-66931 KN, Naval History Division, Navy Department.

Recruiting Poster, 1931. NH-66558 KN, Naval History Division, Navy Department.

Yeomen (F) at the Philadelphia Navy Yard, 1918. NH-53176, Naval History Division, Navy Department.

Aviation Mechanics' School, 1918. A major component of the navy's new personnel system was training sailors to operate and maintain the increasingly sophisticated equipment the service employed. 24-PNA-1376, BUNAV. NA.

Sailors Sleeping in Hammocks aboard the North Dakota, *1911. 19-N-5-a-40, Bureau of Ships, NA.*

Mess on board the U.S.S. Olympia, *1898. Before the introduction of cafeterias, messing was dispersed throughout the ship. Tables were raised*

chapter 9

Recreation and Welfare

Until the twentieth century the navy manifested little interest in the off-duty lives of sailors. After the Spanish-American War, the expense and difficulty involved in manning the service prompted a sensitivity to the needs of the enlisted force. The navy slowly recognized that the morale of its men depended not only on chances for training and promotion but also on the quality of life in the service. The department therefore early turned its attention to recreation; its interest in the welfare of the force, however, remained largely limited to the narrow interpretation of providing diversions to fill the sailors' spare moments while they were directly under naval jurisdiction.

RECREATION

During most of the nineteenth century, sailors relied largely on their own initiative to fill their free time. Some ships possessed libraries, but a semiliterate force had little use for these small facilities. The men generally provided their own athletic equipment, and, except for boat racing, sports received scant official encouragement. Bluejackets sometimes produced plays, although some officers even refused permission for this enterprise.[1] By the twentieth century, changing personnel requirements made the department's traditional indifference to recreation unacceptable.

Sports held a natural attraction for the young men who composed the enlisted force; it is therefore not surprising that athletics were the first pastime the navy promoted. Although the Bureau of Navigation began to furnish gymnastic apparatus to ships in the 1890s, it still refused to supply equipment for baseball or football.[2] In 1900 the department moved toward a more active role when it rewrote the *Regulations for the Government of the Navy* to direct commanding officers to "encourage the men to engage in athletics, fencing, boxing, boating, and other similar sports and exercises." Previously, the *Regulations* had urged officers only to "use all proper means to preserve the health of the crew."[3] In 1903 the navy supported its new regulations with an offer to issue a wide variety of athletic equipment to ships, to provide ten baseball uniforms to any vessel with a team, and to supply trophies to commanders of squadrons.[4] As one officer explained:

> There is no better way to make a good sailor and at the same time a loyal and true man to ship and country, than these athletic contests. They give the "jackie" a certain pride in ship and squadron that otherwise he would not acquire, and when a man gets that fondness for his vessel that comes from victory, hard won, whether in engagements in times of war, or athletic contests in times of peace, that man is bound to be a better man in every way as a result of those contests.[5]

Soon reports from the fleet included accounts of athletic competition. In a 1903 memorandum Rear Admiral Robley D. Evans, then commander in chief of the Asiatic Fleet, detailed sports events that had been conducted at the rendezvous of the fleet at Chefoo. From that report it is obvious that, although prizes had been financed by contributions from the crew, the active support of the officers had been necessary to stage the event and to obtain a playing field. Admiral Evans, in fact, urged the department to purchase fields ashore because the fleet had had to rely on the generosity of a local cricket club for a place to hold the games.[6]

Shortly before Evans' report, the navy had found that its home stations provided few recreational facilities. In April 1903 the Bureau of Navigation canvassed the navy yards about available space and received disheartening replies. Only the Mare Island navy yard at that time possessed an athletic field and a completed sports hall. Boston, Norfolk, and Portsmouth, New Hampshire, reported no facilities at all. Boston did suggest that a dump might be converted to an athletic field, and Norfolk and Portsmouth each reported adequate land that could be used for recreational purposes. Norfolk and Portsmouth also submitted plans for buildings that would have cost an estimated $35,000 and $60,000.[7]

In spite of this discouraging account, the Bureau of Navigation hardly rushed into action. Ten years later, in response to a similar inquiry, Norfolk navy yard reported it had an athletic field but no indoor facilities. Boston had no building and was still in the process of converting an open area into an athletic ground. Some minor advancements, however, had been made in the decade. By 1913 Portsmouth provided men with an athletic field and a reading room. Philadelphia and New York offered excellent grounds, and both yards mentioned their proximity to naval YMCAs. As before, Mare Island ranked above the others. The navy yard there boasted a reading room, pool and billiard tables, bowling alleys, and movie equipment. For outdoor sports, it offered tennis and handball courts, a running track, and athletic fields.[8]

After war was declared in 1917, the department undertook a major step in developing its recreational programs. At that time it formed the Commission on Training Camp Activities, composed of both naval officers and prominent civilians and under the direction of Raymond B. Fosdick, who also chaired a slightly older army Commission on Training Camp Activities. The navy commission was created primarily to coordinate the efforts of private charities and other civilians who wished to participate in the war effort. It also provided a central control for recreational programs and directed the expenditure of congressional funds allocated for recreation.[9]

Before 1917 only the Navy Branch of the YMCA and the Navy Relief Society had taken any major role in the life of enlisted personnel. When the United States entered the war, civilian organizations overwhelmed the men with gifts; they donated pianos, songbooks, instruments, and athletic equipment and built and staffed recreation halls, reading rooms, and canteens.[10] Sailors basked in unaccustomed solicitude.

In addition to equipment, the wartime navy also enjoyed the services of trained recreational personnel. Coaches and song leaders replaced officers. Probably no area was affected more from this influx of civilians than theatrical productions. In the early twentieth century bluejackets had presented stage shows with the approval of the ship's officers, though rarely under the officers' direction. These productions were usually presented in a vaudeville or minstrel format that permitted a variety of acts without the troublesome requirement of a plot. On occasion, satire about the ship on which the men served was included with the songs, skits, old jokes, and boxing exhibitions that formed the staple of the shows.[11] The creation of the Commission on Training Camp Activities in 1917 lent considerable encouragement to thespian pursuits. With professional direction, the quality of performances was enhanced. Costumes, equipment, and theaters were readily available, and public interest in the military created a large audience eager to see the shows. Typical of the major productions that were undertaken was *H.M.S. Pinafore*, which Lieutenant John Davies and Charles Rowes, a singing instructor, produced at the Newport Naval Training Station. The all-male company of eighty was given special barracks in which to rehearse and was able to stage its performances at the Colonial Theater in Newport and at the Schubert Majestic Theater in Providence.[12]

When the war ended, civilians were as eager to terminate their involvement as they previously had been to initiate it. The special instructors departed, the supply of free equipment dried up, and the huge audiences vanished. Despite the exodus of civilians, however, the navy emerged from the war more committed to providing for the recreation of its men than it had ever been before.

In 1919 the Bureau of Navigation absorbed the functions of the Commission on Training Camp Activities. At first it formed the Sixth Division to carry out the programs under Commander Claude B. Mayo, who had been a member of the commission during the war. In 1922 the Sixth Division was renamed the Morale Division, but its functions remained the same.[13]

Commander Mayo and his staff began replacing civilian specialists and programs with naval ones, hoping there could be a gradual and orderly transfer of most projects then in operation.[14] Yet it soon became apparent that Congress would not appropriate money at the rate it had during the war. Mayo sought $1,045,000 for the fiscal year ending June 30, 1920, but the House slashed this amount to $400,000. The final appropriation of $652,354.32, though an improvement over the House bill, was still far less than Mayo had requested.[15] The division also faced a serious personnel shortage. In 1920 Mayo complained to the chief of the Bureau of Navigation that he had pared his manpower requests to below the division's needs, yet men were still being transferred without warning, crippling the work of his office.[16]

The new division would obviously be unable to maintain the wartime level of activity. But although the appropriation for the recreation of the enlisted force plummeted after the armistice, it did continue. Before 1917 the navy had not even had a specific allocation for recreation; the continuation of the allotment into peacetime attests to the entrenchment of this interest. Even in the depression, the appropriation continued in the budget. The long-felt need to provide for the men in off-duty hours had finally produced a mechanism to insure that the program would be guided and developed.

The Morale Division rarely inaugurated new activities in the twenties and thirties but rather provided direction to those already under way. The introduction of motion pictures exemplifies this process. Showing films aboard ships was already commonplace when the Sixth Division was created in 1919. Indeed, virtually from the time movies had first entered American life in the early twentieth century, some crews began to obtain equipment and bookings on their own initiative. Profits from the ship's store, allotted for the men's welfare, were the usual means of financing the shows. Because the larger ships possessed an obvious advantage, the new art rapidly became established on these vessels. Correspondents with the fleet on its round-the-world voyage in 1907-9 reported that the crews enjoyed nickelodeons, though the reporters stressed that the films were wholesome, containing no taint of lewdness.[17]

During World War I some degree of central control was instituted when the Jewish Welfare Board and the Knights of Columbus provided a fund to purchase movies.[18] After the armistice, these agencies withdrew, and the Sixth Division assumed their functions. It quickly acted to insure an orderly and centrally controlled supply of films, establishing the Motion Picture Exchange in 1920 at the Brooklyn navy yard to secure prints from producers and distribute them to the fleets. This system provided small ships a better method of procuring shows.[19]

Along with distribution, the Bureau of Navigation sought to control the content of films. Official entertainment was to be wholesome entertainment, and films were accordingly censored. In 1921, for example, the Motion Picture Exchange deleted three flashes of the lovers from *Infatuation of Youth*. Censorship resided with the commanding officer of the exchange until 1927, when complaints about the type of films reaching the fleet spurred the bureau to transfer final approval of films to the Morale Division in Washington.[20]

By the time sound pictures appeared, the Morale Division, through the Motion Picture Exchange, controlled all distribution for the navy. Silent pictures had been initiated ship by ship, but the introduction of talkies required a decision from the Bureau of Navigation, which was not to be rushed into supporting a fad. After noting that producers were concentrating on talkies, the *Bureau of Navigation Bulletin* of April 6, 1929, lamented that if the trend continued "undoubtedly the scarcity of desirable silent prints will be aggravated each year until in the end the Navy may be faced with the prospect of equipping vessels for 'talkie' projection." The bureau resisted the tide until 1931. In that year it opened schools to train operators for the $332,000 worth of sound motion-picture equipment Congress had authorized.[21]

Athletics and films constituted the major diversions the navy offered its men. Nevertheless, the department began to encourage other kinds of recreation, though it did not attempt to establish the same level of central control as it had in film distribution. The number of ships carrying bands increased. The band often serenaded the crew at noon and after the evening meal, providing music for dancing or listening. Sometimes officers permitted "smokers" or "happy hours," occasions for boxing matches, music, and possibly treats such as ice cream. Generally, a happy hour was limited to the members of the crew; a smoker included visitors from other vessels. On a large ship in harbor, several thousand men might participate in a smoker.[22]

In addition to these all-male entertainments, the ship's crew was increasingly likely to sponsor a formal ball, which wives and girl friends attended. Although the men ran the parties, commanding officers encouraged these events, facilitated the planning, and attended with their wives in order to mix with the crew. Typical of these dances was a 1937 gala presented by the crew of the *Maryland* at the Ambassador Hotel in Los Angeles that featured two orchestras and a floor show.[23]

The new range of officially sanctioned entertainment offered the sailor a diversion for every mood. Among the choices, athletics contined to enjoy the greatest favor. Ultimately, this prominence of sports was created not by pressure and encouragement from the Bureau of Navigation but by the men's own interest. Bluejackets turned naturally and enthusiastically to sports. They devoted their free time to boxing, gymnastics, baseball, and football, unconcerned that they were enhancing ship spirit. They trained for racing-boat crews with little regard for the navy's desire to have its men proficient in handling small craft. They answered swimming call eagerly, caring little that the service wished its men to know how to swim.[24]

Athletic contests also permitted some men to achieve reputations beyond their ships. Winners of all-navy boxing competitions achieved service-wide fame. Other sports, similarly, produced their heroes. C. P. ("Shorty") Walters, for example, was a celebrated racing-boat coxswain. Shorty excelled not only in his ability to train a crew and to prepare a boat, but also in his gamesmanship—as when he pretended not to be able to see the stake boat in order to postpone a race after he had discovered that his boat was leaking.[25]

WELFARE

During the four decades between the Spanish-American War and World War II, the navy's welfare activities generally consisted only of recreational programs. Indeed, the department used the terms "recreation" and "welfare" interchangeably, even though the latter, as a much broader concept, encompasses all efforts to promote happiness or well-being. Despite the larger meaning, during these years the navy continued to conceive its role quite narrowly.

Venereal-Disease Control

Except for general medical care, the single activity that approached a broader definition of welfare was the navy's attempts to reduce the incidence of venereal disease. Venereal disease obviously was not a problem that was unique in the modern navy. What was new was that the twentieth-century service inaugurated efforts to prevent men from becoming infected—measures that had been lacking in the old navy. In the nineteenth century, medical officers had confined their suggestions for control of the disease to the hope that civilian public health officers would clean up red-light districts ashore.[26] The rest of the naval establishment seems to have ignored the question entirely. In the twentieth century, on the other hand, the department took steps to reduce the alarming casualty rate from venereal disease, and it addressed the prevalence of the disease as both a medical and a social problem.

Throughout the first four decades of the twentieth century, chancroid, gonorrhea, and syphilis each ranked among the leading causes of sick days for every year.[27] Although venereal disease was a problem throughout the navy, the rate of infection was not uniform for all classes of personnel or for all duty stations. Among the various occupational groups in the navy, the incidence of infection was well above average among firemen and seamen and below average for men in aviation, musician, and hospital ratings.[28] The lowest level of infection occurred among personnel stationed in the United States. The rate was somewhat higher for the fleet in European waters and much higher for vessels in the Far East. In fact, the Asiatic Fleet reported an incidence of syphilis twice that of any other unit in the navy.[29]

The high rate of infection among sailors in the Orient reflected both fewer public hygiene measures against the disease in the Far East and a greater reliance on prostitutes for sexual activity. Some cynics, in fact, divided the personnel of the Asiatic squadrons into those who have it, those who have had it, and those who will get it. Although this picture may have been overdrawn, venereal disease was common. The *Asheville*, probably typical of many ships in the Orient, had eighty admissions for the disease in the calendar year 1924 from a crew of about two hundred.[30]

Attention to reducing the rate of venereal disease came first from the Bureau of Medicine and Surgery. Despite the fact that the prevalence of the disease among prostitutes on shore clearly had a relation to the likelihood of infection among crew members, in the twentieth century medical officers turned from trying to improve conditions ashore and admitted that "naval authority must, as a rule, confine its efforts for the betterment of health to its own sphere."[31] Prophylaxis after intercourse was one way to reduce the incidence of the disease without attempting to change the habits of the men or the civilian communities. The navy thus began experiments with prophylaxis early in the twentieth century, and the results proved promising. In 1911 the surgeon general recommended issuing a prophylactic packet to the men to take with them on liberty to be used as soon after intercourse as possible.[32]

With the coming of Daniels, venereal disease ceased to be a strictly medical concern. The new secretary immediately rejected issuing prophylactic packets to the men. He believed

> the use of this packet . . . to be immoral; it savors of the panderer; and it is wicked to seem to encourage and approve placing in the hands of men an appliance which will lead them to think that they may indulge in practices which are not sanctioned by moral, military, or civil law, with impunity, and the use of which would tend to subvert and destroy the very foundations of our moral and Christian beliefs and teachings with regard to these sexual matters.[33]

Daniels preferred educational programs that stressed the dangers of venereal disease and explained that "sexual continence is compatible with health and that it is the best prevention of venereal infections."[34]

The Commission on Training Camp Activities, created in 1917 as part of the wartime recreational program, became an instrument for executing Daniels' policy. Relying heavily on moral indoctrination, it sought to build what Daniels considered good character and wholesome manhood. Recruits in training camps heard lectures—usually delivered by chaplains—saw movie presentations, and received pamphlets on the consequences of thoughtless action. Although Daniels felt the training camps offered the best audience, he also proselytized in the service at large. The commission, furthermore, sponsored activities in an attempt to offer the men alternatives to "alcoholic liquor and immorality," and to provide a "safe outlet for youthful energy."[35]

When the Bureau of Navigation assumed responsibility for the commission's programs after the war, it continued the campaign against venereal disease as a major part of its welfare activities. The entry of the commission and later the Bureau of Navigation into venereal-disease control did not mean that the Bureau of Medicine and Surgery was excluded. Even Daniels recognized that not all men would follow his exhortations to live a clean and celibate life and that, as a result, medical treatment was necessary. Although Daniels would not allow packets to be issued before liberty, he did permit medical prophylaxis to be given aboard ship to men who had been exposed. He also considered it a disobedience of orders—and hence a court-martial offense—if a man failed to report to the medical officer for prophylaxis before symptoms appeared.[36]

When Daniels left office, the navy began to modify its policies toward men with venereal disease. In September 1921 the department stopped regarding the failure to take prophylaxis as disobedience; in February 1922 the medical corps resumed issuing prophylactic outfits to men going on liberty. Two years later the surgeon general reported that the use of medical prophylaxis immediately after exposure was found to prevent up to 50 percent of the infections that would ordinarily occur. Yet many men did not use the packets even when issued; in April 1926 the service therefore made it a court-martial offense not to use the kits. In order to circumvent this order, many men administered the prophylaxis to themselves as soon as they went ashore on liberty and before exposure in order to have their names appear on the prophylactic register.[37]

These disciplinary procedures remained in force until 1937. In that year, the Bureau of Navigation removed all punitive actions against men suffering from venereal disease, except loss of pay for time absent from duty, in order that venereal infections would "be treated in the same light as other infections, that is, as a disease, and not an offense against discipline." The bureau hoped that more men would report for treatment and that the serious manpower loss to the disease would end.[38]

Family Life

In no area were the limitations of the navy's enlisted policy more apparent than in the treatment of the men's families. During the years between the Spanish-American War and World War II enlisted families received almost no special aid. In 1907 Captain Albert C. Dillingham, the commanding officer of the training facilities at Norfolk, complained that there "are no men in the world who have less consideration than enlisted men in the United States Navy who are married; there is no institution in the world that considers less the privileges of home life than the Navy."[39]

The situation improved only slightly later. In 1920 Congress permitted paying transportation of dependents, helping at least when men were transferred to new stations. But in 1926 a drive to extend hospitalization care to dependents failed, though in most cases navy doctors did provide outpatient care to sailors' families.[40]

A "Navy Marriage Ceremony," waggishly proposed by *Our Navy*, underscored the realities of life for married enlisted men: long absences and uncertain schedules.

Navy Marriage Ceremony as It Could Be

"Wilt thou, Jack, have this woman as thy wedded wife? To live together insofar as the Bureau of Navigation will allow? Wilt thou love her, comfort, honor, and keep her, take her to the movies and come home regularly to her on the 4:30 boat?"—"I will."

"Wilt thou, Jane, have this sailor as thy wedded husband bearing in mind liberty hours, boat schedule, watches, sudden orders, uncertain mail communication, and all other penalties of Navy life? Wilt thou obey him, serve him, love, honor and wait for him; press his uniforms, and let him smoke Navy plug in the house?"—"I will."

"I, Jack, take thee, Jane, as my wedded wife, from 4:30 p.m. until 7:30 a.m. as far as permitted by my Commanding Officer, liberty subject to change without notice for better, for worse, for earlier, for later, and I promise to send thee a weekly letter on cruise."

"I, Jane, take thee, Jack, as my wedded husband subject to the whim of the officer of the deck, changing residence whenever the ship moves; to have and to hold just as long as my allotment comes regularly and therefore I give my troth."[41]

At the heart of the special difficulties the married sailor faced was the separation inherent in service life. Every married enlisted man had his own tales of prolonged absences and difficulties in getting home in emergencies. The vagaries of assignment are graphically illustrated in the experience of Mrs. R. R. Quintero, the wife of a chief petty officer. Mrs. Quintero met her husband on the street one day, only to learn that he was preparing to leave for duty in Russia.[42] Other sailors also shared the plight of Charles Herget, who was at sea when his wife gave birth to their first child.[43]

The fact that the navy provided no aid in housing for enlisted men's families exacerbated the problems of service life. The department maintained almost no quarters for its married enlisted personnel and was far behind the army in this regard. Even in remote stations like Guam or Samoa, where there clearly was insufficient housing in the private market to accommodate married sailors, the navy made no attempt to supply quarters for enlisted men's families.[44]

Lacking government housing, sailors were often forced to remain separated from their families. In October 1924 Chief Machinist's Mate John Schroeder reported that he had not seen his wife for over two years.[45] Schroeder was stationed in the Orient, where the navy's failure to provide quarters for married enlisted men made it difficult for families to accompany the sailors. Even men with duty in the United States were often unable to have their families with them. A. E. Moore, machinist, first class, was assigned to Charleston, South Carolina, in 1920, but he was unable to move his family from Massachusetts; as a result, he had to endure long periods between visits. After one of his children was injured in April 1920, Moore had to rely on a loan from his shipmates to go home.[46]

When married sailors did attempt to have their families accompany them to their duty stations, they often encountered an unfavorable housing market. In Guam or Samoa, there was little available that was considered suitable for habitation by westerners. In the United States, sailors were often forced into an inflated housing market around naval stations. Facing the ordeal of the search alone, families usually left no record of their plight. A congressional hearing on naval pay in 1920, however, has preserved several individual accounts of apartment hunting in Washington, D.C. Mrs. F. D. Waer, the wife of a gunner's mate, first class, inquired at dozens of light housekeeping apartments before finding a room with kitchen privileges in a private home for herself, her husband, and their two-year old child; these modest accommodations took $35 a month from her husband's $95 per month pay. Mrs. R. R. Quintero finally had to settle for two unfurnished rooms at $35 a month. Mrs. H. H. MacNeal paid $27.50 of her husband's $96 a month pay for an unfurnished room on East Capitol Street. Because of the difficulty in finding quarters they could afford, many enlisted families lived with relatives. When the Waers were first married, they stayed with her mother in Boston. Similarly, Charles Herget and his wife lived with her sister for many years.[47]

In the absence of any official action to improve conditions, enlisted men at least twice in the period formed cooperatives to provide low-cost housing. In 1921 twenty-six chief petty officers and six petty officers from the naval air station at North Island, California, formed a home-building club to assist one another in construction. In 1937 another enterprise, the Navy Development Syndicate in Bremerton, Washington, sold stock to 235 navy men to finance homes to be rented at moderate rates to naval personnel.[48]

Many bluejackets probably chose not to reenlist because of the hardships they faced in attempting to combine family life and a naval career. While some were willing to suffer the disruptions of their homes, others were not. When these latter sailors married, they returned ashore for a more settled existence.[49]

In spite of the many problems faced by married enlisted men, a hardy minority persisted. The exact number is uncertain, since the navy published statistics on marital status only between 1918 and 1921. The information from these years shows that only a small proportion of the enlisted force was married: 7.8 percent in 1918, 6.3 percent in 1919, 7.3 percent in 1920, and 8.2 percent in 1921.[50] Because the war attracted men who ordinarily would not have joined, the figures may not be representative of the entire period between 1899 and 1939. Yet the preponderance of single enlisted men is clear. In addition, most sailors were below the median age of first marriage for the population, and the travel and long absences of naval life did nothing to encourage early attachment. Although the majority of men were always single, it seems likely that during the twenties and thirties, as the average age of the enlisted force increased and as more men served for more than one enlistment, a larger percentage were married.[51]

The experiences of married enlisted men reveal the limits of the navy's concern for the general welfare of its men. In the twentieth century the navy sought to make the conditions of service more attractive by introducing an increasingly extensive program of recreation. As long as a sailor was under direct naval jursidiction, he enjoyed a variety of new programs, such as athletics, movies, and band concerts. In fact, the navy equated welfare with recreation. Because of that narrow outlook, extensive social welfare programs that were aimed at improving the lives of sailors and at helping married enlisted men remain in the service were not developed before World War II.

The failure of the navy to adopt sweeping social welfare programs for the enlisted force, on the other hand, should not obscure the major step involved in the creation of recreational programs. In the nineteenth century no official programs had existed at all. Thus the recognition of the need to institutionalize programs that enhanced service life represented an important change in official thinking that would later make changes in other areas possible.

A major part of the navy's concern with improving service life was directed to the living and working conditions aboard its vessels. The ships of the modern navy provided new possibilities for bettering the life of enlisted men, possibilities the navy department gradually exploited. In addition to the innovations made aboard ships in the twentieth century, many other elements contributed to the type of experience a sailor had in the navy. The work a man performed, where his ship was located, the officers under whom he served, the military actions his ship might be engaged in—these and other factors produced the life of a sailor.

chapter 10

Life of a Sailor

A ship at sea becomes a world unto itself, isolated and self-sufficient. The Navy Department often remained a remote and mysterious force to men afloat. For a sailor, the navy was his vessel. To understand more fully enlisted men and their role in the navy, it is necessary to shift the focus of study to individual units. Here changes were more subtle than at a higher level, and they were blurred in the variety of men, ships, and places.

SHIPBOARD ORGANIZATION

Perhaps the most important factor determining the bluejacket's life was his position at the bottom of the naval hierarchy. The men implemented policy that was formed on high. One sailor neatly captured the reality of his existence in doggerel:

The Captain tells the Exec,
When he wants something done;
The Exec then tells the O.O.D.
And gets him on the run.
The O.O.D. looks wondrous wise
And strokes his downy jaw
Then he calls his trusty bosun's mate
And to him lays down the law.
The bosun's mate calls the coxswain
To see what he can see;
The coxswain gets a seaman
And that poor seaman is me.[1]

The hierarchy of rank was only part of the ordering of a naval vessel. As in the era of sail, in the modern navy every man had a place to be and a task to perform. Upon reporting for duty, a sailor was assigned to one of two watches, either port or starboard. He was simultaneously placed in one of six divisions; this assignment determined his actual duties. There were four "gun divisions," composed of men of the deck ratings, with each division responsible for maintaining a quadrant of the ship. A "powder division" consisted of electricians, shipwrights, carpenters, and men of other specialized ratings who performed their particular trades and cleaned their storerooms and work areas, and an "engineers' division" operated and cared for the fireroom and engine room. If the ship carried a marine detachment, it formed a seventh division.[2]

Most activities aboard ship required smaller units than watches and divisions. For such work, every ship had a watch, quarter, and station bill. Each man on a ship had a number. The bill was a catalog listing the duty station for various drills of the number holder and designating where the sailor ate, slept, and stowed his hammock.[3]

While the bill determined where on the ship the bluejacket performed his tasks, a daily schedule specified when the work was to be done. Table 13 of the Appendix outlines a typical daily schedule. A similar pattern of activity existed on all ships throughout the navy. Although special duty such as coaling ship or target practice disrupted the routine temporarily, at most times and in most places bluejackets lived under this timetable.

An enlisted man's precise duties, of course, depended upon his rating. The deck force—which consisted of seamen and ordinary seamen and such ratings as boatswain's mate, quartermaster, and gunner's mate—supplied lookouts, helmsmen, and messengers. These men also did the daily scrubbing, sweeping, and polishing that a ship needed. Under the watchful eyes of their petty officers, seamen quickly learned that housekeeping required special efforts to meet navy standards. On his first day after completing a training program, Charles Blackford twice failed to sweep the deck to his chief's satisfaction. On the third try, with the chief's assistance, Blackford discovered dirt under lines, inside gun mounts, and in other nooks and crannies he had overlooked.[4]

Seamen in the deck force also scraped and painted the ship inside and out. Many men shared John Kendig's experience, squeezing through narrow manholes to clean and paint the space between the double bottom of a battleship.[5] At such times, no doubt, more than a few sailors ironically recalled navy recruiting posters.

In the engine room, the sixth division—which was composed primarily of coal passers and firemen but also included machinists, oilers, and water tenders—cleaned the area and worked the machinery of the ship. Men in the engine room received a higher starting pay than did seamen entering the deck force. The bonus was well earned; the work of feeding boilers on a coal-burning ship was the most arduous task in the navy. In addition, the men worked in close quarters and in extreme heat. In 1924 during a voyage in the Persian Gulf, for example, the temperature on the cruiser *Trenton* reached 105 degrees in the shade on the top decks and 110 degrees below; men in the fireroom, in contrast, broiled in 145-degree heat. Only men in the galley had to endure similar temperatures.[6]

The laborious engine-room work required individuals of considerable stamina, but in times of expansion the navy assigned this duty to some recruits who were physically unsuited. The surgeon general, recognizing the health hazard to all men, reported his objections to these conditions. In 1907 he wrote that the engineers' force

> is often short-handed and even if not and the individual members are all physically qualified for such duty, which is not always the case, the demands of the Department in and out of port keep the men too long employed below decks and away from the sun and fresh air which they need so badly as an aid in recuperating from their arduous duties.[7]

In spite of the Bureau of Medicine and Surgery's warning, those practices persisted.[8] Apparently only the conversion from coal- to oil-burning ships improved conditions in the engine room.

DRILL

Duty on a man-of-war entailed more than operating and maintaining the ship. Because a naval vessel was supposed to be constantly ready to wage war, a large amount of time was devoted to drilling to prepare for an emergency or for combat.

The most common exercises were general quarters, clearing the ship for action, and fire, battalion, collision, and gunnery drills. General quarters required manning battle stations. Clearing the ship for action, less common than general quarters, involved manning battle stations plus removing anything that would interfere with the sweep of the guns—stanchions, davits, and awnings—or which would splinter if struck by an enemy shell—chests, mess tables, and benches.

The navy also regarded coaling ship as a drill, partly because in time of war rapid refueling was necessary. In elevating coaling to a drill, however, the navy may also have been attempting to lend some prestige to a tiresome and difficult job. Coaling ship required the efforts of all hands. After lighters had brought the coal alongside, gangs of men shoveled the coal into large bags, which were hoisted aboard. The coal was then sent into the holds through canvas chutes. From there, other gangs transferred it into the bunkers. Fine coal dust pervaded the vessel; after the ship was coaled—a task often consuming most of a day—the crew had to clean first the ship and then themselves.

Coaling, however, did offer some compensations. Old, nonregulation clothing was permitted. The ship's band, if there was one, serenaded the workers. And rival gangs or ships competed in emptying their lighters. In general, though, coaling was a job best viewed in retrospect: old hands might look back nostalgically from oil-burners to the exploits of true sailors in the days of coal, but while they were actually carrying out the assignment, most men considered it unpleasant. During World War I a sailor-poet on the *Plattsburg* expressed his sentiments, complete with ethnic slurs:

I'll face Hun submarines
Davy Jones' fierce Jyreens,
I'll stay for a cruise to Khan-kee,
But loading soft coal,
In a coal-burner's hold,
Is a job for spicks—coolies—Not me[9]

DANGER IN THE SAILOR'S LIFE

Military Action

The purpose of drill and training is obviously to prepare for a military encounter. In the four decades following the Spanish-American War, the major military experience was, of course, World War I. Because by April 1917 the war was being fought primarily on land, the navy received less attention than the army. Nevertheless, the navy contributed to the Allied war effort in various ways. American vessels helped lay the North Sea mine barrage, and American torpedo boats participated in the attack on the Austrian base at Durrazzo in September 1918. On shore, naval gun crews operated large railway guns in France. In the air, naval aviators flew numerous missions in both heavier-than-air and lighter-than-air craft.[10]

Even though the navy had varied assignments, its major tasks were antisubmarine patrol and convoy duty; most naval personnel engaged in these duties. On May 4, 1917, six American destroyers under the command of Lieutenant Commander J. K. Taussig reached Queenstown, Ireland, the first Americans to operate in European waters. These vessels and later arrivals spent long, difficult hours at sea but seldom saw the enemy. An occasional encounter did produce a hero—as when Gunner's Mate Osmond K. Ingram of the *Cassin* died trying to disarm depth charges before a torpedo struck his destroyer.[11] But most men seldom engaged in battle. Chief Torpedoman Harry S. Morris, as an example, served on board the destroyer *Downs* and never fired a torpedo during the whole war. In his case, no action may have been a blessing, since he recalled that "the storms were so heavy in the war years that there was a time I couldn't even get the torpedoes out of the tubes. They were rusted in."[12]

The number of navy casualties reflects the routine nature of the service's role in the war. From a force of almost a half million, the navy lost a total of 6,929 men and 438 officers. Of the enlisted deaths, 5,352 were attributed to disease, 1,193 to accidents, and 384 to enemy action. Thirty-eight officers died in battle, 284 of disease, and 116 through accidents. Thus, only 422—or 0.8 percent—of the 53,402 Americans who died in battle during World War I were in the navy.[13]

Even if postwar tabulations showed naval casualties to be negligible, the danger was real. The nature of submarine warfare made it impossible to anticipate an attack, and this uncertainty heightened tension for crews in the war zone. Searching too hard for U-boats, sailors spotted them where none existed. Wreckage, porpoises, waves, the evening star, and nonbelligerent craft were reported as the enemy. Men on duty in dangerous areas for the first time were particularly prone to making false reports. When the gunboat *Yankton* first crossed the Atlantic at the beginning of American entry into the war, the lookouts spotted what they thought was a submarine. The ship lobbed shells at the object; a lookout, mistaking the splashes from these shells for enemy fire, reported that the submarine was returning fire. With that report, the *Yankton* increased its firing, and the enemy hoisted sail and fled. The "submarine" proved to be native fishing boats from the Azores.[14]

In addition to its role in World War I, between 1899 and 1939 the navy engaged in frequent smaller operations. After the Spanish-American War, the service was immediately involved in the Philippine Insurrection from 1899 to 1902. During that same period, it joined a combined English and American landing force in Samoa in 1899 and cooperated with other nations in suppressing the Boxer Rebellion (1900-1901). The service was particularly active in Latin America. It was used in Cuba from 1906 to 1908 and in 1912; in Nicaragua in 1912 and 1925 and from 1926 to 1928; in Mexico in 1914; in Haiti in 1915; in Panama in 1921; and in Honduras in 1924 and 1925. In 1924 the navy again fought in the Philippines as a result of the Moro uprisings; in the same year it formed the Cavite Provisional Company of two officers and 100 enlisted men for service in China.[15]

In addition to these military operations, the Caribbean Special Services Squadron, the Yangtze River Patrol, and the South China Patrol operated in perennially troubled areas. The men on these assignments were involved in frequent military encounters. In a fairly typical experience from 1922 to 1925, the gunboat *Asheville* of the South China Patrol landed nine patrols—four that included navy men and five that were composed solely of marines. The 1937 bombing of the *Panay* by the Japanese, in which two sailors and one civilian were killed and eleven officers and men were wounded, attests to the dangers of operating in a war zone even if one is a nonbelligerent.[16]

Reports of the sailors' performances ashore were generally good. After a 1906 landing in Cienfuegos, Cuba, Commander William F. Fullam expressed satisfaction with and pride in his men, boasting that the managers of two Cuban sugar estates had requested that the marines rather than the sailors be withdrawn.[17] Because Fullam had long advocated training sailors for duty ashore and championed removing marines from ships, his men might have been better prepared than others, and his evaluation may have been overly generous.[18] Nevertheless, comments on enlisted men's performances in other actions were also favorable. In April 1914 bluejackets landed at Veracruz, Mexico. While securing the city, they received fire from snipers, from regular troops, and, because of the confusion, from their own comrades. During the landing, American naval forces sustained casualties of seventeen dead and sixty-seven wounded—compared to estimated Mexican casualties of 125 killed and 200 wounded. Rear Admiral Charles J. Badger, commander in chief of the Atlantic Fleet, wrote proudly to Secretary Daniels that the "restraint of our men under the terrible punishment being dealt among them by individuals hidden on housetops or on balconies or where any cover could be obtained was very remarkable."[19]

Official reports, of course, presented an incomplete account of actions ashore. Danger was often slight or over quickly, and the men then proceeded to perform their military duties with good humor. In 1926 Dom Albert Pagano, a sailor from the cruiser *Galveston*, landed in Bluefields, Nicaragua, where he was placed in charge of a patrol to keep peace in the town. After enforcing an eight o'clock curfew, his men spent the rest of their watch chasing pigs down the streets and switching the flags that merchants flew in front of their shops. A Chinese merchant might have awakened to discover that he was displaying the Union Jack. Later, when Pagano served as a sentry on a boat going up river for bananas, he passed the time by firing at alligators and other wildlife.[20] Although it is not surprising that official accounts omitted such skylarking, to the men it was a memorable part of military encounters.

Accidents

Because relatively few sailors saw military action, even of the lighthearted variety, accidents were far more lethal to enlisted men than was enemy fire. Most mishaps that befell the bluejacket were only indirectly connected with the navy. Falls and injuries sustained during athletic contests and in automobile accidents consistently occupied top positions in statistics the surgeon general collected. These two categories alone comprised almost 70 percent of all accidents. Usually grouped under headings such as "industrial and miscellaneous hazards," most accidents could have happened to civilian workers. Drowning—which accounted for only 0.1 percent of all accidents—was a hazard unique to service on the water, but not unique to the navy. Other accidents, however, arose from the specialized nature of the navy's work. Submarines and airplanes, for example, were experimental and dangerous vehicles that a civilian was unlikely to operate.[21]

Although most naval accidents involved only a few men each, disasters that emphasized the underlying danger of naval service did sometimes occur. A brief examination of a few of these incidents illustrates these hazards. A boiler explosion in 1905 on the gunboat *Bennington* claimed sixty-six lives. In 1923 twenty-three enlisted men died when seven destroyers grounded at Honda, California, during a fog. The world of underseas craft presented a constant risk—a risk recognized in the pay schedule. The first American submarine disaster took place March 25, 1915, when the *F-4* sank off Honolulu, losing the entire crew of one officer and nineteen enlisted men. On September 25, 1925, the *S-51* was struck by the coastal steamer *City of Rome*; of the forty officers and men board, only three enlisted men escaped. In 1927 the submarine *S-4* collided with a Coast Guard cutter in Cape Cod Bay, and when it sank, eighteen men died.[22]

The presence of high explosives on board naval ships meant continuing danger. In 1904 a flashback in the *Missouri*'s twelve-inch turret ignited powder in the handling room, killing eighteen men in the turret and twelve in the handling room and magazines. Two years later on the *Kearsarge*, three bags of powder were accidentally set off during gun drill, and two officers and eight men died. In 1924, powder bags were ignited in a turret of the *Mississippi*, and forty-eight officers and men were killed. An exploding gun on the *Wyoming* in 1937 left seven dead and twelve injured.[23]

Early air travel was also hazardous, but crashes usually involved only one or two enlisted men. Only lighter-than-air craft carried a large enough crew to capture national headlines. On September 2, 1925, for example, the *Shenandoah* broke up in a storm near Byesville, Ohio, leaving eighteen dead. On April 3, 1933, the airship *Akron* crashed into the Atlantic. Among the eighteen officers and fifty-five men who died in this accident was Rear Admiral William A. Moffett, then chief of the Bureau of Aeronautics and previously commandant of the Great Lakes Naval Training Station. And the *Macon*, the *Akron*'s sister ship, crashed February 12, 1935, with a loss of two.[24]

THE SHIP

In any account of the activity of enlisted men, it is important to consider the ships to which men were assigned. Although a standard pattern of daily activity and the rating structure tended to impose a rough unity throughout the navy, the size, age, and location of the bluejacket's ship produced some diversity and profoundly influenced the nature of his service.

Size directly affected comfort and discipline. As a general rule, small ships such as destroyers and submarines offered few amenities. Aboard these vessels, men vied with machinery for space. Because of their size, these ships never felt the full impact of the boom in shipboard recreational facilities that occurred on cruisers and battleships in the forty years after the Spanish-American War. There was no room for a gymnasium, a piano, or much of a library. Even motion pictures were ordinarily shown only when the ships were in port, where the crews of several vessels could be assembled for the screening.

Small vessels also behaved differently in heavy seas from their larger sisters. On destroyers, notorious for their violent pitching in storms, the movements of the ship interfered with sleep, inflicted bumps and bruises, and often prevented the serving of hot meals. Although submarines were less likely than destroyers to be at sea in rough weather, submarine service entailed discomforts in the form of cramped space, noxious fumes, and bad air. Describing his home, one submariner wrote:

Born in the shops of the devil,
Designed by the brains of a fiend;
Filled with acid and crude oil,
And christened "A Submarine."

. . .

We eat where'er we can find it,
And sleep hanging up on hooks;
Conditions under which we're existing
Are never published in books.

Life in these boats is obnoxious
And this is using mild terms;
We are never bothered by sickness,
There isn't any room for germs.[25]

In spite of such complaints, men were devoted to the small boats; many who served on them vowed they would never return to the battleship navy. Indeed, there were enough men of this sentiment that both destroyers and submarines were usually manned solely by volunteers.

A prime attraction of the smaller vessels was the freedom the crews enjoyed from the spit and polish of the larger men-of-war. The ships were "just small enough to make a home for the crew," as one destroyerman explained. He continued:

> Going aboard the black boats in port one is struck with the absence of—of—well, everything which one sees on a white ship. You might stay about for a week and you would never hear a bugle blowing quarters or see the men doing "monkey drill," setting up exercises or standing stiffly at attention.[26]

In a small crew men knew each other better and had closer contact than was possible with the crew as a whole on a battleship or cruiser. On both destroyers and submarines the comradeship of officers and crew was greater than usual in the navy. One enlisted man's magazine said of the submarine service: "Men love the life. With the officers they are as one family, sharing everything equally."[27]

In addition to relaxed discipline, the smaller units permitted the men greater responsibility. With few officers to supervise them, enlisted men on small craft handled their work independently. On a patrol boat, a petty officer might be the senior engineering officer, whereas on a battleship he would have had warrant officers and commissioned officers overseeing his work.[28]

Larger ships, on the other hand, offered their own advantages. As the tonnage of navy vessels increased to accommodate the new guns, space became available for barbershops, libraries, and recreation rooms. Furthermore, since the larger vessels rolled less in heavy seas, the men suffered less from seasickness.[29]

As living conditions aboard ship improved steadily after the Spanish-American War, the battleships and cruisers were usually the first to acquire modern comforts. For example, dishwashing machines first came into use on the battleship *Missouri* in 1904. Similarly, laundries, which freed sailors from scrubbing their own clothing, were introduced on battleships during World War I. Of greater importance, the larger ships generally had superior lighting, ventilation, and heating—problems whose satisfactory solution had eluded the navy throughout its history.[30]

Another benefit the new battleships made possible was improved food storage and preparation. Refrigerated compartments and ice machines, which were installed aboard some warships as early as 1893, increased the likelihood that the men would be served fresh rather than dried or canned meat and vegetables. Mechanical cooling equipment also permitted the introduction of electrical ice-cream makers. These devices enjoyed great popularity among the men. Writing in 1906 of such a machine aboard the *Missouri*, Paymaster George P. Dyer admitted that "some may smile at the association of sailors and ice-cream" but insisted that "the day of the salt-horse, rough-living tar has passed. His place has been taken by clear-eyed, intelligent, American youths who are of the metal to endure hardship if necessary, but who know what clean living and good fare are; and they have the usual American notion of the festive nature of ice-cream."[31]

In addition to acquiring cooling equipment for the fleet, the modern navy also began to centralize meal preparation for the entire crew. The old navy had considered each mess a virtually autonomous unit. The mess (composed of approximately twenty men) took charge of its own supplies, cared for its own equipment, prepared much of its own food, and assessed its members small amounts to purchase items not a part of the navy ration. This system had serious shortcomings. Messes often accused one another of theft of stores; mess treasurers sometimes deserted with their shipmates' money; and the food was often poorly prepared since the mess cooks, who frequently had little interest in their task, generally simply boiled the food. To an extent, the cramped quarters and limited storage of the wooden sailing ships had necessitated this type of dispersed mess arrangement. With the commissioning of the larger, modern ships, it was possible to try new methods. In 1896 the battleship *Indiana* experimented with centralizing all food preparation in a single galley under the supervision of a permanent staff of cooks. The quality of meals improved, and economies of scale made it possible to eliminate special assessments within the messes.[32]

After food preparation became centralized, the men continued to eat in berthing areas. Because food was issued to representatives of the mess six minutes before meal call, hot meals were rare. In 1916 the *New York* experimented with serving men in cafeteria style, but this idea apparently was soon dropped. The cafeteria method of serving and eating was apparently not adopted for another twenty years.[33]

The bigger ships were also first to introduce lockers and bunks for the men. Traditionally sailors kept their clothing in seabags, which were stored away; the men were allowed to get items from their bags only at specified times during the day, and at these times what they needed was invariably at the bottom. In the 1890s the navy began testing lockers aboard the *Philadelphia* but abandoned the experiment. The idea, however, was not dead. Shortly before World War I the men began agitating through their publications for such equipment. Nevertheless, it was apparently not until 1920, when the navy built lockers on the battleship *Tennessee*, that the service conducted another experiment on the feasibility of equipping ships with lockers.[34]

Shortly after this trial, the navy tested both lockers and bunks aboard the *California* and *Oklahoma* in 1924.[35] Previously men had slept in hammocks, which were slung at night and stored in the daytime. With some practice, a sailor could sleep satisfactorily in a hammock but never as comfortably as on a bed. Moreover, it was easy to slip from a hammock to the deck several feet below. In 1926 the surgeon general reported that ninety-four men were injured in such falls that year and that, as a result of these accidents, 1,787 days were lost.[36]

After placing bunks and lockers on the two battleships, the department solicited reactions. Officers reported that both innovations were popular with the crews. Furthermore, because bunks were not removed during the day, crew members could rest on them when they were not on duty—a welcome feature for the men. Despite the men's enthusiasm, the Bureau of Navigation was reluctant to accept service-wide use of bunks. It argued that bunks would be unsuitable during combat since wooden frames splintered when hit by a shell and thus presented a hazard not posed by hammocks; in addition, it said that because ship complements were increased in wartime, bunks permanently occupied space that would be needed for other purposes. The bureau concluded that during peacetime men should sleep in the hammocks they would have to use during wartime. It also considered it not "good practice to have men loafing in their bunks during the day" and suggested that off-duty men sleep on the open deck, as was customary. By 1927, however, the bureau had overcome its reservations and recommended that bunks be installed on all ships where possible. Yet complete conversion did not occur rapidly; it was not until 1946 that the *Bluejackets' Manual* omitted the section on the care of hammocks.[37]

An adequate amount of fresh water contributed greatly to a sailor's contentment; in this area, too, the large ships usually enjoyed an advantage. Because vessels under sail had had to carry and store fresh water, the stock was limited and carefully rationed. The introduction of steam engines meant that ships maintained equipment to distill water for the boilers and that the crew received any surplus. As steam engines grew more efficient and required less water, the distillation equipment increasingly could be used to provide water for the men. Bluejackets transferring from sailing ships to steamships were impressed both by the amount of fresh water available and by the presence of hot water.[38]

Water was more plentiful in the modern navy, but its supply was not unlimited. Some small ships, such as the *Machias*, barely distilled enough water for their boilers; the crews of these ships sometimes were rationed as little as one quart of water per day.[39] More commonly, water rations were small because captains decided to seek the red "E" awarded for engineering efficiency. Since purifying water required fuel, commanding officers often imposed rationing to reduce fuel consumption. In World War I, the *Texas* rationed fresh water to six quarts per man per day. The water supply was also sometimes shut off or the distillation process was sometimes accelerated, producing water that tasted salty. Because excessive control over water created discontent among the crew, some officers pointedly refused to strain for engineering efficiency, feeling that good morale resulted in proficiency in nonengineering areas.[40]

Size alone did not determine the habitability of a ship. The ship's age also influenced the degree of comfort a bluejacket could expect. While living conditions afloat steadily improved, older vessels remained in commission, and the navy could not or would not install all the new features on them. Among the most infamous of the older vessels were the gunboats acquired from the Spanish in 1898, which remained in service in Asia far into the new century. Concerning one such ship, the *Pampanga*, launched in 1888, a 1924 issue of the magazine *Orient* complained:

The coolie-quarters on a slaver would be cabin space in comparison with the crew quarters on the *Pampanga*. If men sleep aboard they must sleep on the top side.
And there is no lifeline, railing, bulkhead or bulwark sufficient to prevent anyone who might toss in his sleep, from rolling over the side.[41]

Vessels permanently assigned to distant patrol were not the only ships to show signs of age. In 1930 four enlisted men deplored conditions on the *Galveston*, which had been completed in 1903:

Just why she is kept in commission nobody knows. There is a lot of talk about cleanliness, and clean and sanitary surroundings, but these things did not exist in the Navy of 25 or 30 years ago, that is compared to the modern battleships of today with a nice work room, clean bunks, and big recreation centres. . . . She loses a good percentage of her crew at every United States port she hits. The majority of the crew would rather face a court-martial or worse rather than make a 10-month cruise on the *Gally*.[42]

As new ships were built, older ones obviously suffered from comparison.

For the men, probably few improvements equalled the introduction of oil as fuel. Oil freed the entire crew from the ordeal of coaling ship and the engine-room force from stoking boilers. As was the case with other innovations, conversion to oil also proved slow. The navy first studied the use of fuel oil in 1904 aboard the torpedo boat *Rodgers*. Another experiment was conducted in 1909 aboard the *Cheyenne*. The chief of the Bureau of Steam Engineering pronounced the results of the *Cheyenne* tests satisfactory. As a consequence, the department began providing every new battleship and many new destroyers and submarines with oil-burning engines. Also in 1909 the Bureau of Navigation established fuel-oil storage facilities. Yet during World War I most of the battleships and many of the destroyers were still fired by coal, and after every maneuver the ships had to recoal in preparation for the next sortie.[43]

In addition to the ship's size and age, its duty station also affected the lives of the men. Different locales had decidedly different advantages and drawbacks.[44] The question of what was the best assignment was the subject of long debate. Men with families preferred vessels that spent much of their time in a United States home port. While family men tried to avoid being assigned to distant stations that required prolonged separation, other sailors had enlisted for travel, and they were determined to see the world. Europe offered both antique charm and, for many, a chance to visit relatives. Service in these waters consisted of cruises from city to city with formal visits at each stop between officers of the various fleets in port. Although this duty put the greatest demand on the officers, the men too experienced an increased attention to spit and polish and to formal ceremony. The Caribbean provided sunny islands and blue seas, but boredom plagued men cruising in the area for any length of time.

Farthest from the United States in both distance and culture was East Asia, which offered a suitably exotic setting. Even in the Orient, though, not every assignment was equally attractive. Some vessels remained all year in Philippine waters, while others escaped the torrid months of southern Asia by taking leisurely voyages to China or Japan. Other ships faced long calls in Chinese ports to protect American interests, even though the men were yearning to travel. Patrol boats on the Upper Yangtze were isolated at all times. During the months of low water when they were trapped up river, it took mail or supplies three months to arrive from the coast by junk.

OFFICERS

A major factor that influenced the quality of service was the type of officer under whom the enlisted man served. Although in some respects many officers were becoming interested in improving the treatment of the men, at the same time they retained a paternalistic attitude toward the enlisted force.

An officer was always aware of his superior and separate status at the top of the ship hierarchy, never imagining the seamen to be his equals. He fulfilled his obligations toward the men, but only rarely did he allow them to penetrate his consciousness as individuals. The lack of references to enlisted men in officers' letters and diaries suggests this impersonal attitude toward the men. Midshipman Hollis T. Winston, for example, kept a log from 1900 to 1903, carefully describing the three ships on which he served, but never mentioning a sailor. Amidst descriptions of armor, engines, and armament, not even a notation of the ship's complement is to be found.[45]

The few enlisted men who did rate a line in officers' memoirs, moreover, appeared only in a limited and stereotyped way. Many were petty officers with long service, often much of it spent in the smaller navy of the years before the Spanish-American War. They were gruff old salts, relics of a bygone era, relating with bewilderment and regret the changes that had taken place since the old days. Some officers were also fond of relating drunken-sailor anecdotes. Usually competent seamen when sober, the men in these stories possessed a weakness for liquor that repeatedly undermined gains they had made. Because the drunken sailor accepted his fate with good humor or as a repentant child, officers wrote of him with fondness.[46]

Enlisted men's absence or appearance only as stereotypes in officers' narratives demonstrates the difficulty seamen encountered in achieving individual recognition. Frequent transfers of both officers and men exacerbated the situation. Furthermore, as officers achieved higher rank, they had little association with enlisted personnel. The contacts that did remain were with men performing direct services for them: i.e., yeomen, officers' stewards and cooks, and messmen.[47] The rest of the force dissolved into a uniformed blur.

The gulf between rank and rate also obscured sailors' perceptions of their superiors. In many cases, frequent transfers clouded seamen's memories of individual officers. Yet, because the seamen were in a subordinate position and dependent on their superiors for promotion, leave, and special favors, it was essential for them to know their officers. With so much of their lives determined by the men over them, sailors studied, recognized, and appreciated differences in officers' behavior.

Good officers made a ship a "home," the highest praise an enlisted man could bestow.[48] Such superiors were not lenient or soft, but fair, open, and as ready to praise as to censure. Under their leadership, sailors performed well and with reasonable contentment. They sometimes expressed their appreciation of a favorite officer by presenting a gift to his wife.[49] Many sailors, furthermore, remembered good superiors long after their service together had ended. One seaman, for example, wrote to the magazine *Bostonian* to commend Commander S. S. Robinson, who had "won the admiration and respect of all the crew" during tours as executive officer of the *Pennsylvania* and navigator of the *Tennessee*.[50] Upon receiving advancement to chief petty officer, R. A. Emery wrote Captain Rufus Johnston to thank him for acting leniently when Emery had been before the mast for fraudulent enlistment five years earlier. Rear Admiral Andrew T. Long received a letter of appreciation from a former crewman of the *Nevada* eleven years after he had commanded it.[51] Cumulatively, testimonials such as these demonstrate the ability of an officer to make a lasting and favorable impression on enlisted men.

Conversely, ships on which officers abused their power were called "madhouses." In one such case, a captain brought a "mad" destroyer around the Horn to the Pacific in 1908. When he transferred to another vessel, it too went mad. Eventually, the Bureau of Navigation removed him from command, but only after many enlisted men had had their records blemished or their ratings reduced.[52]

Overall there were probably more homes than madhouses, and most ships never attained either extreme. Yet a ship need not have degenerated to madness for the bluejackets to experience frustration and bitterness when confronted with the arrogance of rank. In most cases officers, secure on their side of the barrier, were oblivious to the sailors' feelings. Sometimes an officer, perhaps unknowingly, conducted his routine duties in a way that unnecessarily antagonized the men. John Kendig, an electrician on the *Kearsarge*, protested the behavior of his "beloved first luf," who often required extra work and refused small favors such as sleeping topside in hot weather. Because of the *Kearsarge*'s officers, Kendig ominously predicted that "a large percentage of the men will desert when we reach the States."[53]

Sometimes the sailors also resented officers' special privileges. In 1915 a veteran chief petty officer complained of not being allowed to take visitors below decks even though "an officer who has not been on the ship two months can take girls below whom he never saw before." And sometimes, discontent was directed against general assignments. Typical of such feelings were the charges by a sailor in 1904 that at Guantánamo the men were "driven like brutes and treated worse than the most deprived slaves."[54]

By themselves enlisted men's complaints about officers reveal little about the treatment of the men. Sailors have always been, and probably always will be, certain that their officers were personally responsible for all shortcomings in food, work, and weather. Yet, as has been seen, in the decades following the Spanish-American War, both the desertion and reenlistment rates improved. By deserting less often and reenlisting more often, sailors demonstrated their contentment with the service as a whole. Their treatment by officers probably contributed greatly to this overall regard for the service.

Even with the amelioration of many of the conditions under which enlisted men lived, sailors still occupied a clearly inferior position in the naval hierarchy. Their low status prevented even the most sympathetic officers from completely understanding the bluejackets' position, and enlisted frustrations remained unarticulated.

The resourceful sailor, however, was not completely blocked from releasing the tension created by his powerless position. Sometimes through good-natured skylarking he sparred with the system that dictated his impotence. Mark Murnane, a hospital corpsman in World War I, relished sauntering up Sands Street near the Brooklyn navy yard with other enlisted men and saluting officers who were returning from shopping. Forgetting in the surprise of the moment that regulations did not require returning a salute if it was inconvenient to do so, the officer fumbled with packages in an effort to free an arm. To increase the fun, the seamen sometimes separated, and the group passed in intervals of several feet. This sport was especially pleasurable when the officers were young and overly concerned about always being saluted.[55] At other times, sailors took more direct action, though in such a way as to avoid retaliation. Seamen, for example, might drop an unpopular officer's trunk into the sea, leaving the man to guess whether it was an accident or not.[56]

SHIPBOARD DIVERSIONS

Because sailors were too young and too lively to let the work unfold without interruption, the daily schedule presents only an incomplete picture of the lives of enlisted men. Sometimes the men were content with officially sponsored recreational activities; at other times they created their own opportunities to escape the monotony of the shipboard routine.

Officers occasionally permitted certain festivities that relaxed the lines of rank. During New Year's celebrations, for example, costumed bluejackets collected instruments and paraded around the ship. Usually forbidden areas in officers' territory were open to the procession. Some horseplay was tolerated; if an occasional officer was doused, he took it in the good humor of the evening.[57] Probably few men in command formulated detailed theories of behavior concerning these diversions, but most recognized that they improved ship morale because they allowed a brief respite from the restrictions of the usual discipline.

Crossing the equator called for the initiation of men passing over the line for the first time—a ceremony that was one of the most famous breaks from the routine. Celebration of the event on European ships can be traced to 1529.[58] Although American seamen did not invent the ritual, they adopted it enthusiastically. Furthermore, officers supported the undertaking to bolster morale; indeed, should a crew have been reluctant to prepare a proper ceremony, the officers would most likely have ordered it done.

Even though the officers supported the project, the crew themselves staged the event.[59] Spinning elaborate yarns about the coming ordeal, old hands set the mood from the time the ship left port. The day before a ship was to cross the equator, Davy Jones hailed her, requested permission to come aboard—which was immediately granted—climbed from the hawsehole, and made his way to the bridge. Here he greeted the captain and presented a summons. Written in suitably flowery language, this document demanded the presence in Neptune's court of all men entering the domain for the first time. The next day, as their ship reached the equator, she was boarded by Neptune's party, and the bridge was turned over to a member of the court during the stay of his majesty Neptunus Rex. Besides the king, his queen, and Davy Jones, the entourage usually included a royal navigator, a royal officer of the deck, a royal judge, a royal prosecuting attorney, a royal scribe, a royal barber, a royal dentist, and the royal police. If the sponsors of the show were sufficiently numerous and energetic, also in attendance were a royal baby—usually one of the largest men on the ship—a royal electrician, royal handmaidens, and miscellaneous pirates and naval heroes.

While the court made its way to the portion of the deck set aside for the ceremony, the royal police assembled the initiates. All officers and men who had not crossed the line before were required to appear before the assemblage to explain why they dared trespass on Neptune's domain when they were not certified "shellbacks." At each hearing the court quickly tried and convicted the accused. The prisoner was thereupon examined by the royal dentist and shaved by a royal barber, who used a large paint brush and a wooden razor. The royal doctor administered a foul-tasting pill. The chair in which the convicted man sat was then flipped backward, catapulting the victim into a canvas pool, where the royal bears playfully dunked him a few times. Although the pool was lined with several layers of canvas to cushion the deck and the bears tried to break the fall, this finale often produced sprains and broken bones. Assuming he survived unharmed, the new shellback could join the police searching for any men who were hiding.

Although all first-timers were called to the court, not all received the same treatment. Officers were permitted to purchase exemption from the rites, though most of the younger ones apparently did not. Before Secretary Daniels abolished the officers' "wine mess" in 1914, payment had been in beer; after that sad day cigars were substituted.[60] Generally, the first men received greater attention than the others, especially on a large ship which might have had to process several hundred men. Unpopular men or men who tried to hide were generally honored with a more elaborate initiation than the average sailor.

While the sailors welcomed a semiofficial event such as the crossing ceremony, they were not wholly dependent on special occasions for their amusements. Even in the regulated life of a man-of-war, the men had some time to call their own. Freed from both work and organized recreation, they used their ingenuity to pursue a surprisingly wide variety of pastimes. Some men filled their leisure profitably—caring for their outfits, studying for advancement, or earning extra money by doing sewing, laundry, and similar tasks for their shipmates. Others occupied themselves in more frivolous ways with games of chance and skill. Acey-deucey (a form of backgammon), cards, and dice were found on every ship. Although the *Regulations* forbade gambling, that prohibition never deterred the bluejackets. In storerooms or in other secluded spots, they gathered to try their luck. Some small vessels in the Philippines early in the century also permitted cockfighting, but this sport rarely reached the bigger ships.[61]

Games were not the only source of recreation. A ship also presented numerous opportunities for pranks. A recruit arriving on his first ship was sent in search of nonexistent but plausible pieces of equipment: hammock ladders, anchor covers, starboard scythes, starboard monkey wrenches, or red and green oil for running lights.[62] While a sailor fresh from training camp offered ideal prey, other men were not immune. John Kendig was victimized in a typical trick when someone placed an eight-inch shell in his hammock. Determined not to be the only dupe, he transferred it to a friend's hammock. Then, pretending to be asleep, Kendig was able to relish his shipmate's reaction. At another time, Kendig demonstrated the sailor's ability to seize every opportunity for a joke. One night he was awakened when a bear, the ship's mascot, climbed into his hammock. Recognizing a situation too good to let pass, he shifted the animal onto the man in the next hammock. His friend awoke swearing. Also realizing the possibilities of the incident, he in turn transferred the bear to yet another victim, who also awoke enraged, to the amusement of those watching.[63]

In addition to these pastimes, some enlisted men felt that proper relaxation required liquor. The navy, however, did not share this conviction. The grog ration for enlisted men had been discontinued in 1862. On February 3, 1899, Secretary John D. Long issued General Order 508 prohibiting the sale of beer to men on board ships or within the limits of naval stations. Long's order made drinking on board difficult, but not impossible. Using the time-honored tricks of the sea, some sailors resorted to smuggling. They taped flasks inside their trouser legs, hid bottles in ship supplies, and purchased liquor in baskets of fruit from bumboat men. A few bluejackets also smuggled for profit. B. J. Ducret of the cruiser *Princeton* sold liquor at five dollars a bottle—much of it to men in the brig—before a court-martial conviction in 1907 put him out of business. Other men relied on alcohol in supplies aboard ship. The dispensary stocked alcohol, to which the hospital corps had access. Additional spirits were aboard in the form of alcohol for torpedoes and shellac. Drinking shellac, however, was a measure of desperation, because it left an odious taste.[64]

LIBERTY

However enjoyable the pastimes aboard ship, the bluejacket received greatest respite from his duties during liberty. Going ashore released him from the rigid discipline of naval life and made it easier to endure the routine when he returned. Most officers recognized the relation between liberty and morale and tried to grant their men as much liberty as possible.[65]

Although enlisted men were always eager to touch land, not all ports were equally attractive. American cities such as New York and San Francisco were interesting, but they lacked the glamour of foreign climes. European ports were generally considered good liberty; Copenhagen was a favorite. In the Far East, Japanese cities reputedly ranked among the best in the world for the sailor on liberty. Sailors in China favored larger metropolitan areas, such as Shanghai or Tsingtao, because in smaller ports facilities were limited. In smaller cities the men found only "two types of recreation constantly open to the dashing man-of-war's man . . . the gin mill and the dive." The Army-Navy YMCA offered facilities in Manila, Shanghai, Hankow, Tientsin, and Peking, but in other cities the sailor had to operate from his ship. In the Caribbean, Panama was a popular stop, as were some islands in the West Indies.[66]

Sailors also knew which ports were undesirable. In 1909 a sailor on the *Tennessee*, recounting a stop at Chatham Island in the Galápagos, dismissed the islands as "a lemon, not even a native, let alone a village." Guantánamo, which the fleet frequently visited for target practice, was considered dull. Without question, though, the leading contenders for the distinction of worst liberty were Guam and Samoa. Small, isolated, and under navy control, these islands were almost legendary. In describing the relative merits of various cities, one author asserted, "When good sailors die their souls go to Japan—the bad 'uns go to—well say Guam or Tutuila."[67]

Whatever the merits of the city, enlisted men disembarked determined to enjoy themselves. Having joined up to see the world, they set off to investigate new lands with the enthusiasm of compulsive tourists. In each new port seamen took in all the attractions. They gaped at New York skyscrapers, investigated Egyptian pyramids, examined Roman ruins, and roamed through the Vatican. In Japan, or even Tsingtao, bluejackets sought out geisha houses, changed into kimonos, and enjoyed an evening of oriental food and entertainment. Enlisted men were such inveterate sightseers that after Japan's invasion of China, the Japanese army organized tours of the war zone for curious Americans.[68]

Like all travelers, sailors collected mementos of their visits. George Eastman had begun marketing a simple hand camera in 1888, and modern enlisted men recorded their travels on film. Every invading liberty party was armed with Kodaks, which were fired indiscriminately in all directions. The camera captured smiling bluejackets riding rickshaws in China and camels in Egypt. The men also returned from their adventures with trinkets of widely varying worth. On the 1907-9 world cruise, all hands received cloisonné cups from the Empress Dowager of China, but normally sailors purchased cheap souvenirs, which were stuffed into seabags and ditty boxes.[69]

Since sailors were free spenders, merchants made special arrangements for their visits. Often storekeepers raised prices "to untold heights" in honor of the American tourists.[70] The crews' patronage sometimes took precedence over local problems. When skirmishes of contesting revolutionary factions in Lisbon in 1918 prevented liberty, businessmen arranged an afternoon ceasefire so that the men from the visiting American ships could come ashore.[71] Special provisions of this nature were rarely necessary, but the incident reflects both the desire of the sailor to make purchases and the willingness of those ashore to assist him.

Not all relations between sailors and civilians were as cordial as in Lisbon. In fact, enlisted men entered the twentieth century with an image that made them outcasts in many strata of society and targets of discrimination, especially in the United States. As the composition of the enlisted force changed after the Spanish-American War, sailors began to challenge their status in the civilian world. Although the navy participated in some efforts to improve sailor-civilian relations, for the most part the department ignored aspects of enlisted men's lives outside naval jurisdiction. The major impetus for change in the treatment of sailors by civilians came not from the Navy Department as such, but from individual officers and from the men themselves.

RELATIONS WITH CIVILIANS AT HOME

In the nineteenth century, enlisted men usually experienced a cool reception when they went ashore on liberty. Because sailors bore a reputation for drinking and fighting, many neighborhoods of coastal cities tried to exclude them. Consequently, bluejackets restricted their activities to waterfront bars and boardinghouses. Here, while their money lasted, they were honored guests and among friends.[72]

The new enlisted force upset this equilibrium. Sailors became more and more unwilling to confine their leisure time to these traditional areas. Furthermore, their increased numbers could no longer be accommodated in the old facilities even if they had been content to remain there. Not only were individual ships larger, but the vessels now maneuvered as fleets.[73] Because more men were in port at one time than there had been in the nineteenth century, sailors overflowed their old haunts. In 1906, 500 seamen presented Norfolk with an unprecedented number of men on leave at one time. A newspaper observed that the bluejackets "fairly swarmed on the streets."[74] Soon cities faced several times that many young men invading from visiting warships.

Such a deluge of fun-seeking sailors easily overwhelmed existing amusement facilities in all parts of cities, and the men found themselves unwelcome. Regarding sailors as potential troublemakers who would drive away local patronage, proprietors banned them from their establishments. Sailors, for their part, resented exclusion based not on an individual's misconduct but on the uniform of national service.

The mushrooming in the number of sailors in the years following the Spanish-American War intensified friction between seamen and civilians. Not only did the new sailor abandon his traditional locales, but he also protested discriminatory treatment. In one of the first legal actions, Fred J. Buenzle lodged a suit in 1906 against the Newport Amusement Company. Buenzle, a chief yeoman at the Newport Naval Training Station and editor of *Bluejacket*, had purchased a ticket to a dance while he was dressed in civilian clothes. Changing into his uniform, he returned to the hall but was denied admission. He refused to accept a refund and sued the company. Although Buenzle appealed his case to the Rhode Island Supreme Court, he was unable to collect damages beyond the price of the ticket. Nevertheless, the suit attracted national attention when President Theodore Roosevelt contributed $100 in support of Buenzle. The publicity attending *Buenzle* v. *Newport Amusement Company* no doubt encouraged the passage of a 1908 act in Rhode Island prohibiting discrimination against men in uniform.[75]

The practices that led to Buenzle's case were not restricted to Newport. Problems arose wherever enlisted men were present in large numbers. In 1911 the management of the Mammoth Skating Rink in Seattle refused admission to enlisted men.[76] In the same year, Commander George F. Cooper, commanding officer of the *Marietta*, protested to the mayor of Portsmouth, New Hampshire, that bluejackets were forbidden use of the dance floor at the Freeman's Hall. In January 1917 the proprietor of the Olympic Theater in Brooklyn was fined $250 for barring sailors.[77]

In addition to finding themselves unwelcome in many public places, enlisted men discovered they were the prey of land sharks. Sailors encountered artificially inflated prices in waterfront areas close to the yards. Furthermore, in any kind of emergency a seaman found himself exceptionally vulnerable. In a particularly flagrant example in 1910, a San Francisco boatman increased the fare tenfold for a man hurrying to his ship. Sailors wishing to return to the camp at Pelham Bay Park in 1918 found the transportation rate had doubled.[78]

Even if he escaped such overt overcharging, the bluejacket had ample evidence that many citizens valued only his money. In 1910 Portsmouth, New Hampshire, complained that the transfer of the cruiser *Tacoma*, scheduled to be dry-docked for overhauling, to another yard deprived Portsmouth of the $5,000 the men would have spent. Decrying Portsmouth's excessive commercialism, *Our Navy* noted that Vallejo, California, and Bremerton, Washington, welcomed the men as well as their money.[79]

The hypocrisy of some civilians also irritated sailors. The same town that either rejected the men or appreciated only their cash value felt, at the same time, a perfect right to courtesies from the navy. In 1911 Portsmouth, New Hampshire, barred men in uniform from many public places and then felt aggrieved when the sailors were not ordered to march in the Memorial Day parade.[80]

Frequently the police also reflected a city's hostility toward enlisted men. In 1905 the secretary of the naval YMCA in Norfolk charged that enlisted men were deliberately harassed by some policemen who were trying to detect deserters and collect the reward money. A year later, Rear Admiral Evans accused the Portland, Maine, police of an unprovoked assault upon an orderly party of men returning from leave.[81]

Although incidents of discrimination were never completely eradicated, the situation improved during the first years of the twentieth century. Sailors were more likely to receive small kindnesses from civilians, even if only in the form of comfort bags sent by women's clubs.[82] Furthermore, cities began to prepare festivals for visiting fleets. At these celebrations, which began on a large scale with the voyage of the fleet in 1908, the bluejacket was lavished with food, lodging, and entertainment—either free or at minimal cost. Though an element of self-preservation motivated communities faced with an invasion of several thousand young men, the festivals demonstrated an interest in the men that helped counteract the effects of the exploitation the sailors so often experienced.[83]

A factor that undoubtedly contributed to improved relations between sailors and civilians at home was the fact that the type of good times most sailors pursued seems to have changed from earlier days. Observers both inside and outside the service noted sailors' improved behavior. An officer visiting New York's Metropolitan Museum in 1906 saw at least a hundred uniformed navy men touring the exhibits:

> Clean, clear cut, picturesquely dressed, they wandered through the rooms studying the catalogues which nearly every one of them had bought; absolutely unconscious of the attention they attracted and of the fact that they were doing something that sailors were not expected to do.[84]

In 1913 the secretary of the Brooklyn Naval YMCA reported to Rear Admiral Hugo Osterhaus, the commander in chief of the Atlantic Fleet, that it had been over a month since a drunken sailor had entered the Y. The admiral responded that he had not seen a drunken sailor for so long that he had "forgotten what one looks like."[85] After a visit of the fleet to San Diego in 1925, the mayor of the city expressed his appreciation for the conduct of the enlisted men. Although 20,000 young persons had descended upon the city, "there was nothing but good reported of them from all quarters."[86] In 1929 Admiral Henry A. Wiley, commander in chief of the United States Fleet, was pleased, though perhaps also surprised, at the men's good behavior in Panama. The concentration of the fleet there doubled the population of Panama City, but only scattered incidents of drunkenness were reported.[87]

All of these evaluations of behavior, of course, were largely subjective; indeed, the whole question of deportment ashore defies statistical analysis. Nevertheless, these observations and many similar ones seem to reflect a noticeable change in enlisted conduct.

Every encounter between sailors and civilians was not happy. Some friction between the two groups continued, and the twentieth century saw its share of disturbances involving enlisted men. Sailors reacted to an overcharging of two members of a liberty party in 1908 by stoning the offending restaurant; two years later bluejackets drove an orator from his outdoor podium after he had characterized "most of the men who man our warships" as "bums, derelicts and pikers."[88]

During World War I soldiers and sailors became the heroes of the hour. A smothering hospitality replaced the former discrimination. Shortly after war was declared, Mrs. Joseph M. Gazzam, wife of a prominent Philadelphia lawyer, announced that she was inviting fifty sailors to her home for tea to demonstrate that men in uniform would no longer be ostracized. As social leaders in other cities emulated Mrs. Gazzam, the bluejacket found himself no longer a pariah but besieged with invitations. The Winter Club at Lake Forest, Illinois, was among the many private facilities that welcomed enlisted men. The uniform also commanded benefits such as low-cost or free entertainment, meals, and lodging, all provided by charitable and fraternal organizations. Furthermore, sailors received spontaneous gestures of goodwill, including admission to fashionable parties.[89]

Not all the solicitude followed a course the men appreciated, for the war was used as an excuse to create a dry zone around camps and stations. A federal law passed in 1917 prohibited the sale of liquor to men in uniform.[90] Although the sailors in the twentieth century did not make drinking their sole occupation ashore, they still enjoyed imbibing when on liberty. Despite the hopes of the prohibition forces of the country, however, the new law did not eradicate the vice among enlisted men but merely changed the locale of drinking. Now the men had to patronize back rooms, thoughtfully provided by proprietors of bars near military installations.[91]

War brought recognition to enlisted men; peace ended it. After the armistice, civilians quickly reverted to normal relations, and sailors were plummeted from the social heights they had enjoyed. Symbolic of this reversal was the transfer in 1919 of weekly dances for sailors from the Evanston Country Club to Patten Gymnasium of Northwestern University.[92] Downtown commercial interests, too, no longer welcomed enlisted men. Early in January 1919 the Morrison Hotel of Chicago barred sailors. Although offended bluejackets quickly retorted that it was not the kind of hotel any self-respecting sailor wanted to patronize, it was obvious that times had changed. By late 1929, of the numerous New York City facilities that had catered to servicemen during the war, only the National Navy Club survived.[93]

Although the conclusion of the war ended special consideration from civilians, sailors nevertheless found their position more satisfactory than it had been in the nineteenth century or even earlier in the twentieth century. Wartime had improved their public image; their enhanced prestige undoubtedly was carried over to the postwar era. In addition, bluejackets had gained a legal protection that had not existed for sailors of the old navy. A survey by the Bureau of Navigation revealed that by 1920 Rhode Island, New York, Massachusetts, Maine, Connecticut, and California had passed statutes prohibiting discrimination against men in uniform.[94] Because these six states contained the majority of ports and bases the navy used, they were the areas in which the concentration of enlisted men was large enough to arouse civilian hostility.

Discrimination against sailors became rarer in the 1920s and 1930s, even though some, of course, still existed. In 1932 the officer in charge of the Los Angeles recruiting station reported an alleged false arrest of a shipfitter, first class, for drunken driving, commenting that police in small communities around Los Angeles "are not as lenient with enlisted men as they are with civilians." He also believed that some police ran a racket on arrests of naval personnel.[95] And, of course, enlisted men still found prices raised in their honor. Nevertheless, during these two decades, the relationship between civilians at home and sailors attained a new level of cordiality. Each group could exist without overly offending the other.

RELATIONS WITH CIVILIANS ABROAD

Unlike their counterparts in the army, enlisted men of the navy frequently visited foreign countries and had continuing contact with civilians of other nations. Surprisingly, sailor-civilian relations abroad were free of much of the friction that existed in the United States. Indeed, the men often lamented that the uniform was better received abroad than at home.[96]

One factor in the absence of hostility was that the Americans rarely overwhelmed foreign seaports. The larger warships generally visited only major harbors, and merchants and guides in these cities were expert in handling foreign seamen. If American enlisted men were willing to accept some overcharging, they encountered little trouble. Advance planning for cities to accommodate any unusually large number of men who were to visit also helped reduce tension.[97]

Not all the behavior of enlisted men in foreign ports, of course, was admirable. Sailors had a reputation for brawling that was not totally undeserved, and Americans saw their share of action even in the twentieth century. In 1908, for example, a disturbance occurred in Rio de Janeiro between "drunken native negroes and a few of the sailors from the American fleet." Five years later, citizens of Naples complained of the bluejackets' conduct.[98] Trouble was most common, however, in Asian ports. Contact with a radically different culture and the ineffective law enforcement in many cities freed the men from their normal restraints. In addition, seamen from various national fleets competed for female companionship. Here, as in other parts of the world, the free-spending Americans offended sailors from other fleets, who received less pay, and fights resulted.[99] Yet, although disruptions were common, they were usually confined to areas near the waterfront that were accustomed to the ways of sailors. The population there accepted the frays as a normal part of business.

During World War I many sailors were stationed in England and, in lesser numbers, in other Allied nations. No longer did they stay for just liberty; rather, they formed permanent garrisons. Their large numbers also increased chances for misunderstanding. Never before had the American navy stationed so many men in another country.

Initial developments augured well for smooth relations between the Americans and their hosts. A large, enthusiastic crowd greeted the first destroyers to arrive in Queenstown, Ireland, in May 1917, despite official secrecy about the arrival time. Going ashore, the men found the townspeople open and friendly. As the American presence grew, the men reached other cities—London, Paris, and Edinburgh. Here, too, they often received a warmhearted, spontaneous welcome.[100]

Although a widespread cordiality often existed, the potential for hostility was also present. Consequently, the navy counseled the men about their conduct. Before the end of 1917 the enlisted force was cautioned not to make inflammatory statements such as "We have come over here to finish the War for you because you cannot do it yourselves." Some months later, Vice Admiral Henry B. Wilson also found it necessary to instruct his men to act as befitted guests in someone's home.[101]

At times the undercurrent of hostility that some segments of the civilian population felt toward Americans erupted. In late 1917 mobs in the town of Cork attacked sailors who were with Irish girls, and the navy was forced to place Cork off-limits to men on leave.[102] Although incidents rarely provoked such extreme official reaction, in many cities some residents engaged in sporadic harassment of Americans. As Allied prospects in the war improved and the American presence grew, the comradeship that had been felt during less hopeful days faded. Confrontations involving American bluejackets and their hosts increased. Newcastle ruffians, for example, battled sailors from several ships; in 1918 the crew of the battleship *Texas* escalated the skirmishes to open war. After a series of attacks that the Americans felt were particularly unjustified, the bluejackets went ashore to deal with the Newcastle rowdies. During the night small bands of sailors engaged gangs of Englishmen, withdrew when the police arrived, only to re-form and attack again. The men dubbed the encounter the "Battle of Newcastle," considering it "the biggest, the bloodiest and the best battle of the entire war."[103]

The problem of relations during the war was further complicated by white Americans' hostility toward racially mixed couples. In November 1917 the chief of police of Newport, Monmouthshire, reported incidents involving the crew of the *Benham*, which was in port for repair from early September to November 1917. After a period of good relations, "a collision took place between a number of the crew and some coloured men, and so far as can be ascertained the origin of the trouble was the dislike of the American Seamen to coloured men cohabiting and associating with white women." After the trouble the local populace showed "signs of unfriendliness" toward the Americans.[104] Similarly, an enlisted man from the *Texas* witnessed a near riot caused by the reaction of sailors to a black enlisted man's arriving at a train station with two white women.[105]

In many ways, of course, the incidents of wartime resembled the brawls of peacetime. What makes them different was that they were more common, if only because there were more Americans spending more time abroad. Furthermore, since they detracted from Allied unity in the crusade against the Hun, they embarrassed the war effort. The navy never found the key to smoothing all contacts between enlisted men and Allied civilians. Only the withdrawal of the men after the armistice ended the difficulty.

Whether at home or abroad, an enlisted man found that his uniform identified him as a member of a particular group and that he was treated on the basis of this membership rather than as an individual. A bluejacket could protest discrimination, but his lot was determined by the reputation of the enlisted force as a whole. Improvements in the relationships between sailors and civilians could result only from a change in the enlisted force. In the twentieth century the enlisted force became more skilled and, of greater significance, more representative of the country it served. As civilians began to accord seamen greater respect, sailors gradually shed their status as outcasts.

Many ingredients, then, went into shaping enlisted men's lives. The large ships of the new navy increasingly offered facilities and comforts sailors had never before enjoyed: barbershops, reading rooms, recreation areas, dishwashers, laundries, improved heating, lighting, and ventilation, lockers and bunks, and greater supplies of fresh water. Larger ships also meant less seasickness, and the introduction of oil as a fuel relieved the men of the unpleasant task of coaling the ship. Yet the navy was never quite the same for any two men. The kind of ship on which they served, when and where they served, what their specialties were, the officers under whom they served, the reputation of the force as a whole, and their own characters all influenced the final experience. Nevertheless, in the years between the Spanish-American War and World War II, the lives of most sailors were not unpleasant. Reminiscing in 1970, Chief Morris offered what may have been a typical attitude:

> Some of the experiences were good and some not. I don't regret any of it; I enjoyed it. In the old days in the Navy it was a little hard, but we didn't know any better. We enjoyed it: what did we know about it? Whether we got $9 a month or $90, it didn't mean anything to us.[106]

The action of D. N. Burke, boilermaker, first class, offers evidence that Morris' opinion was commonly held. Taking a substantial cut in pay, Burke returned to the navy in 1920 after working in the merchant marine, because, he said, there were "no good shipmates" there as in the navy.[107] The sentiments Morris and Burke expressed seem to have applied to most men, including those who did not make the navy a career. Sailors enjoyed the excitement of the sea, the adventure of travel, and the pleasure of good shipmates.

chapter 11

Conclusion

Today a youth from the plains of Kansas joins the navy at a recruiting office near his home and then travels to Illinois for initial training. Throughout his career he will find extensive provisions for his comfort, education, and leisure time; if he remains in uniform long enough, he can expect generous retirement benefits. Neither the navy nor the recruit views today's treatment as unusual or the prospects as exceptional. Yet no part of this now familiar pattern existed before the Spanish-American War. Furthermore, all of these innovations had been established in the navy by 1940.

This metamorphosis in personnel policy was forced on the department when the navy began simultaneously to adopt a new technology of war and expand the size of the fleet. Many skills used aboard nineteenth-century ships were unsuited to the world of steam and electricity found on a battleship. The twentieth-century navy needed sailor-technicians, and large numbers of them. In seeking to attract, train, and hold the men required, it had to develop new enlisted personnel policies.

The fundamental change the department undertook was the recruitment of the enlisted force from across the nation. In the nineteenth century the navy had drawn sailors from the ports of the world. These men identified primarily with their trade of mariner rather than with the flag under which they served. Although in one sense the old navy was more cosmopolitan than the new, in another sense it was surprisingly parochial. Most nineteenth-century sailors spent their lives either at sea or within waterfront districts, the Navy Department itself also confined its activities to seaport areas. Considered in this way, the navy of that era can be regarded as a regional enterprise. When the department changed its recruiting methods after 1898 and brought to the service young men from all parts of the country, the new enlistees altered the character of naval personnel. Recruits began to share a primary identity as Americans, not as seamen, and the navy, with a recruiting network spread across the country, became a national institution. Furthermore, as sailors came to represent diverse areas of the United States, bluejackets gradually shed their former status as social outcasts.

Because the young men who flocked to the new navy were not familiar with their duties aboard ship, the department had to develop a new, large-scale training system. In place of the small apprentice program, which had been the old navy's only significant educational activity, the service in the twentieth century began instructing all recruits in elementary seamanship. This training provided a sufficient number of men for the expanding fleet but did not secure individuals in the skilled ratings required aboard a modern warship. To satisfy this need, the department developed shore schools and correspondence courses. Taken together, these efforts mark the emergence of the service as a major educational establishment.

The creation of a new recruiting and training network meant that the department had invested considerable effort and expense in securing and developing its enlisted force. Bluejackets of the old navy had been enlisted through a simple recruiting system that usually operated as a minor adjunct of other naval operations; for the most part they could be replaced by other mariners already suitable for assignment aboard ship. Sailors in the new navy, on the other hand, were enlisted through a specially created nationwide recruiting service; all had undergone initial training, and many had been taught advanced trades. The modern navy thus possessed an incentive to improve enlisted life in order to encourage men to remain in the service. It began lending official support to athletics and sponsoring other recreational activities. Taking advantage of the increased size of modern warships, it introduced dishwashers, laundries, lockers, bunks, and reading and recreational rooms. It also offered better food service and installed improved heating, lighting, and ventilation systems. Features such as these tangibly demonstrate the willingness of the navy to foster the morale and contentment of the enlisted force. Similarly, the department began giving some offenders a second chance through probation in an attempt to modernize its criminal justice system and adapt it to its new personnel.

The same type of enlistee who transformed the navy into a national institution also made possible the creation of a career enlisted force. Since at least 1825 the department had sought men who would regard the service as their life's work. After studying reforms in the treatment of enlisted personnel between 1828 and 1862, Harold Langley concludes that during those years "the foundations were laid for a career enlisted service."[1] Yet, although important reforms such as the abolition of flogging were made during that period, this conclusion is nevertheless premature. In the late nineteenth century, sailors continued to move easily between the navy and merchant marine as the mood struck them. The nineteenth-century navy had also been plagued by a high desertion rate. By the 1920s and 1930s, in contrast, the department had developed a career enlisted force for the first time in its history: reenlistment rates were high, desertion rates were low, and the service enjoyed a sizable core of skilled manpower. More importantly, bluejackets considered themselves primarily navy men, not seamen. The merchant sailor, however, remained akin to his nineteenth-century counterpart—often coming from a seafaring tradition and transferring from one firm to another.[2]

At the same time that it was developing its recruiting and training systems, the navy found itself able to exclude aliens and blacks—men who had formed an important part of the old navy. Noncitizens were barred from first enlistment in 1907. Blacks, after having their opportunities in the service steadily reduced in the early twentieth century, were prohibited from first enlistment entirely from 1919 to 1932. When blacks were again permitted to join in 1933, they were restricted to servant billets.

Discontent with the presence of blacks and aliens in the enlisted force did not originate in the twentieth century. Yet because the old navy was able to operate within its limited personnel system, it did not drastically alter its policies and continued to employ these two groups. The ships of the new navy, on the other hand, demanded manpower that the old system could not possibly supply. The department thus had to revamp the way it raised men. In the process, it adopted new methods of recruiting and training that enabled it to secure adequate numbers of white Americans and to end its former reliance on aliens and blacks.

A prime example of the new techniques the navy adopted can be seen in the recruiting process. As a part of its efforts to attract young men from the interior of the country, the service employed concepts that were coming into extensive use in the twentieth century. For example, in its advertising campaigns the Bureau of Navigation borrowed the idea of salesmanship from the civilian sector. Recruiters were schooled in this concept; a Madison Avenue firm was hired to develop a recruiting brochure designed primarily to sell naval life. In addition, navy advertising exploited all the available mass media—newspapers, magazines, posters, direct-mail circulars, and the newly developed motion pictures. Advertising content was also steadily modified to present a simple, eye-catching format. As was the case with civilian advertising, the department wished more to attract attention and arouse interest than to give extensive information.[3] Service life had become a commodity to be marketed in much the same way as consumer wares.

A byproduct of this recruiting process was that the modern navy also became involved in nationwide public relations efforts. Although officers in the nineteenth century certainly had been concerned about public attitudes toward the navy, they had not possessed any means of influencing those opinions. The new recruiting system enabled the service to disseminate pronavy information throughout the country in connection with an easily justifiable function. This discovery of public relations occurred at roughly the same time that the business world became interested in such activity.[4]

Well before World War I, public relations was an entrenched part of the recruiting process.

Just as the department adopted new techniques to attract large numbers of recruits, it also made use of other modern developments to shape the enlisted force to its ends. What emerges from an account of the various practices the navy employed is a case study of a bureaucracy's attempts to gain control over an expanding organization. Fingerprinting, for example, permitted a certainty of identification that had been absent in the nineteenth century. Intelligence and aptitude tests allowed the Bureau of Navigation to set easily verifiable criteria for selection of personnel. Written examinations for advancement to higher ratings injected a new element of central control into the promotion process. On the other hand, classification by such methods undoubtedly meant the exclusion of men from the navy or from advancement who would have been acceptable in an earlier era.

A similar impulse toward standardizing the treatment of enlisted personnel can be seen in other policies of the modern navy. Departmental review of discharges and court decisions was one component of that movement. In the area of education, formal instruction at recruit training facilities and in advanced courses helped the department provide a uniform learning experience for its men. The development of correspondence-type navy training courses helped insure that even the education the men undertook on their own time met service needs. Supervision of instruction was enhanced by central preparation of such training aids as drill books, movies, and slide films, and the issuance of a common manual to all recruits. Even the recreational and entertainment programs that the department incorporated into its structure—although usually welcomed by the men—produced a degree of central direction in leisure-time activities and tended to reduce individual initiative and differences.

Although the consequences of the measures the navy adopted were permanent and far-reaching, innovations in the personnel system were introduced not as part of an overall design but in response to immediate problems. During the formation of the modern force, the department acted in self-imposed isolation. New ideas arose only as conditions in the service itself demanded, seldom as the result of learning from the experiences of others. The army, for example, instituted many reforms that the navy was later to adopt. Among other measures, it began offering retirement to its men in 1885; permitted noncommissioned officers to receive commissions after 1878 and created avenues for other enlisted men to become officers in 1892; inaugurated one-man courts in 1890; and expanded its recruiting efforts in 1891. In addition, by 1890 the army was trying to train every recruit for four months before transferring him to a field unit.[5]

The difference in the timing of these reforms reflected the army's own manpower crisis. Instead of responding to the needs of a changing technology and a rapidly expanding force, the nineteenth-century army was seeking to reduce a high and increasing desertion rate from a force whose technology and enlisted strength remained relatively constant. Indeed, the army lagged behind the navy in providing technical education for its men—apparently instruction of that type was not instituted until World War I.[6]

Both the army and the navy shared certain characteristics as military institutions. Yet in many ways the changes that took place in the navy in the early twentieth century were closer to those in industry than to what was happening in the other services. Factories were becoming larger, and machinery was growing more sophisticated. Such similarities invite a search for some pattern of interaction between the navy and the civilian world. The available evidence, however, does not facilitate generalization.

The question of skilled manpower demonstrates the complexity of relationships between the navy and the civilian economy. Both the service and private industry needed technicians, and to some degree they competed for the same men. The navy responded to this rivalry in different ways. Sometimes it sought to exploit temporary weaknesses in private enterprise, as when the Bureau of Navigation urged recruiters to give extra attention to areas where workers were to be laid off. Recruiters also extolled service life in order to entice men away from civilian employment. Navy publicity claimed that the hours of labor in the service compared favorably with those in factories; it also noted that the department offered medical and retirement benefits that were almost nonexistent elsewhere.[7]

Although one facet of the navy's response to its manpower problems was to vie with industry for personnel, another thrust was to withdraw from the competition. The formation of extensive educational facilities within the navy meant that the service no longer had to recruit men familiar with a trade. The very creation of an independent source of supply, however, seems to indicate that in the end the navy was not able to compete effectively against the lures of private employment for skilled manpower. The department therefore strove to build its own closed world.

In developing this separate system, the navy demonstrated its ability to isolate itself from much of society. One result of that independence was that the service did not experience some of the side effects of industrialization that the civilian sector felt. In the twentieth century, for example, organized labor achieved new strength—enrolling such important industries as steel in the 1920s and automobiles in the 1930s. Yet there is no evidence of sailors' organizing to present a united expression of their particular needs within the navy. The formation of civilian unions, of course, had encountered resistance; indeed, workers were subject to prosecution for conspiracy until the passage of the Wagner Act in 1935. Within the military, organization by enlisted personnel outside the normal chain of command was regarded with hostility, and this attitude has persisted.[8]

The depression of the thirties also reveals the freedom of navy personnel from events that had a major impact on the rest of the nation. For the civilian world, economic collapse led to dramatic innovations. Analyzing the "Roosevelt Revolution," one historian has argued that the "six years from 1933 through 1938 marked a greater upheaval in American institutions than any similar period in our history."[9] Virtually the entire federal government underwent rapid expansion. In this age of change, navy personnel policy remained almost static. Even the activities of a pronavy president were limited to matériel and did not affect personnel. Although the number of applicants for enlistment increased in the thirties, any alteration in the quality of men could have produced only a marginal improvement. By the late twenties the service possessed an enlisted force characterized by high morale and good performance. Secure, almost complacent, the navy could watch the "upheaval in American institutions" from the sidelines.

The personnel system that the department developed in the first part of the twentieth century formed the basic structure under which the navy has subsequently operated. After World War II erupted, the strength of the enlisted force swelled to thirty times its prewar level.[10] The influx of thousands of men and women diluted the career force, but the bluejackets of the thirties provided the experienced petty officers that the enlarged navy required. By 1940 such developments as inland recruiting, training stations, trade schools, and recreational offerings were taken for granted. With the advent of war, they provided the framework that permitted the service to attract, train, and utilize thousands of new men and women, and the navy had only to concern itself with extending and refining the programs it already possessed.

So satisfactory was this personnel system in fulfilling the needs of the modern navy that it has remained at the core of the navy's manpower policies to the present day. Even when Admiral Elmo R. Zumwalt, Jr., chief of naval operations from 1970 to 1974, instituted a number of well-publicized reforms to make enlisted life more attractive to modern youths, he left unchanged the essential methods of training and recruiting that the service had developed in the first decades of the twentieth century.[11] Today's navy is able to operate within the personnel structure formed three quarters of a century ago because its basic requirement remains the same—the maintenance of a skilled force for a large, technically advanced fleet.

Appendix

Table 1 • **Authorized Strength, United States Navy, 1880-1940**

Fiscal Year	Men	Apprentices or Apprentice Seamen[a]	Total
1880	7,500	750	8,250
1881	7,500	750	8,250
1882	7,500	750	8,250
1883	7,500	750	8,250
1884	7,500	750	8,250
1885	7,500	750	8,250
1886	7,500	750	8,250
1887	7,500	750	8,250
1888	7,500	750	8,250
1889	7,500	750	8,250
1890	7,500	750	8,250
1891	7,500	750	8,250
1892	7,500	750	8,250
1893	7,500	750	8,250
1894	7,500	1,500	9,000
1895	8,250	750	9,000
1896[b]	8,250	750	9,000
1897[b]	9,250	750	10,000
1898	11,000	750	11,750
1899[c]	12,750	1,000	13,750
1900	17,500	2,500	20,000
1901	17,500	2,500	20,000
1902	22,500	2,500	25,000
1903	25,500	2,500	28,000
1904	28,500	2,500	31,000
1905	31,500	2,500	34,000
1906	34,500	2,500	37,000
1907	34,500	2,500	37,000
1908	36,000	2,500	38,500
1909	42,000	2,500	44,500
1910	42,000	2,500	44,500
1911	44,000	3,500	47,500
1912	44,000	3,500	47,500
1913	48,000	3,500	51,500
1914	48,000	3,500	51,500
1915	48,000	3,500	51,500
1916	48,000	3,500	51,500
1917[d]	68,700	6,000	74,700
1918	68,700	6,000	74,700
	140,000[e]	10,000	150,000
1919	191,485	24,000	215,485
1920			
July 1, 1919-September 30, 1919			241,000
October 1, 1919-December 31, 1919			191,000
January 1, 1920-June 30, 1920[f]			170,000

Table 1 *continued*

Fiscal Year	Men	Apprentices or Apprentice Seamen[a]	Total
1921			......
1922	106,000	6,000	112,000
1923			86,000
1924			86,000
1925			86,000
1926			82,000
1927			82,500
1928			83,250
1929			84,000
1930			84,500
1931			84,500
1932			79,700
1933			79,700
1934			79,700
1935			81,500
1936			88,000
1937			96,500
1938			
Beginning of fiscal year			100,000
End of fiscal year			105,000
1939			110,100
1940[g]			116,000

SOURCE: Enlisted strength from 1880 to 1920 was specifically authorized by Congress and given in the naval appropriation acts for those years. See U.S., *Statutes at Large*, vols. 20-41. For the years from 1922 to 1940 Congress did not specify an exact level but authorized a lump sum for navy pay based on an enlisted force of a particular size. Each *Annual Report of the Chief of the Bureau of Navigation* for those years cites the allowed strength on which the budget was based.

[a]The apprentice rating was abolished in 1904, and the apprentice seaman rating was established the same year. Published statistics for the years 1920-40 do not list apprentice seamen separately.

[b]The secretary of the navy was empowered to enlist 1,000 additional men if necessary.

[c]The secretary of the navy was empowered to enlist additional men as needed for the war.

[d]The president was empowered to increase the force to 87,000.

[e]On May 22, 1917, Congress increased its original authorization because the United States had entered the World War. Wartime figures in this table do not include members of the reserve on active duty.

[f]The president was empowered to increase the force to 191,000.

[g]After a presidential declaration of a national emergency on September 8, 1939, the authorized strength was raised to 145,000.

Table 2 • **Applications for Enlistment, 1899-1940**

Year	Applied for Enlistment	Rejected for Physical Disability	Rejected for Other Causes	Disqualification Waived	Failed to Enlist	First Enlistments	Reenlistments	Total Enlistments	Men Enlisted as a Percentage of Applicants
1899	41,756	33,500		214	276	......	......	8,270	19.8
1900	40,854	6,965	25,276	297	787	......	......	8,123	19.9
1901	38,998	11,464	16,723	231	1,146	......	......	9,896	25.4
1902	37,043	10,721	14,984	414	1,458	......	......	10,294	27.8
1903	47,765	18,302	14,246	741	3,024	......	......	12,934	27.1
1904	40,709	13,648	12,058	594	2,217	......	......	13,380	32.9
1905	41,239	14,491	13,606	266	1,689	9,306	2,413	11,719	28.4
1906	40,918	16,518	9,381	389	1,970	11,200	2,218	13,418	32.8
1907	45,691	16,674	11,784	504	3,408	12,227	2,102	14,329	31.4
1908	81,442	29,919	26,242	467	467	17,852	4,077	21,929	26.9
1909	91,588	38,782	31,786	397	2,704	14,683	4,039	18,713	20.4
1910	76,074	33,072	25,136	406	3,516	10,915	3,841	14,756	19.4
1911	79,458	37,746	21,747	347	4,588	11,875	3,849	15,724	19.8
1912	73,364	36,999	14,793	507	3,829	11,516	5,720	17,743	24.2
1913	75,457	39,070	13,348	650	5,121	12,088	5,830	17,918	23.7
1914	88,943	47,240	16,142	552	6,613	13,780	5,168	18,948	21.3
1915	102,561	61,370	16,999	425	6,488	11,413	6,291	17,704	17.3
1916	89,812	51,522	8,645	706	8,425	13,169	8,051[a]	21,220	23.6
1917	281,957	127,512	22,911	4,170	38,441	84,229	8,864[a]	93,093	33.0
1918	380,260	186,755	27,245	2,137	59,982	95,259	11,019[a]	106,278	27.9
1919	160,977	68,968	6,550	538	26,684	50,495	8,280[a]	58,775	36.5
1920	160,057	56,683	5,782	680	17,722	43,381	36,489[a]	79,870	49.9

1921	135,993	47,758	4,585	316	11,264	54,517	17,869[a]	72,386	53.2
1922	39,569	14,044	2,973	81	1,664	7,412	13,476	20,888	52.8
1923	81,150	32,347	2,205	19	4,950	28,679	12,969	41,648	51.3
1924	81,257	32,506	6,239	168	7,107	21,688	10,549	35,237	43.4
1925	46,271	17,543	4,156	24	4,869	12,147	7,532	19,679	42.5
1926	45,513	19,928	4,621	24	4,341	10,686	5,913	16,599	36.5
1927	83,044	41,589	6,036	166	5,358	20,699	9,362	30,061	36.2
1928	84,243	43,039	8,536	20	6,719	17,002	8,947	25,949	30.8
1929	81,126	41,440	9,188	20	8,465	13,906	8,127	22,033	27.1
1930	95,062	55,350	10,390	44	8,747	12,643	7,932	20,575	21.6
1931	110,526	69,734	14,376	78	6,712	8,833	10,871	19,704	17.8
1932	122,136	69,865	27,484	111	6,128	7,061	11,598	18,659	15.3
1933	117,326	68,463	27,805	85	2,786	4,572	13,272	18,272	15.6
1934	133,503	68,841	37,269	108	7,046	11,612	8,735	20,347	15.2
1935	177,602	99,632	49,093	174	8,181	10,781	9,915	20,696	11.7
1936	155,446	79,486	40,664	251	8,223	18,039	9,034	27,073	17.4
1937	130,825	60,259	28,252	180	7,671	15,494	9,149	24,643	20.4
1938	165,714	85,228	44,132	304	10,945	16,333	9,076	25,409	15.3
1939	140,873	73,941	33,743	277	8,440	14,699	10,050	24,749	17.6
1940	193,848	86,296	37,556	557	15,741	38,788	15,467	54,255	28.0

SOURCE: Each *Annual Report of the Chief of the Bureau of Navigation* for the years 1899-1940 gives the numbers of men used in this table. Percentages have been calculated from those statistics.

NOTE: This table uses the figures as given by the Bureau of Navigation even though these numbers are sometimes not internally consistent. Over the years the bureau also varied its treatment of the "Disqualification Waived" category.

[a]Includes extensions of enlistment.

Table 3 • **Place of Birth of the Enlisted Force**

Place	Percentage of Total Force		
	1890[a]	1906	1915
United States			
New England:[b]			
Maine	1.6	.9	.6
New Hampshire	.5	.6	.4
Vermont	.6	.3	.2
Massachusetts	7.1	7.5	6.3
Rhode Island	1.2	1.6	1.2
Connecticut	1.6	1.6	1.7
Total	12.6	12.5	10.4
Middle Atlantic:			
New York	10.3	11.3	12.9
New Jersey	2.9	2.8	4.3
Pennsylvania	5.0	8.4	9.5
Total	18.2	22.5	26.7
East North Central:			
Ohio	.5	5.2	4.3
Indiana	.2	2.7	3.1
Illinois	.6	5.1	5.1
Michigan	1.1	2.9	2.4
Wisconsin	...	1.6	2.1
Total	2.4	17.5	17.0
West North Central:			
Minnesota	.2	1.5	1.2
Iowa	.3	1.9	1.9
Missouri	...	3.0	2.9
North Dakota	...	.1	.2
South Dakota	...	.4	.3
Nebraska	...	1.1	1.2
Kansas	.2	1.7	1.6
Total	.7	9.7	9.3
South Atlantic:			
Delaware	...	.4	.3
Maryland	5.6	3.1	2.8
Washington, D.C.	1.1	1.0	.9
Virginia	4.5	2.5	2.5
West Virginia	.2	.4	.6
North Carolina	.6	1.0	.7
South Carolina	.6	.7	.9
Georgia	...	.8	2.0
Florida	.5	.3	.5
Total	13.1[a]	10.2	12.2

Table 3 *continued*

Place	Percentage of Total Force		
	1890[a]	1906	1915
East South Central:[b]			
Kentucky	...	1.5	1.8
Tennessee	.2	.7	.3
Alabama	.2	.5	1.0
Mississippi	...	.2	.8
Total	.4	2.9	3.9
West South Central:			
Arkansas	.2	.4	.8
Louisiana	...	.5	1.1
Oklahoma	...	.1	.5
Texas	.5	1.9	3.3
Total	.7	2.9	5.7
Mountain:			
Montana	...	.1	.2
Idaho	...	.1	.1
Wyoming	...	.1	.1
Colorado	...	.6	.8
New Mexico	...	.1	.1
Arizona	...	.1	.1
Utah	...	.2	.3
Nevada	...	.1	.1
Total	...	1.4	1.8
Pacific:			
Washington	...	.3	.5
Oregon	...	.3	.5
California	2.2	1.9	2.3
Total	2.2	2.5	3.3
Total United States	50.3	82.3	90.3
Foreign			
Canada	1.5	1.2	.4
Denmark	2.4	.5	.2
England	3.9	1.1	.3
Finland	1.3	.3	.1
Germany	5.6	2.9	1.0
Ireland	10.5	2.7	.7
Italy	2.1	.8	.3
Norway	4.5	1.0	.3
Scotland	2.1	.3	.1
Sweden	6.1	1.3	.5
China	2.4	.9	.4
Japan	2.3	1.3	.3
Philippines	.2	.9	3.3
Other	4.8	2.5	1.6
Total foreign	49.7	17.7	9.7

Table 3 *continued*

SOURCE: Data for 1890 was compiled from a sample of muster rolls for the quarter ending June 30 of that year. The muster rolls are a part of the Records of the Bureau of Naval Personnel, Record Group 24, National Archives and Records Service, Washington, D.C. Percentages for 1906 and 1915 were calculated from tables on the place of birth of the men in the force as of June 30 of those years, given in *Annual Report of the Chief of the Bureau of Navigation, 1906,* pp. 415-16, and *1915*, pp. 211-12.

[a]Since percentages for 1890 are derived from a sample of the enlisted force, some states or territories that are not represented in the sample probably would have appeared as the place of birth of a few men if the entire force had been tallied.

[b]The states are classified by region according to Census Bureau divisions listed in U.S., Department of Commerce, Bureau of the Census, *Historical Statistics of the United States, Colonial Times to 1957* (Washington: GPO, 1960), p. 4.

Table 4 • **Citizenship of the Enlisted Force, 1899-1940**

Fiscal Year	Native-born		Naturalized		Citizens of U.S. Insular Possessions		Noncitizens	
	No.	Percent	No.	Percent	No.	Percent	No.	Percent
1899[a]	7,383	60.1	2,441	19.9	.....	...	2,456	20.0
1900[a]	6,397	67.0	1,199	12.6	.....	...	1,952	20.4
1901[a]	7,724	72.0	1,178	11.0	.....	...	1,823	17.0
1902[a]	9,402	76.4	1,216	9.8	.....	...	1,691	13.7
1903[a]	13,392	78.8	1,245	7.3	.....	...	2,364	13.9
1904[a]	19,197	76.8	2,999	12.0	323	1.2	2,459	9.8
1905	24,913	80.8	3,415	11.1	291	.9	2,217	7.2
1906	26,443	82.2	3,496	10.9	382	1.2	1,842	5.7
1907	27,733	84.0	3,385	10.3	531	1.6	1,368	4.1
1908	33,991	87.0	3,254	8.3	620	1.6	1,183	3.0
1909	39,012	88.4	3,227	7.3	1,103	2.4	787	1.8
1910	40,091	89.0	3,169	7.0	1,170	2.6	646	1.4
1911	42,752	89.8	3,050	6.4	1,240	2.6	570	1.2
1912	42,859	90.2	2,875	6.1	1,326	2.8	455	2.8
1913	43,367	90.2	2,842	5.9	1,347	2.8	512	1.1
1914	47,939	91.0	2,571	4.9	1,694	3.2	463	.9
1915	47,664	90.7	2,518	4.8	1,960	3.7	419	.8
1916	49,252	90.8	2,560	4.7	2,065	3.8	357	.7
1917	95,099	94.7	2,891	2.9	2,246	2.2	213	.2
1918								
USN	199,589	95.6	4,954	2.4	3,800	1.8	328	.2
USNRF	199,756	93.9	9,760	4.6	294	.1	2,850	1.3
NNV	13,640	93.4	377	2.7	.....	...	44	.3
Total	412,985	94.9	15,091	3.5	4,094	.9	3,222	.7
1919								
USN	159,196	93.9	3,900	2.3	6,129	3.6	350	.2
USNRF	76,198	93.8	3,513	4.3	200	.2	1,357	1.7
Total	235,394	93.8	7,413	2.9	6,329	2.5	1,707	.7
1920								
USN	98,273	91.3	3,112	2.9	308	.3	5,908	5.5
USNRF	1,089	80.7	93	6.9	20	1.5	147	10.9
Total	99,362	91.2	3,205	2.9	328	.3	6,055	5.5
1921	109,457	91.8	3,567	3.0	5,829	4.9	352	.3
1922	80,509	90.9	2,734	3.1	5,018	5.7	319	.4
1923	73,434	91.4	2,256	2.8	4,375	5.4	290	.4
1924	80,412	92.1	2,251	2.6	4,458	5.1	206	.2
1925	77,769	92.3	2,082	2.5	4,218	5.0	220	.3
1926	75,714	92.1	2,058	2.5	4,203	5.1	186	.2
1927	77,438	92.7	1,975	2.4	3,973	4.7	180	.2
1928	78,172	92.7	1,917	2.3	4,092	4.9	174	.2

Table 4 *continued*

Fiscal Year	Native-born		Naturalized		Citizens of U.S. Insular Possessions		Noncitizens	
	No.	Percent	No.	Percent	No.	Percent	No.	Percent
1929	79,026	92.6	1,860	2.2	4,278	5.0	157	.2
1930	78,549	92.5	1,842	2.2	4,398	5.2	149	.2
1931	74,667	92.3	1,772	2.2	4,347	5.4	124	.1
1932	75,022	92.5	1,773	2.2	4,168	5.1	157	.2
1933	73,432	92.7	1,732	2.2	3,922	4.9	157	.2
1934	74,930	93.2	1,647	2.0	3,645	4.5	137	.2
1935	77,904	94.0	1,535	1.8	3,271	3.9	129	.1
1936	88,739	95.3	1,493	1.6	2,708	2.9	137	.1
1937	96,096	95.9	1,465	1.5	2,460	2.5	159	.1
1938	100,975	96.3	1,471	1.4	2,249	2.1	193	.2
1939	106,185	96.4	1,536	1.4	2,233	2.0	242	.2
1940	135,222	96.9	1,873	1.3	2,220	1.6	239	.2

SOURCE: *Annual Report of the Chief of the Bureau of Navigation* for the years 1899-1940. Statistics are based on men in the force as of June 30 of each year.

[a]Does not include apprentices.

Table 5 • **Color of the Enlisted Force, 1906-40**

Year	White	Negro	Chinese	Japanese	Filipino	Samoan	Chamorro (Guam)	Hawaiian	American Indian	Puerto Rican	Other	Total
1906	29,511	1,456	348	406	285	81	28	13	2	22	13	32,165
1907	30,221	1,484	394	365	399	79	37	...	2	24	10	33,027
1908	35,971	1,867	286	271	455	81	38	...	2	46	1	39,018
1909	40,675	1,768	327	256	901	79	51	16	7	48	1	44,129
1910	41,765	1,535	314	261	969	81	76	25	6	44	..	45,076
1911	44,280	1,529	305	230	1,042	81	70	21	7	47	..	47,612
1912	44,261	1,438	258	210	1,125	83	72	18	4	46	..	47,515
1913	44,739	1,491	266	206	1,137	87	77	19	..	46	..	48,068
1914	49,052	1,431	248	198	1,464	87	98	25	18	46	..	52,667
1915	48,908	1,265	235	167	1,726	78	110	14	15	43	..	52,561
1916	50,496	1,262	228	143	1,823	84	117	20	20	41	..	54,234
1917	96,571	1,285	195	120	2,001	87	158	47	36	39	..	100,539
1918	201,220	3,203	188	121	3,451	90	195	203	25	105	..	208,671
1919												
USN	158,454	4,307	179	102	5,970	71	71	175	49	197	..	169,575
USNRF	79,583	1,361	30	6	164	2	25	52	7	28	..	81,258
Total	238,037	5,668	219	108	6,134	73	96	227	56	225	..	250,833
1920												
USN	98,040	3,018	195	96	5,594	87	210	181	51	129	..	107,601
USNRF	1,172	29	...	...	148	...	...	...	..	...	..	1,349
Total	99,212	3,037	195	96	5,742	87	210	181	51	129	..	108,950
1921	110,024	2,385	196	88	5,545	139	249	296	86	197	..	119,205
1922	80,888	1,867	174	69	4,837	92	214	232	59	148	..	88,580
1923	75,899	1,322	165	42	4,378	91	194	119	26	119	..	82,355
1924	81,083	1,112	153	43	4,438	92	195	95	28	88	..	87,327
1925	77,524	925	144	29	4,193	93	185	79	30	79	..	84,289

Table 5 *continued*

Year	White	Negro	Chinese	Japanese	Filipino	Samoan	Chamorro (Guam)	Hawaiian	American Indian	Puerto Rican	Other	Total
1926	76,562	775	120	19	4,240	91	190	66	26	72	..	82,161
1927	78,375	681	132	12	3,949	92	183	59	24	59	..	83,566
1928	79,137	607	121	10	4,087	83	185	52	14	59	..	84,355
1929	79,996	533	128	10	4,227	78	216	54	16	63	..	85,321
1930	79,570	462	118	5	4,375	83	201	47	18	59	..	84,938
1931	75,638	465	102	3	4,313	81	196	38	23	51	..	80,910
1932	76,018	441	134	2	4,133	107	176	37	27	45	..	81,120
1933	74,296	505	139	2	3,925	102	171	34	29	40	..	79,243
1934	75,515	708	122	1	3,667	105	139	32	32	38	..	80,359
1935	78,009	1,152	114	1	3,246	102	129	25	28	33	..	82,839
1936	88,137	1,936	122	...	2,595	94	122	17	27	27	..	93,077
1937	95,294	2,104	121	...	2,397	88	121	10	25	20	..	100,180
1938	99,903	2,384	119	...	2,116	85	226	13	22	20	..	104,888
1939	104,756	2,807	138	...	1,961	83	405	13	17	16	..	110,196
1940	132,889	4,007	136	...	1,833	86	557	14	16	16	..	139,554

SOURCE: *Annual Report of the Chief of the Bureau of Navigation* for the years 1906-40. Statistics are based on men in the force as of June 30 of each year.

NOTE: The title of the table and the column categories were used by the Bureau of Navigation.

Table 6 • **Reenlistments and Extensions of Enlistment, 1905-39**

Fiscal Year	Rate of Reenlistment and Extension	Rate of Unemployment for Calendar Year
1905	54	3.1
1906	43.1	.8
1907	32.2	1.8
1908	57	8.5
1909	65	5.2
1910	61	5.9
1911	57	6.2
1912	54	5.2
1913	57	4.4
1914	65	8.0
1915	72	9.7
1916	72	4.8
1917	78.6	4.8
1918	83.4	1.4
1919	35.9	2.3
1920	35.6	4.0
1921	78.6	11.9
1922	72.2	7.6
1923	49	3.2
1924	76.7	5.5
1925	72	4.0
1926	75	1.9
1927	61.7	4.1
1928	68.5	4.4
1929	72.8	3.2
1930	71.9	8.7
1931	78.5	15.9
1932	90.07	23.6
1933	93.25	24.9
1934	76.10	21.7
1935	80.86	20.1
1936	83.67	16.9
1937	81.75	14.3
1938	72.21	19.0
1939	80.81	17.2

SOURCE: Reenlistment rates: *Annual Report of the Chief of the Bureau of Navigation* for the years 1905-39. Unemployment rates: U.S., Department of Commerce, Bureau of the Census, *Historical Statistics of the United States, Colonial Times to 1957* (Washington: GPO, 1960), p. 73.

Table 7 • **Length of Service of the Enlisted Force, 1907-40**

Fiscal Year	Less than Four Years		Four to Eight Years		Eight to Twelve Years		Twelve to Sixteen Years		Sixteen to Twenty Years		Twenty Years or More		Total
	No.	Per-cent	No.	Per-cent	No.	Per-cent	No.	Per-cent	No.	Per-cent	No.	Per-cent	
1907	25,761	78.0	4,405	13.3	1,275	3.9	632	1.9	374	1.1	580	1.8	33,027
1908	29,734	76.1	5,862	15.0	1,642	4.2	668	1.7	446	1.1	696	1.9	39,048
1909	32,798	76.5	6,483	15.1	1,749	4.1	748	1.8	433	1.0	650	1.5	42,861
1910	33,526	74.4	7,327	16.3	2,063	4.6	914	2.0	516	1.1	730	1.6	45,076
1911	34,634	72.7	8,055	16.9	2,704	5.7	931	2.0	538	1.1	750	1.6	47,612
1912	32,206	67.8	9,289	19.6	3,516	7.4	1,078	2.3	542	1.1	884	1.8	47,515
1913	31,085	64.7	10,040	20.9	4,015	8.3	1,385	2.9	658	1.4	885	1.8	48,068
1914	34,027	64.6	10,909	20.7	4,529	8.6	1,588	3.0	745	1.4	869	1.7	52,667
1915	32,240	61.3	11,615	22.1	4,928	9.4	2,096	4.0	818	1.6	864	1.6	52,561
1916	32,372	59.7	11,426	21.1	5,617	10.4	2,842	5.2	1,065	2.0	912	1.6	54,234
1917	79,858	79.4	10,771	10.7	5,414	5.4	2,653	2.6	1,083	1.1	760	.8	100,539
1918													
USN	182,943	87.7	13,826	6.6	6,317	3.0	3,283	1.6	1,535	.7	767	.4	208,671
USNRF	209,112	98.3	2,134	1.0	369	.2	76	.1	258	.1	711	.3	212,660
NNV	14,018	99.7	41	.2	7	.1	.....	...	.....	...	1	...	14,067
Total	406,073	93.3	16,001	3.7	6,693	1.5	3,359	.8	1,793	.4	1,479	.3	435,398
1919													
USN	148,705	87.7	10,826	6.4	5,229	3.1	2,941	1.7	1,248	.7	626	.4	169,575
USNRF	79,100	97.3	1,550	1.9	195	.2	60	.1	138	.2	215	.3	81,258
Total	227,805	92.5	12,376	4.1	5,424	1.7	3,001	.9	1,386	.5	841	.3	250,833
1920													
USN	90,235	83.9	7,452	7.0	4,872	4.5	3,207	3.0	1,343	1.2	492	.4	107,601
USNRF	1,155	85.6	76	5.6	18	1.3	8	.6	34	2.5	58	4.4	1,349
Total	91,390	83.9	7,528	6.9	4,890	4.5	3,215	2.9	1,377	1.3	550	.5	108,950

1921	99,401	83.4	8,826	7.4	5,444	4.6	3,604	3.0	1,481	1.2	449	.4	119,205
1922	68,646	77.5	9,152	10.3	5,169	5.8	3,693	4.2	1,564	1.8	356	.4	88,580
1923	63,620	77.3	10,288	12.5	4,901	5.9	2,438	3.0	903	1.1	205	.2	82,355
1924	67,213	77.0	11,110	12.7	5,138	5.9	2,662	3.1	995	1.1	209	.2	87,327
1925	60,776	72.1	13,699	16.3	5,375	6.4	2,948	3.5	1,070	1.3	421	.4	84,284
1926	47,280	57.5	20,723	25.2	7,789	9.5	4,750	5.8	1,409	1.7	210	.3	82,161
1927	48,029	57.5	19,575	23.4	9,276	11.1	5,063	6.1	1,450	1.7	173	.2	83,566
1928	46,245	54.8	18,115	21.5	13,285	15.7	4,915	5.8	1,600	1.9	195	.3	84,355
1929	48,078	56.3	15,129	17.7	14,791	17.3	5,254	6.2	1,841	2.2	228	.3	85,321
1930	47,819	56.3	14,205	16.7	13,740	16.2	6,825	8.0	2,129	2.5	220	.3	84,938
1931	40,806	50.4	15,929	19.7	13,368	16.5	8,260	10.2	2,336	2.9	211	.3	80,910
1932	34,232	42.2	20,033	24.7	12,335	15.2	11,879	14.6	2,369	2.9	272	.4	81,120
1933	27,709	34.8	22,714	28.5	11,624	14.6	14,544	18.2	2,742	3.4	389	.5	79,722
1934	28,436	35.4	23,714	29.5	11,263	14.0	12,743	15.9	3,810	4.7	393	.5	80,359
1935	31,237	37.7	21,012	25.4	12,805	15.5	11,988	14.5	5,415	6.5	382	.4	82,839
1936	42,767	45.9	17,188	18.5	14,245	15.3	11,145	12.0	7,323	7.9	409	.4	93,077
1937	52,004	51.9	13,395	13.4	15,546	15.5	10,499	10.5	8,309	8.3	425	.4	100,178
1938	56,744	54.1	12,424	11.8	16,908	16.1	10,438	10.0	7,590	7.2	784	.8	104,888
1939	58,980	53.5	15,307	13.9	15,624	14.2	11,389	10.3	8,013	7.3	883	.8	110,196
1940	80,377	57.6	22,541	16.2	13,449	9.6	12,434	8.9	8,565	6.1	2,188	1.6	139,554

SOURCE: Each *Annual Report of the Chief of the Bureau of Navigation* for the years 1907-40 gives the numbers of men used in this table. Percentages have been calculated from those statistics.

Table 8 • **Advanced Schools**

Year	Schools and Locations
1883	Gunnery (Washington, e)
1885	Gunnery (Newport, e)
1897	Gun captains (U.S.S. *Amphitrite,* e)
1899	Electrical (New York, e, trans. to Hampton Roads 1918; Boston, e); gunnery (U.S.S. *Lancaster*, U.S.S. *Fortune*: m)
1901	Petty officers (Newport, e)
1902	Artificer—carpenter's mate, shipwright, plumber and fitter, blacksmith, painter (Norfolk, New York: e); master at arms, musician, ship's cook, yeoman (Norfolk, m, yeoman trans. to Newport 1907)
1903	Machinist (New York, m); machinist and fireman for torpedo-boat service (Newport, m)
1905	Electrical (Mare Island, m, dis. 1922); hospital corps (Mare Island, m, trans. to San Diego 1929; Norfolk, m); yeoman (New York, San Francisco: m); coppersmith (Norfolk, m)
1906	Machinist (Norfolk, e, absorbed by Charleston 1912)
1907	Cooks, bakers, and commissary stewards (Newport, e, dis. 1920); musician (Newport, e); yeoman (Newport, trans. from Norfolk, dis. 1925)
1908	Cooks, bakers, and commissary stewards (Norfolk, m)
1909	Cooks, bakers, and commissary stewards (San Francisco, e); torpedo (Newport, e, created from gunnery school)
1911	Machinist's mate (Charleston, e, trans. to Hampton Roads 1920); musician (San Francisco, e)
1914	Coppersmith (Charleston, m); fuel oil (Philadelphia, m, dis. 1926); hospital corps (Newport, e); messmen (Norfolk, m)
1915	Aeronautics (Pensacola, e); coppersmith (Philadelphia, m); deep-sea diving (Newport, e, dis. 1923); gas engine (Charleston, m); hospital corps (San Francisco, e)
1916	Hospital corps (Great Lakes, e, dis. 1920); signal (Great Lakes, Newport, Norfolk: e, dis. 1922)
1918	Artificer—carpenter, shipwright, shipfitter, blacksmith, painter (Mare Island, m, dis. 1922); aviation aerography (Pensacola, m); aviation armorer (Great Lakes, m); aviation carpenter's mate (Pensacola, m); aviation carpenter's mate, postgraduate course (Philadelphia, m); aviation instrument repair (New York, m, trans. from Pensacola); aviation machinist's mate (Pensacola, San Diego: m); aviation mechanic (Great Lakes, m, trans. to Norfolk 1933); aviation quartermaster (Great Lakes, Hampton Roads, San Diego: m); aviation quartermaster, postgraduate course (Philadelphia, m); cooks and bakers (Philadelphia, m); deep-sea diving (New London, e); electrical (Hampton Roads, trans. from New York); gunnery engineer (Pensacola, m); gyrocompass (Hampton Roads, m); listener, mechanics for submarine tenders, mining and mine sweeping (New London, m); molders and patternmakers (Mare Island, m); optical (Washington, m); radio telephone (New London, m); searchlight control (New York, m); storekeeper (Newport, m); signalman (Hampton Roads, m)
1919	Naval Academy Preparatory (Hampton Roads, San Diego: e)
1920	Artificer—blacksmith, patternmaker, molder, painter, shipfitter, shipwright (Hampton Roads, m); baker (Hampton Roads, m); bugler (Hampton Roads, Newport, San Francisco: m); cook (Hampton Roads, m);

Table 8 *continued*

Year	Schools and Locations
	coppersmith (Great Lakes, e); fuel oil (Mare Island, m, dis. 1927); gyrocompass (Mare Island, e); machinist's mate (Great Lakes, e, dis. 1923; Hampton Roads, trans. from Charleston); mess attendant, pharmacist's mate (Hampton Roads, m); photography (Washington, e, dis. 1925); radio (Great Lakes, m); signalman (San Francisco, m); submarine (New London, m); yeoman (Hampton Roads, m, dis. 1925)
1921	Optical (Mare Island, m)
1922	Aviation carpenter's mate, aviation machinist's mate, aviation metalsmith (Great Lakes, m); aircraft radio (Pensacola, m); aviation rigger (Great Lakes, m); carpenter's mate (Hampton Roads, m); musician (Hampton Roads, m); all commissary schools, dis.; radio (Newport, San Francisco: m)
1923	Photography (Pensacola, m); pigeon training (Washington, e); radio (Hampton Roads, m); torpedo (San Diego, m)
1924	Aviation parachute (Lakehurst, e); coppersmith (Hampton Roads, m); radio (San Diego, m); submarine (New London, e, for men with no submarine experience); yeoman, musician (San Diego, m)
1925	Aerography (Washington, m, trans. to Lakehurst, 1929); bugle (San Diego, m); cooks and bakers (Hampton Roads, e, dis. 1933); electrician (San Diego, e); fire controlman (Washington, m); gyrocompass (New York, e); pharmacist's mate (Washington, m); radio material (San Diego, Washington: e); sound (San Diego, e, dis. 1933; New London, e, dis. 1933)
1926	Aviation general utility (Great Lakes, e); recruiter (Hampton Roads, San Diego: e); stenography (Hampton Roads, e, dis. 1933; San Diego, e)
1927	Aviation instrument (Philadelphia, m); aviation pilot (Pensacola, m); boilermaker (Hampton Roads, m); cooks and bakers, buglemaster (San Diego, e)
1928	Deep-sea diving (Washington, e); dental technician (Washington, m)
1929	Aerography (Lakehurst, trans. from Washington); aviation electroplating (Great Lakes, m); aviation pilot elimination (Hampton Roads, San Diego: e); gyrocompass (San Diego, m); hospital corps (San Diego, trans. from San Francisco); radio (Cavite, P.I., m)
1930	Aviation ordnance man (Hampton Roads, e); interior communication (Washington, e); lighter-than-air craft (Lakehurst, m); officers' stewards and cooks (Hampton Roads, e, dis. 1933)
1931	Slide film (Washington, m); sound motion-picture technician (New York, San Diego: e)
1932	Mess attendants (Hampton Roads, e); officers' stewards and cooks (San Diego, e)
1933	Aviation mechanic (Norfolk, trans. from Great Lakes)
1935	Diesel engine (New London, e); musician (Washington, e)
1936	Aviation machinist's mate, aviation metalsmith (Norfolk, m)
1939	Automatic pilot (El Segundo, Calif., New York: m); bombsight (Dahlgren, Va., Pearl Harbor, San Diego: m); echo sounding (Boston, m); gas mask (Englewood Arsenal, Md., m); parachute (San Diego, m); sound motion-picture technician (Cavite, P.I., m); torpedo (Pearl Harbor, m); welder (San Diego, m)

SOURCE: The Navy Department did not keep a central file concerning the opening and closing of its schools. The information for this table was collected from scattered references to schools in the *Annual Report of the Chief of the Bureau of Navigation* for the years 1890-1940 and in the General Correspondence files of the Records of the Bureau of Naval Personnel, National Archives and Records Service, Washington, D.C. Given the limitations of the sources, this table is meant not to be definitive but to demonstrate the growth and increasing diversity of the navy's educational system.

NOTE: It is often not possible to determine when a school was officially opened. For some schools, the date in the table represents the official establishment, but for others the year is the first mention of the school that I have found in the records. The former are marked with an "e" and the latter with an "m." (Schools marked "m," of course, may have been established in an earlier year.) Other abbreviations used in the table are "dis." for "discontinued" and "trans." for "transferred." These designations are used only when the sources provide a specific date for the closing or moving of a school; not all schools without these markings can be assumed to have remained in operation until 1939. Charleston is Charleston, South Carolina, Lakehurst is in New Jersey, and Washington is Washington, D.C.

Table 9 • **Rating Changes, 1866-1939**

Year	Established	Disestablished	Changed
1866[a]	Machinist		Surgeon's steward to apothecary
1867			Paymaster's steward to paymaster's writer
1868		Surgeon's steward in charge	
1869	Boilermaker; coppersmith; seaman gunner; ship's printer; ship's tailor	Boatswain's mate in charge	
1870	Bayman; ship's barber	Gunner's mate in charge	Baker to ship's baker; paymaster's writer to paymaster's yeoman 1c, 2c, 3c
1871	Bugler; ordinary seaman, engineer's force; seaman, engineer's force		
1874	Engineer's yeoman		
1876	Jack of the dust; ordinary seaman 2c; ship's lamplighter		
1878			Paymaster's yeoman 1c, 2c, 3c to paymaster's yeoman
1879	Blacksmith	Coppersmith	
1880	Engineer's blacksmith; engineer's force blacksmith; finisher	Machinist	
1883	Apprentice 1c, 2c, 3c[b]; cook to commandant of yard; electrician	Signal quartermaster; ordinary seaman, engineer's force	
1884	Coxswain to commandant of yard; equipment yeoman; musician C; oiler; ship's yeoman; steward to commandant of navy yard; water tender	Armorer; armorer's mate; assistant cook; bag room keeper; cooper; electrician; nurse (male); ship's baker; ship's carpenter; yeoman; seaman, engineer's force	Boilermaker to machinist 2c, 3c; boy 1c, 2c, 3c to boy; engineer's blacksmith and engineer's force blacksmith included in blacksmith; finisher to machinist 1c, 2c; machinist 1c to

Table 9 *continued*

Year	Established	Disestablished	Changed
			machinist; painter 1c to painter
1885	Attendant; captain of maintop	Lamp cleaner; ordinary seaman 2c	Master of bands to bandmaster; ship's barber to barber; carpenter and caulker to two ratings (carpenter, caulker); ship's lamplighter to lamplighter; ship's tailor to tailor
1891	Gun captain		
1893	Boatswain's mate 1c, 2c; coppersmith (reestablished); gunner's mate 1c, 2c, 3c; mess attendant; plumber and fitter; sailmaker; quartermaster 1c, 2c, 3c; ship's cook 4c; shipwright; writer 2c, 3c	Barber; boy; captain of the: afterguard, forecastle, hold, maintop, mizzentop; carpenter; caulker; coxswain to commandant of yard; engineer's yeoman; equipment yeoman; jack of the dust; lamplighter; paymaster's yeoman; quarter gunner; ship's corporal; tailor	Carpenter's mate to carpenter's mate C, 1c, 2c, 3c; coal heaver to coal passer; musician C to first musician; ship's printer to printer; ship's cook to ship's cook 1c, 2c, 3c; ship's writer to writer 1c; ship's yeoman to yeoman; attendant to mess attendant
1895			Machinist to machinist C, 1c, 2c
1896	Yeoman C		Writer 1c, 2c, 3c to yeoman 1c, 2c, 3c
1897			Gun captain to gun captain C, 1c, 2c
1898	Electrician (reestablished) C, 1c, 2c		Apothecary to hospital steward; bayman to hospital apprentice and hospital apprentice 1c
1899	Landsman for training[c]		
1900	Electrician 3c	Sailmaker; schoolmaster	
1902	Baker 1c, 2c; commissary steward; painter 1c; shipfitter 1c, 2c		Mess attendant to mess attendant 1c, 2c, 3c; painter included in

Table 9 *continued*

Year	Established	Disestablished	Changed
			painter 2c and 3c; painter 2c included in landsman
1903	Turret captain C, 1c; water tender C		
1904	Apprentice seaman	Apprentice 1c, 2c, 3c; landsman for training[c]; gun captain C, 1c, 2c	Machinist C, 1c, 2c to machinist's mate C, 1c, 2c
1916	Storekeeper		
1917	Blacksmith 1c; engineman 1c, 2c; molder 1c, 2c; patternmaker 1c, 2c; special mechanic C, lc		Blacksmith to blacksmith 2c; coal passer to fireman 3c; coppersmith to coppersmith 1c, 2c; hospital steward to pharmacist's mate; ordinary seaman to seaman 2c; hospital apprentice to hospital apprentice 2c
1918	Chief winch (in use during World War I)		Printer to printer C, 1c
1920	Bugler 1c		Bugler to bugler 2c
1921	Aviation carpenter's mate; aviation machinist's mate C, 1c, 2c; aviation metalsmith; aviation rigger; baker 3c; motor machinist C, 1c, 2c; photographer; printer 2c 3c; radioman; shipfitter C, 3c; signalman; torpedoman; water tender 1c, 2c	Cook to commandant of yard; cook to CINC; coxswain to CINC; landsman; master at arms; oiler; plumber and fitter; seaman gunner; special mechanic C, 1c; steward to commandant of navy yard; steward to CINC; ship's cook 4c	Boilermaker to boilermaker 1c, 2c; electrician to electrician's mate; sailmaker's mate to sailmaker's mate 1c, 2c, 3c; seaman to seaman 1c, 2c; shipwright included in seaman 1c
1923			Cabin cook to officers' cook 1c; cabin steward to officers' steward 1c; steerage cook and wardroom cook to officers' cook 2c; warrant officers' cook to

Table 9 *continued*

Year	Established	Disestablished	Changed
			officers' cook 3c; steerage steward and wardroom steward to officers' steward 2c; warrant officers' steward to officers' steward 3c
1924	Aerographer; aviation pilot		
1926	Aviation machinist's mate 3c; aviation ordnanceman; blacksmith 3c; boilermaker 3c; machinist's mate 3c; molder 3c; motor machinist 3c; telegrapher	Motor machinist C, 1c, 2c, 3c	Aviation rigger to aviation machinist's mate
1927	Aviation pilot C, 1c; boilermaker C; buglemaster; metalsmith C		
1928		Boilermaker C, 1c, 2c, 3c	
1929		Blacksmith 3c; machinist 3c; molder 3c	
1931		Commissary steward; engineman 1c, 2c	
1936			Blacksmith 1c, 2c, and coppersmith 1c, 2c to metalsmith 1c, 2c
1939			Sailmaker's mate included in boatswain's mate and coxswain

SOURCE: Compiled from U.S., Navy Department, Bureau of Naval Personnel, Recorder, Permanent Board for Control of the Enlisted Rating Structure, *Compilation of Enlisted Ratings and Apprenticeships, U.S. Navy, 1775 to the Present* (mimeographed, September 1967). The symbols C, 1c, 2c, and 3c stand for chief, first class, second class, and third class, respectively.

[a]The ratings in existence at the end of 1865 were armorer; armorer's mate; assistant cook; bag room keeper; baker; boatswain's mate; boatswain's mate in charge; boy 1c, 2c, 3c; captain of the: afterguard, forecastle, hold, mizzentop; carpenter and caulker; carpenter's mate; coal heaver; coxswain; coxswain to CINC; cooper; fireman 1c, 2c; gunner's mate; gunner's mate C; gunner's mate in charge; lamp cleaner;

Table 9 *continued*

landsman; master-at-arms; master of bands; nurse (male); cabin steward; cabin cook; cook to CINC; steerage cook; wardroom cook; warrant officers' cook; ordinary seaman; painter 1c, 2c; paymaster's steward; quarter gunner; quartermaster; quartermaster C; sailmaker's mate; schoolmaster; seaman; ship's carpenter; ship's cook; ship's corporal; ship's writer; signal quartermaster; steerage steward; steward to CINC; surgeon's steward; surgeon's steward in charge; wardroom steward; warrant officers' steward; yeoman.

[b]From 1875 to 1883 the apprentice program had used the ratings of boy 1c, 2c, 3c to designate youths under training.

[c]Even though landsman for training was not technically a new rating but was a grouping within the older landsman category, the importance of the landsman for training designation in the development of naval personnel policy warrants its inclusion in this table. See chapter 4.

Table 10 • **General Court-Martial Trials: Selected Offenses of Enlisted Men**

Fiscal Year	Absence over Leave or without Leave	Assaulting a Superior	Conduct to the Prejudice of Good Order and Discipline	Desertion	Disobeying an Order	Drunkenness
1904	231	..	...	394	...	...
1905	147	..	...	447	...	...
1906	241	..	...	622	52	...
1907	324	..	...	574	38	18
1908	468	..	41	969	...	40
1909	256	4	59	950	39	38
1910	332	10	41	651	21	17
1911	276	10	31	590	33	14
1912	291	3	40	600	43	16
1913	181	4	45	671	28	15
1914	135	8	57	843	18	26
1915	398	3	15	709	17	26
1916	319	6	41	599	7	15
1917	385	13	42	697	17	15
1918	1,416	47	137	1,174	85	141
1919	2,928	19	173	535	125	243
1920	1,570	26	49	849	87	68
1921	1,799	31	91	1,476	86	86
1922	426	18	67	620	39	70
1923	398	13	30	345	23	53
1924	752	11	29	1,080	19	42
1925	593	16	50	935	15	73
1926	371	18	34	609	15	52
1927	388	25	31	798	14	44
1928	421	20	46	884	16	50
1929	273	16	29	681	19	45
1930	204	13	20	720	11	35
1931	110	..	35	621	9	41
1932	72	1	31	503	5	34
1933	52	4	31	285	5	40
1934	69	1	32	229	9	31
1935	39	2	21	136	7	30
1936	30	..	17	114	1	22
1937	35	2	22	104	6	29
1938	49	1	42	163	6	34
1939	17	2	17	103	2	12

SOURCE: *Annual Report of the Judge Advocate General* for the years 1904-39.

Table 10 *continued*

Fraudulent Enlistment	Scandalous Conduct Tending to the Destruction of Good Morals	Sodomy	Robbery and Theft	Abusive, Obscene, or Threatening Language	Falsehood	Sleeping on Watch
64	...	..	...	..	..	..
33	...	..	...	..	..	..
135	...	4	...	..	..	..
145	38	4	26	..	..	2
145	23	14	23	..	..	..
168	28	4	31	16	4	2
135	33	5	33	7	2	5
151	33	9	25	7	2	1
169	35	5	26	4	1	2
181	43	9	35	1	1	..
122	29	7	38	4	..	3
81	21	7	36	6	2	3
81	47	3	55	6	3	..
72	47	7	23	7	2	18
14	205	19	101	42	9	94
7	243	16	124	45	11	67
76	111	37	214	16	5	1
58	144	20	160	10	6	2
6	81	10	92	2	3	4
53	51	3	42	2	3	..
26	52	1	45	..	1	..
2	42	7	38	..	1	8
3	53	2	52	..	3	3
...	49	10	34	..	5	5
1	58	1	53	..	1	1
...	53	5	47	..	3	2
...	67	2	40	..	4	1
3	48	1	19	5	9	..
2	28	2	7	5	4	1
...	46	2	8	..	10	..
...	39	..	12	1	10	..
...	28	..	9	1	6	1
...	25	4	9	1	3	2
...	31	..	12	1	2	..
...	26	4	14	4	5	..
...	18	..	10	..	..	..

Table 11 • **Desertion, 1900-1940**

Fiscal Year	Enlisted Force June 30	Number of Desertions	Desertions as Percentage of Enlisted Force
1900	16,832	2,452	14.5
1901	18,825	3,158	16.8
1902	21,433	3,037	14.1
1903	27,245	4,136	15.1
1904	29,321	4,488	15.3
1905	30,804	4,427	14.4
1906	32,163	4,867	15.1
1907	33,027	5,105	15.5
1908	39,048	6,054	15.5
1909	42,861	3,836	8.8
1910	45,076	3,549	7.9
1911	47,612	3,284	6.9
1912	47,515	3,055	6.4
1913	48,068	3,237	6.7
1914	52,667	2,728	5.2
1915	52,561	2,320	4.4
1916	54,234	2,064	3.8
1917	100,539	2,826	2.8
1918	435,406	3,133	.7
1919	250,833	6,138	2.5
1920	108,950	10,036	9.5
1921	119,205	10,261	8.6
1922	85,580	not available	
1923	82,355	5,820	7.1
1924	87,327	7,787	8.9
1925	84,289	4,657	4.9
1926	82,161	2,675	3.2
1927	83,566	3,123	3.8
1928	84,355	2,906	3.5
1929	85,321	2,055	2.4
1930	84,938	1,884	2.2
1931	80,910	1,123	1.4
1932	81,120	757	.9
1933	79,243	604	.8
1934	80,359	580	.7
1935	82,839	332	.4
1936	93,077	318	.3
1937	100,178	467	.5
1938	104,888	473	.5
1939	110,196	338	.3
1940	139,554	442	.3

SOURCE: *Annual Report of the Chief of the Bureau of Navigation* for the years 1900-1940.

Table 12 • **Enlisted Men Tried by Courts-Martial, 1909-39**

Fiscal Year	Enlisted Force[a]	General Courts-Martial		Summary Courts-Martial		Deck Courts	
		Number	Percent	Number	Percent	Number	Percent
1909	57,769	1,781	3.08	7,630	13.21	1,320	2.28
1910	54,791	1,339	2.44	8,457	15.43	10,915	19.92
1911	61,832	1,226	1.98	8,246	13.33	10,763	17.40
1912	65,286	1,265	1.94	9,202	14.09	7,214	11.05
1913	65,126	1,295	1.99	9,946	15.27	7,285	11.18
1914	67,015	1,342	2.00	7,542	11.25	5,603	8.36
1915	71,511	1,384	1.93	9,084	12.70	5,515	7.71
1916	72,885	1,239	1.70	8,274	11.35	4,570	6.27
1917	81,097	1,423	1.75	7,979	9.83	4,003	4.93
1918	378,858	4,428	1.17	14,552	3.84	10,654	2.81
1919	393,802	4,900	1.24	21,101	5.36	15,819	4.02
1920	137,456	3,217	2.34	20,311	14.78	12,321	8.96
1921	not available						
1922	98,946	1,624	1.74	12,702	12.74	9,990	10.01
1923	83,185	1,154	1.39	9,795	11.77	7,135	5.58
1924	85,603	2,204	2.57	9,057	10.58	5,452	6.37
1925	85,945	1,880	2.18	9,384	10.91	6,045	7.00
1926	82,128	1,307	1.59	8,619	10.49	5,331	6.49
1927	82,932	1,485	1.79	8,224	9.91	5,343	6.44
1928	84,010	1,612	1.92	8,639	10.28	4,945	5.88
1929	84,443	1,269	1.50	7,719	9.14	4,693	5.55
1930	85,270	1,181	1.38	6,058	7.10	4,100	4.70
1931	82,564	866	1.05	6,252	7.55	3,728	4.36
1932	80,711	692	.86	5,387	6.70	3,476	4.31
1933	80,735	457	.57	5,048	6.25	3,168	3.92
1934	78,260	394	.50	4,352	5.56	2,836	3.62
1935	81,510	261	.32	3,100	3.80	2,455	3.01
1936	86,574	223	.26	3,090	3.53	2,039	2.33
1937	96,360	228	.24	3,127	3.25	2,057	2.13
1938	102,509	352	.34	3,869	3.77	2,442	2.38
1939	107,594	265	.25	3,677	3.42	2,653	2.47

SOURCE: *Annual Report of the Judge Advocate General* for the years 1909-39.

[a]For 1909-16 this column gives the total number of men in the navy during the fiscal year; for 1917-39 it lists the average number of men under naval jurisdiction during each year.

Table 13 • **Daily Schedule of a Man-of-War**

2:00 a.m.	Relieve wheel and lookouts.
3:50	Call the watch section.
4:00	Relieve the watch. Muster the watch section and lifeboat's crew. Light smoking lamp. Call ship's cooks of the watch. Five minutes before sunrise station details at running lights. Turn off at sunrise. Relieve lookouts and station masthead lookouts.
5:00	Call idlers and section of the watch sleeping in. Coffee.
5:20	Pipe sweepers.
5:30	Turn to; out smoking lamp. Execute morning orders.
6:00	Relieve the wheel and lookout. Trice up clothesline.
6:45	Hammock stowers haul back hammock cloths.
7:00	Up all hammocks.
7:15	Hammock stowers stop down hammock cloths. Mess gear. Light smoking lamp.
7:30	Breakfast. Shift into the uniform of the day during the meal hour.
8:00	Relieve the watch (both sections on deck). Muster watch and life-boat's crew.
8:15	Turn to. Out smoking lamp. Deck and gun bright work.
8:30	Sick call.
8:45	Knock off bright work. Sweep down. Stow away ditty boxes and wash deck gear. Take down towel lines. Clear up decks for quarters.
9:10	Officers' call. Divisions fall in for quarters.
9:15	Quarters for muster and inspection. Physical drill, and drills as prescribed.
10:00	Relieve wheel and masthead.
11:30	Retreat from drill. Pipe down washed clothes, if dry. Sweep down.
11:45	Mess gear.
12:00 noon	Dinner.
12:30 p.m.	Relieve the watch.
1:00	Turn to. Pipe sweepers. Out smoking lamp.
1:45	Drill call, if ordered.
2:00	Relieve wheel and masthead.
2:15	Retreat from drill. Pipe sweepers. Turn to.
3:30	Pipe down wash clothes, if up.
4:00	Relieve the watch. Muster watch and lifeboat's crew.
4:30	Sweep down. Knock off ship's work. Light smoking lamp. Five minutes before sunset station details at running lights. Turn on running lights with senior ship present. Station deck lookouts. Muster life-boat's crew. Inspect lifeboats.
5:30	Clear up decks. Stow away ditty boxes.
5:45	Mess gear.
6:00	Supper. Relieve the wheel and lookouts.
6:30	Turn to. Sweep down. Wet down after main deck.
7:00	Band concert for crew until 8:00.
7:30	Hammocks. No smoking below decks.
8:00	Call the watch. Relieve the wheel and lookouts. Relieve the watch. Muster watch and lifeboat's crew. Turn out all but standing lights and lights in officers' quarters and chief petty officers' mess room.
9:00	Out smoking lamp. Turn out lights in chief petty officers' mess room.

Table 13 *continued*

10:00	Relieve the wheel and lookout. Turn out lights in officers' quarters unless an extension has been granted.
11:50	Call the watch.
Midnight	Relieve the watch, Muster the watch and lifeboat crew.

SOURCE: *The Bluejacket's Manual, 1918,* 6th ed. (New York: Edwin N. Appleton, 1918), pp. 131-32.

Abbreviations Used in the Notes

ADM	Admiral
BUEQUIP	Bureau of Equipment and Recruiting
BUNAV	Bureau of Navigation
CAPT	Captain
CDR	Commander
CINC	Commander in chief
CNO	Chief of naval operations
CO	Commanding officer
GC	General Correspondence
GPO	Government Printing Office
JAG	Judge advocate general
LC	Manuscript Division, Library of Congress, Washington, D.C.
LCDR	Lieutenant commander
LT	Lieutenant
NA	National Archives and Records Service, Washington, D.C.
NHF	Naval Historical Foundation Collection, Washington, D.C.
NTS	Naval training station
RADM	Rear admiral
RG 24	Records of the Bureau of Naval Personnel, Record Group 24
RG 38	Records of the Office of the Chief of Naval Operations, Record Group 38
RG 45	Naval Records Collection of the Office of Naval Records and Library, Record Group 45
RG 52	Records of the Bureau of Medicine and Surgery, Record Group 52
RG 80	Records of the Department of the Navy, Record Group 80
RG 125	Records of the Office of the Judge Advocate General (Navy), Record Group 125
RG 181	Records of Naval Districts and Shore Establishments, Record Group 181
RG 350	Records of the Bureau of Insular Affairs, Record Group 350
SECNAV	Secretary of the navy
SHC	Southern Historical Collection, University of North Carolina, Chapel Hill
USNIP	*United States Naval Institute Proceedings*

NOTE: There was no standard form of naval abbreviations during the period between the Spanish-American War and World War II. Where appropriate, I have followed the usage of Bill Wedertz, ed., *Dictionary of Naval Abbreviations* (Annapolis, Md.: U.S. Naval Institute, 1970).

Notes

CHAPTER 1

1. U.S., Navy Department, BUNAV, *The Making of a Man-o'-Warsman* (New York: Street & Finney, 1906).

2. For general histories of the navy and the development of a modern fleet, see Harold and Margaret Sprout, *The Rise of American Naval Power, 1776-1918* (Princeton: Princeton University Press, 1939); Charles Oscar Paullin, *Paullin's History of Naval Administration, 1775-1911: A Collection of Articles from the U.S. Naval Institute "Proceedings"* (Annapolis, Md.: U.S. Naval Institute, 1968); E. B. Potter and Chester W. Nimitz, eds., *Sea Power: A Naval History* (Englewood Cliffs, N.J.: Prentice-Hall, 1960); Dudley W. Knox, *A History of the United States Navy* (New York: G. P. Putnam's Sons, 1948); and Donald W. Mitchell, *History of the Modern American Navy from 1883 through Pearl Harbor* (New York: Alfred A. Knopf, 1946).

3. The navy had had some experience with steam before 1842. During the War of 1812, Robert Fulton had designed a steam-powered battery called the *Demologos* (later renamed the *Fulton*), but the war ended before the ship was completed, and the vessel was used only as a receiving ship. In 1837 the navy launched the *Fulton II* as an experiment with steam. The success of the *Fulton II* led to the construction of the *Mississippi* and *Missouri*. Potter and Nimitz, *Sea Power*, pp. 237-38.

4. U.S., Department of Commerce, Bureau of the Census, *Historical Statistics of the United States, Colonial Times to 1957* (Washington: GPO, 1960), pp. 736-37.

5. N. H. Farquhar, "Inducements for Retaining Trained Seamen in the Navy, and Best System of Rewards for Long and Faithful Service," *USNIP* 11 (1885): 176, 178.

6. Even though the navy required some men to operate the steam equipment it did use, its needs for these men did not upset the existing personnel system, for they could either be trained on the job or enlisted from the men who worked the machinery in the merchant marine. In addition, the engine-room force composed a comparatively small proportion of the crew.

7. See, for example, "The Great Naval Review," *Review of Reviews* 7 (1893): 391; and "The Display of the Ships," *New York Times*, April 28, 1893, p. 4.

8. *New York Times*, March 26, 1917, p. 1; and Josephus Daniels, *Our Navy at War* (Washington: Pictorial Bureau, 1922), p. 33.

9. Daniels, *Our Navy at War*, pp. 311-12. The 1918 number includes members of the reserve on active duty.

10. U.S., Navy Department, BUNAV, *Annual Report of the Chief of the Bureau of Navigation, 1920*, pp. 573, 579 (hereafter cited as *Annual Report of the Chief BUNAV*, with the appropriate year).

11. See Appendix, table 1, for authorized strength and Appendix, table 5, for actual strength.

12. Harold Wool, *The Military Specialist: Skilled Manpower for the Armed Forces* (Baltimore: Johns Hopkins Press, 1968), pp. 19-22.

CHAPTER 2

1. Earl English, Chief BUEQUIP, to Commodore J. H. Upshur, Commandant New York, May 29, 1883, Press Copies of Letters Sent to the Commandant of the New York Navy Yard, 19:337-38, Records of the BUEQUIP, RG 24, NA. Emphasis in the original.

2. Enlistment on vessels composed 33.2 percent of enlistments in 1870, 55.8 percent in 1880, and 42.2 percent in 1890. Compiled from a random sample of enlistment returns for the years 1870, 1880, and 1890. Enlistment returns were submitted weekly by rendezvous and quarterly by vessels. The forms enumerate the men who had enlisted either at the rendezvous or aboard ship over the given period and contain information such as the individual's place of birth, age, previous occupation, and physical description.

3. Silas Casey to CAPT R. W. Shufeldt, Chief BUEQUIP, July 27, 1875, Letterbook of Portsmouth, p. 2, Silas Casey Papers, Box 2, NHF, LC.

4. RADM Jno. Rodgers to CAPT R. W. Shufeldt, Chief BUEQUIP, May 5, 1873, and Geo. M. Robeson, SECNAV, to President, May 8, 1875, Letters Received from the SECNAV, 3:109-12, Records of the BUEQUIP, RG 24, NA.

5. See, for example, the comments of John Rodgers, Commandant Mare Island, to RADM Wm. Reynolds, Chief BUEQUIP, December 12, 1874, No. 136, Letters Received from the Commandant of the Mare Island Navy Yard, 2:unnumbered, Records of the BUEQUIP, RG 24, NA; and Thos. S. Phelps, Commandant Mare Island, to Commodore Earl English, Chief BUEQUIP, January 4, 1883, Letters Received from the Commandant of the Mare Island Navy Yard, 6:164, Records of the BUEQUIP, RG 24, NA.

6. CAPT Wm. A. Parker, CO Receiving Ship *Independence*, to Commodore M. Smith, Chief BUEQUIP, February 8, 1868, Letters Received from Officers, 48:13-14, Records of the BUEQUIP, RG 24, NA.

7. Statement by Jno. Simon (signed with X), August 2, 1869, Letters Received from Officers, 58:26-27, Records of the BUEQUIP, RG 24, NA. See also telegrams from Belknap, Commandant Mare Island, to Commodore Schley, Chief BUEQUIP, January 21, 1889, Correspondence of Mare Island Navy Yard with BUEQUIP, 11:292, RG 181, NA.

8. Muster rolls were forms on which commanding officers of vessels or shore stations listed the men serving under them at a particular date—in the case of the sample analyzed, men who were aboard ship during the quarters ending June 30 of 1870, 1880, and 1890. The forms contain information such as previous occupation, rating, place of birth, and physical description.

There was a slight shift in occupations from 1870 to 1890. The number of men who listed mariner as their previous occupation in the muster rolls fell from 38.3 percent in 1870 to 34.7 percent in 1890, while men with previous occupations useful in the engine room rose from 8.3 percent to 13.0 percent. Enlistment returns show essentially the same pattern. This change reflects the gradual retirement of older ships during the 1880s and the beginning of modernization of the fleet.

Even with the slight shift in the type of men enlisted, as reflected in previous occupations, it was still possible for traditional methods to obtain recruits familiar with the duties of the deck or engine-room forces because of their service in the merchant marine. The movement of sailors, of course, went in both directions, and the department undoubtedly lost men who had learned or upgraded their skills in the navy and then transferred to civilian employment; unfortunately, it is not possible to determine the size of this group.

9. Harold D. Langley, *Social Reform in the United States Navy, 1798-1862* (Urbana: University of Illinois Press, 1967), p. 71.

10. Muster rolls, in fact, usually show a gap of only a few days between the date of enlistment and the date a recruit was received on board ship.

11. CDR E. K. Owen to Commodore Wm. Reynolds, Chief BUEQUIP, October 31, 1870, Letters Received from Officers, 66:302, and reply of Wm. Reynolds to RADM O. H. Davis, November 14, 1870, Press Copies of Letters Sent to the Commandant of the Norfolk Navy Yard, 3:297, Records of the BUEQUIP, RG 24, NA.

I have found no written policies limiting blacks during the latter half of the nineteenth century. In contrast, in 1842 Secretary of the Navy Abel P. Upshur had informed the House of Representatives that "not more than one-twentieth part of the crew of any vessel is allowed to consist of negroes." U.S., Congress, House, *Colored Persons in the Navy of the United States* (27th Cong., 2d sess., 1842), H. Doc. 282. It is possible, of course, that there was an unwritten code restricting black enlistment in the latter part of the nineteenth century.

12. Information on black sailors is derived from my enumeration of blacks recorded in enlistment returns for 1870, 1880, and 1890. A study of muster rolls for the quarters ending June 30 of the same years shows that blacks made up about the same proportion of the entire enlisted force. As a part of a sailor's physical description, these forms requested information on "complexion." Blacks were listed as "Negro," "mulatto," and, more rarely, as "black," "quadroon," or "octoroon." It is also probable that a few men described as "dark" could be considered blacks, but none has been included in the count because there is no satisfactory method to distinguish these individuals from dark-skinned Caucasians. These statistics are thus conservative.

13. My study of muster rolls shows that the proportion of blacks who were apprentices increased from 3.2 percent in 1880 to 13.6 percent in 1890.

14. From my study of blacks listed in muster rolls for 1870, 1880, and 1890. The three categories of cook, steward, and landsman accounted for 75.4 percent of black enlisted men in 1870, 76.9 percent in 1880, and 52.9 percent in 1890. (In contrast, these billets constituted only 32 percent of all enlisted men in 1870, 22.2 percent in 1880, and 18.2 percent in 1890.)

The decrease in those three categories from 1880 to 1890 results from an increase in the number of blacks serving as coal heavers and apprentices. Black coal heavers rose from 0.6 percent of black enlisted men in 1880 to 6.1 percent in 1890; this change does not represent a breakthrough for blacks so much as the navy's change from its practice of assigning landsmen to the job to a policy of using men specifically designated as "coal heaver." On the other hand, the proportion of blacks who were apprentices increased, as has been seen.

15. Jonathan H. Paynter, *Joining the Navy; or, Abroad with Uncle Sam* (Hartford, Conn.: American Publishing Co., 1895), p. 19. Paynter served as cabin boy aboard the *Juniata* and *Ossippee* in 1884. For the establishment of the messmen rating, see William S. Edwards, "Enlisted Ratings Established in the Naval Service by the Act of 1 July 1797 and Subsequent Action" (Bureau of Naval Personnel, 1951; typescript in Navy Department Library), p. 16.

16. CAPT S. P. Quackenbush, CO Receiving Ship *New Hampshire*, to Commodore T. H. Stevens, Commandant Norfolk, December 5, 1874, Letters Received from the Commandant of the Norfolk Navy Yard, 2:unnumbered, Records of the BUEQUIP, RG 24, NA. The bureau reply did not refer to race but merely said that the required men would be sent to Norfolk from New York. Acting Chief BUEQUIP to Commodore T. H. Stevens,

December 7, 1874, Press Copies of Letters Sent to the Commandant of the Norfolk Navy Yard, 5:266, Records of the BUEQUIP, RG 24, NA.

17. The proportion of black enlistees who were born in Virginia and Maryland increased from 38.1 percent in 1870 to 54.6 percent in 1880 and 56.1 percent in 1890. In contrast, the percentage of blacks who were born in New York and Pennsylvania declined from 13.9 percent in 1870 to 6.2 percent in 1880 and 5.2 percent in 1890. The changes are even more dramatic when compared to the pre-Civil War navy. In 1855, Virginia and Maryland had been the place of birth of 32.1 percent of black enlistees and New York and Pennsylvania of 28.2 percent. From my study of blacks listed in enlistment returns for 1855, 1870, 1880, and 1890.

18. S. B. Luce to SECNAV, November 12, 1872, GC, Box 7, Stephen B. Luce Papers, NHF, LC.

19. 2d Endorsement, signed by F. M. Ramsay, Chief BUNAV, October 17, 1894, No. 35161, Press Copies of Letters Sent, 66:39, RG 24, NA. A similar statement is found in F. M. Ramsay to CO U.S.S. *Richmond*, January 10, 1896, No. 51117, BUNAV Press Copies of Letters Sent, 83:654-55, RG 24, NA.

20. LCDR Francis A. Bunce to Commodore John Rodgers, November 26, 1865, Box 11, John Rodgers (1812-82) Papers, which are part of Rodgers Family Papers, NHF, LC.

21. The abolition of the grog ration in 1862 and of flogging in 1850 were the most important changes in the life of sailors in the first part of the nineteenth century. The impetus for both reforms came from humanitarians outside the service; neither measure, however, produced the improvement in the enlisted force that its advocates had anticipated. For a history of both efforts, see Langley, *Social Reform in the United States Navy*, pp. 131-269.

22. Albert Leary Gihon, "Practical Suggestions in Naval Hygiene," in U.S., Navy Department, Bureau of Medicine and Surgery, *Medical Essays* (Washington: GPO, 1873), p. 1.

23. Charles F. Goodrich, "Hygienic Notes on Ships' Bilges," *USNIP* 2 (1876): 96.

24. U.S., Navy Department, Bureau of Medicine and Surgery, *Annual Report of the Surgeon General, 1881* (Washington: GPO, 1881), p. 517. For similar remarks on heads, see ibid., p. 563; Gihon, "Naval Hygiene," p. 40; and "The Laws of Hygiene as Applied to Berthing, Messing, Ventilation, and Interior Arrangements of Men-of-War," discussion by the Naval Institute, Boston Branch, September 30, 1880, in *USNIP* 6 (1880): 352.

25. Gihon, "Naval Hygiene," p. 45.

26. *Annual Report of the Surgeon General, 1881*, p. 405.

27. Gihon, "Naval Hygiene," p. 39. See also "The Laws of Hygiene," p. 352; and *Annual Report of the Surgeon General, 1884*, p. 363. For examples of experimentation with mechanical ventilation, see G. W. Baird, "The Ventilation of Ships," *USNIP* 6 (1880): 256-57.

28. U.S., Navy Department, Bureau of Equipment and Recruiting, *Annual Report of the Chief of the Bureau of Equipment and Recruiting, 1876* (Washington: GPO, 1876), p. 107 (hereafter cited as *Annual Report of the Chief BUEQUIP*, with the appropriate year). Among the examples Shufeldt later cited to point up discrepancies in space allotments were the *Swatara*, which had 324 cubic feet per officer and 58 cubic feet per man, and the *Miantonomoh*, which had 1,158 cubic feet per officer and 81 cubic feet per man. Ibid., *1877*, unnumbered page after p. 122.

29. U.S., Navy Department, *Annual Report of the Secretary of the Navy, 1866* (Washington: GPO, 1866), p. 34 (hereafter cited as *Annual Report of the SECNAV*, with the appropriate year).

30. Chief BUNAV to Commandant Mare Island, June 30, 1893, No. 21928, Press Copies of Letters Sent, 48:311, RG 24, NA. Chief BUNAV to CO Receiving Ship *Independence*,

Mare Island, June 30, 1893, No. 21928, Press Copies of Letters Sent, 48:312, RG 24, NA. CAPT H. Harrison, Commandant Mare Island, to CO Receiving Ship *Independence*, July 5, 1893, Correspondence of Commandant of Mare Island to CO Receiving Ship *Independence*, 3:389-90, RG 181, NA.

31. Both ideas were recommended almost yearly. See, for example, *Annual Report of the Chief BUEQUIP, 1875*, p. 85, and *1885*, pp.196-97. *Annual Report of the SECNAV, 1866*, p. 36, *1876*, p. 11, and *1877*, pp. 25, 28.

32. The continuous-service payment was established under a general order of April 7, 1855. See also Gihon, "Naval Hygiene," p. 124. In 1899 the bonus was increased to four months' pay, and the period of eligibility for reenlistment under continuous service was extended to four months after expiration of enlistment. Act of March 3, 1899, in U.S., *Statutes at Large*, 30:1008. A sample of enlistment returns shows that 5.1 percent of the men enlisting in 1870 had continuous service, 12.9 percent in 1880, and 14.6 percent in 1890. Reenlistment rates are not available for the nineteenth century.

33. For a history of the Naval Pension Fund, see U.S., House, Committee on Naval Affairs, *Hearings: Sundry Legislation Affecting the Naval Establishment, 1925-26* (69th Cong., 1st sess., 1926), pp. 119-20. For the assignment of men to receiving ships, see "Crews of Receiving and Stationary Ships," Order 17, signed by Chief BUNAV, October 1, 1891, Press Copies of Letters Sent, 19:133, RG 24, NA, and Chief BUNAV to CO U.S.S. *Constellation*, October 17, 1894, Press Copies of Letters Sent, 67:472, RG 24, NA.

34. The navy did not always publish the number of desertions, but it did so often enough to give a good idea of the problem. In 1876, 1,203 men deserted, 818 in 1877, 669 in 1878, 941 in 1886, 773 in 1887, 1,121 in 1888, 749 in 1889, 1,388 in 1891, 1,360 in 1892, and 1,259 in 1893. *Annual Report of the Chief BUEQUIP* for the years 1878 and 1886-89, and *Annual Report of the Chief BUNAV* for the years 1891-93.

35. CAPT Wm. G. Temple to Commodore William Reynolds, Chief BUEQUIP, April 17, 1871, Letters Received from Officers, 70:247-48, Records of the BUEQUIP, RG 24, NA. The *Tennessee* had a crew of 413 men. Log of *Tennessee*, in Logs of United States Naval Ships and Stations, RG 24, NA. CDR Francis A. Roe to Commodore Melancton Smith, Chief BUEQUIP, September 27, 1866, Letterbook of U.S.S. *Madawaska* and U.S.S. *Tacony*, Box 3, Francis A. Roe Papers, NHF, LC.

36. The man actually jumped from a railroad car window while crossing the Isthmus of Panama. John Rodgers, Commandant Mare Island, to RADM Wm. Reynolds, Chief BUEQUIP, November 28, 1874, No. 133, Letters Received from the Commandant of the Mare Island Navy Yard, 2:unnumbered, Records of the BUEQUIP, RG 24, NA.

37. For comments on the advance-wage system, see M. Smith, Chief BUEQUIP, to Geo. M. Robeson, October 20, 1869, Letters Received from the SECNAV, 1:378, Records of the BUEQUIP, RG 24, NA; Earl English, Chief BUEQUIP, to Commodore A. K. Hughes, Commandant Norfolk, April 26, 1882, Press Copies of Letters Sent to the Commandant of the Norfolk Navy Yard, 10:54, Records of the BUEQUIP, RG 24, NA; Wm. Reynolds, Chief BUEQUIP, to RADM C. H. Davis, Commandant Norfolk, January 6, 1873, Press Copies of Letters Sent to the Commandant of the Norfolk Navy Yard, 4:312-13, Records of the BUEQUIP, RG 24, NA; and Earl English, Chief BUEQUIP, to Commodore J. H. Upshur, Commandant New York, April 14, 1883, Press Copies of Letters Sent to the Commandant of the New York Navy Yard, 19:298, Records of the BUEQUIP, RG 24, NA.

38. M. Smith, Chief BUEQUIP, to Commodore Chas. C. Bell, Commandant New York, November 27, 1865, No. 442, Press Copies of Letters Sent to the Commandant of the New York Navy Yard, 2:23, Records of the BUEQUIP, RG 24, NA.

39. M. Smith, Chief BUEQUIP, to Commodore C. H. Bell, Commandant New York, March 9, 1866, No. 92, Press Copies of Letters Sent to the Commandant of the New York Navy Yard, 2:147, Records of the BUEQUIP, RG 24, NA.

40. CDR A. C. Rhind, Receiving Ship *Vermont*, to Commodore C. H. Bell, Commandant New York, March 6, 1866, Letters Received from Officers, 27:291-93, Records of the BUEQUIP, RG 24, NA. Emphasis in the original.

41. John Rodgers, Commandant Boston, to Commodore M. Smith, Chief BUEQUIP, April 25, 1867, and enclosures, Letters Received from Commandants of Navy Yards, 24:4-5 and following unnumbered pages, Records of the BUEQUIP, RG 24, NA. CAPT P. C. Johnson to Commodore Earl English, Chief BUEQUIP, October 31, 1879, No. 144, Letters Received from the Commandant of the Mare Island Navy Yard, 4:unnumbered, Records of the BUEQUIP, RG 24, NA.

42. *Annual Report of the Chief BUEQUIP, 1866*, pp. 151-52.

43. U.S., Navy Department, *Regulations for the Government of the Navy, 1870* (Washington: GPO, 1870), p. 223.

44. Computed from the shipping articles of the men who formed the random sample of enlistment returns for the years 1870, 1880, and 1890. These articles constituted the contract of enlistment between the sailor and the navy. Advances were recorded on them. Unfortunately, the 1870 and 1880 shipping articles for the rendezvous at Philadelphia, Norfolk, San Francisco, Washington, D.C., and Portsmouth, N.H., could not be located, though the forms for Boston and New York as well as for virtually all cruising vessels are in the National Archives. This means that shipping articles could not be located for 21.0 percent of the 1870 sample and 15.7 percent of the 1880 sample. The missing men are not included in the totals on which the percentages are based.

45. Compiled from sample of muster rolls for the quarters ending June 30 of 1870, 1880, and 1890. Muster rolls note whether each man was on board at the end of the quarter or whether he had deserted, died, or been discharged or transferred during that time period. With this data it is possible to calculate the approximate desertion rate for the year.

46. The sample of muster rolls shows that 75 percent, 85.7 percent, and 68 percent of the men who deserted for the quarters ending June 30 of 1870, 1880, and 1890, respectively, had enlisted within twelve months before the end of the quarter.

47. Watters to Commodore M. Smith, Chief BUEQUIP, February 29, 1868, Letters Received from Officers, 48:124-28, Records of the BUEQUIP, RG 24, NA.

48. Ibid. Desertion, of course, did not end with the twentieth century, though the rate was substantially reduced (see chapter 8).

49. *Annual Report of the SECNAV, 1889*, p. 24. N. H. Farquhar, "Inducements for Retaining Trained Seamen in the Navy, and Best System of Rewards for Long and Faithful Service," *USNIP* 11 (1885): 176.

50. Matthew Radom, "The 'Americanization' of the U.S. Navy," *USNIP* 63 (1937): 231. See also Albert Gleaves, *Life and Letters of Rear Admiral Stephen B. Luce* (New York: G. P. Putnam's Sons, 1925), p. 145.

51. W. F. Fullam, "The System of Naval Training and Discipline Required to Promote Efficiency and Attract Americans," *USNIP* 16 (1890): 479.

52. Luce to SECNAV, November 12, 1872, GC, Box 7, Stephen B. Luce Papers, NHF, LC.

53. U.S., Navy Department, *Annual Report of Admiral David D. Porter, 1873* (Washington: GPO, 1873), p. 273.

54. Frank Bennett, "American Men for the Navy," *United Service*, 2d ser. 11 (1894): 101-5.

55. Enlistment returns show that in 1870 50.9 percent of the men entering the navy were native-born, 57.5 percent in 1880, and 48.2 percent in 1890. A muster-roll sample supports these figures: 47.3 percent in 1870, 55.7 percent in 1880, and 50.3 percent in 1890.

The majority of foreign-born sailors came from relatively few countries. Great Britain was the place of birth for 12.4 percent of all enlisted men in 1870, for 7.5 percent in 1880, and for 6.1 percent in 1890; Ireland for 16.7 percent in 1870, 13.4 percent in 1880, and 10.5 percent in 1890; and the Scandinavian countries for 3.0 percent in 1870, 7.5 percent in 1880, and 14.3 percent in 1890. Asian nations were the homeland for 0.7 percent in 1870, 2.1 percent in 1880, and 4.8 percent in 1890. Since the navy confined Orientals almost entirely to cook and servant billets, where they were highly prized by officers, opponents of foreigners in the enlisted ranks rarely included Asians in their complaints.

Peter Karsten provides a useful discussion of the role of Social Darwinism in officers' aversion to foreigners. Peter Karsten, *The Naval Aristocracy: The Golden Age of Annapolis and the Emergence of Modern American Navalism* (New York: Free Press, 1972), pp. 213-14.

56. Luce to SECNAV, November 12, 1872, GC, Box 7, NHF, LC. Luce added that he thought one-third of the sailors who professed to be Americans were not.

57. Enlistment returns study, 1870, 1880, and 1890. The entries on "place of usual residence" are probably the least reliable information on the forms. For those seamen for whom this block was completed, 89.8 percent in 1870, 78.0 percent in 1880, and 92.8 percent in 1890 gave a location in the United States as their usual residence. Unfortunately, the data is missing for 68.5 percent of all enlistees in 1870 and for 30.7 percent in 1880 and 61.2 percent in 1890. Some recruiters obviously ignored the block entirely. It is also possible that recruiters sometimes listed everyone as a resident of the city in which the rendezvous was located.

58. *Annual Report of the Chief BUNAV, 1890*, p. 124.

59. *Annual Report of the Chief BUNAV, 1897*, p. 222.

60. U.S., Navy Department, Office of the Judge Advocate General, *Annual Report of the Judge Advocate General, 1894* (Washington: GPO, 1894), pp. 74-75 (hereafter cited as *Annual Report of the JAG*, with the appropriate year). Act of July 26, 1894, in U.S., *Statutes at Large*, 28:124. The law removed the requirement for a previous declaration of intention to become a citizen.

61. M. Smith, Chief BUEQUIP, to Commodore A. H. Kilty, Commandant Norfolk, August 3, 1869, Press Copies of Letters Sent to the Commandant of the Norfolk Navy Yard, 3:66, Records of the BUEQUIP, RG 24, NA.

62. David D. Porter to Commodore M. Smith, Chief BUEQUIP, June 24, 1869, Letters Received from the SECNAV, 1:327-28, Records of the BUEQUIP, RG 24, NA. "Circular Relative to Seamen Gunners," July 1, 1869, Press Copies of Miscellaneous Letters Sent, 2:181-82, Records of the BUEQUIP, RG 24, NA.

63. U.S., Congress, Senate, *Documents from the Department of the Navy* (19th Cong., 1st sess., 1825), Sen. Doc. 2, p. 101. Langley, *Social Reform in the United States Navy*, p. 99.

64. J. D. Elliah to LT B. Montgomery, April 1828, NR-Recruiting and Enlistment, Subject File, RG 45, NA. Langley, *Social Reform in the United States Navy*, p. 125.

65. *Annual Report of the SECNAV, 1879*, p. 19.

66. CDR Francis J. Higginson to Chief BUEQUIP, March 23, 1889, NR-Recruiting and Enlistment, Subject File, RG 45, NA.

67. Compiled from a sample of muster rolls for the quarters ending June 30, 1870, 1880, and 1890. California, the District of Columbia, Massachusetts, New Hampshire, New York State, Pennsylvania, and Virginia were the place of birth of 64.7 percent of the native-born enlisted men in 1870, 62.1 percent in 1880, and 61.4 percent in 1890. The addition of Connecticut and Maryland raises the figures to 79.1 percent in 1870; 76.5 percent in 1880, and 75.9 percent in 1890.

68. Langley, *Social Reform in the United States Navy*, pp. 98-112. Radom, "'Americanization' of the U.S. Navy," pp. 231-33. S. B. Luce, "Manning of Our Navy and Mercantile Marine," *USNIP* 1 (1874): 26.

69. *Annual Report of the SECNAV, 1866,* p. 33.

70. CDR F. A. Roe to RADM Stephen C. Rowan, August 6, 1869, Letterbook of the U.S.S. *Delaware,* Francis A. Roe Papers, Box 3, NHF, LC.

71. *Annual Report of Admiral David D. Porter, 1871,* p. 31. Luce, "Manning of Our Navy," p. 27.

72. *Annual Report of the SECNAV, 1875,* p. 18. The minimum age was lowered to fifteen in 1879 and to fourteen in 1881. *New York Times,* May 2, 1875. "Circular Relating to the Enlistment of Boys," April 1, 1875, March 31, 1879, and March 15, 1881, in M. S. Thompson, comp., *General Orders and Circulars Issued by the Navy Department from 1863 to 1887* (Washington: GPO, 1887), pp. 137-38, 177-78, and 195-96.

73. *Annual Report of the SECNAV, 1875,* p. 18.

74. Ibid. *Annual Report of the Chief BUEQUIP, 1875,* p. 85.

75. Act of May 12, 1879, in U.S., *Statutes at Large,* 21:3.

76. Commodore S. B. Luce to Commodore Earl English, Chief BUEQUIP, June 9, 1884, Letters Received from the CO of the Training Squadrons and the Training Station at Newport, R.I., 2: unnumbered, Records of the BUEQUIP, RG 24, NA.

77. Gleaves, *Luce,* pp. 149-67.

78. Luce to R. W. Thompson, SECNAV, November 19, 1880, File "1880," Box 8, GC, Stephen B. Luce Papers, LC.

79. Gleaves, *Luce,* p. 149.

80. Luce to Thompson, November 19, 1880, File "1880," Box 8, GC, Stephen B. Luce Papers, LC.

81. Thompson to Commodore Earl English, Chief BUEQUIP, November 27, 1880, and English to SECNAV, December 4, 1880, Records Relating to the Establishment of a Headquarters for Training Naval Apprentices, Records of the BUEQUIP, RG 24, NA. U.S., Navy Department, Bureau of Yards and Docks, *Federal Owned Real Estate under the Control of the Navy Department* (Washington: GPO, 1937), p. 323.

82. R. W. Shufeldt to R. W. Thompson, March 11, 1878, Press Copies of Letters Sent to the SECNAV, 2:382-83, Records of the BUEQUIP, RG 24, NA. RADM R. H. Wyman to W. H. Hunt, January 20, 1882, Letters Received by the SECNAV from COs of Squadrons, RG 45, NA Microfilm Publication M89, roll 293, frames 16-17. Chief BUNAV to CO U.S.S. *Michigan,* October 24, 1890, No. 9917, Press Copies of Letters Sent, 2:241-42, RG 24, NA. Earl English to Nathan Goff, Jr., January 18, 1881, Press Copies of Letters Sent to the SECNAV, 3:59-60, Records of the BUEQUIP, RG 24, NA.

83. R. W. Shufeldt to CDR Silas Casey, July 16, 1875, Box 1, Silas Casey Papers, NHF, LC.

84. Commodore S. B. Luce to Commodore Earl English, December 29, 1881, Letters Received from the CO of the Training Squadrons and the Training Station at Newport, R.I., 1:141, Records of the BUEQUIP, RG 24, NA. Earl English to Commodore Thos. S. Phelps, January 4, 1882 [date written as 1881], Press Copies of Letters Sent to the Commandant of the Mare Island Navy Yard, 5:283-85, Records of the BUEQUIP, RG 24, NA.

85. Chief BUNAV to F. W. Sanborn, District Attorney of Orange County, Calif., May 28, 1892, 31:63, Press Copies of Letters Sent, RG 24, NA.

86. Chief BUNAV to Commandant Mare Island Navy Yard, March 13, 1896, No. 4100, GC, RG 24, NA. Mare Island was only a temporary location for apprentice training since first steps were being taken to acquire Yerba Buena Island from the army.

87. SECNAV to Secretary of War, March 24, 1897, No. 8937, GC, RG 24, NA. Chief BUNAV to Commandant Mare Island Navy Yard, May 4, 1896, No. 10181, GC, RG 24, NA. George Perkins to Commodore A. S. Crowninshield, September 2, 1897, No. 8937, GC, RG 24, NA. Bureau of Yards and Docks, *Real Estate,* p. 51. U.S., Congress, Senate,

Congressional Record (54th Cong., 1st sess., 1896), 28, pt. 5:4460-62. Acting SECNAV to Secretary of War, October 28, 1898, No. 8937, GC, RG 24, NA.

88. "Circular Relating to the Enlistment of Boys in the U.S. Naval Service," April 8, 1875, in Thompson, *General Orders and Circulars*, p. 137.

89. Edward L. Beach, "The Training Ship," *USNIP* 28 (1902): 26-27. S. B. Luce, "Naval Training," *USNIP* 16 (1890): 389. General Order 271, May 11, 1881, in Thompson, *General Orders and Circulars*, p. 198.

90. CAPT D. B. Harmony to Commodore Earl English, Chief BUEQUIP, October 21, 1879, Letters Received from the CO of the Training Squadrons and the Training Station at Newport, R.I., 1:358, Records of the BUEQUIP, RG 24, NA.

91. Chief BUNAV to A. J. Knapp, June 12, 1893, No. 21321, Press Copies of Letters Sent, 47:96, RG 24, NA.

92. Acting Chief BUNAV to Ira Otterson, New Jersey State Reform School, April 26, 1894, Press Copies of Letters Sent, 59:225, RG 24, NA.

93. Commodore S. B. Luce to Commodore Earl English, June 13, 1883, Letters Received from the CO of the Training Squadrons and the Training Station at Newport, R.I., 1:243, Records of the BUEQUIP, RG 24, NA. For desertion by boys, see also Luce to English, June 30, 1881, Letters Received from the CO of the Training Squadrons and the Training Station at Newport, R.I., 1:unnumbered, Records of the BUEQUIP, RG 24, NA.

94. Commodore S. B. Luce to Commodore Earl English, June 30, 1883, Letters Received from the CO of the Training Squadrons and the Training Station at Newport, R.I., 1:262, Records of the BUEQUIP, RG 24, NA.

95. Chief BUNAV to Mrs. M. Levy, May 25, 1891, No. 3256, Press Copies of Letters Sent, 10:496, RG 24, NA.

96. Fullam, "Naval Training and Discipline," p. 480. The 2.3 percent is derived from my sample of muster rolls for the quarter ending June 30, 1890.

97. LCDR O. W. Farenholt, "Suggestions How to Man the New Ships, Train Apprentices, and Keep Them in the Naval Service," November 24, 1890, No. 9917, GC, RG 24, NA. *Annual Report of the SECNAV, 1889*, p. 23.

CHAPTER 3

1. For a history of the Bureau of Navigation, see Henry P. Beers, "The Bureau of Navigation, 1862-1942," *American Archivist* 6 (1943): 212-52; and Charles Oscar Paullin, *Paullin's History of Naval Administration, 1775-1911: A Collection of Articles from the U.S. Naval Institute "Proceedings"* (Annapolis, Md.: U.S. Naval Institute, 1968), pp. 259-63, 329, 383-84. For the 1889 reorganization, see *Annual Report of the SECNAV, 1889*, pp. 37-40.

2. Beers, "Bureau of Navigation," p. 236.

3. R. R. Belknap, "The Bureau of Navigation," in U.S., Navy Department, Naval Academy, Post-Graduate Department, *The Navy Department* (Washington: GPO, 1913), pp. 29-30.

4. *Annual Report of the SECNAV, 1917*, pp. 64-65, and *1923*, pp. 29-30. *Annual Report of the Chief BUNAV, 1919*, pp. 386-87, *1922*, p. 95, and *1923*, p. 219. *Bureau of Navigation News Bulletin*, No. 17, March 10, 1923. BUNAV Circular Letter 23-23 to All Ships and Stations, March 21, 1923, GC, Fleet Training Division, RG 38, NA. W. R. Shoemaker, *A Lecture Delivered before the War College Class, April 28, 1925, on Navy Personnel* (Washington: GPO, 1925), p. 26. Clifford M. Drury, *The History of the Chaplain Corps, United States Navy*, 6 vols. (Washington: GPO, 1949-60), 1:164-65.

5. Beers, "Bureau of Navigation," p. 212.

6. Naval Appropriation Act for 1916, in U.S., *Statutes at Large*, 38:929.

7. Any annual report of the chief of naval operations gives a good summary of the activities of the office.

8. For this lobbying effort, see chapter 10.

9. For an example of the enlisted correspondence with congressmen, see Military File, Series C, Box 72, La Follette Family Collection, LC.

10. The successive secretaries of the navy from 1898 to 1939 and the years they entered office were John D. Long, 1897; William H. Moody, 1902; Paul Morton, 1904; Charles J. Bonaparte, 1905; Victor H. Metcalf, 1906; Truman H. Newberry, 1908; George von Lengerke Meyer, 1909; Josephus Daniels, 1913; Edwin Denby, 1921; Curtis D. Wilbur, 1924; Charles F. Adams, 1929; and Claude A. Swanson, 1933, who served until 1939. U.S., Navy Department, *Register of Commissioned and Warrant Officers of the Navy of the United States and of the Marine Corps* for the years 1897-1940 (Washington: GPO, 1897-1940; hereafter cited as *Navy Register*, with the appropriate year).

11. The Lizzie Borden prosecutor was Moody; the author of children's stories, Denby. Harvard graduates were Long, Moody, Bonaparte, Meyer, and Swanson; Yale graduates Metcalf and Newberry; other cabinet, Moody (attorney general), Bonaparte (attorney general), Metcalf (secretary of commerce and labor), and Meyer (postmaster); members of the House of Representatives, Moody and Metcalf; senators, Swanson and Newberry; and descendants of Napoleon and John Adams, Charles J. Bonaparte and Charles F. Adams. Biographical sketches of all the secretaries are available in the *National Cyclopedia of American Biography* (hereafter cited as *NCAB*) and the *Dictionary of American Biography* (hereafter cited as *DAB*).

12. Henry F. Pringle, "Wilbur—Benevolent Blunderer," *Outlook* 148 (January 25, 1928): 123.

13. Elting E. Morison, ed., *The Letters of Theodore Roosevelt*, 8 vols. (Cambridge: Harvard University Press, 1951-54), 1:603.

14. Lawrence Shaw Mayo, ed., *America of Yesterday as Reflected in the Journal of John Davis Long* (Boston: Atlantic Monthly Press, 1923), p. 157. The parenthetical addition is in the original.

15. Joseph Bucklin Bishop, *Charles Joseph Bonaparte: His Life and Public Services* (New York: Charles Scribner's Sons, 1922), p. 112.

16. Elting E. Morison, *Admiral Sims and the Modern American Navy* (Boston: Houghton Mifflin Co., 1942), p. 229.

17. U.S., Navy Department, *Regulations for the Government of the Navy, 1913* (Washington: GPO, 1913), p. 17.

18. M. A. DeWolfe Howe, *George von Lengerke Meyer: His Life and Public Services* (New York: Dodd, Mead & Co., 1919), pp. 482-83. For more details on Meyer's reforms, see chapter 8.

19. For Daniels' own retrospective account of his tenure, see *The Wilson Era: Years of Peace, 1910-1917* (Chapel Hill: University of North Carolina Press, 1944), and *The Wilson Era: Years of War and After, 1917-1923* (Chapel Hill: University of North Carolina Press, 1946). More contemporary observations can be found in E. David Cronon, ed., *The Cabinet Diaries of Josephus Daniels, 1913-1921* (Lincoln: University of Nebraska Press, 1963), and in Josephus Daniels, *Our Navy at War* (Washington: Pictorial Bureau, 1922).

20. Robert Greenhalgh Albion and Robert Howe Connery, *Forrestal and the Navy* (New York: Columbia University Press, 1962), p. 229.

21. *Fleet Review* 3 (April 1913): 18. See also Daniels, *Years of Peace*, pp. 247-63.

22. Daniels to J. B. Baker, March 18, 1913, Letter Press Book, 3:unnumbered, Semi-Official, Josephus Daniels Papers, LC.

23. Blue was born in North Carolina but was appointed to the Naval Academy from South Carolina.

24. Cronon, *Cabinet Diaries of Josephus Daniels*, p. 14. Joseph L. Morrison, *Josephus Daniels: The Small-d Democrat* (Chapel Hill: University of North Carolina Press, 1966), p. 52. Daniels, *Years of Peace*, pp. 279-84.

25. Donald W. Mitchell, *History of the Modern American Navy from 1883 through Pearl Harbor* (New York: Alfred A. Knopf, 1946), p. 159.

26. For a discussion of desertion, see chapter 8.

27. Jonathan Daniels, *The End of Innocence* (Philadelphia: J. B. Lippincott Co., 1954), p. 130.

28. See chapter 6 for additional discussion of Daniels' educational program.

29. See chapter 8 for a discussion of the system of naval justice.

30. Daniels, "The Worth of the Christian Character," an address delivered January 11, 1914, at Grace M. E. Church, Washington, D.C., Speeches, Box 475, Josephus Daniels Papers, LC.

31. Chief Torpedoman Harry S. Morris to Harrod, March 30, 1971. The Oral History Project of the U.S. Naval Institute, Annapolis, Md., interviewed Chief Morris, who served as an enlisted man from 1903 to 1956. The correspondence quoted here expanded upon that interview and was in reply to an inquiry.

32. The successive chiefs of the bureau from 1898 to 1939 and the dates they entered office were Arent S. Crowninshield, 1897; Henry C. Taylor, 1902; George A. Converse, 1904; Willard H. Brownson, 1907; John E. Pillsbury, 1908; William P. Potter, 1909; Reginald F. Nicholson, 1909; Philip Andrews, 1912; Victor Blue, 1913; Leigh C. Palmer, 1916; Victor Blue, 1918; Thomas Washington, 1919; Andrew T. Long, 1923; William R. Shoemaker, 1924; Richard H. Leigh, 1927; Frank B. Upham, 1930; William D. Leahy, 1933; Adolphus Andrews, 1935; and James O. Richardson, 1938, who served until 1939. Virgil E. Baugh, comp., *Records of the Bureau of Naval Personnel*, National Archives Preliminary Inventory No. 123 (Washington: National Archives, 1960), p. 4.

33. For all the men, Navy Department, *Navy Register* is invaluable in tracing their careers. The *NCAB* also gives information on Taylor, 9:15; Converse, 36:293; Brownson, 25:56; Pillsbury, 20:287; Blue, 15:128; Long, 38:444; Leigh, 35:255; A. Andrews, 48:467; and Leahy, F:44.

34. Seven of the men died or retired before further sea duty.

35. For a biography of Luce, see Albert Gleaves, *Life and Letters of Rear Admiral Stephen B. Luce* (New York: G. P. Putnam's Sons, 1925); *DAB*, 11:488; and Navy Department, *Navy Register*.

36. Gleaves, *Luce*, pp. 77-80, 134-38, 149. Luce, "Naval Training, II," *USNIP* 36 (1910): 103-23.

37. For Fullam see *NCAB*, 20:478-79, and Navy Department, *Navy Register* for the years 1873-1919. For Dillingham see *NCAB*, 20:383, and Navy Department, *Navy Register* for the years 1865-1910.

38. These two articles by Dillingham were published, respectively, in *USNIP* 33 (1907): 137-51, and *USNIP* 35 (1909): 1019-28.

39. *USNIP* 16 (1890): 473-95. Among Fullam's other articles were "The Employment of Petty Officers in the Navy" *USNIP* 28 (1902): 467-73, and "The Training of Landsmen for the Navy," *USNIP* 28 (1902): 475-84.

40. Fullam, *The Petty Officer's Drill Book* (Annapolis, Md.: U.S. Naval Institute, 1902). Idem, *Hand-Book for Infantry and Artillery* (Annapolis, Md.: U.S. Naval Institute, 1899). Idem, *The Recruit's Handy Book* (Annapolis, Md.: U.S. Naval Institute, 1903).

CHAPTER 4

1. *Annual Report of the Chief BUNAV, 1891*, p. 149. For other expressions of concern about manning the new ships, see *Annual Report of the SECNAV, 1895*, p. xxix;

Memorandum for Information of the Assistant Secretary of the Navy from F. W. Ramsay, Chief BUNAV, January 19, 1896, Press Copies of Letters Sent, 66:358-59, RG 24, NA; H. A. Herbert, SECNAV, to J. Frederick Talbott, Chairman, House Subcommittee on Naval Affairs, February 5, 1895, and Herbert to Joseph D. Sayers, Chairman, House Committee on Appropriations, February 11, 1895, Press Copies of Letters Sent, 72:109-11, 113-15, RG 24, NA. For authorized strength from 1880 to 1940, see Appendix, table 1. *Chicago Tribune*, September 23, 1897, p. 7.

2. See Appendix, table 1.

3. H. A. Herbert to S. M. Cullom, March 19, 1895, No. 41520, Press Copies of Letters Sent, 72:220, RG 24, NA.

4. *Chicago Tribune*, June 21, 1897, p. 1.

5. Chief BUNAV to Officer in Charge Branch Hydrographic Office Cleveland, Ohio, June 9, 1897, and LT G. H. Stafford to Chief BUNAV, June 15, 1897, No. 67872, GC, RG 24, NA. BUNAV to Branch Hydrographic Office Chicago, June 9, 1897, and W. J. Wilson to BUNAV, June 12, 1897, No. 67873, GC, RG 24, NA.

6. *Chicago Tribune*, August 3, 1897, p. 5, and August 22, 1897, pt. 2, p. 2. LCDR John M. Hawley to SECNAV, September 13, 1897, No. 5013, GC, RG 80, NA.

7. LCDR John M. Hawley to SECNAV, September 13, 1897, No. 5013, GC, RG 80, NA. LT Simon Cook to Chief BUNAV, November 22, 1897, and reply from BUNAV, November 26, 1897, No. 86360, GC, RG 24, NA.

8. *Chicago Tribune*, March 27, 1898, p. 55, and April 3, 1898, p. 51.

9. *Annual Report of the Chief BUNAV, 1900*, p. 451.

10. *Army and Navy Journal* 36 (June 10, 1899): 979, and 36 (July 15, 1899): 1086.

11. *Annual Report of the Chief BUNAV, 1901*, pp. 511-12.

12. Statistics for 1890 were compiled from a sample of enlistment returns for Boston, New York, Philadelphia, Norfolk, San Francisco, Portsmouth, N.H., and Washington, D.C. U.S., Congress, House, Committee on Naval Affairs, *Hearings: Estimates Submitted by the Secretary of the Navy, 1911* (61st Cong., 2d sess., 1911), p. 4 (hereafter cited as *Hearings: Estimates Submitted by the SECNAV*, with the appropriate year), gives data for the years 1907-10. In 1908 interior recruiting stations supplied 70 percent of 15,404 enlistments; in 1909, 68 percent of 11,296; and in the first eleven months of 1910, 61 percent of 10,025. It is assumed that these figures are first enlistments since they are less than the total number of enlistees for those years. See Appendix, table 2.

13. *Annual Report of the Chief BUNAV, 1903*, p. 486, and *1906*, p. 416.

14. *Annual Report of the SECNAV, 1919*, p. 81.

15. See Appendix, table 2, for first enlistments. In fiscal year 1932 BUNAV shut its main recruiting stations in Boston, Brooklyn, New York City, Seattle, Philadelphia, Chicago, Milwaukee, San Francisco, Newark, and Atlanta. In 1933 all rent-paying stations were closed, leaving the thirty-one main and seventy-nine substations in operation at the end of the fiscal year. Later in the thirties, recruiting picked up, and at the end of fiscal year 1938 there were thirty-five main stations and 254 substations. *Annual Report of the Chief BUNAV, 1932*, p. 173, *1933*, pp. 19-20, and *1938*, p. 12.

16. Newton Baker to Daniels, July 30, 1918, Correspondence, 1913-21, "Baker, N.D. (2)," Box 35, Josephus Daniels Papers, LC. BUNAV, Recruiting Division, to All Recruiting Offices, September 19, 1918, No. 5525-3240, GC, RG 24, NA. E. H. Crowder, *The Spirit of Selective Service* (New York: Century Co., 1920), pp. 167, 171.

17. BUNAV to CO Navy Recruiting Offices, March 16, 1909, No. 2019-65, GC, RG 24, NA. LCDR H. A. Wiley to Officer in Charge Recruiting Stations, February 1, 1910, No. 6974-26, GC, RG 24, NA.

18. *Annual Report of the SECNAV, 1916*, p. 45. The division was along the 103d degree west longitude, which is the western boundary of the Texas Panhandle extended north and south.

19. For changes that were made in district organization, see House, Committee on Naval Affairs, *Hearings: Estimates Submitted by the SECNAV, 1917* (64th Cong., 2d sess., 1917), p. 590; *Annual Report of the SECNAV, 1919*, p. 81; Chief BUNAV to Navy Recruiting Service, August 24, 1922, No. 57358-61, GC, RG 24, NA; and *Annual Report of the Chief BUNAV, 1926*, p. 150.

20. BUNAV to Recruiting Stations, July 10, 1917, No. 5525-1963, GC, RG 24, NA. Examples of these first monthly quotas were Raleigh, 8; Providence, 12; Albany, N.Y., 20; San Diego, 8; Portland, Maine, 12; Philadelphia, 30; Boston, 24; Los Angeles, 16; Peoria, 14; Richmond, 12; San Francisco, 25; and New Orleans, 31. For other uses of quotas, see *Annual Report of the Chief BUNAV, 1922*, pp. 102-3; Chief BUNAV to Recruiting Service, October 10, 1925, No. P14-4(82), GC, RG 24, NA; and *Bureau of Navigation Bulletin*, No. 115, October 12, 1929.

21. Chief BUNAV to CINCs Atlantic and Pacific Fleets, October 29, 1909, No. 5525-228, GC, RG 24, NA. Acting Chief BUNAV to CINC Atlantic Fleet, December 14, 1909, No. 5525-229, GC, RG 24, NA.

22. BUNAV to Navy Recruiting Bureau, Seven Recruiting Inspectors, All Main Recruiting Stations, July 6, 1920, No. 1120-2736, GC, RG 24, NA.

23. Chief BUNAV to Recruiting Service, August 1, 1922, No. 57358-48, GC, RG 24, NA. Chief BUNAV to Navy Recruiting Service, November 10, 1922, No. 57358-106, GC, RG 24, NA. File number 57358-106 also contains two folders of reports from the stations on the competitions being held. *Annual Report of the Chief BUNAV, 1926*, p. 149.

24. Chief BUNAV to Recruiting Service, July 15, 1931, No. P14-4/P16-3(531), GC, RG 24, NA. Chief BUNAV to Navy Recruiting Service, August 10, 1922, No. 57358-55, GC, RG 24, NA.

25. *Annual Report of the Chief BUNAV, 1926*, p. 149.

26. Chief BUNAV to Navy Recruiting Service, May 19, 1922, No. 57358-24, GC, RG 24, NA. Hoffman, "Recruiting Salesmanship," *USNIP* 47 (1921): 825-48.

27. CDR L. M. Stevens, "An Angle of Recruiting," *USNIP* 55 (1929): 218.

28. LT F. H. Gilmer, "Psychology and the Navy," *USNIP* 47 (1921): 77-79. Discussion by LCDR K. C. McIntosh, ibid., pp. 393-95.

29. For the use of aptitude tests, see chapter 6.

30. Robert E. Coontz, *From the Mississippi to the Sea* (Philadelphia: Dorrance & Co., 1930), p. 275.

31. W. H. Brownson, Chief BUNAV, to CINC Pacific Fleet, November 1, 1907, No. 5525-59, GC, RG 24, NA. Victor Blue to All CINCs and COs All Vessels in Home Waters, June 19, 1913, No. 5525-707, GC, RG 24, NA.

32. L. C. Palmer to All CINCs, Force Commanders, Squadron Commanders, Flotilla Commanders, COs, Publicity Bureau, All Main and Substations, January 17, 1917, No. 5525-1150, GC, RG 24, NA.

33. BUNAV Circular Letter 67-19, May 18, 1919, No. 5525-3677, GC, RG 24, NA. CINC Atlantic Fleet to Fleet, September 6, 1919, No. 125135(91), Fleet: Atlantic 1919, Box 382, GC, RG 52, NA.

34. Chief BUNAV to Navy Recruiting Service, May 18, 1922, No. 57358-23, GC, RG 24, NA. U.S., Navy Department, BUNAV, *Bureau of Navigation Manual, 1925* (Washington: GPO, 1925), p. 275.

35. LCDR A. Sharp, BUNAV, to McCarty and Furlong, January 6, 1903, No. 525-2, GC, RG 24, NA. McLean to BUNAV, January 2, 1903, No. 525-4, GC, RG 24, NA.

36. Arthur Kyle Davis, ed., *Virginia Communities in Wartime*, Publications of the Virginia War History Commission, vol. 6 (Richmond: Virginia History Commission, 1926), p. 310.

37. Catheryna Cooke Gilman to Frank E. Kellogg, May 1, 1917, No. 3328-193, GC, RG 24, NA.

38. Chief BUNAV to Recruiting Officer Boston, December 31, 1912, No. 5525-636, GC, RG 24, NA.

39. See Theodore Roosevelt to Coordinator for General Supply, December 30, 1921, No. 15183-142:1, GC, RG 80, NA; and U.S., Congress, House, Committee on Appropriations, *Hearings: Navy Department Appropriation Bill, 1925* (68th Cong., 1st sess., 1924), p. 133.

40. LCDR H. B. Wilson to Postmaster Wadham Mills, New York, September 29, 1905, No. 4955-216, GC, RG 24, NA. Postmaster General to SECNAV, January 8, 1908, No. 5704-48, GC, RG 24, NA.

41. Ensign M. M. Frucht to Chief BUNAV, December 17, 1906, No. 5525-1, GC, RG 24, NA.

42. BUNAV Circular Letter, August 30, 1916, No. 5525-1114, GC, RG 24, NA. Edwin Denby, SECNAV, to Postmaster General, January 23, 1923, and reply Postmaster General to SECNAV, January 30, 1923, No. 57358-161, GC, RG 24, NA.

43. Herman Melville, *White-Jacket; or, the World in a Man-of-War* (London: Oxford University Press, 1966), p. 396. For an example of a poster from ca. 1837, see NR-Recruiting and Enlistment, Subject File, RG 45, NA.

44. LT G. W. Steele, Jr., to Chief BUNAV, July 3, 1907, No. 5735-41, GC, RG 24, NA. See chapter 7 for the establishment of a clothing allowance.

45. LT C. R. Train, Recruiting Station Philadelphia, to Chief BUNAV, December 28, 1908, No. 5525-171, GC, RG 24, NA.

46. LCDR W. H. Webb to Chief BUNAV, January 28, 1903, No. 684-5, GC, RG 24, NA.

47. LT A. W. Pressey, Recruiting Office Indianapolis, to BUNAV, April 8, 1908, No. 5735-84, p. 5, GC, RG 24, NA.

48. In 1912 of a total of $22,211.92 for advertising space, the BUNAV spent $15,652.92 on classified columns in newspapers and only $6,559.00 on magazines. House, Committee on Naval Affairs, *Hearings: Estimates Submitted by the SECNAV, 1913* (62d Cong., 3d sess., 1913), pp. 305-6.

49. J. Pillsbury to Robert Johnson Mooney, March 24, 1905, No. 684-108, GC, RG 24, NA.

50. BUNAV to Associated Billposters and Distributors Co., New York, March 25, 1905, No. 545-638, GC, RG 24, NA. LCDR H. B. Wilson to Officer in Charge Recruiting Party No. 2, April 1, 1905, No. 4955-1, GC, RG 24, NA. St. Louis Bill Posting Co. to Bryan and Co., March 3, 1903, No. 545-77, GC, RG 24, NA. File numbers 545 and 4955 contain correspondence with private billing agents.

51. Acting Chief BUNAV to Recruiting Officers, August 23, 1904, and LCDR J. B. Luby to BUNAV, August 26, 1904, No. 545-349, GC, RG 24, NA.

52. Navy Recruiting Station Buffalo to Chief BUNAV, July 9, 1903, No. 545-139, GC, RG 24, NA. "Recruiting Posters, World War I," *USNIP* 98 (February 1972): 68-72.

53. LCDR H. B. Wilson to Street and Finney, October 30, 1905, No. 684-136, GC, RG 24, NA. Frank Finney to Wilson, July 9, 1906, No. 684-183, GC, RG 24, NA. Wilson to Street and Finney, December 18, 1906, No. 684-188, GC, RG 24, NA. U.S., Navy Department, BUNAV, *The Making of a Man-o'-Warsman* (New York: Street & Finney, 1906).

54. BUNAV to Recruiting Stations, February 5, 1910, No. 7045-1, GC, RG 24, NA. H. A. Wiley to Officer in Charge Recruiting Office Cincinnati, January 21, 1910, No. 6974-18, GC, RG 24, NA. File number 6973 contains correspondence concerning obtaining names from men on ships, and number 6974 has additional correspondence establishing the direct-mail system. Chief BUNAV to Recruiting Office Indianapolis, December 2, 1911, No. 5735-375, GC, RG 24, NA.

55. LT A. W. Pressey to BUNAV, April 8, 1908, No. 5735-84, GC, RG 24, NA.

56. McIntosh to George von L. Meyer, January 30, 1911, No. 5525-437, GC, RG 24, NA. Chief BUNAV to Recruiting Officer Dallas, April 12, 1911, No. 5525-460, GC, RG 24, NA. See also A. R. Renwick to SECNAV, February 20, 1912, and reply by CDR J. R. Y.

Blakely, February 24, 1912, No. 1020-58, GC, RG 24, NA; and Philip Andrews, Acting SECNAV, to F. C. Stevens, July 24, 1912, No. 6974-210, GC, RG 24, NA.

57. LT A. W. Pressey to Chief BUNAV, January 11, 1908, No. 5735-73, GC, RG 24, NA. LCDR W. R. Shoemaker to Officer in Charge Navy Recruiting Station Indianapolis, July 13, 1908, No. 5735-115, GC, RG 24, NA. LT A. Staton to BUNAV, April 27, 1910, No. 5525-361, GC, RG 24, NA. *Recruiting Bureau Bulletin*, No. 11, October 15, 1920, File "Recruiting," Box 5, GC, Morale and Recreation Section, Records of the Morale Division, RG 24, NA.

58. "A Battleship That Will Never Sail the Seven Seas," *Scientific American* 116 (June 9, 1917): 569. SECNAV to Recruiting Office New York, June 23, 1920, No. 15183-102:1, GC, RG 80, NA. Francis C. Gallatin to Daniels, June 16, 1920, No. 15183-102:2, GC, RG 80, NA.

59. Chief BUNAV to Commandant Training Stations at Great Lakes, Mare Island, Norfolk, and Newport, November 14, 1919, No. 5525-4450, GC, RG 24, NA.

60. *New York Times*, July 28, 1919, p. 8.

61. LCDR Wells Hawks, "The Navy on the Mississippi," *Navy Life* (October 1919): 21-22.

62. Shoemaker to Officer in Charge Recruiting Station Salt Lake City, July 23, 1926, No. L3/NL35(27), GC, RG 24, NA.

63. Ernest Lee Jahncke to Samuel Eckles, Chief Engineer, Department of Highways, March 31, 1930, No. P14-4/L3(66), GC, RG 24, NA.

64. Hoffman, "Recruiting Salesmanship," pp. 847-48.

65. Ibid., p. 847. BUNAV, *Making of a Man-o'-Warsman*, pp. 4-6, 31.

66. LCDR A. Wiley, BUNAV, to Officer in Charge Navy Recruiting Station New York, May 11, 1910, No. 6974-66, GC, RG 24, NA.

67. BUNAV to Publicity Station New York, April 17, 1914, No. 6974-241, GC, RG 24, NA.

68. LCDR H. B. Wilson to CO Recruiting Pary No. 1, June 2, 1905, No. 684-105, GC, RG 24, NA. The 1903 poster is No. 547-177, GC, RG 24, NA. CDR Shoemaker to Associated Billposters and D. P. Co., January 13, 1909, No. 5704-86, GC, RG 24, NA.

69. Officer in Charge Eastern Recruiting Districts to All Officers and Petty Officers on Recruiting Duty in the Eastern Recruiting District, February 23, 1916, No. 5704-433, GC, RG 24, NA. Josephus Daniels, *The Wilson Era: Years of Peace, 1910-1917* (Chapel Hill: University of North Carolina Press, 1944), p. 248.

CHAPTER 5

1. Table 2 of the Appendix lists the number of applicants and the numbers enlisted and rejected for the years 1899-1940.

2. For age requirements in the nineteenth and twentieth centuries, see U.S., Navy Department, *Regulations for the Government of the Navy, 1865* (Washington: GPO, 1865), p. 179; and *Bluejacket's Manual, 1915* (Annapolis, Md.: U.S. Naval Institute, 1915), p. 65. For the ending of the apprentice program, see chapter 6.

3. House, Committee on Naval Affairs, *Hearings: Estimates Submitted by the SECNAV, 1910* (61st Cong., 1st sess., 1910), pp. 571-72.

4. R. H. Leigh, *A Lecture . . . Delivered before the War College Class, May 2, 1924, on Naval Personnel* (Washington: GPO, 1924), p. 24. *Annual Report of the Chief BUNAV, 1936*, p. 10, *1937*, p. 10, and *1938*, p. 13.

5. Chief BUNAV to Recruiting Service, February 4, 1929, No. P14-4/A2-11(84), GC, RG 24, NA. BUNAV Circular Letter 30-29, April 30, 1929, No. P14-4(363), GC, RG 24, NA. Chief BUNAV to Officer in Charge Navy Recruiting Station Buffalo, December 9, 1932, No. P14-4(604), GC, RG 24, NA.

6. Frank B. Upham, Chief BUNAV, to Miss C. Leboon, July 23, 1932, No. P14-4(R) (170), GC, RG 24, NA.

7. Charles A. Costello, "The Principal Defects Found in Persons Examined for Service in the United States Navy," *American Journal of Public Health* 7 (May 1917): 489-92. For the nineteenth century, see Albert Leary Gihon, "Practical Suggestions in Naval Hygiene," in U.S., Navy Department, Bureau of Medicine and Surgery, *Medical Essays* (Washington: GPO, 1873), pp. 5-21.

8. *Bluejacket* 10 (June 1910): 358. James O. Pryor to BUMED, November 10, 1920, No. 126930(112), GC, RG 52, NA.

9. CO NTS Hampton Roads to BUNAV, September 25, 1922, No. 57364-170, GC, RG 24, NA.

10. *Annual Report of the Surgeon General, 1906*, p. 1039, and *1908*, p. 874.

11. CO NTS Hampton Roads to BUNAV, September 25, 1922, No. 57364-170, GC, RG 24, NA.

12. *Annual Report of the Chief BUNAV, 1936*, p. 10.

13. Grace F. Pennel, *Monograph on Military Personnel and Related Records of the War Department, 1912-1939* (St. Louis: National Personnel Records Center, Military Reference Branch, 1966), p. 48.

14. *Annual Report of the Surgeon General, 1907*, p. 1183. The search for a better method of detecting undesirable applicants produced a number of suggestions. The Indianapolis recruiting office in 1921 combined fingerprinting with a card index of deserters arranged by height. In 1920 the BUNAV announced a scheme of classifying noses into nine types and started plans to distribute photographs based on this system. At another time an officer recommended that the navy use a polygraph at all recruiting stations, but this idea was rejected because of its cost. J. F. Lankford and F. O. Huntsinger, "Apprehending Repeaters," *Hospital Corps Quarterly* 5 (January 1921): 45-46. BUNAV to Recruiting Bureau, Seven Recruiting Inspectors, All Main Recruiting Stations, February 14, 1920, No. 5525-4771, GC, RG 24, NA. E. Moses to JAG, January 20, 1923, and 1st Endorsement by E. R. Stitt, BUMED, to JAG, January 27, 1923, No. 15183-167, GC, RG 80, NA.

15. In 1914 BUNAV estimated that 95 percent of the fraudulently enlisted men had tattoos and recommended that recruiting officers be alert for the following: shoulders with tattoos of birds, animals, grotesque figures, butterflies, and stars; the inscriptions "U.S.A.," "U.S.M.C.," "U.S.N."; the motto "Death before Dishonor," or "Pig" on the foot; "Manila PI" or the name of other foreign ports; tattoos of sailor's head, eagle and shield, crossed guns, apprentice knots, or other marks characteristic of military service; tombstones and weeping willows; the phrase "In memory of my mother" or "In memory of my father"; a star or other marks over the umbilicus; tattooing below the waist; obscene tattooing; tattooing on buttocks. J. R. Y. Blakeley to Recruiting Offices Chicago, Baltimore, Cleveland, Cincinnati, May 16, 1914, No. 5525-803, GC, RG 24, NA.

16. BUNAV to Recruiting Stations Boston, New York, Baltimore, Buffalo, Indianapolis, Cleveland, Detroit, Chicago, Minneapolis, St. Louis, Chattanooga, New Orleans, Omaha, Kansas City, Dallas, Los Angeles, *Wolverine*, February 17, 1910, No. 7045-3, GC, RG 24, NA.

17. BUNAV Form No. 1, No. 5525-360, GC, RG 24, NA.

18. The four-year enlistment became law in 1899 after a century of experimentation with other terms. In 1797 the maximum period was only one year. Because a single year often proved too short for the completion of a cruise, in 1798 Congress permitted the president to extend enlistments over one year if the vessel was on the high seas and for an additional ten days after reaching port. In 1809 the maximum period became two years, though seamen could be discharged earlier if their services were no longer needed. In 1837 Congress approved a maximum period of five years, and for the next sixty years the navy used its

discretion within this five-year limit—usually signing men for three years or for the duration of a cruise. John F. Callan and A. W. Russell, comps., *Laws of the United States Relating to the Navy and Marine Corps from the Formation of the Government to 1859* (Baltimore: John Murphy & Co., 1859), pp. 90, 91, 170, 301. Act of March 3, 1899, in U.S., *Statutes at Large*, 30:1008.

19. J. H. Shaw to Daniels, March 27, 1917, and reply April 2, 1917, by LCDR L. B. Porterfield, No. 5525-1346, GC, RG 24, NA. Great Lakes NTS to BUNAV, April 7, 1917, No. 5525-1522, GC, RG 24, NA.

20. BUNAV to Recruiting Station Minneapolis, September 22, 1920, No. 5525-5524, GC, RG 24, NA. H. R. Stark, CO NTS Hampton Roads, to BUNAV, August 21, 1920, and BUNAV to Navy Recruiting Bureau, Navy Recruiting Inspectors, All Main Recruiting Stations, September 1, 1920, No. 5525-5453, GC, RG 24, NA. *Bureau of Navigation News Bulletin*, No. 23, May 1, 1923.

21. *Annual Report of the SECNAV, 1921*, p. 4. BUNAV Circular Letter, October 6, 1923, No. 57358-03-50, GC, RG 24, NA.

22. Letters to BUNAV, March to July 1923, No. 57358-185, GC, RG 24, NA.

23. BUNAV Circular Letter 13-39, May 2, 1939, No. P14-4(1104), GC, RG 24, NA.

24. *New York Times*, July 18, 1919, p. 4. The navy received many men from the army and took obvious delight in enlistments from other services. *Great Lakes Bulletin*, January 7 and 10, 1919.

25. *Annual Report of the SECNAV, 1920*, p. 88. *Great Lakes Bulletin*, January 8, 1920. Memorandum from Acting Chief BUNAV to Confidential Clerk of SECNAV, September 16, 1904, No. 525-172, GC, RG 24, NA. John A. Sleicher to Daniels, November 29, 1916, No. 5525-1097, GC, RG 24, NA. E. H. Campbell, Acting Chief BUNAV, to Carl Cramer, January 8, 1925, No. 57365-398, GC, RG 24, NA.

26. Henry A. Wiley, *An Admiral from Texas* (Garden City, N.Y.: Doubleday, Doran & Co., 1934), p. 132.

27. House, Committee on Naval Affairs, *Hearings: Estimates Submitted by the SECNAV, 1911* (61st Cong., 2d sess., 1911), p. 3.

28. Chief BUNAV to Officers in Charge Recruiting Stations Cincinnati, Indianapolis, Chicago, Minneapolis, Des Moines, St. Louis, February 13, 1923, No. 57358-01-3, GC, RG 24, NA.

29. Milton MacKaye, "The Modern Bluejacket," *Outlook and Independent* 152 (July 31, 1929): 533.

30. For an expression of this attitude, see Harry W. Rickels to Paul Morton, March 21, 1905, No. 525-238, GC, RG 24, NA.

31. See Appendix, table 3. Authorized strength during this period grew from 8,250 men and boys in 1890 to 51,500 in 1915 (see Appendix, table 1).

32. *Annual Report of the Chief BUNAV, 1916*, pp. 229-32.

33. See Appendix, table 4, for the citizenship of the enlisted force from 1899 to 1940. For the 1907 citizenship requirement, see LCDR H. B. Wilson to Officer in Charge Navy Recruiting Station Boston, January 5, 1907, No. 1120-70 (filed with No. 963-254), GC, RG 24, NA. In spite of the long agitation to free the enlisted force from aliens, the department made an exception to its policy of exclusion and sometimes permitted ships in Asiatic waters to enlist Chinese as servants, since some officers thought Chinese could "perform their duties much more satisfactorily than men of any other race." BUNAV to CINC Asiatic Fleet, July 26, 1923, No. 57886-02-20, GC, RG 24, NA.

34. Semiannual Report, A. C. Dillingham to BUNAV, July 25, 1907, No. 5274-10, GC, RG 24, NA.

35. Surgeon General to SECNAV (Division of Personnel), April 25, 1911, No. 5525-466, GC, RG 24, NA.

36. Paul Schubert, *Come on "Texas"* (New York: Jonathan Cape & Harrison Smith, 1930), p. 193.

37. From a sample of shipping articles of men enlisting in 1870.

38. *Bureau of Navigation Bulletin*, No. 33, October 30, 1923.

39. RADM W. C. Wise to SECNAV (BUNAV), October 14, 1904, No. 525-180, GC, RG 24, NA.

40. Robert B. Dashiel to A. Staton, March 27, 1920, Folder No. 6, Box 1, A. Staton Papers, SHC. *Bureau of Navigation Bulletin*, No. 143, October 25, 1930.

41. A few reports of many such incidents are as follows: *New York Times*, March 18, 1923, p. 18; "A Hick Judge in a Hick Town," *Our Navy* 18 (September 1, 1924): 10; No. 57358-242, GC, RG 24, NA; No. 5525-122, GC, RG 24, NA; and No. P14-4(1034), GC, RG 24, NA.

42. Edward Frensdorf to Daniels, April 13, 1918, and reply by Daniels, June 25, 1918, No. 5525-2978, GC, RG 24, NA.

43. 2d Endorsement by Chief BUNAV, January 9, 1901, on CAPT W. C. Wise to Chief BUNAV, January 7, 1901, No. 24215, GC, RG 24, NA.

44. David J. Boyd to Chief BUNAV, April 21, 1904, No. 525-134, GC, RG 24, NA.

45. H. C. Smith to SECNAV, May 21, 1908, and SECNAV to H. C. Smith, May 27, 1908, No. 5525-130, GC, RG 24, NA.

46. LCDR W. R. Shoemaker to Officer in Charge Navy Recruiting Station New York, May 23, 1908, No. 5325-28, GC, RG 24, NA.

47. Philip Andrews, Chief BUNAV, to Reverend J. Milton Waldron, February 7, 1913, No. 5325-60, GC, RG 24, NA. The *Army and Navy Journal* 50 (January 18, 1913): 605, reported plans to select sailors for the inaugural parade from the battleships of the Atlantic Fleet. Assuming this letter refers to the same vessels, these blacks represented twenty-one ships with a total designed complement of 17,268 men. U.S., Navy Department, Office of the Chief of Naval Operations, Naval History Division, *Dictionary of American Naval Fighting Ships* (Washington: GPO, 1959), 1:189-202.

48. CAPT W. H. Brownson to Chief BUNAV, October 2, 1900, No. 235,913, GC, RG 24, NA.

49. "Negro U.S.N." to President T. Roosevelt, October 11, 1905, No. 3328-60, GC, RG 24, NA.

50. Wm. A. Sinclair and N. F. Mossell to William Howard Taft, December 30, 1909, and Chief BUNAV to Constitution League, March 26, 1910, No. 1159-342, GC, RG 24, NA.

51. On federal racial policy in the Wilson era, see, for example, George C. Osborn, "The Problem of the Negro in Government, 1913," *Historian* 23 (1961): 330-47, and Nancy J. Weiss, "The Negro and Segregation," *Political Science Quarterly* 84 (1969): 61-79.

52. BUNAV to Thomas D. Schall, May 15, 1917, No. 5525-1699, GC, RG 24, NA.

53. Daniels to Frelinghuysen, April 11, 1917, No. 5525-1447, GC, RG 24, NA.

54. Dennis Denmark Nelson, *The Integration of the Negro into the United States Navy, 1776-1947* (Washington: Navy Department, 1948), pp. 22, 25. Jack D. Foner in his *Blacks and the Military in American History* (New York: Praeger Publishers, 1974), pp. 103-6, working primarily from black newspapers, has partially sketched the process of segregation before World War I.

55. House, Committee on Naval Affairs, *Hearings: Estimates Submitted by the SECNAV, 1916* (64th Cong., 1st sess., 1916), 1:928.

56. CO NTS Hampton Roads to BUNAV, March 16, 1922, and reply BUNAV to CO NTS, March 20, 1922, No. 19270-1919, GC, RG 24, NA. The commanding officer of the training station had sixteen black petty officers, six of whom were in excess of complement, and requested permission to keep them all at his station, since, he said, when "transferred to another ship or station, they often do not fit in anywhere." The bureau replied that it did not feel the service could afford to have any extra men ashore. It instructed that four of the

blacks with twenty years' service (a chief carpenter's mate, chief gunner's mate, chief water tender, and machinist's mate, first class) were to accept early retirement by transfer to the naval reserve. If they declined retirement, they were to be transferred to the Pacific Fleet. One ship's cook, first class, had thirty-five years of service and was to be retired. One chief gunner's mate was to be kept in excess of complement for a year until he was eligible for the reserve. Significantly, two commissary stewards were assigned to cruising vessels. The remaining eight (four water tenders, first class, one chief carpenter's mate, one chief machinist's mate, and two engineers, first class) were to remain at Hampton Roads, in excess of complement if need be. The bureau said that they would "only be ordered to other duty when it is considered that their services can be used with satisfaction to all concerned."

57. The date of August 4, 1919, is from Memorandum for Captain Nimitz from Randall Jacobs, April 29, 1937, No. MB(187), GC, RG 24, NA. I have been unable to find the order itself, but in July and August 1919 the Bureau of Navigation closed enlistments in many ratings. I assume that the exclusion of blacks was accomplished by allowing one such "temporary" suspension of enlistment of messmen in the United States to remain in force throughout the twenties. Enlistments in the Philippines continued as needed during the entire period.

58. A. Claude, Memorandum for Chief BUNAV, October 18, 1932, No. NC66(1), GC, RG 24, NA.

59. CDR R. R. M. Emmet, Memorandum for CAPT Noyes, October 19, 1932, No. NC66(1), GC, RG 24, NA.

60. H. S. Gearing, Memorandum for CAPT Claude, December 2, 1932, No. NC66(1), GC, RG 24, NA.

61. D. A. Weaver to CAPT Abram Claude, November 28, 1932, No. NC66(1), GC, RG 24, NA.

62. H. S. Gearing, Memorandum for CAPT Claude, December 2, 1932, No. NC66(1), GC, RG 24, NA. See also under the same file number A. W. Johnson, Memorandum for Chief BUNAV, November 8, 1932, and W. T. Cluverius to CAPT Abram Claude, November 25, 1932.

63. Chief BUNAV to CO NTS Norfolk, December 17, 1932, No. NC66(1), GC, RG 24, NA.

64. The first monthly quotas were as follows: Macon, Ga., 2; Raleigh, N.C., 2; Richmond, Va., 2; Birmingham, Ala., 2; Little Rock, Ark., 2; and Nashville, Tenn., 2. Chief BUNAV to CO NTS Norfolk, December 6, 1932, No. NC66(1), GC, RG 24, NA.

65. William D. Leahy, Chief BUNAV to A. C. MacNeal, June 3, 1935, No. P14-4(746), GC, RG 24, NA.

66. H. J. Williams to Walter White, October 26, 1936, and November 12, 1936, C3-77, Administrative Files, National Association for the Advancement of Colored People Papers, LC.

67. Executive Officer, U.S.S. *Wyoming*, to Chief BUNAV, May 21, 1935, No. MB(154), GC, RG 24, NA.

68. Commander Base Force to Chief BUNAV, February 27, 1938, No. MB(188), GC, RG 24, NA.

69. Chief BUNAV to Governor of Guam, May 8, 1937, No. MB(187), GC, RG 24, NA. BUNAV to CINCUS, CINCAF, COMBASEFOR, June 4, 1938, No. MB(187), GC, RG 24, NA. There is other correspondence on this subject under the same file number. For the month of July 1937, the other quotas for messmen were Northeast District, 3; Southeast, 16; South, 16; Central, 5; West, 0. No. MB(190), GC, RG 24, NA.

70. Memorandum for Chief of Bureau from CAPT J. B. Oldendorf, July 25, 1938, No. MB(209), GC, RG 24, NA. Agreement between the United States and the Republic of the

Philippines, December 13, 1952, in U.S., Department of State, *United States Treaties and Other International Agreements* (Washington: GPO, 1955), 5:373-78.

71. RADM Adolphus Andrews, Chief BUNAV, to A. C. MacNeal, September 19, 1935, P14-4(770), GC, RG 24, NA.

72. For an example of Filipinos serving as musicians, see *Army and Navy Journal* 50 (1912): 192, which gives an account of a parade in New York to which the *Georgia* sent an all-Filipino bugle corps. For an example of the bureau's general policy of preventing Filipinos from transferring out of the messmen branch, see CO U.S.S. *Connecticut* to BUNAV, September 20, 1919, and reply by L. T. DuBose, September 24, 1919, No. 2158-1308, GC, RG 24, NA. The *Connecticut* reported requests from Filipino mess attendants to transfer to other ratings, such as fireman; the bureau replied that no changes other than advancement were allowed without its approval. In a 1920 case, the bureau stated that it was "contrary to the Bureau's policy to rate filipinos in any branches other than the messmen and musicians branches." BUNAV to CO NTS, Naval Operating Base, Hampton Roads, January 8, 1920, No. 2158-1351, GC, RG 24, NA.

73. BUNAV Circular Letter 222-18, November 23, 1918, No. 19334-4, GC, RG 24, NA. CO *Rizal* to BUNAV, June 25, 1919, No. 49044-19, GC, RG 24, NA. SECNAV to Secretary of War, November 22, 1917, No. 27311-2, GC, RG 350, NA. Clipping from *Official U.S. Bulletin*, September 21, 1918, No. 27311-12, GC, RG 350, NA. Clipping from Newark, N.J., *Star*, May 12, 1919, No. 27311-15, GC, RG 350, NA. At the end of the war, the Philippines entered a financial depression, and the United States government never collected the $2 million that had been agreed on. Frank McIntyre, Chief of Bureau of Insular Affairs, to Frank W. Carpenter, May 24, 1927, No. 27311-18, GC, RG 350, NA.

74. See Chief BUNAV Adolphus Andrews (signed by J. B. Oldendorf) to E. K. McDermott, April 25, 1938, No. P14-4(986), GC, RG 24, NA; Chief BUNAV Adolphus Andrews to Prentiss B. Taylor, February 23, 1938, No. P14-4(952), GC, RG 24, NA; and Chief BUNAV Adolphus Andrews to Senator Champ Clark, April 22, 1938, No. P14-4(981), GC, RG 24, NA.

75. The Insular Forces were composed of small vessels patrolling the new American possessions in the Pacific. Members of the force served as a special part of the navy; they received less pay than other navy men and were assigned only to duty around the islands. See Memorandum, Chief BUNAV to SECNAV, April 3, 1901, No. 123423, GC, RG 80, NA. Under this same file number is a copy of an executive order dated April 5, 1901, establishing the force.

76. For navy policy toward American Indians and Puerto Ricans, see BUNAV to Secretary of the Interior, April 19, 1911, No. 5525-461, GC, RG 24, NA; LCDR Alexander Sharp to Elias Brevoort, March 30, 1903, No. 525-47, GC, RG 24, NA; LCDR H. P. Jones to BUNAV, January 21, 1905, No. 525-225, GC, RG 24, NA; LT L. E. Bass to BUNAV, January 29, 1908, and 1st Endorsement by LCDR W. R. Shoemaker, February 4, 1908, No. 5525-90, GC, RG 24, NA; and JAG to BUNAV, August 3, 1914, No. 5525-816, GC, RG 24, NA.

77. Clifford Merrill Drury, *History of the Chaplain Corps, United States Navy*, 6 vols. (Washington: GPO, 1949-60), 1:169-70.

78. The character is Mendel, who first appears in the narrative at pp. 149-52. Marcus Goodrich, *Delilah* (New York: Farrar & Rinehart, 1941).

79. Sammy Bear, "I Found Tolerance in the Navy," *Our Navy* 25 (June 1, 1931): 3.

80. Drury, *History of the Chaplain Corps*, 1:168-69, 3:107, 265.

81. Ibid., 1:198, 241.

82. Ibid., 1:100, 117. The places of birth are from a muster-roll sample for the quarter ending June 30, 1870. For a listing of Catholic chaplains commissioned before 1917, see Dom Aidan Henry Germain, "Catholic Military and Naval Chaplains, 1776-1917" (Ph.D. diss., Catholic University, 1929), pp. 144-48. For a listing of all chaplains, see U.S., Navy

Department, *Navy Register, 1913*, p. 92. There were also Catholics among officers. Peter Karsten has found that 11.1 percent of students at Annapolis between 1885 and 1895 were Catholic. Karsten, *The Naval Aristocracy; The Golden Age of Annapolis and the Emergence of Modern American Navalism* (New York: Free Press, 1972), p. 75.

83. Barker to SECNAV, December 27, 1897, No. 83002, GC, RG 24, NA. A copy of the published article is filed with Barker's letter.

84. *New York Times*, June 24, 1921, p. 1; and June 25, 1921, pp. 2, 10. *Army and Navy Journal* 58 (1921): 1159.

85. Josephus Daniels, *The Wilson Era: Years of War and After, 1917-1923* (Chapel Hill: University of North Carolina Press, 1946), p. 211. SECNAV to Chief BUNAV, March 14, 1917, No. 6757-420, GC, RG 24, NA. JAG to Chief Bureau of Supplies and Accounts, April 26, 1917, No. 26254-2225:1, GC, RG 80, NA. SECNAV to Pay Inspector Barron P. DuBois, April 27, 1917, No. 26254-2225:1, GC, RG 80, NA.

86. Comptroller of the Treasury to Pay Inspector B. P. DuBois, May 24, 1917, No. 26254-2225:2, GC, RG 80, NA. Act of August 29, 1916, in U.S., *Statutes at Large*, 39:587, 592.

87. Chief BUNAV L. C. Palmer to Commandants of All Districts, March 19, 1917, No. 26254:2225, GC, RG 80, NA.

88. Memorandum for Mr. Henkel, Chief Clerk, from J. T. Scully, May 3, 1924, No. 9875-5666, GC, RG 24, NA. Eunice C. Dessez, *The First Enlisted Women, 1917-1918* (Philadelphia: Dorrance & Co., 1955), pp. 11-13, 25. Josephus Daniels, *Our Navy at War* (Washington: Pictorial Bureau, 1922), pp. 328-29.

89. 2d Endorsement, Acting Chief BUNAV to JAG, July 20, 1908, No. 4778-2, GC, RG 24, NA.

90. Dessez, *First Enlisted Women*, p. 21.

91. L. K. Karr, Yeoman (F), 1st class, to Auditor for Navy Department, June 6, 1917, No. 26254-2225:3, GC, RG 80, NA. SECNAV to Commandant Naval Station Key West, June 19, 1917, No. 26254-2225:3, GC, RG 80, NA. JAG to Chief Bureau of Supplies and Accounts, April 26, 1917, No. 26254-2225:1, GC, RG 80, NA. For a description of the uniform adopted, see Dessez, *First Enlisted Women*, pp. 45-51.

92. Committee on Public Information, Division of Woman's War Work, June 14, 1918, for release June 30, 1918, NA-3, "Women in Naval Reserve Force," Subject File, 1911-27, Box 277, RG 45, NA. For other commendations of the women see Robert E. Coontz, *From the Mississippi to the Sea* (Philadelphia: Dorrance & Co., 1930), p. 385, and Letter of Recommendation for Kate Abrams from Josephus Daniels, October 25, 1919, Kate Abrams' Scrapbook, SHC.

93. *Our Navy* 12 (March 1919): 22. A similar protest is found in *Our Navy* 12 (October 1918): 20.

94. E. David Cronon, ed., *The Cabinet Diaries of Josephus Daniels, 1913-1921* (Lincoln: University of Nebraska Press, 1963), p. 253. The woman had been reduced in rank because she left—presumably without permission—when she was sick. Daniels again disapproved a court finding for a yeoman (F) in March 1918, writing that the "Department considers it inadvisable to try female yeomen by court-martial, as in contravention to public policy." SECNAV to CO NTS Newport, March 26, 1918, No. 27217-2648, GC, RG 80, NA.

95. House, Committee on Naval Affairs, *Hearings: Estimates Submitted by the SECNAV, 1918* (65th Cong., 1st sess., 1918), p. 12. I have found no testimony on how the navy would have treated major offenses by women.

96. *Navy Life* (August 1919), p. 53.

97. Act of July 11, 1919, in U.S., *Statutes at Large*, 41:138. See also BUNAV to Commandants Naval Districts, July 3, 1919, No. 1159-1425, GC, RG 24, NA, and BUNAV to L. R. G. Gignilliat, December 14, 1920, No. 9878-3932, GC, RG 24, NA.

98. Dessez, *First Enlisted Women*, p. 69.

99. Ibid., pp. 67, 72-75. Mrs. Henry F. Butler, *I Was a Yeoman* (F) (Washington: Naval Historical Foundation, n.d.), p. 13. Joy Bright Hancock, *Lady in the Navy: A Personal Reminiscence* (Annapolis, Md.: U.S. Naval Institute, 1972), p. 28.

100. Chief BUNAV to Officer in Charge Navy Recruiting Station New Haven, Conn., February 12, 1942, No. QR/P14-4(933), GC, RG 24, NA.

101. Charles Minor Blackford, *Torpedoboat Sailor* (Annapolis, Md.: U.S. Naval Institute, 1968), pp. 3, 48-49. Murry Wolffe, *Memoirs of a Gob* (New York: Exposition Press, 1949), p. 7.

102. *Annual Report of the Surgeon General, 1908*, p. 840. *New York Times*, April 20, 1914, p. 1, and April 21, 1914, p. 4.

103. *Bureau of Navigation News Bulletin*, No. 23, May 1, 1923.

104. See Appendix, table 2.

105. L. J. Gulliver, "Better Iron Men for the Navy," *USNIP* 56 (1930): 528.

106. *Annual Report of the Surgeon General, 1908*, p. 840.

107. LT Joseph D. Little to BUNAV, November 2, 1910, No. 5525-405, GC, RG 24, NA. B. W. McNeely to All Recruiting Stations and Substations, August 9, 1916, No. 5525-1024, GC, RG 24, NA. Mansfield to BUNAV, January 17, 1919, No. 5525-2315, GC, RG 24, NA.

108. House, Committee on Naval Affairs, *Hearings: Estimates Submitted by the SECNAV, 1907* (59th Cong., 2d sess., 1907), p. 9.

109. *New York Times*, December 24, 1916, pt. 1:14.

110. Karsten, *Naval Aristocracy*, p. 77.

111. See Appendix, table 2, for the number of navy enlistments, and U.S., Department of Commerce, Bureau of the Census, *Historical Statistics of the United States, Colonial Times to 1957* (Washington: GPO, 1960), p. 73, for unemployment statistics.

112. Act of March 3, 1899, in U.S., *Statutes at Large*, 30:1008.

113. Act of August 22, 1912, in U.S., *Statutes at Large*, 37:331.

114. It is difficult to compile comparable figures for the nineteenth century because the previous-service blank on enlistment returns often was not filled in. For 1890, the completed blanks show 24.6 percent of the men with four or more years' service, but 51 percent of the blanks were not completed. If the empty space indicated no previous service, then only 11.6 percent had four or more years of service. Muster rolls do not give previous service.

115. Blackford, *Torpedoboat Sailor*, pp. 155-56.

116. *Annual Report of the SECNAV, 1920*, p. 87. BUNAV to COs All Ships and Stations, July 11, 1921, No. 5525-6116, GC, RG 24, NA.

117. Chief BUNAV to Navy Recruiting Service, June 15, 1923, No. 57358-01-36, GC, RG 24, NA. BUNAV Circular Letter 40-23, June 7, 1923, No. 507, GC, Fleet Training Division, RG 38, NA.

118. The *Annual Report of the Chief BUNAV, 1926*, p. 150, is the first report to mention such literature.

119. *Bureau of Navigation Bulletin*, No. 90, October 29, 1928.

120. "Be Glad You're In," *Our Navy* 25 (Mid-March 1932): 12.

121. *Annual Report of the Chief BUNAV, 1933*, p. 5. In *Annual Report of the Chief BUNAV, 1937*, p. 3, the bureau requested that Congress reinstate the payment, but this recommendation was not in the 1938 report.

122. Josephus Daniels, "A Message to the Boys of America," *St. Nicholas* 45 (July 1918): 785.

CHAPTER 6

1. Acting Chief BUNAV to Selby M. Cullom, July 28, 1896, No. 18923, GC, RG 24, NA. Although it is often convenient to speak of landsman for training as a rating, it was actually a special category created within the existing landsman rating.

2. Stevens Vail, "Making a Man of War's Man," *Junior Munsey* 11 (December 1901): 365.

3. *Annual Report of the Chief BUNAV, 1900*, p. 451.

4. CAPT Harry Glass to CDR W. S. Cowles, BUNAV, January 12, 1901, No. 249724, GC, RG 24, NA.

5. Chief BUNAV to CINC Atlantic Training Squadron, September 21, 1903, No. 3791-4, GC, RG 24, NA.

6. The similarity of names caused some confusion. As late as 1922 Senator Henry Cabot Lodge did not realize that the navy no longer trained boys as apprentices. U. S., Congress, Senate, Committee on Naval Affairs, *Hearings: United States Naval Training Stations at Norfolk, Va., and Newport, R.I.* (67th Cong., 2d sess., 1922), pp. 2-3. RADM W. C. Wise to BUNAV, December 1903, No. 562-34, GC, RG 24, NA. The original landsman rating was not affected by the 1904 consolidation, but survived until 1921. See Appendix, table 9. For the ending of the apprentice system, see *Annual Report of the Chief BUNAV, 1905*, p. 376.

7. S. B. Luce, "Naval Training II," *USNIP* 36 (1910): 108.

8. Ibid., p. 116.

9. Memorandum for RADM Taylor, March 31, 1902, No. 312552, GC, RG 24, NA.

10. *New York Times*, June 8, 1903, p. 6, and June 18, 1903, p. 16.

11. *Annual Report of the Chief BUNAV, 1905*, p. 376.

12. LCDR H. A. Wiley to Commandant Newport Training Station, April 5, 1907, and reply CAPT A. Dillingham to BUNAV, April 13, 1907, No. 5274-8, GC, RG 24, NA.

13. Memorandum on Training Ships for Recruits, February 20, 1912, No. 1024-149, GC, RG 24, NA.

14. Fullam to ADM William B. Caperton, December 5, 1916, File "Correspondence Dec. 1916-Feb. 1917," William F. Fullam Papers, LC.

15. F. E. Chadwick, "Letter," *USNIP* 27 (1901): 270.

16. Luce to CAPT G. C. Hanus, February 13, 1907, in Albert Gleaves, *Life and Letters of Rear Admiral Stephen B. Luce* (New York: G. P. Putnam's Sons, 1925), p. 166. See also H. C. Taylor to Luce, January 11, 1888, File "Jan.-July 1888," GC, Luce Papers, LC.

17. S. B. Luce, "Naval Training," *USNIP* (1890): 369. Vestiges of this attitude, of course, still survive. All midshipmen at the Naval Academy are taught to sail, and the United States Coast Guard as well as several foreign navies maintain some sailing ships for practice cruises with future officers. Sailing clubs for navy enlisted men are also encouraged.

18. CDR Silas W. Terry to Luce, January 11, 1888, File "Jan.-July, 1888," GC, Luce Papers, LC. Terry had commanded the apprentice training ship *Portsmouth* from 1885 to 1886. This letter, as the Taylor letter cited in note 16 above, is one of several written to Luce in reply to his inquiry whether sail or auxiliary steam made the better training ship. The responses are overwhelmingly in favor of sail alone.

19. Charles D. Sigsbee, "Discussion" [of Chadwick, "Letter"], *USNIP* 27 (1901): 272.

20. E. W. Eberle, "Discussion" [of H. S. Knapp, "The Training of Landsmen"], *USNIP* 29 (1903): 230.

21. *Annual Report of the Chief of the Bureau of Construction and Repair, 1903*, pp. 785-86.

22. The older stations were often referred to by several names. Newport was also called Coaster's Harbor Island and Narragansett Bay; Norfolk appears as St. Helena and the receiving ship *Franklin*; and San Francisco was also known as Yerba Buena Island and Goat Island. For the development of the Newport and San Francisco stations, see chapter 2.

23. CAPT A. C. Dillingham to BUNAV, July 25, 1907, No. 5274-10, GC, RG 24, NA. *Man-O'-Warsman*, 1 (November 1908): 6.

24. CAPT A. C. Dillingham to BUNAV, October 12, 1907, No. 1389-113, GC, RG 24, NA.

25. A. S. Crowninshield to SECNAV, February 20, 1902, No. 312552, GC, RG 24, NA. Naval Appropriation Act for 1914, in U.S., *Statutes at Large*, 37:895.

26. SECNAV to Eugene Hale, April 29, 1902, No. 312552, GC, RG 24, NA.

27. Ibid. A. S. Crowninshield to SECNAV, February 20, 1902, No. 312552, GC, RG 24, NA.

28. CAPT J. J. Hunker, CDR W. S. Cowles, and LCDR V. L. Cottman to SECNAV, April 23, 1901, No. 259682, GC, RG 24, NA.

29. Acting SECNAV to Commandant Naval Station Port Royal, July 5, 1901, No. 259682, GC, RG 24, NA. Chief BUNAV to Commandant Naval Station Port Royal, July 8, 1901, No. 259682, GC, RG 24, NA.

30. BUNAV sent the training ship *Topeka* to Port Royal to serve as a station ship, and recruits at Port Royal operated on it during the last half of 1901. See the log of the *Topeka*, May 26 to November 18, 1901, Logs of U.S. Naval Ships and Stations, RG 24, NA.

31. House, Committee on Naval Affairs, *Hearings: Estimates Submitted by the SECNAV, 1907* (59th Cong., 1st sess., 1906), p. 17. *Annual Report of the Commandant of the Marine Corps, 1916*, p. 770.

32. U.S., Congress, Senate, *Additional Naval Training Station on the Great Lakes* (57th Cong., 1st sess., 1902), Sen. Doc. 45, p. 19.

33. Ibid., pp. 3-4.

34. U.S., Congress, House, *Site for a Naval Training Station on the Great Lakes* (58th Cong., 1st sess., 1903), H. Doc. 6, p. 10.

35. U.S., Navy Department, Bureau of Yards and Docks, *Federal Owned Real Estate under the Control of the Navy Department* (Washington: GPO, 1937), p. 154. The navy accepted the property but refused to name the station for Graeme Stewart, who had purchased the farm for the Commercial Club. Memorandum to SECNAV from Chief BUNAV, January 8, 1906, No. 1965-59, GC, RG 24, NA.

36. CAPT A. Ross to BUNAV, July 1, 1905, No. 1965-26, GC, RG 24, NA. Contract with Jarvis Hunt, December 17, 1904, No. 1965-12, GC, RG 24, NA. RADM A. Ross to Chief BUNAV, August 6, 1908, No. 1965-94, GC, RG 24, NA.

37. Meyer to Gustav Kunsterman, October 13, 1909, No. 1965-138, GC, RG 24, NA. Ross to BUNAV, July 1, 1911, No. 1965-328, GC, RG 24, NA.

38. Report by the President of the Board for the Inspection of Shore Stations, August 12, 1910, No. 1965-206, GC, RG 24, NA.

39. Dillingham, "U.S. Naval Training Service," *USNIP* 36 (1910): 345.

40. House, Committee on Naval Affairs, *Hearings: Estimates Submitted by the SECNAV, 1916* (64th Cong., 1st sess., 1916), 1:957. *Annual Report of the Chief BUNAV, 1917*, p. 159.

41. House, Committee on Naval Affairs, *Hearings: Estimates Submitted by the SECNAV, 1919* (63d Cong., 3d sess., 1919), 1:640.

42. Bureau of Yards and Docks, *Real Estate*, pp. 155-56, 325. The exposition had gone into receivership and had offered to sell its land and buildings in 1908, but the navy did not buy them at that time. With the war, Congress appropriated money for the purchase, and the navy commissioned it as the Naval Operating Base at Hampton Roads on October 12, 1917. The station at St. Helena was used only as an auxiliary point for men on general detail. Finally on May 20, 1919, all activities on St. Helena ceased, and on June 23, 1919, the land became part of the navy yard. U.S., Congress, Senate, Committee on Naval Affairs, *Hearings: Naval Training Station on Hampton Roads, Virginia* (60th Cong., 1st sess., 1908). F. B. Upham to Harry Cooper, January 12, 1931, No. 1389-601, GC, RG 24, NA.

43. House, Committee on Naval Affairs, *Hearings: Estimates Submitted by the SECNAV, 1912* (62d Cong., 2d sess., 1912), p. 21. Bureau of Yards and Docks, *Real Estate*, p. 47. House, Committee on Naval Affairs, *Hearings: Estimates Submitted by the SECNAV, 1919* (63d Cong., 3d sess., 1919), p. 627. The 278 acres included forty acres under water.

44. *Annual Report of the Chief BUNAV, 1923,* p. 219.

45. A. H. Scales to LCDR C. S. Roberts, February 27, 1919, Scrapbook, 15:unnumbered, Scales Papers, SHC.

46. House, Committee on Naval Affairs, *Hearings: Estimates Submitted by the SECNAV, 1920* (66th Cong., 2d sess., 1920), p. 2311.

47. Senate, Committee on Naval Affairs, *Hearings: Naval Training Station at Norfolk, Va., and Newport, R.I.* (67th Cong., 2d sess., 1922), pp. 20-23.

48. W. C. Barker, BUNAV, to Clark Burdick, March 18, 1921, No. 6075-1846, GC, RG 24, NA.

49. Memorandum for Chief BUNAV, July 20, 1921, No. 6075-1875, GC, RG 24, NA. BUNAV, Memorandum for All Bureaus, October 17, 1921, No. 6075-1893, GC, RG 24, NA. Chief BUNAV to CO NTS Newport, July 1, 1922, No. 16456-19, GC, RG 24, NA. *Bureau of Navigation News Bulletin,* No. 26, June 5, 1923.

50. Curtis D. Wilbur to Carl R. Chindbloom, August 31, 1925, No. NM3/A4-2(22), GC, RG 24, NA.

51. U.S., Congress, House, Committee on Appropriations, *Hearings: Navy Department Appropriation Bill, 1925* (68th Cong., 1st sess., 1924), pp. 207, 208, 242, 247. For the Rodman Board report, see *Annual Report of the SECNAV, 1923,* pp. 80-96; training stations are discussed on page 90 of the report.

52. Chief BUNAV to CO NTS Great Lakes, May 9, 1933, No. NM3/A4-2(222), GC, RG 24, NA. 28 ALNAV, SECNAV to All Ships and Stations, June 27, 1935, No. NM3/(278), GC, RG 24, NA. House, Committee on Appropriations, *Hearings: Navy Department Appropriation Bill, 1934* (72d Cong., 2d sess., 1933), p. 161. Idem, *Hearings: Navy Department Appropriation Bill, 1936* (74th Cong., 1st sess., 1935), pp. 94, 157.

53. Chief BUNAV to CO U.S.T.S. *Lancaster,* January 16, 1900, No. 202424, GC, RG 24, NA. CAPT A. C. Dillingham to BUNAV, January 23, 1907, No. 5274-4, GC, RG 24, NA. CAPT A. C. Dillingham to BUNAV, October 17, 1907, No. 5274-12, GC, RG 24, NA.

54. Report of the Commandants of Naval Training Stations, May 20, 1920, No. 4111-1370, GC, RG 24, NA.

55. The *Annual Report of the Chief BUNAV, 1905,* p. 380, reported that one-third of all desertions were by men holding the rating of coal passer.

56. *Annual Report of the Chief BUEQUIP, 1877,* p. 124.

57. RADM W. C. Wise to BUNAV, April 1904, No. 3791-27, GC, RG 24, NA.

58. Report of Inspection of Norfolk, CAPT A. C. Dillingham to BUNAV, March 12, 1907, No. 1389-101, GC, RG 24, NA.

59. *Annual Report of the Surgeon General, 1902,* pp. 908-9, and *1905,* p. 1187.

60. Ibid., *1910,* p. 646.

61. General Order 271, May 11, 1881, in M. S. Thompson, comp., *General Orders and Circulars Issued by the Navy Department from 1863 to 1887* (Washington: GPO, 1887), p. 198. *Annual Report of the Chief BUNAV, 1900,* p. 451.

62. *Annual Report of the Chief BUNAV, 1903,* p. 483. Chief BUNAV to Benjamin R. Tillman, March 6, 1906, No. 1024-77, GC, RG 24, NA. *Annual Report of the Chief BUNAV, 1915,* p. 193.

63. House, Committee on Appropriations, *Hearings: Navy Department Appropriation Bill, 1924* (67th Cong., 4th sess., 1922), p. 43. U.S., Navy Department, BUNAV, *Yearbook of Enlisted Training, 1930* (Washington: GPO, 1931), p. 1. Chief BUNAV to Commandants Naval Training Stations, April 28, 1931, No. P11-1/MM(223), GC, RG 24, NA.

64. San Francisco fared better—it gave an average of four months' training. The course at Newport averaged three months, ten days. Semiannual Report, A. C. Dillingham to BUNAV, July 25, 1907, No. 5274-10, GC, RG 24, NA.

65. House, Committee on Naval Affairs, *Hearings: Estimates Submitted by the SECNAV, 1912* (62d Cong., 2d sess., 1912), p. 9. *Annual Report of the Chief BUNAV, 1914*, p. 150.

66. Lyman A. Cotten, uncensored letter to his wife, April 22, 1917, Folder 98, Box 6, Lyman A. Cotten Papers, SHC. See also his Diary, April 17, 1917, 17:116, Box 35.

67. For comments on receiving ships, see *Annual Report of the Chief BUNAV, 1900*, p. 459, and *Annual Report of the Surgeon General, 1904*, p. 1165. For an example of disease at training camps, see *Annual Report of the Surgeon General, 1903*, pp. 1198-203.

68. S. H. Dickson to Commandant Navy Yard and Station Norfolk, March 25, 1908, No. 1389-119, GC, RG 24, NA.

69. *Man-O'-Warsman* 1 (November 1908): 47-48.

70. Lyman A. Cotten, uncensored letter to his wife, May 2, 1917, Folder 99, Box 6, Lyman A. Cotten Papers, SHC.

71. William F. Fullam, "The Training of Landsmen for the Navy," *USNIP* 28 (1902): 475.

72. *Annual Report of the Chief BUNAV, 1903*, p. 483.

73. C. F. Martin, ed., *A Booklet Descriptive and Illustrative of the United States Naval Training Station, Great Lakes, Illinois* (n.p., 1916), p. 5.

74. BUNAV, *Yearbook of Enlisted Training*, p. 1.

75. Some of the many accounts of men in training camps are G. L. Peirce to Executive Officer Newport, May 26, 1908, No. 6075-87, GC, RG 24, NA; Ernest Durr, "The Training of Recruits," *USNIP* 43 (1917): 104; LT William Woodworth Phelps, "Making a Man-of-Warsman," *Our Naval Apprentice* 4 (October 1904): 49-52; *Naval Training*, Signal Corps film in Audiovisual Archives Division, NA; U.S., Navy Department, BUNAV, *The United States Navy: The Enlistment, Instruction, Pay, and Advancement of Young Men* (Washington: GPO, 1917), pp. 20-21; *Great Lakes Bulletin*, August 11, 1911; and Orton P. Jackson and Frank E. Evans, "The Training of a Man-O'-War's-Man," *St. Nicholas* 44 (July 1917): 834-37.

76. CAPT John G. Quinby to the Parents of Apprentice Seamen, enclosed in Daniels to Naval Recruiting Stations, September 9, 1913, No. 1024-202, GC, RG 24, NA.

77. A. C. Dillingham, "Methods Employed at Training Stations for Training Apprentice Seamen for the Fleet," *USNIP* 33 (1907): 140.

78. Ibid. Jackson and Evans, "The Training of a Man-O'-War's-Man," p. 834.

79. See, for example, "A Young American Citizen and Ex Sailor" to SECNAV Daniels, August 13, 1915, No. 6075-940, GC, RG 24, NA; and "The Fighting Boys of Uncle Sam" to Daniels, October 19, 1918, Subject File "Intelligence," Box 398, Josephus Daniels Papers, LC.

80. CO NTS San Diego to SECNAV, July 23, 1931, Annual Report, No. A9-1/NM5(199), GC, RG 24, NA.

81. Memorandum for Surgeon General from JAG, November 16, 1914, No. 7657-245:2, GC, RG 80, NA. Chief BUNAV to Recruiting Stations, February 12, 1923, No. 47358-01-5, GC, RG 24, NA.

82. BUNAV to CO NTS Great Lakes, August 29, 1923, No. 55402-525, GC, RG 24, NA. *Annual Report of the Chief BUNAV, 1924*, pp. 152-53. C. G. Smith to CO NTS Hampton Roads, May 6, 1925, No. P11-1/P2-5(6), GC, RG 24, NA.

83. Chief BUNAV to All Ships and Stations, January 9, 1929, No. P11-1(804), GC, RG 24, NA.

84. BUNAV Circular Letter 55-31, June 24, 1931, No. P11-1(1076), GC, RG 24, NA. BUNAV Circular Letter 8-38, February 8, 1938, No. P11-1(1750), GC, RG 24, NA.

85. Dillingham, "Methods Employed at Training Stations," p. 137.

86. *Bureau of Navigation News Bulletin*, No. 45, May 16, 1924.

87. C. F. Goodrich, "Naval Education," *USNIP* 5 (1879): 341.

88. See *Our Naval Apprentice* 1 (March 1902): 11, and *Bluejacket* 10 (January 15, 1910): inside front cover, for such advertisements.

89. E. A. Sietz to President of the United States, January 24, 1906, No. 1024-76, GC, RG 24, NA.

90. *Annual Report of the Chief of the Bureau of Ordnance, 1883*, p. 413, and *1885*, p. 207. Chief BUNAV to CO *Amphitrite*, November 2, 1897, and December 16, 1897, No. 156617, GC, RG 24, NA.

91. *Annual Report of the SECNAV, 1899*, p. 25.

92. Chief BUNAV to Commandants Newport and Yerba Buena, March 9, 1901, No. 256249, GC, RG 24, NA. This letter indicates that BUNAV intended to establish a similar course at Yerba Buena, but instruction was apparently not begun. See *Annual Report of the Chief BUNAV, 1901*, p. 514, and *1903*, pp. 485-86.

93. *Fleet Review* 3 (February 1913): 3-6

94. See Appendix, table 8, for a list of advanced schools established before 1940.

95. *Annual Report of the Chief BUNAV, 1919*, p. 380. F. W. Milner to W. G. Sullivan, Officer in Charge Fuel Oil School, Fore River Shipbuilding Corporation, May 6, 1918, No. N9M/G404, GC, Training Division, RG 24, NA. Willard Connely, "Making Sailors without Ships," *Independent* 92 (November 10, 1917): 283.

96. BUNAV, *Yearbook of Enlisted Training*, pp. 3, 60-61. *Annual Report of the Chief BUNAV, 1925*, p. 160, and *1927*, p. 173.

97. Report by CAPT E. S. Houston of gunnery ship *Amphitrite* in *Annual Report of the SECNAV, 1900*, p. 541. Report of the Commandant of NTS Newport, in *Annual Report of the SECNAV, 1901*, p. 598.

98. "Annual Report of Naval Training Station, Newport, Rhode Island," in *Annual Report of the Chief BUNAV, 1903*, p. 586.

99. See, for example, Memorandum for LCDR Root from Office of the Director of Naval Communication Service, October 1, 1917, No. 5525-2283, GC, RG 24, NA.

100. LT Louis Nulton to BUNAV, January 12, 1905, No. 525-216, GC, RG 24, NA.

101. Newton A. McCully, Diary, September 28, 1923, Newton Alexander McCully Papers, SHC.

102. *Bureau of Navigation News Bulletin*, No. 28, August 1, 1923.

103. CO Newport to BUNAV, November 16, 1914. SECNAV to Universal Film Co., November 21, 1914. Universal Film Mfg. Co. to Daniels, November 25, 1914. Daniels to Jack Cohn, December 16, 1914, No. 6075-909, GC, RG 24, NA.

104. *Annual Report of the Chief BUNAV, 1926*, p. 158. BUNAV, *Yearbook of Enlisted Training*, p. 85. The other titles were *Resuscitation of the Apparently Drowned, Diesel Oil Engines, Electrical Transmission of Speech, Norfolk Gas Engines, Storage Batteries*, and *Oil-Burning Boilers*.

105. *Annual Report of the Chief BUNAV, 1930*, p. 181. CDR D. E. Cummings, "Enlisted Training in the Navy," *USNIP* 55 (1929): 884-85.

106. *Annual Report of the Chief BUNAV, 1933*, p. 31. The other new slide films were *Packing, Steam and Water Cycle, Boat Building*, and *Boots—Nomenclature and Types*.

107. William Exton, Jr., "Motion Picture Training Films in the Navy," *USNIP* 69 (1943): 933.

108. *Annual Report of the SECNAV, 1913*, p. 6.

109. Daniels to COs Ships in Commission and Reserve, June 7, 1913, No. 1024-192, GC, RG 24, NA. The answers are filed under the same number. A memorandum of July 10, 1913, tabulates the results.

110. Board to Outline Scheme of Instruction for Apprentice Seamen to CO NTS Newport, June 20, 1913, No. 1024-194, GC, RG 24, NA.

111. General Order 172, November 6, 1914.

112. *Annual Report of the SECNAV, 1916*, p. 53.

113. See, for example, E. K. Roden, "Our Navy as a Schoolhouse: Success of the New System in the First Year of Its Operation," *Scientific American* 114 (February 26, 1916): 218-19; and Walter B. Norris, "The Educational Developments of the Navy," *Education* 35 (April 1915): 503-10.

114. LT H. Hoogewerffe, in CAPT Irwin to CDR Mayo, August 13, 1919, Subject 250, Morale, Replies to Admiral's Letter, GC, Sixth Division, RG 24, NA. Chief Yeoman Ray W. Byrns, Letter to Editor, *Our Navy* 8 (September 1914): 22.

115. House, Committee on Naval Affairs, *Hearings: Estimates Submitted by the SECNAV, 1916* (64th Cong., 1st sess., 1916), 1:898.

116. Oscar D. Conger to "My Dear Eagle," July 25, 1919, Subject 250, Morale, Replies to Admiral's Letter, GC, Sixth Division, RG 24, NA.

117. Cotten, Diary, March 8, 1917, 17:14, Box 35, Lyman Cotten Papers, SHC.

118. Cotten, uncensored letter to his wife, September 21, 1917, Folder 101, Box 7, Lyman A. Cotten Papers, SHC. Emphasis in the original.

119. U.S., Congress, House, Committee on Naval Affairs, *Hearings: Sundry Legislation Affecting the Naval Establishment, 1920-21* (66th Cong., 3d sess., 1921), p. 144.

120. Daniels to Reed Smoot, January 5, 1921, No. 55402-147, GC, RG 24, NA.

121. Ibid. BUNAV to CINC Pacific Fleet, July 12, 1921, No. 55402-238, GC, RG 24, NA. House, Committee on Naval Affairs, *Hearings: Sundry Legislation Affecting the Naval Establishment, 1920-21*, pp. 144, 148.

122. R. H. Leigh to CO U.S.S. *Sands*, March 4, 1924, No. 55402-632, GC, RG 24, NA. See also BUNAV to CO U.S.S. *Shirk*, February 26, 1925, No. P11-1/DD318(16), GC, RG 24, NA.

123. CO U.S.S. *Pecos* to CINC Asiatic Fleet, September 12, 1928, No. P11-1/MM(117), GC, RG 24, NA.

124. *Annual Report of the SECNAV, 1926*, p. 23.

125. *Bureau of Navigation News Bulletin*, No. 70, March 29, 1926.

126. Chief BUNAV to CO U.S.S. *New Mexico*, October 28, 1930, No. P11-1/BB40(1005), GC, RG 24, NA. *Bureau of Navigation Bulletin*, No. 144, November 8, 1930.

CHAPTER 7

1. Enlisted strength is from U.S., Department of Commerce, Bureau of the Census, *Historical Statistics of the United States, Colonial Times to 1957* (Washington: GPO, 1960), p. 737. The list of ratings was compiled from U.S., Navy Department, Bureau of Naval Personnel, Recorder, Permanent Board for Control of the Enlisted Rating Structure, *Compilation of Enlisted Ratings and Apprenticeships, U.S. Navy, 1775 to the Present* (mimeographed, September 1967). The division of ratings by branch is based on the pay table for 1890 in U.S., Navy Department, *Navy Register, 1890*, pp. 169-70.

2. The ratings not named in the text were able seaman, boatswain's yeoman, boy, captain's clerk, cockswain, cooper, gunner's yeoman, master at arms, master's mate, ordinary seaman, quarter gunner, quartermaster (for frigates), sailmaker's mate, and yeoman of the gunroom. Permanent Board for Control of the Enlisted Rating Structure, *Compilation of Enlisted Ratings*.

3. See Bureau of the Census, *Historical Statistics*, p. 737, for enlisted strength. The number of ratings was calculated from Permanent Board for Control of the Enlisted Rating Structure, *Compilation of Enlisted Ratings*.

4. The number of ratings was fifty-nine in 1866. Permanent Board for Control of the Enlisted Rating Structure, *Compilation of Enlisted Ratings*.

5. The continuing rivalry between engineering and line officers, which Peter Karsten discusses in his *Naval Aristocracy*, may also have affected the configuration of the enlisted

force. Karsten, *The Naval Aristocracy: The Golden Age of Annapolis and the Emergence of Modern American Navalism* (New York: Free Press, 1972), pp. 65-69.

6. U.S. Navy Regulation Circular No. 41, January 8, 1885, in M.S. Thompson, comp., *General Orders and Circulars Issued by the Navy Department from 1863 to 1887* (Washington: GPO, 1887), p. 242.

7. See Appendix, table 9.

8. The numbers of ratings were calculated from Permanent Board for Control of the Enlisted Rating Structure, *Compilation of Enlisted Ratings*. Enlisted strengths are from *Annual Report of the Chief BUNAV, 1897,* p. 221, *1910,* p. 294, and *1930,* p. 203.

9. See Appendix, table 9.

10. Calculated from Permanent Board for Control of the Enlisted Rating Structure, *Compilation of Enlisted Ratings*. The placement of ratings of the artificer branch into engine-room and nonengine-room categories was based on the grouping of the ship's complement in the 1910 log of the U. S. S. *Connecticut* in Logs of United States Naval Ships and Stations, 1801-1946, RG 24, NA.

11. In fact, the electrician rating had been established in 1883, only to be disestablished the next year, and finally to be reestablished permanently in 1898. See Appendix, table 9.

12. See Appendix, table 9, for the creation of the radioman rating. The New York electrician school included the care and use of the radio in its curriculum. CDR. R. H. Leigh to Commandant Navy Yard New York, June 30, 1907, No. 2836-18, GC, RG 24, NA.

13. For presidential authority, see John F. Callan and A. W. Russell, comps., *Laws of the United States Relating to the Navy and Marine Corps from the Formation of the Government to 1859* (Baltimore: John Murphy & Co., 1859), p. 86. For the 1900 pay table, see Navy Department, *Navy Register, 1900,* pp. 183-84.

14. "Schedule of Rates of Pay on the Pacific Coast," enclosure to CDR V. L. Cottman to Chief BUNAV, June 4, 1903, No. 562-18, GC, RG 24, NA. For the 1903 pay table, see Navy Department, *Navy Register, 1903,* pp. 197-98.

15. Naval Appropriation Act for 1909, in U.S., *Statutes at Large,* 35:128.

16. Act of May 22, 1917, in U.S., *Statutes at Large,* 40:87.

17. Act of July 11, 1919, in U.S., *Statutes at Large,* 41:140.

18. Paul F. Brissenden, *Earnings of Factory Workers, 1899 to 1927: An Analysis of Pay-roll Statistics* (1929; reprint ed., New York: Burt Franklin, 1971), pp. 68, 96. Bureau of the Census, *Historical Statistics,* pp. 91, 92.

19. "Navy Pay and a Fifty Cent Dollar," *Scientific American* 121 (November 8, 1919): 456.

20. Act of May 18, 1920, in U.S., *Statutes at Large,* 41:602.

21. Act of June 10, 1922, in U.S., *Statutes at Large,* 42:629-30. See also "Comments by the Navy Representatives of the Service Committee on the Pay Bill," no date (ca. 1922), No. 24447-41, GC, RG 24, NA.

22. See, for example, *Our Navy* 23 (Mid-November 1929): 35.

23. Report of the Interdepartment Pay Board, July 19, 1929, p. 41, No. L16-4(155), GC, RG 24, NA.

24. *Annual Report of the SECNAV, 1933,* p. 15.

25. "The Pay Cuts," *Our Navy* 27 (May 1, 1933): 29.

26. *Annual Report of the SECNAV, 1933,* p. 16. *Annual Report of the Chief BUNAV, 1933,* p. 6.

27. See, for example, A. Consier, Pharmacist's Mate, 1st class, to Louis Howe, Secretary to the President, June 16, 1933, No. L16-4(292), GC, RG 24, NA.

28. *Annual Report of the SECNAV, 1934,* p. 15, and *1935,* p. 16.

29. A bonus for submarine duty was instituted by President Theodore Roosevelt after a trip on the *Plunger* on August 26, 1905. Before that time submariners did not get extra pay, and the duty counted as shore rather than sea duty for promotion. *New York Times,*

August 27, 1905, p. 5. Aviation pay was established by an act of June 10, 1922, in U.S., *Statutes at Large*, 42:632.

30. Act of June 10, 1922, in U.S., *Statutes at Large*, 42:630.

31. See chapter 2 for a discussion of the reenlistment bonus. The death gratuity was established by an act of May 13, 1908, in U.S., *Statutes at Large*, 35:128.

32. Revenue Act of 1918, in U.S., *Statutes at Large*, 40:1151.

33. See, for example, BUNAV to All Ships and Stations, June 2, 1921, No. 5570-1618, GC, RG 24, NA, which announced a Minnesota bonus of fifteen dollars for each month served by citizens of Minnesota.

34. Naval Appropriation Acts for 1891 and 1901, in U.S., *Statutes at Large*, 26:190 and 31:686.

35. LCDR H. B. Wilson to Officer in Charge Recruiting Station Boston, November 16, 1906, No. 1882-36, GC, RG 24, NA. W. A. Moffett to BUNAV, January 4, 1917, No. 1882-87, GC, RG 24, NA.

36. House, Committee on Naval Affairs, *Hearings: Estimates Submitted by the SECNAV, 1918* (65th Cong., 1st sess., 1918), p. 32. Naval Appropriation Act for 1919, in U.S., *Statutes at Large*, 40:707.

37. U.S., Congress, House, Committee on Appropriations, *Hearings: Navy Department Appropriation Bill for 1935* (73d Cong., 2d sess., 1934), p. 299. Act of June 30, 1932, in U.S., *Statutes at Large*, 47:451.

38. Officer in Charge Springfield, Mass., Recruiting Office to BUNAV, March 4, 1926, enclosing a clipping from the Newport Naval Training Station newspaper, No. L16-4/MM(55), GC, RG 24, NA.

39. Report of the Interdepartment Pay Board, July 19, 1929, No. L16-4(155), GC, RG 24, NA.

40. BUNAV Circular Letter 6-29, No. 014-2 MN (84), GC, RG 24, NA. U.S., Navy Department, *Regulations for the Government of the Navy, 1905* (Washington: GPO, 1905), pp. 191-94, and *1909*, pp. 179-82. U.S., Navy Department, BUNAV, *Manual, 1925* (Washington: GPO, 1925), pp. 11-14, and *1942*, pp. 84-89.

41. LT Mark L. Bristol to CINC Atlantic Fleet, February 17, 1903, No. 562-9, GC, RG 24, NA.

42. General Order 134 of June 26, 1903, for example, required that men seeking permanent appointment as chief petty officer demonstrate their competence before a board of three officers from a ship other than the one on which they were serving.

43. See W. S. Sims to Daniels, September 27, 1918, File "Sims, Adm. W. S. (1)," Correspondence, Box 43, Josephus Daniels Papers, LC. E. D. McEathron, "Selection of 'Strikers,'" *USNIP* 60 (1934): 655.

44. Ernest Driscoll, Letter to Editor, *Our Navy* 21 (July 1, 1927): 21. See also Charles Herget, "Dear Shipmate" (Xeroxed memoirs of naval service, Turnersville, New Jersey, 1967), pp. 51-58, recounting his efforts to get promoted to chief petty officer between 1928 and 1932.

45. *Annual Report of the Chief BUNAV, 1899*, p. 404, and *1902*, p. 405.

46. John W. Swift, *An Iowa Boy around the World in the Navy: A True Story of Our Navy, 1898-1902* (Des Moines: Kenyon Printing & Manufacturing Co., 1902), pp. 12, 63.

47. See chapter 6, note 92, and Appendix, table 8, for the creation of the petty officers' school. Circular Letter, October 20, 1903, No. 1020-15, GC, RG 24, NA. *Annual Report of the Chief BUNAV, 1913*, p. 133.

48. L. C. Palmer, Chief BUNAV, to Commandants All Navy Yards and Naval Stations and All Superintending Constructors, September 19, 1917, No. 5524-287, GC, RG 24, NA. Ray Millholland, *The Splinter Fleet of the Otranto Barrage* (New York: Bobbs-Merrill Co., 1936), pp. 15-16.

49. BUNAV Circular Letter 12-22, March 28, 1922, No. 57354-17, GC, RG 24, NA.
50. BUNAV to All Ships and Stations, February 7, 1924, No. 4111-1413-9, GC, RG 24, NA.
51. Act of March 3, 1899, in U.S., *Statutes at Large*, 30:1007.
52. Act of March 3, 1901, in U.S., *Statutes at Large*, 31:1129. House, Committee on Naval Affairs, *Hearings: Estimates Submitted by the SECNAV, 1907* (59th Cong., 2d sess., 1907), p. 427.
53. Stevens Vail, "Making of a Man of War's Man," *Junior Munsey* 11 (December 1901): 367. For biographies of two men commissioned early in the century, see *Our Naval Apprentice* 2 (July 1902): 8-9, and (December 1902):3.
54. U.S., Congress, Senate, Committee on Naval Affairs, *Hearings: Naval Investigation* (66th Cong., 2d sess., 1921), 2:2768.
55. Naval Appropriation Acts for 1915, 1917, and 1918, in U.S., *Statutes at Large*, 38:410, 39:576, and 39:1182.
56. General Order 124, October 19, 1914.
57. Philip D. Gallery, "The Naval Academy Preparatory Class," *USNIP* 63 (1937): 376-77.
58. *Our Navy* 14 (October 1920): 11. One such man was LT H. V. Barr, who joined the navy in 1892 at age sixteen as an apprentice, third class. Barr rose to gunner's mate in the Spanish-American War. In World War I he received a commission, which he retained after the war. Barr, "From Gob to Striper," *"Tennessee" Tar* (September 1920), Box 5, A. Staton Papers, SHC.
59. *Bluejacket's Manual, 1922* (Annapolis, Md.: U.S. Naval Institute, 1922), pp. 46-47.
60. Ibid., p. 48.
61. Chief BUNAV to SECNAV, February 29, 1932, No. P19-1(406), GC, RG 24, NA.
62. Acting Chief BUNAV to Lamar Jeffers, December 3, 1925, No. P19-1(66), GC, RG 24, NA.
63. See, for example, BUNAV, *Manual, 1925*, pp. 215-16; and Chief BUNAV to J. R. Mitchell, January 28, 1937, No. P19-1(600), GC, RG 24, NA.
64. A. Staton to CAPT Charles F. Russel, December 10, 1933, Folder 60, Box 4, A. Staton Papers, SHC.
65. General Order 414, July 3, 1893.
66. See Memorandum, received December 5, 1906, No. 1120-108, GC, RG 24, NA.
67. Chief BUNAV to Dr. Frank M. Wright, December 10, 1934, No. P19-1(528), GC, RG 24, NA. Memorandum for the Recruiting Service by CAPT F. H. Poteet, December 19, 1927, No. P19-1(216), GC, RG 24, NA.
68. K. G. Gastleman, BUNAV, to Cornelius A. McGlennon, April 30, 1919, No. 1120-1379, GC, RG 24, NA. Circular for Information of Commanding Officers of Navy Recruiting Stations, September 9, 1916, No. 1120-519, GC, RG 24, NA.
69. BUNAV to JAG, April 20, 1917, No. 1120-566, GC, RG 24, NA. BUNAV, *Manual, 1925*, p. 197.
70. See, for example, SECNAV to LT Paul Foley, CO U.S.S. *Dixie*, February 17, 1910, No. 1120-187, GC, RG 24, NA.
71. Chief BUNAV to CO U.S.S. *Franklin*, April 9, 1906, No. 1120-104, GC, RG 24, NA. W. R. Shoemaker, *A Lecture Delivered before the War College Class, April 28, 1925, on Navy Personnel* (Washington: GPO, 1925), p. 35. Acting Chief BUNAV to Ross A. Collins, September 29, 1923, No. 57364-363, GC, RG 24, NA.
72. *Annual Report of the SECNAV, 1914*, p. 42. An act of August 29, 1916, offered easy exit for men enlisting after that date. After one year of service at sea, men not in debt to the government, not under charges, and not undergoing punishment could receive a discharge at their own request without cost in June or December. The provision was withdrawn for

men enlisting after March 3, 1917. The war ended the possibility for most men. Navy Department, *Regulations for the Government of the Navy, 1918*, p. 247.

73. *Annual Report of the Chief BUNAV, 1914*, p. 156, and *1915*, p. 210.

74. *Our Navy* 8 (October 1914): 16.

75. Commandant Great Lakes NTS to BUNAV, January 28, 1914, and reply February 11,1914, No. 1120-374, GC, RG 24, NA. CO Newport NTS to BUNAV, October 8, 1915, No. 1120-474, GC, RG 24, NA.

76. See House, Committee on Appropriations, *Hearings: Navy Department Appropriation Bill for 1931* (71st Cong., 2d sess., 1930), p. 115, table of men leaving the service for reasons other than expiration of enlistment, 1925-29; and idem, *Hearings: Navy Department Appropriation Bill for 1935* (73d Cong., 2d sess., 1934), p. 118, table "Attrition by Causes," 1930-33.

77. U.S., Congress, House, *Report on HR 5670* (48th Cong., 1st sess., 1884), H. Rept. 616.

78.*Annual Report of the Chief BUEQUIP, 1885*, p. 197.

79. For examples of petitions see U.S., Congress, House and Senate, *Congressional Record* (53d Cong., 3d sess., 1895), 27, pt. 1: 232, 310, 384, 477, 532, 576, 620, 763, 889, pt. 2:1008, 1131, 1164, 1201, 1243, 1275, 1327, 1520, 1764, 1813, pt. 3:2111, 2203, 2274. Writers' Program, Ohio, *The Army and Navy Union, U.S.A.* (n.p.: Army & Navy Union, 1942), pp. 27-28.

80. House, *Congressional Record* (55th Cong., 3d sess., 1899), 32, pt. 1:719.

81. *Annual Report of the JAG, 1899*, p. 133. Act of March 3, 1899, In U.S., *Statutes at Large*, 30:1008.

82. *Annual Report of the JAG, 1899*, p. 133.

83. House, Committee on Naval Affairs, *Hearings: Estimates Submitted by the SECNAV, 1909* (60th Cong., 2d sess., 1909), p. 789. A. C. Dillingham, "How Shall We Induce Our Men to Continue in the Navy," *USNIP* 35 (1909): 1022, 1023, 1025.

84. *Annual Report of the SECNAV, 1911*, p. 53. See also *Annual Report of the Chief BUNAV, 1913*, p. 121.

85. U.S., Navy Department, BUNAV, *The United States Navy: The Enlistment, Instruction, Pay, and Advancement of Young Men* (Washington: GPO, 1917), p. 19. Chief BUNAV to J. F. Lippett, December 22, 1925, No. P19-2/MM(13), GC, RG 24, NA.

CHAPTER 8

1. Marcus Goodrich, *Delilah* (New York: Farrar & Rinehart, 1941), p. 85.

2. Peter Karsten, *The Naval Aristocracy: The Golden Age of Annapolis and the Emergence of Modern American Navalism* (New York: Free Press, 1972), pp. 5-19.

3. Thomas Beyer, *The American Battleship and Life in the Navy* (Chicago: Laird & Lee, 1908), p. 177. U.S., Navy Department, *The Bluejacket's Manual, 1918*, 6th ed., rev. 1916 (New York: Edwin N. Appleton, 1918), pp. 91-97.

4. The following are examples of offenses for which regulations prescribed such differences in the punishments of officers and men: refusing to obey the lawful order of a superior officer; cruelty toward or oppression or maltreatment of any person subject to his orders; lewd or indecent behavior; neglect of duty; and using profane, obscene, or abusive language toward another person in the service. U.S., Navy Department, *Naval Courts and Boards, 1917* (Washington: GPO, 1917), pp. 218-24.

5. Karsten, *Naval Aristocracy*, pp. 89, 92, 359.

6. L. H. Thebaud, *Naval Leadership with Some Hints to Junior Officers and Others* (Annapolis, Md.: U.S. Naval Institute, 1924), pp. 79-80.

7. Fred J. Buenzle, with A. Grove Day, *Bluejacket: An Autobiography* (New York: W. W. Norton & Co., 1939), p. 40.

8. Clergy of Provincetown to Secretary Bonaparte, March 16, 1906, and RADM R. D. Evans to BUNAV, April 17, 1906, No. 3328-69, GC, RG 24, NA.

9. Adolphus Andrews, "Naval Personnel of Today," *USNIP* 62 (1936): 1404.

10. Thebaud, *Naval Leadership*, p. 81.

11. U.S., Navy Department, *Regulations for the Government of the Navy, 1913* (Washington: GPO, 1913), p. 148.

12. I was unable to find a record of such a case.

13. U.S., Navy Department, *The Bluejackets' Manual, 1927*, 7th ed., rev. 1927 (Washington: GPO, 1928), p. 11, discourages attempts to seek congressional aid. See also Henry A. Wiley, *An Admiral from Texas* (New York: Doubleday, Doran & Co., 1934), pp. 155-57.

14. U.S., Congress, House, Committee on Naval Affairs, *Hearings: Sundry Legislation Affecting the Naval Establishment, 1920-21* (66th Cong., 3d sess., 1921), p. 819.

15. *Great Lakes Bulletin*, July 29, 1918.

16. Navy Department, *Bluejacket's Manual, 1918*, p. 17. Emphasis in the original. Other editions of the manual contain similar statements.

17. Ibid., pp. 14-15.

18. Leland Pearsons Lovette, *Naval Customs, Traditions, and Usage* (Annapolis, Md.: U.S. Naval Institute, 1934), pp. 59-71. Charles Richard Williams, "On the History of Discipline in the Navy," *USNIP* 45 (1919): 355.

19. Navy Department, *Bluejackets' Manual, 1927*, p. 212.

20. J. H. McGilliam, "Gobs Should Be Proud of Right to Salute: It Implies Equality," *Great Lakes Bulletin*, June 30, 1919. See also Asiatic Fleet Circular 11, December 17, 1919, No. 125135(71), File "Fleet Asiatic," Box 382, GC, RG 52, NA.

21. Navy Department, *Bluejacket's Manual, 1918*, p. 19. Emphasis in the original.

22. U.S., Navy Department, Office of the Judge Advocate General, *Manual for the Government of Naval Prisons: General Instructions Relating to Prisoners* (Washington: GPO, 1918), p. 3.

23. Ibid.

24. Navy Department, *Regulations for the Government of the Navy, 1909*, p. 189.

25. Ibid.

26. See chapter 2.

27. William F. Fullam, *Recruit's Handy Book* (Annapolis, Md.: U.S. Naval Institute, 1903), pp. 13-14. Navy Department, *Bluejacket's Manual, 1918*, pp. 25-27. Idem, *Regulations for the Government of the Navy, 1905*, p. 201.

28. See, for example, *Bureau of Navigation News Bulletin*, No. 37, January 2, 1924.

29. On July 1 and 2, 1903, BUNAV sent letters to ships and stations asking for reasons for desertion. Two of the more complete replies are from CAPT C. F. Goodrich to BUNAV, July 8, 1903, and CAPT A. Snow to BUNAV, July 6, 1903, No. 918-40, GC, RG 24, NA. *New York Times*, November 12, 1905, pt. 3:4. RADM C. D. Sigsbee to CINC Atlantic Fleet, April 19, 1906, No. 918-198, GC, RG 24, NA. R. H. Leigh to BUNAV, December 14, 1920, No. 918-1236, GC, RG 24, NA. CO U.S.S. *Florida* to BUNAV, March 9, 1921, No. 918-1236, GC, RG 24, NA. The results of a study of desertion during 1923 are in U.S., Congress, House, Committee on Appropriations, *Navy Department Appropriation Bill for 1925* (68th Cong., 1st sess., 1924), pp. 148-53.

30. Leutze to BUNAV, July 6, 1903, No. 918-40, GC, RG 24, NA. For a similar statement see, LCDR E. H. Tillman to BUNAV, October 14, 1903, No. 918-57, GC, RG 24, NA.

31. CO U.S.S. *Asheville* to BUNAV, December 22, 1920, No. 918-1236, GC, RG 24, NA. BUNAV to All Ships and Stations, November 20, 1920, requested opinions on the reasons for desertions and on steps to reduce it. File number 918-1236 contains two folders of replies. Most letters stress the low quality of recruits.

32. See *Bostonian* 4 (May 1910): 426-27. "An Enlisted Man" on the U.S.S. *Maryland* to Bonaparte, October 27, 1905, No. 918-178, GC, RG 24, NA. RADM J. B. Coghlan to SECNAV, January 18, 1904, No. 525-116, GC, RG 24, NA. George Steinberg to SECNAV, September 20, 1903, No. 918-67, GC, RG 24, NA.

33. Record of Proceedings of a Board of Investigation to Inquire into the Large Numbers of Desertions from the U.S.S. *Wyoming* . . . , October 2, 1903, No. 918-53, GC, RG 24, NA. Blaming the recruiter was still putting the primary blame on the type of men entering the service and not on the navy itself.

34. See note 31 above.

35. The unemployment rate is from U.S., Department of Commerce, Bureau of the Census, *Historical Statistics of the United States, Colonial Times to 1957* (Washington: GPO, 1960), p. 73. See Appendix, table 11, for desertion rates.

36. Board to Examine into the General Nature of the Administration of the Laws Affecting Navy Discipline and Punishment, June 15, 1929, Folder 42, Box 3, A. Staton Papers, SHC.

37. House, Committee on Naval Affairs, *Hearings: Sundry Legislation Affecting the Naval Establishment, 1920-21*, p. 805. The accused, for example, had a right to counsel, but only the judge advocate and the accused could address the court unless the convening authority ordered otherwise. Navy Department, *Regulations for the Government of the Navy, 1905*, p. 486.

38. For general references on courts-martial, see U.S., Navy Department, *Naval Courts and Boards, 1937* (Washington: GPO, 1937), pp. 189-344, and idem, *Bluejackets' Manual, 1927*, pp. 246-48.

39. SECNAV to BUNAV, July 13, 1903, No. 963-24, GC, RG 24, NA.

40. Act of February 16, 1909, in U.S., *Statutes at Large*, 35:621.

41. Ibid. The deck court could sentence an enlisted man to solitary confinement on bread and water for not more than twenty days, solitary confinement for not more than twenty days, loss of liberty on foreign station, reduction to the next inferior rate, extra duties, and loss of pay for not more than twenty days.

42. "The Deck Court and the Enlisted Man," *Our Navy* 7 (January 1914): 17.

43. See Appendix, table 12.

44. Compiled from *Annual Report of the JAG* for the years 1904-39.

45. Frederick L. Sawyer, *Sons of Gunboats* (Annapolis, Md.: U.S. Naval Institute, 1946), pp. 90-91.

46. *Annual Report of the SECNAV, 1920*, p. 91. BUNAV Circular Letter 17-24, March 10, 1924, No. 507, GC, Division of Fleet Training, RG 38, NA. For examples of use of the commendatory mast, see Diary of Lyman A. Cotten, August 31, 1924, 26:89-90, Lyman A. Cotten Papers, SHC; and A. Staton to Mrs. R. J. Marian, February 22, 1931, Folder 54, Box 3, A. Staton Papers, SHC.

47. There is a sizable, though by no means complete, collection of ship logs with the records of BUNAV in the NA. I selected logs from the years 1900, 1910, 1920, and 1930 and examined the entries for May and December of each year. There were a total of 389 infractions under twenty-two captains. There are obvious limits to this method—the sample is small, and no attempt was made to match the selection with the distribution of ships and assignments in the navy. Nevertheless, in the absence of other records, this study does offer some understanding of the conduct of the mast.

48. Conduct books are in RG 24, NA. The length of time represented for each man varied from less than a month to two years; the period for most men was less than one year. Only a few conduct books remain; there are none for the years after 1905.

49. George F. Wiley, Letter to Editor, *Bostonian* 4 (July 1910): 490. James B. Connolly, *Navy Men* (New York: John Day Co., 1939), p. 30.

50. R. E. Krause, "Morale for Our 'New Navy,'" *USNIP* 47 (1921): 523.

51. The Senate passed an amendment to the 1909 navy appropriation bill that would have abolished all use of irons. Secretary of the Navy Truman Newberry protested that such a provision would deprive "the captain of the power to use practically the only means under his control to place in restraint unmanageable members of the crew." As a result, the final version of the act allowed the navy to continue limited use of irons. U.S., Congress, Senate, *Congressional Record* (60th Cong., 1st sess., 1908), 42, pt. 6:5117-18. Truman Newberry to George Foss, April 28, 1908, in House, Committee on Naval Affairs, *Hearings: Estimates Submitted by the SECNAV, 1908-1909* (60th Cong., 2d sess., 1908), pp. 1123-24. Act of May 13, 1908, in U.S., *Statutes at Large*, 35:132.

52. Evans, 1st Endorsement, March 17, 1906, No. 3711-14, GC, RG 24, NA. See also LT B. B. Bierer to BUNAV, December 26, 1903, No. 3711-7, GC, RG 24, NA. Memorandum by Robert Russell, JAG, to BUNAV, August 15, 1910, No. 3711-25, GC, RG 24, NA. A. C. Dillingham, "Methods Employed at Training Stations for Training Apprentice Seamen for the Fleet," *USNIP* 33 (1907): 143. *Great Lakes Bulletin*, September 14, 1918.

53. Asiatic Fleet Circular Letter 1-24, January 2, 1924, No. 125135(11), Folder "1924-25," GC, RG 52, NA.

54. *Bluejacket* 10 (February 1, 1910): 120. Commander U.S. Naval Aviation Forces, Foreign Service, to CO All U.S. Air Stations, Circular Letter 22, April 17, 1918, which cites Circular Letter 17 from Force Commander (W. S. Sims), April 9, 1918, No. L4-a-1918, Discipline (General), Logistics File, 1911-27, RG 45, NA.

55. B. B. Bieber, "A Proposed System of Punishment for Certain Offenses against Navy Regulations," *USNIP* 30 (1904): 201-2.

56. Navy Department, *Navy Courts and Boards, 1937*, pp. 242-43. Idem, *Regulations for the Government of the Navy, 1913*, pp. 56, 65-66, 85-86.

57. Act of February 16, 1909, in U.S., *Statutes at Large*, 35:621.

58. BUNAV Circular Letter 3-24, December 11, 1924, No. A17-21/L16-4(2), GC, RG 24, NA. *Bureau of Navigation Bulletin*, No. 200, October 14, 1933.

59. BUNAV Circular Letter 13-22, April 11, 1922, No. A2-11(1), GC, RG 24, NA. See also Acting Chief BUNAV to CINC Atlantic Training Squadron, August 27, 1903, No. 3711-2, GC, RG 24, NA.

60. *Annual Report of the JAG, 1901*, p. 118.

61. Ibid., *1911*, pp. 171-72.

62. Meyer to Taft, August 14, 1911, in M. A. DeWolfe Howe, *George von Lengerke Meyer: His Life and Public Services* (New York: Dodd, Mead & Co., 1919), pp. 482-83.

63. *Annual Report of the JAG, 1912*, pp. 61-62. Charles B. Hatch, "The U.S. Naval Disciplinary Barracks, Port Royal, South Carolina," *USNIP* 38 (1912): 1382.

64. Hatch, "U.S. Naval Disciplinary Barracks, Port Royal," pp. 1379-84. Annual Report of CO Puget Sound Naval Disciplinary Barracks, June 30, 1912, Drawer "Ordnance, Athletics, Entertainments," Jacket 19, Folder 1, "Reports and Returns," Records of Naval Disciplinary Barracks, Puget Sound, Wash., RG 125, NA.

65. Daniels to Commandant Navy Yard Puget Sound, January 13, 1916, in Drawer "Receipts 1912-14," Naval Disciplinary Barracks, Puget Sound, RG 125, NA. The program at Puget Sound was transferred to the receiving ship *Philadelphia* in the same yard, where it continued at a reduced level until January 1916. Daniels to Commandant Navy Yard Puget Sound, April 24, 1914, No. 1-140, Jacket 1, Folder 2, in Drawer "Transfers, Ratings, and Enlistments," Naval Disciplinary Barracks, Puget Sound, RG 125, NA. Daniels to Commandant Navy Yard Puget Sound, August 15, 1914, JAG to SECNAV, August 12, 1914, 6-16, 6-19, Folder 1, Jacket 6, "Disciplinary Barracks, Policy, Etc.," in Drawer "Pay, Transportation, Etc.," Navy Disciplinary Barracks, Puget Sound, RG 125. *Annual Report of the JAG, 1914*, pp. 114-15.

66. *Annual Report of the JAG, 1915*, pp. 133-34.

67. Ibid., p. 137.

68. *Annual Report of the SECNAV, 1915*, pp. 27-28. *Annual Report of the JAG, 1916*, p. 163.

69. *Annual Report of the JAG, 1915*, p. 137.

70. Navy Department, *Regulations for the Government of the Navy, 1913*, p. 147. U.S., Navy Department, Office of the JAG, *Manual for the Government of United States Naval Prisons* (Washington: GPO, 1918).

71. *Annual Report of the JAG, 1906*, p. 115, and *1908*, p. 88.

72. Frank Tannenbaum, *Osborne of Sing Sing* (Chapel Hill: University of North Carolina Press, 1933), p. 279.

73. Frank H. Potter, "A Repair Shop for Men," *Outlook* 120 (1918): 540. E. David Cronon, ed., *The Cabinet Diaries of Josephus Daniels* (Lincoln: University of Nebraska Press, 1963), p. 116. Josephus Daniels, *The Navy and the Nation* (New York: George H. Doran Co., 1919), p. 79. Tannebaum, *Osborne*, pp. 279-80.

74. Tannenbaum, *Osborne*, pp. 284-85.

CHAPTER 9

1. Harry R. Skallerup, *Books Afloat and Ashore: A History of Books, Libraries, and Reading among Seamen during the Age of Sail* (Hamden, Conn.: Archon Books, 1974), pp. 49-50, 88-97. U.S., Navy Department, BUNAV, *Catalogue of Library Books Issued to Vessels of the U.S. Navy* (Washington: GPO, 1886). Robert Erwin Johnson, *Thence round Cape Horn: The Story of United States Naval Forces on Pacific Station, 1818-1923* (Annapolis, Md.: U.S. Naval Institute, 1963), p. 19.

2. CDR M. R. S. Mackenzie to BUNAV, October 11, 1896, and reply Chief BUNAV to CO U.S.S. *Machias*, November 28, 1896, No. 37076, GC, RG 24, NA. LCDR E. P. Wood to BUNAV, January 20, 1897, and reply Chief BUNAV to CO U.S.S. *Petrel*, February 4, 1897, No. 46939, GC, RG 24, NA.

3. U.S., Navy Department, *Regulations for the Government of the Navy, 1896* (Washington: GPO, 1896), p. 87. Idem, *Regulations for the Government of the Navy, 1905* (Washington: GPO, 1905), p. 98.

4. Special Order 37, February 26, 1903.

5. *New York Times*, March 8, 1903, p. 11.

6. RADM R. D. Evans to SECNAV, September 18, 1903, No. 2807-14, GC, RG 24, NA.

7. Chief BUNAV to Commandants Navy Yards at Portsmouth, New York, Norfolk, Mare Island, Boston, April 22, 1903, No. 2807-4, GC, RG 24, NA. Replies are filed under the same file number: Boston, April 27; Norfolk, May 6; Portsmouth, May 7; Mare Island, April 29. I have been unable to find replies from New York and Philadelphia. See also *New York Times*, July 25, 1903, p. 6.

8. LCDR Semmes Read to SECNAV, May 29, 1913, No. 2807-55, GC, RG 24, NA. This letter was sent to recommend that recreation grounds and buildings be provided at every station, and BUNAV sent a copy to all yards for comment. The replies are under the same file number: Puget Sound, June 23; Boston, June 16; Mare Island, June 14; Philadelphia, June 13; New York, June 19; Portsmouth, June 23; Norfolk, June 14.

Although the YMCA had had occasional contact with naval personnel since 1856, it did not form a special Army and Navy Department until 1898. The creation of this unit coincided with a general YMCA building program; by 1914 benefactors had provided nine navy YMCA buildings for American sailors around the world. C. Howard Hopkins, *History of the Y.M.C.A. in North America* (New York: Association Press, 1951), pp. 26-27, 208-10, 411, 454-56.

9. *Annual Report of the SECNAV, 1918*, pp. 88-89.

10. See, for example, File 14, Correspondence with Madame Frances Alda, Chairman of Music, Department of Navy Recreation, Women's Naval Service, Inc., and File 18,

Correspondence with S. A. Ackley, Executive Secretary, Southeastern Department, National War Work Council, YMCA, GC, Sixth Division, 1918-20, RG 24, NA.

11. See, for example, "Program for *Monocacy*'s Twentieth Century Minstrels," Tongku, China, February 23, 1903, Folder 14, Macay-McNeely Papers, SHC.

12. File 84, Franklin B. Coates, GC, Sixth Division, RG 24, NA, contains correspondence with and about Coates, who served as drama director of the Atlantic Fleet. Louis Glasper, "We Sail the Ocean Blue," *Newport Recruit* 6 (August 1918): 9-13.

13. BUNAV Circular Letter 33-19, March 11, 1919, in Subject ZN, "Commission on Training Camp Activities," Subject File, RG 45, NA. *Annual Report of the Chief BUNAV, 1922*, p. 104, is the first annual report to use the designation "Morale Division."

14. BUNAV to Commandant 14th Naval District (Aide for Morale), October 24, 1919, in "Honolulu-Hawaii, General For Sta," Box 3, Sixth Division, Correspondence with Foreign Stations, RG 24, NA. *Annual Report of the Chief BUNAV, 1921*, p. 31.

15. U.S., Congress, Senate, Committee on Naval Affairs, *Hearings: Naval Appropriations, 1920* (66th Cong., 1st sess., 1919), p. 125. Act of July 11, 1919, in U.S., *Statutes at Large*, 41:134.

16. Memorandum for ADM Washington from Mayo, February 16, 1920, File 240 "Memorandum—Chiefs of Bureau," GC, Sixth Division, RG 24, NA.

17. Robert A. Hart, *The Great White Fleet: Its Voyage around the World, 1907-1909* (Boston: Little, Brown & Co., 1965), p. 66.

18. Senate, Committee on Naval Affairs, *Hearings: Naval Appropriations, 1920*, p. 26.

19. *Annual Report of the SECNAV, 1920*, p. 94. W. R. Ryan, "Movies in the United States Navy Give Fun to Thousands," n.d., File "Motion Pictures Nov 1923-June 1924," Box 3, GC, Morale and Recreation Section, 1920-24, RG 24, NA.

20. LCDR R. R. M. Emmet to LT Jos. O'Reilly, August 8, 1921, No. N14-RRME-FVA, Box 2, GC, Morale and Recreation Section, 1920-24, RG 24, NA.

21. *Bureau of Navigation Bulletin*, No. 101, April 6, 1929. *Annual Report of the Chief BUNAV, 1931*, p. 207.

22. At least one sailor regarded the bands as a mixed blessing because they discouraged the crew's own efforts at music. David Perry, "Sorrows of Sailors," *Our Navy* 9 (March 1916): 20. Films undoubtedly also reduced the number of sailor-produced theatricals.

23. "The Big *Mary* Knows How," *Our Navy* 31 (Mid-October 1937): 8-9.

24. See, for example, Thomas Beyer, *The American Battleship and Life in the Navy* (Chicago: Laird & Lee, 1908), p. 77, and Letter from "Dave," *Our Navy* 8 (May 1914): 33.

25. C. P. ("Shorty") Walters, "Race Boats and Boating," *Our Navy* 7 (May 1913): 9-14.

26. Joseph Wilson, *Naval Hygiene: Human Health and the Means of Preventing Disease* (Philadelphia: Lindsay & Blakiston, 1879), p. 220. Albert Leary Gihon, "Practical Suggestions in Naval Hygiene," in U.S., Navy Department, Bureau of Medicine and Surgery, *Medical Essays* (Washington: GPO, 1873), p. 122.

27. The surgeon general published statistics on the incidence of disease in the navy. During calendar year 1923, as an example, gonorrhea, syphilis, and chancroid ranked in the top six causes of sickness and disability in the navy. Gonorrhea led all diseases both in the number of cases and in days lost; syphilis was second in days lost. *Annual Report of the Surgeon General, 1924*, p. 463.

28. George Winfield Mast, "A Ten Year Study of Syphilis in the United States Navy, 1929-1938, Inclusive" (Ph.D. diss., University of Iowa, 1942), pp. 27-A, 46. The lowest incidence was among apprentice seamen, who were almost always confined to training stations.

29. Ibid., pp. 32, 16-A. The surgeon general also published statistics on the incidence of venereal disease by location. See, for example, *Annual Report of the Surgeon General, 1922*, p. 305, and *1925*, p. 433.

30. B. F. Dixon, "Excerpts from a Gunboat Cruise," *Hospital Corps Quarterly* 11 (January 1927): 9, 11.

31. James Duncan Gatewood, *Naval Hygiene* (Philadelphia: P. Blakiston's Son & Co., 1909), p. 41.

32. *Annual Report of the Surgeon General, 1911*, p. 437. For a description of prophylaxis, see Gatewood, *Naval Hygiene*, p. 46.

33. Daniels to All Commanding Officers, February 27, 1915, in File "Prophylaxis," Box 434-38, Subject File, Josephus Daniels Papers, LC. This letter is also reprinted in Daniels, "Venereal Disease in the Navy," *Social Hygiene* 1 (June 1915): 483.

34. Ibid.

35. *Annual Report of the SECNAV, 1918*, p. 89. Daniels, "Venereal Disease in the Navy," pp. 482-83. Daniels, *The Wilson Era: Years of War and After, 1917-1923* (Chapel Hill: University of North Carolina Press, 1946), p. 195. Daniels, *The Navy and the Nation* (New York: George H. Doran Co., 1915), p. 65. E. David Cronon, ed., *The Cabinet Diaries of Josephus Daniels, 1913-1921* (Lincoln: University of Nebraska Press, 1963), p. 316. Charles E. Riggs, "A Study of Venereal Prophylaxis in the Navy," *Social Hygiene* 3 (July 1917): 305-6.

Dean C. Mathews to Major Snow, March 28, Snow to Mathews, March 29, Mathews to Snow, April 27, 1918; Snow to CDR Claude Mayo, June 19, 1919, File 345, "Social Hygiene—Motion Pictures," GC, Sixth Division, RG 24, NA. "The Rookie Puts One Over on the Old Shellback," ca. 1918, File 70, "Chaplain's Round Table," GC, Sixth Division, RG 24, NA. Activities of Social Hygiene Section, July 19, 1920, No. 51, Correspondence of Ensign Joseph Levansaler, RG 24, NA.

36. General Order 530, May 12, 1920.

37. Mast, "Syphilis," pp. 13-14. *Annual Report of the Surgeon General, 1924*, pp. 468-69.

38. *Bureau of Navigation Bulletin*, No. 251, August 28, 1937.

39. Dillingham to BUNAV, July 25, 1907, No. 5274-10, GC, RG 24, NA.

40. U.S., Congress, House, Committee on Naval Affairs, *Hearings: Sundry Legislation Affecting the Naval Establishment, 1925-26* (69th Cong., 1st sess., 1926), pp. 89-90, 358.

41. *Our Navy* 31 (May 1, 1937): 54.

42. U.S., Congress, Joint Special Committee, *Hearings: Readjustment of Service Pay* (67th Cong., 2d sess., 1921), p. 254.

43. Charles Herget, "Dear Shipmate" (Xeroxed memoir of naval service, Turnersville, New Jersey, 1967), p. 64.

44. *Our Navy* 27 (Mid-September 1933): 12. G. H. Blackmun, "Living Conditions in Guam," *Hospital Corps Quarterly* 11 (October 1927): 247. Will Grimes, "American Samoa," *Hospital Corps Quarterly* 12 (July 1928): 155.

45. A Staton to CDR R. S. Crenshaw, October 16, 1924, Folder 14, Box 1, A. Staton Papers, SHC.

46. Congress, Joint Special Committee, *Hearings: Readjustment of Service Pay*, p. 264.

47. Ibid., pp. 251-55. Herget, "Dear Shipmate," p. 46.

48. *Trident* 2 (April 1, 1921): 13-15. M. Dodds Bryant, "The Navy Development Syndicate," *Our Navy* 31 (June 1, 1937): 16-17.

49. A 1954 study suggests that prolonged sea duty continues to be a drawback of navy life. The Bureau of Naval Personnel found that the first-term reenlistment rate was three times greater for those who had spent less than ten months of a four-year enlistment afloat than for those who had spent thirty or more months afloat. Harold Wool, *The Military Specialist: Skilled Manpower for the Armed Forces* (Baltimore: Johns Hopkins Press, 1968), p. 136.

50. *Annual Report of the Chief BUNAV, 1918*, p. 454, *1919*, p. 446, *1920*, p. 579, and *1921*, table 20.

51. The median age of first marriage for males was 24.6 years in 1920 and 24.3 years in 1930. In 1920 only 27 percent of the enlisted force were above that median age (twenty-five or older); the proportion of sailors twenty-five years or older had increased to 46 percent by 1930 and to 57 percent by 1935. U.S., Department of Commerce, Bureau of the Census, *Historical Statistics of the United States, Colonial Times to 1957* (Washington: GPO, 1960), p. 15. *Annual Report of the Chief BUNAV, 1920*, p. 579, *1930*, p. 205, and *1935*, p. 120.

CHAPTER 10

1. "Passing the Buck a la Navy," *Typhoon* 1 (September 14, 1921): 2.
2. For ship routine, see Thomas Beyer, *The American Battleship and Life in the Navy* (Chicago: Laird & Lee, 1908), pp. 34-50; Charles A. Gove, *An Aid for Executive and Division Officers* (Annapolis, Md.: U.S. Naval Institute, 1899), pp. 7-10; C. Aloysious Stumpf, *On a Cruise with the U.S. Pacific Fleet to the Orient: An Account of the American Bluejacket Afloat and Ashore* (Boston: Roxburgh Publishing Co., 1915), pp. 15-16.
3. See Gove, *Aid*, for a printed form of watch, quarter, and station bills. A. Bainbridge Hoff, *A Battle Ship's Order Book* (Annapolis, Md.: U.S. Naval Institute, 1908) also discusses bills. RG 24 has a collection of bills from a few ships.
4. Charles Minor Blackford, *Torpedoboat Sailor* (Annapolis, Md.: U.S. Naval Institute, 1968), pp. 9-10.
5. John L. Kendig, Log, January 22, 1907, 1:8, Logs, Journals, and Diaries of Officers of the United States Navy at Sea (hereafter cited as Logs and Diaries), RG 45, NA.
6. Alfred Young, *The Cruise of the U.S.S. "Trenton": A True Story of the Events Happening to and on Board the U.S.S. "Trenton" during Her Shakedown Cruise, from Saturday, 24 May 1924, to Monday, 29 September 1924* (n.p., n.d.), p. 107.
7. *Annual Report of the Surgeon General, 1907*, p. 1249.
8. See *Annual Report of the Surgeon General, 1908*, p. 947. C. F. Stokes, Surgeon General, to Department, May 10, 1911, No. 1159-406, GC, RG 24, NA. CNO to Chief Bureau of Medicine and Surgery, May 22, 1925, No. 125135-0, GC, Box 376, RG 52, NA.
9. "On Coaling Ship." *U.S.S. "Plattsburg" in the Great War*, p. 23, Subject 338, "Ships Papers," GC, Sixth Division, RG 24, NA. For further comments on coaling see Kendig, Log, December 27, 1907, p. 30; Clarence O'C. McDonagh, Sr., "Log, April 8, 1917, to August 12, 1919" (typescript), September 26, 1917, p. 6; Paul Schubert, *Come on "Texas"* (New York: Jonathan Cape & Harrison Smith, 1930), p. 15; "Coaling Ship," *Our Navy* 4 (June 1910): 18-19; Robert D. Jones, *With the American Fleet from the Atlantic to the Pacific* (Seattle: Harrison Publishing Co., 1908), p. 91.
10. For the participation of the American navy in the war see Thomas G. Frothingham, *The Naval History of the World War: The United States in the War, 1917-1918* (Cambridge: Harvard University Press, 1926), and William S. Sims, *The Victory at Sea* (Garden City, N.Y.: Doubleday, Page & Co., 1920). Also useful are Willis J. Abbot, *Bluejackets of 1918* (New York: Dodd, Mead & Co., 1921), and Josephus Daniels, *Our Navy at War* (Washington: Pictorial Bureau, 1922).
11. Abbot, *Bluejackets of 1918*, pp. 133-38; Daniels, *Our Navy at War*, pp. 54-55, 63.
12. Harry S. Morris, Interview Conducted by Etta Belle Kitchen, January 31, 1970, Oral History Project, United States Naval Institute, Annapolis, Md., p. 35.
13. U.S., Department of Commerce, Bureau of the Census, *Historical Statistics of the United States, Colonial Times to 1957* (Washington: GPO, 1960), p. 735.
14. Malcolm F. Willoughby, *"Yankton": Yacht and Man-of-War* (Cambridge, Mass.: Crimson Printing Co., 1935), pp. 190-92. For other false alarms, see Ray Millholland, *The Splinter Fleet of the Otranto Barrage* (New York: Bobbs-Merrill Co., 1936), pp. 61-62, and George M. Battey, Jr., *70,000 Miles on a Submarine Destroyer* (Atlanta: Webb & Vary Co., 1919), pp. 33, 45.

15. Compiled from *Annual Report of the SECNAV* for the years 1899 to 1939. U.S., Veterans' Administration, *List of Wars, Military Expeditions, Campaigns, and Other Disturbances in Which the United States Army, Navy, and Marine Corps Have Participated* (Washington: GPO, 1922).

16. B. F. Dixon, "Excerpts from a Gunboat Cruise," *Hospital Corps Quarterly* 11 (January 1927): 1-28. Thaddeus V. Tuleja, *Statesmen and Admirals: Quest for a Far Eastern Naval Policy* (New York: W. W. Norton & Co., 1963), p. 172.

17. Fullam to CAPT. Richard Wainwright, October 9, 1906, "Correspondence October-November 1906," William F. Fullam Papers, LC.

18. Fullam, "The System of Naval Training and Discipline Required to Promote Efficiency and Attract Americans," *USNIP* 16 (1890): 475-78; idem, "The Organization, Training, and Discipline of the Navy Personnel as Viewed from the Ship," *USNIP* 22 (1896): 109-14.

19. Jack Sweetman, *The Landing at Veracruz, 1914* (Annapolis, Md.: U.S. Naval Institute, 1968), pp. 93-123; Badger to Daniels, April 29, 1914, in folder "Badger, Rear Admiral," Navy Period Correspondence, 1913-21, Box 35, Josephus Daniels Papers, LC.

20. Dom Albert Pagano, *Bluejackets* (Boston: Meador Publishing Co., 1932), pp. 29, 44.

21. Thomas Jerrell Carter, "Injury Statistics, Enlisted Personnel, United States Navy, 1935-1936," (Ph.D. diss., Johns Hopkins University, 1940), pp. 39-40. Accident statistics can also be found in most annual reports of the surgeon general.

22. For the *Bennington*, see Holden A. Evans, *One Man's Fight for a Better Navy* (New York: Dodd, Mead & Co., 1940), pp. 161-78; and *Annual Report of the Surgeon General, 1906*, pp. 1048-49. For the Honda accident, Charles A. Lockwood and Hans Christian Adamson, *Tragedy at Honda* (Philadelphia: Chilton Co., 1960). For the *F-4, Annual Report of the SECNAV, 1915*, pp. 66-67. For the *S-51, Annual Report of the Chief of Naval Operations, 1926*, p. 68. For the *S-4, Annual Report of the Surgeon General, 1928*, p. 377.

23. For the *Missouri*, see *Annual Report of the Chief of the Bureau of Ordnance, 1904*, p. 576; and Elting E. Morison, *Admiral Sims and the Modern American Navy* (Boston: Houghton Mifflin Co., 1942), pp. 138-41. For the *Kearsarge, Annual Report of the Surgeon General, 1906*, p. 1049. For the *Mississippi, Annual Report of the SECNAV, 1924*, pp. 26-27. For the *Wyoming, Annual Report of the SECNAV, 1938*, p. 17.

24. For the *Shenandoah*, see Archibald D. Turnbull and Clifford L. Lord, *History of United States Naval Aviation* (New Haven: Yale University Press, 1949), pp. 249-51. For the *Akron*, ibid., pp. 282-83; Richard K. Smith, *The Airships "Akron" and "Macon": Flying Aircraft Carriers of the United States Navy* (Annapolis, Md.: U.S. Naval Institute, 1965), pp. 77-84; and *Bureau of Aeronautics News Letter*, No. 302, April 15, 1933. For the *Macon*, Smith, *Airships "Akron" and "Macon,"* pp. 153-57.

25. "A Submarine," in Henry B. Beston, *Full Speed Ahead: Tales from the Log of a Correspondent with Our Navy* (Garden City, N.Y.: Doubleday, Page & Co., 1919), pp. 42-43.

26. Alfred E. Bennett, "The Dungaree Navy," *Our Navy* 3 (July 1909): 6.

27. "Life on a Submarine," *Man-o'-Warsman* 2 (November 1909): 714.

28. Jones, *With the American Fleet*, pp. 224-25. John Stapler, "Gunboats," *USNIP* 42 (1916): 861-72. Herbert Corey, "Across the Equator with the American Navy," *National Geographic Magazine* 39 (June 1921): 581, 583, 587. B. F. Dixon, "The Romance of the Enlisted Doctors," *Hospital Corps Quarterly* 9 (July and October 1925): 23-24.

29. Samuel Harvard Barboo, "A Historical Review of the Hygiene of Shipboard Food Service in the United States Navy, 1775-1965" (Ph.D. diss., University of California, Los Angeles, 1966), pp. 96-97. Hugh Rodman, *Yarns of a Kentucky Admiral* (Indianapolis: Bobbs-Merrill Co., 1928), p. 68.

30. For dishwashing machines, see Barboo, "Shipboard Food Service," p. 66, and Fleet Surgeon Battle Fleet to Chief BUMED, May 25, 1925, submitting "Annual Report of Fleet

Surgeon, 1924," No. 125135-0, Box 376, GC, RG 52, NA; for laundries, *Fleet Review* 11 (August 1920): 3; and for lighting, ventilation, and heating, *Annual Report of the Surgeon General, 1908*, pp. 930-32, and *1927*, pp. 342-43.

31. Dyer, "The Modern General Mess," *USNIP* 32 (1906):636. For the introduction of refrigerated storage and ice machines, see Barboo, "Shipboard Food Service," pp. 58-61.

32. For centralized meal preparation see Barboo, "Shipboard Food Service," pp. 61-66; Benton C. Decker, "The Consolidated Mess of the Crew of the U.S.S. *Indiana*," *USNIP* 23 (1897): 463-67; and Daniel Delehanty, "A Proposed System of Messing the Crews of Our Men-of-War," *USNIP* 14 (1888): 739-49. The navy felt that the ration itself was generous and compared favorably with other navies. See Albert Leary Gihon, "Practical Suggestions in Naval Hygiene," in U.S., Navy Department, Bureau of Medicine and Surgery, *Medical Essays* (Washington: GPO, 1873), pp. 68-69; and J. H. Skillman, "The Evolution of the Navy Ration," *USNIP* 60 (1934): 1678-79. Barboo, "Shipboard Food Service" gives a history of the navy ration from 1775 to 1965.

33. Barboo, "Shipboard Food Service," pp. 93-94. E. D. Foster, "Cafeteria Afloat," *USNIP* 63 (1937): 19-24.

34. Fred J. Buenzle, with A. Grove Day, *Bluejacket: An Autobiography* (New York: W. W. Norton & Co., 1939), p. 177, contains an account of the experiment on the *Philadelphia*. For enlisted support of lockers see M. C. S., on *Minnesota*, Letter to Editor, *Fleet Review* 4 (May 1913): 57; unsigned, Letter to Editor, *Our Navy* 7 (February 1914): 25; and W. W. MacDonald, Chief Electrician, Letter to Editor, *Fleet Review* 5 (May 1914): 64. *Fleet Review* 11 (August 1920): 3, describes lockers on the *Tennessee*.

35. D. L. Hasbrouk, CO *California*, to Bureau of Construction and Repair, November 26, 1924, No. 8956-101, GC, RG 24, NA. W. Pitt Scott, CO *Oklahoma*, to Commander Battleship Divisions, Battle Fleet, November 20, 1924, No. 8956-101, GC, RG 24, NA.

36. *Annual Report of the Surgeon General, 1926*, p. 481. Most hammock-related injuries occurred early in a sailor's enlistment. In 1935 and 1936, hammocks caused only 1.7 percent of injuries for the entire navy but 31 percent for men who had been in the service less than a month. Carter, "Injury Statistics," p. 42.

37. D. L. Hasbrouk to Bureau of Construction and Repair, November 26, 1924, No. 8956-101, GC, RG 24, NA. H. A. Wiley, Commander Battleship Divisions, Battle Fleet, to Commander in Chief Battle Fleet, November 29, 1924, No. 8956-101, GC, RG 24, NA. W. R. Shoemaker, Chief BUNAV, to Bureau of Construction and Repair, February 14, 1925, No. CV2(7), GC, RG 24, NA. Fleet Surgeon, Battle Fleet, to Chief BUMED, "Annual Sanitary Report of Fleet Surgeon," May 25, 1925, No. 125135-0, Box 376, GC, RG 52, NA. Correspondence to and by BUNAV on bunks, 1925-27, No. S33(8), GC, RG 24, NA: see especially CO *California* to CO Battleship Division, Battle Fleet, July 30, 1926; BUNAV to Bureau of Construction and Repair, February 14, 1925; Chief BUNAV to SECNAV, May 20, 1927. *Annual Report of the Surgeon General, 1926*, p. 315.

38. Buenzle, *Bluejacket*, pp. 176-77.

39. Murry Wolffe, *Memoirs of a Gob* (New York: Exposition Press, 1949), p. 13.

40. Mark Raymond Murnane, *Ground Swells: Of Sailors, Ships, and Shellac* (New York: Exposition Press, 1949), p. 77. Daniel V. Gallery, *Eight Bells and All's Well* (New York: W. W. Norton & Co., 1965), p. 64.

41. "Heirlooms," *Orient* 1 (September 1924): 10. See also *Annual Report of the Surgeon General, 1922*, p. 284.

42. "Four Future Admirals," Letter to Editor, *Our Navy* 23 (Mid-January 1930): 10.

43. *Annual Report of the SECNAV, 1904*, pp. 16-17. *Annual Report of the Chief BUNAV, 1909*, p. 311. *Annual Report of the Chief, Bureau of Steam Engineering, 1909*, p. 714.

44. Ralph Clifford Luks, "With the Navy in the Yangtze Kiang Valley, China," *Our Navy* 18 (May 1, 1924): 4-7. Wolffe, *Memoirs*, p. 33. Crew of *Galveston*, Letter to Editor,

Our Navy 10 (May 1916): 74. "Song Sung at Christmas Dinner, 1902," Hollis Taylor Winston Book, p. 185, George T. Winston Papers, SHC.

45. Hollis Taylor Winston Book, George T. Winston Papers, SHC. Similar journals from Richard Wainwright and Charles E. Courtney are in Logs and Diaries, RG 45, NA.

46. See, for example, Andrew T. Long, "Around the World in Sixty Years" (typed memoirs), pp. 78, 199, Box 2, Andrew T. Long Papers, SHC. Edward Simpson, *Yarnlets: The Human Side of the Navy* (New York: G. P. Putnam's Sons, 1934), pp. 31-34.

47. Officers' papers contain numerous letters relating to filling such billets. See, for example, Andrew T. Long to RADM Philip Andrews, May 16, 1923, Folder 25, Box 2, Andrew T. Long Papers, SHC; William Sims to Rufus Z. Johnston, August 21, 1917, Scrapbook, Box 1, Rufus Z. Johnston Papers, SHC; Osborne B. Hardison to LCDR D. E. Wilson, March 14, 1939, Folder 9, Osborne Bennet Hardison Papers, SHC.

48. Richard McKenna, *The Sand Pebbles* (New York: Harper & Row, 1962), pp. 23-25.

49. Albert Gleaves, ed., *The Life of an American Sailor: Rear Admiral William Hemsley Emory, United States Navy* (New York: George H. Doran Co., 1923), pp. 273-74. The gift was made to the wife because regulations forbade presents to a superior. U.S., Navy Department, *Regulations for the Government of the Navy, 1909* (Washington: GPO, 1909), p. 65.

50. "A Sailor," Letter to Editor, *Bostonian* 4 (July 1910): 489.

51. Emery to Johnston, February 12, 1926, Scrapbook, Box 1, Rufus Johnston Papers, SHC. Also Roderick J. Johnson to Johnston, June 22, 1930, Folder 2, Rufus Johnston Papers, SHC; Frank R. Olin to Long, November 28, 1929, Folder 28, Box 2, Andrew T. Long Papers, SHC.

52. "Madhouse," *Our Navy* 7 (October 1913): 18-19.

53. John Kendig, Log, February 12, 14, and 26, and March 2, 1908, 2:159, 164, Logs and Diaries, RG 45, NA.

54. "A C.P.O. with Three Cruises," Letter to Editor, *Our Navy* 8 (April 1915): 14. Anonymous letter to William Moody, n.d., received by BUNAV December 14, 1904, No. 3328-38, GC, RG 24, NA.

55. Murnane, *Ground Swells*, pp. 108-9.

56. Robert E. Coontz, *True Anecdotes of an Admiral* (Philadelphia: Dorrance & Co., 1935), pp. 24-25.

57. James B. Connolly, *Navy Men* (New York: John Day Co., 1939), pp. 272-73.

58. Henning Henningsen, *Crossing the Equator: Sailors' Baptism and Other Initiation Rites* (Copenhagen, Denmark: Munksgaard, 1961), p. 15.

59. For accounts of crossing the equator, see Stumpf, *On a Cruise with the U.S. Pacific Fleet*, pp. 66-79; Young, *Cruise of the U.S.S "Trenton,"* pp. 26-28; Corey, "Across the Equator," pp. 610-11; Lyman A. Cotten, Diary, July 5 and 6, 1925, Lyman A. Cotten Papers, SHC; "Crossing the Line," *Fleet Review* 1 (August 1910): 37-38.

60. The use of intoxicants was banned by General Order 99. See also Josephus Daniels, *The Wilson Era: Years of Peace, 1910-1917* (Chapel Hill: University of North Carolina Press, 1944), p. 386.

61. Navy Department, *Regulations for the Government of the Navy, 1909*, pp. 168, 471. Frederick L. Sawyer, *Sons of Gunboats* (Annapolis, Md.: U.S. Naval Institute, 1946), pp. 82, 85-86.

62. See, for example, Murnane, *Ground Swells*, p. 57.

63. John L. Kendig, Log, October 22, 1907, and June 6, 1908, 1:80, 3:191-93, Logs and Diaries, RG 45, NA.

64. Harold D. Langley, *Social Reform in the United States Navy, 1798-1862* (Urbana: University of Illinois Press, 1967), pp. 211-12. Murnane, *Ground Swells*, pp. 287, 292. Stanton H. King, *Dog-Watches at Sea* (Boston: Houghton, Mifflin & Co., 1901), pp. 236, 253. *San Francisco Examiner*, June 10, 1907, p. 2.

65. *Regulations for the Government of the Navy* permitted a commanding officer to give liberty to half the crew at a time or to three-quarters if the ship was secured to a wharf in a navy yard. The regulations denied liberty only to men under punishment or in debt to the government. Navy Department, *Regulations for the Government of the Navy, 1913,* pp. 255-56, 264.

66. "Welcome to Lil'l ol' New York," *Our Navy* 24 (May 1, 1930): 14-15. L. F. Veit, "With the Destroyers in Europe," *Our Navy* 19 (November 1, 1925): 21. RADM W. C. Cowles to SECNAV, May 20, 1914, File: "Admiral Cowles," Correspondence, 1913-21, Box 38, Josephus Daniels Papers, LC. Charles Herget, "Dear Shipmate" (Xeroxed memoir of naval service, Turnersville, New Jersey, 1967), pp. 21, 26. Dixon, "Excerpts from a Gunboat Cruise," p. 5.

67. J. M. Acuff, "Tennessee Notes," *Our Navy* 3 (May 1909): 20. W. S. Pierce, "The American Sailor in Japan," *Our Navy* 8 (November 1914): 9-13—the same article was republished in *Our Navy* 19 (Mid-June 1926): 6-8. Tutuila is the major island of American Samoa and contains the harbor of Pago Pago.

68. Young, *Cruise of the U.S.S. "Trenton,"* p. 85. Millholland, *Splinter Fleet*, pp. 287-88. C. J. B., Letter to Editor, *Bluejacket* 5 (March 1906): 224-25. "U.S. Asiatic Fleet at Chefoo," *Orient* 1 (August 1924): 7-8. F. P. Baird, "'Beefing' in the Asiatics," *Our Navy* 32 (April 1, 1938): 8-9.

69. Stumpf, *On a Cruise with the U.S. Pacific Fleet*, pp. 181-82. Willoughby, *"Yankton,"* pp. 92, 125. Franklin Matthews, *Back to Hampton Roads* (New York: B. W. Huebsch, 1909), p. 225.

70. Young, *Cruise of the U.S.S. "Trenton,"* p. 84.

71. Millholland, *Splinter Fleet*, pp. 287-88.

72. William H. Rideing, "Jack Ashore," *Harper's New Monthly Magazine* 47 (July 1873): 161-63.

73. A comparison of the two battleships called the *Texas* illustrates the increasing number of men on naval vessels. The first *Texas*, commissioned in 1895, had a designed complement of 362 men. The second, commissioned in 1914, carried 984 men. U.S., Navy Department, Office of the Chief of Naval Operations, Naval History Division, *Dictionary of American Naval Fighting Ships*, 6 vols. to date (Washington: GPO, 1959-), 1:189, 195.

74. *Norfolk Virginian-Pilot*, December 26, 1906, p. 1.

75. *Fred J. Buenzle* v. *Newport Amusement Association*, in *Reports of Cases Argued and Determined in the Supreme Court of Rhode Island* (Providence: E. L. Freeman Co., 1909), 19:23-33. For Buenzle's account, see Buenzle, *Bluejacket*, pp. 316-18. Roosevelt's contribution is also noted in "President Aids Tar's Suit," *New York Times*, September 25, 1906, p. 8. The Rhode Island act is given in General Order 70 of June 15, 1908.

76. "Sailorphobia in Seattle," *Our Navy* 4 (April 1911): 20-21.

77. Cooper to Mayor of Portsmouth, March 8, 1911, No. 3328-93, GC, RG 24, NA. *New York Times*, January 13, 1917, p. 15.

78. "Shore-Boats and Boatmen," *Our Navy* 4 (June 1910): 24. *New York Times*, February 12, 1918, p. 12. See also "Navy Men Overcharged," *Fleet Review* 14 (February 1923): 14.

79. *Our Navy* 4 (May 1910): 14-15.

80. R. K. Crank, "The Navy as a Career," *Forum* 56 (November 1916): 630.

81. *Norfolk Virginian-Pilot*, December 27, 1905, p. 4. *New York Times*, September 14, 1906, p. 3.

82. See, for example, Mrs. I. M. Keepers to Josephus Daniels, October 26, 1915, No. 1651-30, GC, RG 24, NA.

83. For one man's reaction to a 1908 celebration, see John L. Kendig, Log, May 1 and 12, 1908, Logs and Diaries, RG 45, NA.

84. Marbury Johnston, "Discipline in the Navy," *USNIP* 38 (1912): 852.

85. Frank Hunter Potter, "A School for Bluejackets," *Army and Navy Journal of the Philippines* 1 (October 4, 1913): 11.

86. United States Fleet Letter 32-25, April 4, 1925, No. 125135(41), File "Fleet, United States Serial, 1925," GC, RG 52, NA.

87. Henry A. Wiley, *An Admiral from Texas* (Garden City, N.Y.: Doubleday, Doran & Co., 1934), pp. 300-301.

88. *Baltimore Afro-American*, May 2, 1908, p. 2. *Enlisted Man* 1 (November 1910): 3.

89. *New York Times*, May 28, 1917, p. 4. *Great Lakes Bulletin*, July 1, 1918, p. 2. Schubert, *Come on "Texas,"* p. 88.

90. Act of October 6, 1917, in U.S., *Statutes at Large*, 40:393. This act extended to the navy provisions of the May 1917 Selective Service Act that prohibited the sale of intoxicants to army personnel in uniform and banned bars and bawdyhouses near army camps.

91. Murnane, *Ground Swells*, p. 94.

92. *Great Lakes Bulletin*, June 17, 1919, p. 2.

93. "Morrison Hotel Bars Sailors," *Chicago Tribune*, January 17, 1919, in Scrapbook, V. A. H. Scales Papers, SHC. "Concerning the Morrison," *Great Lakes Bulletin*, January 13, 1919, p. 4. Milton MacKaye, "The Modern Bluejacket," *Outlook and Independent* 152 (July 31, 1929): 558.

94. "State Laws Protecting Men in Uniform from Discrimination," a tabulation of answers from inquiries sent to all states by the Sixth Division, Box 5, GC, Morale and Recreation Section, 1920-24, RG 24, NA. Arkansas, Delaware, Georgia, Nevada, New Mexico, Ohio, and Oklahoma did not respond. The remaining states reported no such legislation. Discrimination against men in uniform by theaters or public places of amusement in the District of Columbia, Alaska, and the insular possessions of the United States was prohibited by a March 1, 1911, act of Congress, in U.S., *Statutes at Large*, 36:963-64.

95. G. W. D. Dashell to Chief BUNAV, December 21, 1932, No. A17-4(7), GC, RG 24, NA.

96. Young, *Cruise of the U.S.S. "Trenton,"* p. 48.

97. Samuel Wheeler Beach, *The Great Cruise of 1925* (San Francisco: International Printing Co., 1925), pp. 179-82.

98. *New York Times*, January 15, 1908, p. 4, and November 17, 1913, p. 3.

99. Herget, "Dear Shipmate," pp. 26-27. Sidney Knock, *"Clear Lower Decks": An Intimate Study of the Men of the Royal Navy* (London: Philip Allan, 1932), pp. 34-36.

100. Daniels, *Our Navy at War*, pp. 54-55. *New York Times*, May 17, 1917, pp. 1-2. Blackford, *Torpedoboat Sailor*, p. 76.

101. Force Commander to Commander U.S. Patrol Squadron Based on Gibraltar, December 8, 1917, L4-a, "Discipline General—1917," Logistics File, 1911-27, RG 45, NA. *New York Times*, October 14, 1918, p. 17.

102. *New York Times*, September 5, 1917, p. 6. Blackford, *Torpedoboat Sailor*, p. 84.

103. Murnane, *Ground Swells*, pp. 393-404. Schubert, *Come on "Texas,"* p. 174.

104. Chas. E. Gower, Chief Constable, Newport, Monmouthshire, to the Under Secretary of State, Home Office, Whitehall, London, November 23, 1917, L4-b-1917, "Discipline (On Shore)," Logistics File, 1911-27, RG 45, NA.

105. Murnane, *Ground Swells*, p. 391.

106. Morris, "Interview," p. 66.

107. U.S., Congress, Joint Special Committee, *Hearings: Readjustment of Service Pay* (67th Cong., 2d sess., 1921), p. 266.

CHAPTER 11

1. Harold D. Langley, *Social Reform in the United States Navy, 1798-1862* (Urbana: University of Illinois Press, 1967), p. 279.

2. For social characteristics of merchant sailors, see James C. Healey, *Foc's'le and Glory-hole: A Study of the Merchant Seaman and His Occupation* (New York: Merchant Marine Publishers Association, 1936), pp. 55-57; Jeanne G. Gilbert and James C. Healey, "The Economic and Social Background of the Unlicensed Personnel of the American Merchant Marine," *Social Forces* 21 (1942): 40-43; Robert Straus, *Medical Care for Seamen: The Origin of Public Medical Service in the United States* (New Haven: Yale University Press, 1950), pp. 127-30; and Elmo Paul Hohman, *Seamen Ashore: A Study of the United Seamen's Service and of Merchant Seamen in Port* (New Haven: Yale University Press, 1952), pp. 210-40.

3. The use of slogans and illustrations had become common in commercial advertising during the 1890s. For an account of this trend, see Frank Presbrey, *The History and Development of Advertising* (1929: reprint ed., New York: Greenwood Press, 1968), pp. 356-65, 490-511.

4. The first firm specializing in public relations was established in 1900 in Boston; Alan R. Raucher, *Public Relations and Business, 1900-1929* (Baltimore: Johns Hopkins Press, 1968), pp. 11-15.

5. Jack D. Foner, *The United States Soldier between Two Wars: Army Life and Reforms, 1865-1898* (New York: Humanities Press, 1970), pp. 70-71, 84, 110-12.

6. For desertion in the nineteenth-century army, see Foner, *United States Soldier*, pp. 7-10, 97, 223-24. For army technical training, see Harold Wool, *The Military Specialist: Skilled Manpower for the Armed Forces* (Baltimore: Johns Hopkins Press, 1968), pp. 17-18.

7. The navy established a retirement system in 1899; yet as late as 1929 only 15 percent of civilian wage earners were covered by a pension plan. Don D. Lescohier, "Working Conditions," in John R. Commons et al., *History of Labor in the United States, 1896-1932*, 4 vols. (New York: Macmillan Co., 1918 and 1935), 3:388.

8. Although I have found no mention of the idea of unions among sailors for the years before 1940, officers were so opposed to any grievance procedure outside the normal chain of command that it is safe to assume most would have been hostile to unions. For today's debate over unionization, see John E. Kane et al., "Is Military Unionism an Idea Whose Time Has Come?" *USNIP* 102 (November 1976): 36-44, and (December 1976): 24-28.

9. William E. Leuchtenburg, *Franklin D. Roosevelt and the New Deal, 1932-1940* (New York: Harper & Row, 1963), p. xii.

10. U.S., Department of Commerce, Bureau of the Census, *Historical Statistics of the United States, Colonial Times to 1957* (Washington: GPO, 1960), p. 737.

11. For Zumwalt's account of the changes he instituted, see Elmo R. Zumwalt, Jr., *On Watch: A Memoir* (New York: Quadrangle/New York Times Book Co., 1976), pp. 167-272.

Bibliography

PRIMARY SOURCES

1. GOVERNMENT ARCHIVES

General Records of the Department of the Navy, Record Group 80.*
  Alphabetical File of the Assistant Secretary, 1921-40, 1916-38.
  Confidential Correspondence, 1917-19.
  General File, 1897-1940.
  Minutes of the Council of the Secretary of the Navy, 1921-25.
  Office File of Assistant Secretary Franklin D. Roosevelt, 1913-14.
Naval Records Collection of the Office of Naval Records and Library, Record Group 45.
  Logistics File, 1911-27.
  Logs, Journals, and Diaries of Officers of the United States Navy at Sea.
  Subject File, 1775-1910.
  Subject File Extension, 1911-27.
Records of the Bureau of Insular Affairs, Record Group 350.
  General Correspondence.
Records of the Bureau of Medicine and Surgery, Record Group 52.
  General Correspondence, 1912-25.
Records of the Bureau of Naval Personnel, Record Group 24.
  Records of the Bureau of Equipment and Recruiting.
    Composite Shipping Articles of Apprentices on Naval Vessels.
    Composite Shipping Articles of Enlisted Men on Naval Vessels.
    Letters Received from Officers, 1862-85.
    Letters Received from the Commandant of the Boston Navy Yard, 1872-85.
    Letters Received from the Commandant of the Naval Station at Mound City, Ill., 1872-73.
    Letters Received from the Commandant of the New York Navy Yard, 1872-85.
    Letters Received from the Commandant of the Norfolk Navy Yard, 1872-85.
    Letters Received from the Commandant of the Philadelphia Navy Yard, 1872-85.
    Letters Received from the Commandants of Navy Yards, 1862-72.

*Unless otherwise noted, all record groups are in the National Archives in Washington, D.C.

Letters Received from the Commanding Officer of the Training Squadrons and the Training Station at Newport, R.I., 1881-85.
Letters Received from the Secretary of the Navy, 1862-85.
Letters Sent to the Training Squadrons and the Training Station at Newport, R.I., 1881-85.
Press and Typewritten Copies of Letters Sent to Officers, 1863-85.
Press Copies of Letters Sent to Commandant of the Boston Navy Yard, 1864-85.
Press Copies of Letters Sent to the Commandant of the Mare Island Navy Yard, 1864-85.
Press Copies of Letters Sent to the Commandant of the New York Navy Yard, 1864-85.
Press Copies of Letters Sent to the Commandant of the Norfolk Navy Yard, 1864-85.
Press Copies of Letters Sent to the Commandant of the Philadelphia Navy Yard, 1864-85.
Press Copies of Miscellaneous Letters Sent, 1862-85.
Reports of Conduct of Enlisted Men and Duplicates of Composite Shipping Articles.
Records Relating to the Establishment of a Headquarters for Training Naval Apprentices, 1880-83.
Records of the Bureau of Navigation.
Circulars, Circular Letters, General Orders, and Squadron Orders, April-August 1905.
Descriptive List of Men Enlisted at the Naval Rendezvous at Baltimore, 1846-52.
General Correspondence, 1889-1940.
Letters Sent That Concern Recruiting, 1905-11.
Logs of United States Naval Ships and Stations.
Muster Rolls of Ships.
Press Copies of Letters Sent, 1890-96.
Press Copies of Letters Sent to Congressmen, 1890-96.
Press Copies of Letters Sent to the President and to Cabinet Officers, 1890-96.
Quarterly Returns of Enlistments on Vessels.
Records of the Chaplains Division.
General Correspondence, 1916-40.
Records of the Morale Division, 1918-24.
Correspondence of Ensign Joseph Levansaler, 1919-21.
Correspondence of the Commission on Training Camp Activities, 1918-20.
Correspondence Relating to Ports, 1918-20.
Correspondence with Foreign Stations, 1920.
General Correspondence, 1918-20.
General Correspondence of the Morale and Recreation Section, 1920-24.
Reports from Ships and Stations concerning Expenditures for Recreation, 1920-22.
Records of the Training Division, 1917-40.
General Administrative Correspondence, 1918-23.
Records of the Welfare and Recreation Section, 1923-40.
Reports on Morale Factors among Enlisted Men, 1924-25.
Weekly Trade School Reports, 1922-24.
Watch, Quarter, and Station Bill Books.
Weekly Returns of Enlistments at Naval Rendezvous.
Records of the Joint Army and Navy Boards and Committees, Record Group 225.
General Correspondence of the Joint Board, 1903-38.
Records of Naval Districts and Shore Establishments, Record Group 181, Washington National Records Center, Suitland, Md.

Correspondence of the Commandant of Mare Island with the Commanding Officer of the Receiving Ship *Independence*.
Records of the Office of the Chief of Naval Operations, Record Group 38.
General Correspondence, Division of Fleet Training, 1914-26.
Records of the Office of the Judge Advocate General (Navy), Record Group 125.
Records of Naval Disciplinary Barracks, Port Royal, S.C., 1911-15.
Records of Naval Disciplinary Barracks, Puget Sound, Wash., 1912-15.

2. PERSONAL MANUSCRIPT COLLECTIONS

Manuscript Division, Library of Congress, Washington, D.C.
Josephus Daniels Papers.
La Follette Family Papers.
National Association for the Advancement of Colored People Papers.
Benjamin F. Tracy Papers.
Curtis Dwight Wilbur Papers.
Naval Historical Foundation, Washington, D.C.
Reginald R. Belknap Papers.
Claude Charles Bloch Papers.
Washington Irving Chambers Papers.
Edmund Ross Colhoun Papers.
Edward John Dorn Papers.
William Hemsley Emory Papers.
William F. Fullam Papers.
Julius A. Furer Papers.
Albert Gleaves Papers.
Hilary Pollard Jones Papers.
Ernest J. King Papers.
John Lowe Papers.
Stephen B. Luce Papers.
Charles Butler McVay Papers.
Charles Francis O'Neil Papers.
Porter Family Papers.
Mary Edith Powell Collection
Rodgers Family Papers.
Francis Asbury Roe Papers.
Nathan Sargent Papers.
Southern Historical Collection, University of North Carolina, Chapel Hill, N.C.
Alderman Family Papers.
Edwin Alexander Anderson Papers.
Bagley Family Papers.
Victor Blue Papers.
William Gerard Chapman Papers.
Lyman A. Cotten Papers.
Francis Asbury Dickens Family Papers.
Percy Wright Foote Papers.
Osborne Bennet Hardison Papers.
William Curry Harlee Papers.
Rufus Zenas Johnston Papers.
Andrew T. Long Papers.
Macay-McNeely Papers.

Newton Alexander McCully Papers.
A. Stanton Merrill Papers.
Sallie Rowan Saufley Papers.
Archibald Henderson Scales Papers.
Adolphus Staton Papers.
William Victor and James H. Tombs Papers.
Trenholm Family Papers.
George Tayloe Winston Papers.

3. NEWSPAPERS

Army and Navy Journal. 1870-1920.
Baltimore Afro-American. 1893-1908.
Chicago Tribune. 1897-1905.
New York Times. 1870-1940.
Norfolk Virginian-Pilot. 1869-1910.
San Francisco Examiner. 1906-1910.

4. GOVERNMENT PUBLICATIONS

Belknap, R. R. *Organization, Routine, and Orders, U.S.S. "North Dakota."* Washington: GPO, 1912.

Chadwick, F. E. *Report of the Training Systems for the Navy and Mercantile Marine of England and on the Naval Training System of France Made to the Bureau of Equipment and Recruiting, U.S. Navy Department, September 1879*. Washington: GPO, 1880.

Leigh, R. H. *A Lecture (Including Some Additions to More Fully Cover the Subject) Delivered before the War College Class, May 2, 1924, on Navy Personnel*. Washington: GPO, 1924.

Shoemaker, W. R. *A Lecture Delivered before the War College Class, April 28, 1925, on Navy Personnel*. Washington: GPO, 1925.

Thompson, M. S., comp. *General Orders and Circulars Issued by the Navy Department from 1863 to 1887*. Washington: GPO, 1887.

U.S. Congress, House. *Documents, Letters, etc., in Connection with Appointment of Charles F. Stokes as Commander of the U.S.H.S. "Relief," and Resignation of Willard H. Brownson as Chief of the Bureau of Navigation*. 60th Cong., 1st sess., H. Doc. 552, 1908.

______. *Retirement of Enlisted Men and Noncommissioned Officers in the Army*. 48th Cong., 1st sess., H. Rept. 616, 1884.

______. *Site for a Naval Training Station on the Great Lakes*. 58th Cong., 1st sess., H. Rept. 6, 1903.

U.S. Congress, House, Committee on Appropriations. *Hearings: Navy Department Appropriation Bill* (1924-41). 67th Cong., 4th sess.-76th Cong., 3d sess., 1922-40.

U.S. Congress, House, Committee on Naval Affairs. *Hearings: Estimates Submitted by the Secretary of the Navy* (1907-20). 59th Cong., 2d sess.-66th Cong., 2d sess., 1907-20.

______. *Hearings: Sundry Legislation Affecting the Naval Establishment* (1920-39). 66th Cong., 2d sess.-76th Cong., 1st sess., 1921-39.

U.S. Congress, Joint Army and Navy Selective Service Committee. *American Selective Service: A Brief Account of Its Historical Background and Its Probable Future Form*. Washington: GPO, 1939.

U.S. Congress, Joint Special Committee. *Hearings: Readjustment of Service Pay*. 67th Cong., 2d sess., 1921.

U.S. Congress, Senate. *Additional Naval Training Station on the Great Lakes, a Preliminary Report*. 57th Cong., 2d sess., Sen. Doc. 45, 1902.

______. *Compilation of Annual Naval Appropriation Laws from 1883 to 1903, Including Provisions for the Construction of All Vessels of the "New Navy."* Compiled by Pitman Pulsifer. 58th Cong., 2d sess., Sen. Doc. 100, 1904.

______. *Documents from the Department of the Navy* 19th Cong., 1st sess., Sen. Doc. 2, 1825.

______. *Increase of Pay of Personnel of Army, Navy, Marine Corps, Coast Guard, Coast and Geodetic Survey, and Public Health Service*. 66th Cong., 2d sess., Sen. Rept. 521, 1920.

U.S. Congress, Senate, Committee on Appropriations. *Hearings: Navy Department Appropriation Bill* (1924-29). 67th Cong., 2d sess.-70th Cong., 1st sess., 1922-28.

U.S. Congress, Senate, Committee on Naval Affairs. *Administration of Justice in the Navy*. 62d Cong., 2d sess., Sen. Rept. 152, 1911.

______. *Naval Investigation*. 66th Cong., 2d sess., 1921.

______. *Hearings: Naval Omnibus Bill*. 67th Cong., 4th sess.-68th Cong., 1st sess., 1923-24.

______. *Hearings: Naval Training Station on Hampton Roads, Virginia*. 60th Cong., 1st sess., 1908.

______. *Hearings: Under-age Discharges in the Naval Service or Marine Corps*. 67th Cong., 1st sess., 1926.

______. *Hearings: United States Naval Training Stations at Norfolk, Virginia, and Newport, Rhode Island*. 67th Cong., 2d sess., 1922.

______. *U.S. Naval Reserve*. 64th Cong., 1st sess., Sen. Rept. 412, 1916.

U.S. Department of Commerce, Bureau of the Census. *Historical Statistics of the United States, Colonial Times to 1957*. Washington: GPO, 1960.

U.S. Navy Department. *Annual Report of the Secretary of the Navy* (1870-1940). Washington: GPO, 1870-1940.

______. *General Instructions Relating to Naval Prisoners*. Washington: GPO, 1909.

______. *Jamestown Exposition Property and Other Property for the Naval Base at Hampton Roads, Virginia: Statements before the Subcommittees of the House and Senate*. Washington: GPO, 1917.

______. *Regulations for the Government of the Navy* (1865-1940). Washington: GPO, 1865-1940.

U.S. Navy Department, Bureau of Equipment and Recruiting. *Annual Report of the Chief of the Bureau of Equipment and Recruiting* (1865-89). Washington: GPO, 1865-89.

______. *Instructions concerning the Enlistment, Training, etc., of Naval Apprentices*. Washington: GPO, 1886.

______. *Instructions Relating to Enlistments, Discharges, etc., U.S. Navy*. 1882.

U.S. Navy Department, Bureau of Medicine and Surgery. *Annual Report of the Surgeon General* (1870-1940). Washington: GPO, 1870-1940.

______. *Medical Essays*. Washington: GPO, 1873.

U.S. Navy Department, Bureau of Naval Personnel. *The Navy's Demobilization Program*. Washington: NavPers 15637, 1945.

______. *Science and Art of Navy Recruiting*. Washington: NavPers 15940, 1963.

U.S. Navy Department, Bureau of Navigation. *Annual Report of the Chief of the Bureau of Navigation* (1889-1940). Washington: GPO, 1889-1940.

______. *Bureau of Navigation Manual* (1925, 1942). Washington: GPO, 1925, 1942.

______. *Catalogue of Library Books Issued to Vessels of the U.S. Navy*. Washington: GPO, 1886.

______. *Circular Regarding Enlistment and Promotion of Electricians*. 1906.

______. *Circular Regarding Enlistment of Machinist's Mates*. 1904.

______. *Circular Regarding the Enlistment of Yeoman*. 1905.
______. *Circular Relating to the Enlistment of Men for the United States Navy*. Washington: GPO, 1907.
______. *Course in History, Geography, Arithmetic, etc., for the Use of Enlisted Men*. Washington: GPO, 1915.
______. *Hints to Instructors of Recruits*. Washington: GPO, 1923.
______. *Instruction Governing the Handling of Enlisted Personnel*. Washington: GPO, 1920.
______. *Lectures Delivered to Civilian Volunteers, Naval Training Cruise for Civilians*. Washington: GPO, 1916.
______. *The Making of a Man-o'-Warsman*. New York: Street & Finney, 1906.
______. *The United States Navy: The Enlistment, Instruction, Pay, and Advancement of Young Men*. Washington: GPO, 1917.
______. *Yearbook of Enlisted Training (Edition of 1930)*. Washington: GPO, 1931.
U.S. Navy Department, Bureau of Navigation, Sixth Division. *Morale*. 1920.
U.S. Navy Department, Bureau of Provisions and Clothing. *Pay Tables for the Use of Paymasters and Others of the United States Navy*. Washington: GPO, 1871.
U.S. Navy Department, Bureau of Supplies and Accounts. *Instructions for Carrying into Effect the Joint Service Pay Bill (Act of 10 June 1922)*. Washington: GPO, 1922.
______. *Pay Tables for the Use of Pay Officers and Others of the United States Navy*. Washington: GPO, 1905.
U.S. Navy Department, Bureau of Yards and Docks. *Federal Owned Real Estate under the Control of the Navy Department*. Washington: GPO, 1937.
U.S. Navy Department, Judge Advocate General. *Annual Report of the Judge Advocate General* (1893-1940). Washington: GPO, 1893-1940.
______. *Manual for the Government of United States Naval Prisons: General Instructions Relating to Prisoners*. Washington: GPO, 1918.
U.S. Navy Department, Naval Academy, Post-Graduate Department. *The Navy Department: Duties and Functions of Its Bureaus*. Washington: GPO, 1913.
U.S. Navy Department, Office of Naval Intelligence. *The United States Navy as an Industrial Asset: What the Navy Has Done for Industry and Commerce*. 1922.
U.S. Veterans' Administration. *List of Wars, Military Expeditions, Occupations, Campaigns, and Other Disturbances in Which the United States Army, Navy, and Marine Corps Have Participated*. Washington: GPO, 1922.
Wright, Carroll Q. *Advice and Instruction for Recruits in the United States Navy*. Washington: GPO, 1906.

5. SHIP AND NAVAL INSTALLATION NEWSPAPERS

"Agamemnon" Daily News. 1917.
All Atlantic. U.S.S. *Pennsylvania*, 1921.
Arizonian. U.S.S. *Arizona*, 1918.
Arklight. U.S.S. *Arkansas*, 1919-21.
At Em "Arizona." 1920-21, 1923.
Atlantic Shuttle. U.S.S. *Mount Vernon*, 1918.
Big D Log. U.S.S. *Delaware*, 1920-21.
Big U. U.S.S. *Utah*, 1919-21.
Bos'n's Pipe. U.S. Naval Training Station, Hampton Roads, Va., 1920-21.
Brooklynite. U.S.S. *Brooklyn*, 1920.
"California" Cub. 1921-22.
Catapult. U.S.S. *Maryland*, 1922.

"Charleston" Daily Roll. 1919.
Compass. U.S.S. *Connecticut*, 1921.
Crash Dive. Submarine Division 5, Hampton Roads, Va., 1920.
Ess Dee. U.S.S. *South Dakota*, 1919-20.
Fighting Top. U.S.S. *Wyoming*, 1920-21.
Fleet Mender. U.S.S. *Vestal*, 1920-21.
Golden Gate Sentinel. U.S. Naval Training Station, San Francisco, Calif., 1920-21.
Great Lakes Bulletin. U.S. Naval Training Station, Great Lakes, Ill., 1918-21, 1929-42.
Great Lakes Recruit. Great Lakes Athletic Association, 1917-19.
Hatchet. U.S.S. *George Washington*, 1918-19.
Hoist. U.S. Naval Training Station, San Diego, Calif., 1927-40.
Hoosier. U.S.S. *Indianapolis*, 1938-41.
"Idaho" Yarns. 1919-21.
Live Wire. U.S.S. *Nevada*, 1920-21.
Mariner. U.S.S. *Nebraska*, 1918.
"Mississippi" Bulletin. 1919-21.
"New Jersey" Mosquito. 1918.
"New Mexico" Harpoon. 1922.
Newport Recruit. U.S. Naval Training Station, Newport, R.I., 1918-19.
Norfolk Naval Recruit. U.S. Naval Training Station, Norfolk, Va., 1918-19.
Oriental Patrol. U.S.S. *Huron*, 1920-21.
Oscillator. U.S. Naval Radio School, Harvard University, 1917-19.
Radio Sparks. Great Lakes Radio School, 1918.
Ramrod. U.S.S. *Minneapolis*, 1918.
Rifle. U.S. Navy Rifle Range, Mt. Pleasant, S.C., 1918.
Salvo. U.S.S. *Pittsburgh*, 1919-21.
Sea Bag. U.S.S. *Oklahoma*, 1920.
Searchlight. U.S.S. *Pennsylvania*, 1920-21.
"Seattle" Intelligencer. 1918.
Short Circuit. Mare Island, Calif., 1919.
Sidelights. U.S.S. *Henderson*, 1919.
Sirkle Sea. U.S.S. *Charleston*, 1920-21.
"Tennessee" Tar. 1920-21.
Texan. U.S.S. *Texas*, 1920-21.
Trident. Receiving Ship at New York, 1920-21.
Trident. U.S.S. *Von Steuben*, 1919.
Typhoon. Asiatic Destroyer Squadron, 1921-22.
U.S.S. "Bridgeport" Bulletin. 1920-21.
U.S.S. "Florida" Daily Log. 1921.
Wolverine. U.S.S. *Michigan*, 1921.
Yerba Buena Gazette. U.S. Naval Training Station, San Francisco, Calif., 1918-19.

6. SOUVENIR BOOKS OF SHIPS AND STATIONS

Alden, J. D. *The Cruise of the U.S.S. "Badger," June 5 to October 6, 1898, with the Battalion of the East during the War with Spain: Based on the Log of the "Badger."* n.p., 1941.
Alderman, "Josh." *An Historical Souvenir of the United States Cruiser "Cleveland" Commemorating the Second Anniversary of Her Recommissioning, February 8, 1917-February 8, 1919*. n.p., 1919.
Annual of the U.S.S. "Arkansas," Flagship First Division, U.S. Atlantic Fleet. n.p., 1913.
Beach, Samuel Wheeler. *The Great Cruise of 1925*. San Francisco: International Printing Co., 1925.

____ . *Mediterranean Cruise of the U.S.S. "Chester": A Story of the Queen of the Seas, Its First Crew, Its First Voyage, and of Its Sister Ships of the 10,000 Ton Class*. Portsmouth, Va.: Printcraft Press, 1931.

Byrns, Ray W., ed. *Souvenir of the United States Naval Training Station, San Francisco, Christmas 1914*. San Francisco: U.S. Naval Training Station, 1914.

The Cruise of the U.S.S. "Eagle" during the Spanish-American War. Philadelphia: Patterson & White, 1898.

The Cruise of the U.S.S. "Sacramento" from the Declaration of War, April 6, 1917, to Arrival at New Orleans, January 8, 1919. n.p., 1919.

Lippincott, Haines H. *The Long Cruise of Nineteen Hundred Twenty-five*. n.p., 1926.

Log of the U.S.S. "Yosemite." Detroit: John F. Eby & Co., 1899.

Martin, C. F., ed. *A Booklet Descriptive and Illustrative of the United States Naval Training Station, Great Lakes, Illinois*. n.p., 1916.

Polley, Clad E., and Hill, Myron O., *U.S.S. "Augusta" under Fire: Fire over Pootung; Sino-Japanese Incident, 1937-38, Shanghai, China*. n.p., 1938.

Scholz, John. *Log of the Winter Cruise of the North Atlantic Squadron, November 8th, 1902-May 1st, 1903*. North Tarrytown, N.Y.: Fred Gerhardt, 1903.

Stumpf, C. Aloysious. *On a Cruiser with the U.S. Pacific Fleet to the Orient: An Account of the American Bluejacket Afloat and Ashore*. Boston: Roxburgh Publishing Co., 1915.

The U.S.S. "Yankee" on the Cuban Blockade, 1898. New York: Published by members of the crew, 1928.

U.S.T.S. "Monongahela" and U.S. Naval Training System. Newport, R.I.: Frank H. Child, 1892.

War Log of the U.S.S. "St. Louis," February 4, 1917, to July 2, 1919. n.p., 1919.

Wilkinson, Sydney E. *Greetings from the U.S.S. "Michigan."* Portsmouth, Va.: Whitson & Shephard Particular, 1911.

______. *The U.S.S. "Nevada" and Her Experiences in the War: A Diary*. New York: Schoen Printing Co., 1918.

"World Cruise of the U.S. Battleship Fleet, December 1907-February 1909." Scrapbook, Navy Department Library, Washington, D.C.

Young, Alfred. *The Cruise of the U.S.S. "Trenton": A True Story of the Events Happening to and on Board the U.S.S. "Trenton" during Her Shakedown Cruise, from Saturday, 24 May 1924, to Monday, 29 September 1924*. n.p., n.d.

7. ENLISTED MAGAZINES

Bluejacket, 1904-12.

Bostonian, 1909-10; superseded by *Enlisted Man*.

Bureau of Navigation Bulletin, 1922-40.

Enlisted Man, 1910-11.

Fleet Review: The Journal of the Enlisted Man, 1910-23.

Hospital Corps Quarterly, 1917-30.

Man-O'-Warsman, 1908-11.

Navy Life, 1919-20.

Orient, 1920-24.

Our Naval Apprentice, 1901-4; superseded by *Bluejacket*.

Our Navy, 1909-40.

8. ENLISTED MEMOIRS

a. Unpublished

Herget, Charles. "Dear Shipmate." Xerox copy of typescript, Turnersville, N.J., 1967, in possession of Herget.

Kendig, John L. "Log." Handwritten diary, 1907-9, in Logs, Journals, and Diaries of Officers of the United States Navy at Sea, Record Group 45, National Archives, Washington, D.C.

Kleinatland, J. S. "A Saga of World War I." Typescript, Naval History Division, Washington, D.C., n.d.

McDonagh, Clarence O'C., Sr. "Log." Xerox copy of typescript, Hughesville, Md., n.d., in possession of McDonagh.

Morris, Harry S. "Interview," conducted by Etta Belle Kitchen. Oral History Project, U.S. Naval Institute, Annapolis, Md., 1970.

b. Published

Blackford, Charles Minor. *Torpedoboat Sailor*. Annapolis, Md.: U.S. Naval Institute, 1968.

Buenzle, Fred J., with A. Grove Day. *Bluejacket: An Autobiography*. New York: W. W. Norton & Co., 1939.

Butler, Mrs. Henry F. *I Was a Yeoman (F)*. Washington: Naval Historical Foundation Publication, 1967.

Corzine, W. L. *Sailors in Nightgowns*. New York: Pageant Press, 1939.

Coyne, William M. *A Sailor's Log of Facts Not Fables*. Boston: Christopher Publishing House, 1934.

Eadie, Tom. *I Like Diving: A Professional's Story*. Boston: Houghton Mifflin Co., 1929.

Frey, Hugo. *Hugo's Odyssey: The Lure of the South Sea Islands*. Los Angeles: Institute Press, 1942.

Hancock, Joy Bright. *Lady in the Navy: A Personal Reminiscence*. Annapolis, Md.: U.S. Naval Institute, 1972.

King, Stanton H. *Dog-Watches at Sea*. Boston: Houghton Mifflin & Co., 1901.

Lederer, William J. *All the Ships at Sea*. New York: W. W. Norton, 1950.

Lee, Ping-Quan, as told to Jim Miller. *To a President's Taste: Being the Reminiscences and Recipes of the Ex-President's Steward on the Presidential Yacht*. Emmaus, Pa.: Rodale Press, 1939.

Murdock, Lawrence B. *They Also Served*. New York: Carlton Press, 1967.

Murnance, Mark Raymond. *Ground Swells: Of Sailors, Ships, and Shellac*. New York: Exposition Press, 1949.

Pagano, Dom Albert. *Bluejackets*. Boston: Meador Publishing Co., 1932.

Paynter, Jonathan H. *Joining the Navy; or, Abroad with Uncle Sam*. Hartford, Conn.: American Publishing Co., 1895.

Swift, John W. *An Iowa Boy around the World in the Navy: A True Story of Our Navy, 1898-1902*. Des Moines: Kenyon Printing & Manufacturing Co., 1902.

Wolffe, Murry. *Memoirs of a Gob*. New York: Exposition Press, 1949.

9. BOOKS

Abbot, Willis J. *Bluejackets of 1918*. New York: Dodd, Mead & Co., 1921.

Ageton, Arthur A. *Naval Leadership and the American Bluejacket*. New York: McGraw-Hill Book Co., 1944.

Allen, Edward Frank. *Keeping Our Fighters Fit for War and After*. New York: Century Co., 1918.

Battey, George M., Jr. *70,000 Miles on a Submarine Destroyer; or, the Reid Boat in the World War*. Atlanta: Webb & Vary Co., 1919.

Belknap, Reginald R. *Routine Book, Including General Features of Organization, Administration, and Ordinary Station Bills*. Annapolis, Md.: U.S. Naval Institute, 1918.

Beston, Henry B. *Full Speed Ahead: Tales from the Log of a Correspondent with Our Navy*. Garden City, N.Y.: Doubleday, Page & Co., 1919.

Beyer, Thomas. *The American Battleship and Life in the Navy*. Chicago: Laird & Lee, 1908.

Bichowsky, F. Russell. *Is the Navy Ready?* New York: Vanguard Press, 1935.

Bluejacket's Manual. 1st-3d, 5th-6th eds. 1902, 1904, 1915, 1917, 1918.

Bluejackets' Manual. 7th, 8th, 10th eds. 1928, 1938, 1940.

Buranelli, Prosper. *Maggie of the Suicide Fleet*. Garden City, N.Y.: Doubleday, Doran & Co., 1930.

Callan, John F., and Russell, A. W., comps. *Laws of the United States Relating to the Navy and Marine Corps from the Formation of the Government to 1859.* Baltimore: John Murphy & Co., 1859.

Clarke, Ida Clyde. *American Women and the World War*. New York: D. Appleton & Co., 1918.

"Commander." *Clear the Decks! A Tale of the American Navy To-day*. Philadelphia: J. B. Lippincott Co.., 1918.

Connolly, James B. *Navy Men*. New York: John Day Co., 1939.

Coontz, Robert E. *From the Mississippi to the Sea*. Philadelphia: Dorrance & Co., 1930.

______. *True Anecdotes of an Admiral*. Philadelphia: Dorrance & Co., 1935.

Cronon, E. David, ed. *The Cabinet Diaries of Josephus Daniels, 1913-1921*. Lincoln: University of Nebraska Press, 1963.

Crowder, E. H. *The Spirit of Selective Service*. New York: Century Co., 1920.

Dagget, Mabel Potter. *Women Wanted: The Story Written in Blood Red Letters on the Horizon of the Great War*. New York: George H. Doran Co., 1918.

Daniels, Josephus. *The Navy and the Nation: War-time Addresses.* New York: George H. Doran Co., 1919.

______. *Our Navy at War*. Washington: Pictorial Bureau, 1922.

______. *The Wilson Era: Years of Peace, 1910-1917.* Chapel Hill: University of North Carolina Press, 1944.

______. *The Wilson Era: Years of War and After, 1917-1923.* Chapel Hill: University of North Carolina Press, 1946.

Denlinger, Sutherland, and Gary, Charles D. *War in the Pacific: A Study of Navies, People, and Battle Problems*. New York: Robert M. McBride & Co., 1936.

Dewey, George. *Autobiography*. New York: Charles Scribner's Sons, 1913.

Evans, Holden A. *One Man's Fight for a Better Navy*. New York: Dodd, Mead & Co., 1940.

Evans, Robley D. *An Admiral's Log*. New York: Appleton, 1910.

______. *A Sailor's Log*. New York: Appleton, 1901.

Forest, F. F. *On a Cruise with Pat in the U.S. Navy*. n.p., 1920.

Fullam, William F. *Hand-Book for Infantry and Artillery, United States Navy*. Annapolis, Md.: U.S. Naval Institute, 1899.

______. *The Petty Officer's Drill Book, United States Navy.* Annapolis, Md.: U.S. Naval Institute, 1902.

______. *The Recruit's Handy Book*. Annapolis, Md.: U.S. Naval Institute, 1903.

Gallery, Daniel V. *Eight Bells and All's Well*. New York: W. W. Norton & Co., 1965.

Gatewood, James Duncan. *Naval Hygiene*. Philadelphia: P. Blakiston's Sons & Co., 1909.

Gills, W. Armistead. *The Crew or the Cruiser?* Richmond, Va.: Garrett & Massie, 1933.

Goodrich, Caspar F. *Rope Yarns from the Old Navy*. New York: Naval History Society, 1931.

Goodrich, Marcus. *Delilah*. New York: Farrar & Rinehart, 1941.

Gove, Charles A. *An Aid for Executive and Division Officers*. Annapolis, Md.: U.S. Naval Institute, 1899.

Green, Fitzhugh. *Uncle Sam's Sailors*. New York: D. Appleton & Co., 1926.

Hill, H. W., ed. *President-Elect Herbert Hoover's Good Will Cruise to Central and South America: This Being a Log of the Trip aboard the U.S.S. "Maryland."* San Francisco: Book Press, 1929.

Hoff, A. Bainbridge. *A Battle Ship's Order Book*. Annapolis, Md.: U.S. Naval Institute, 1908.

Husband, Joseph. *A Year in the Navy*. Boston: Houghton Mifflin Co., 1919.

Jackson, Orton P., and Evans, Frank E. *The Marvel Book of American Ships*. New York: Frederick A. Stokes Co., 1917.

Jones, Harry W. *A Chaplain's Experiences Ashore and Afloat: The "Texas" under Fire*. New York: A. G. Sherwood & Co., 1901.

Jones, Robert D. *With the American Fleet from the Atlantic to the Pacific*. Seattle: Harrison Publishing Co., 1908.

Kerrick, Harrison S. *Military and Naval America*. Garden City, N.Y.: Doubleday, Page & Co., 1916.

Knock, Sidney. *"Clear Lower Deck": An Intimate Study of the Men of the Royal Navy*. London: Philip Allan, 1932.

Long, John D. *The New American Navy*. 2 vols. New York: Outlook Co., 1903.

Lovette, Leland Pearsons. *Naval Customs, Traditions, and Usage*. Annapolis, Md.: U.S. Naval Institute, 1934.

Magruder, Thomas P. *The United States Navy*. Philadelphia: Dorrance & Co., 1928.

Mayo, Lawrence Shaw, ed. *America of Yesterday as Reflected in the Journal of John Davis Long*. Boston: Atlantic Monthly Press, 1923.

McKenna, Richard. *The Sand Pebbles*. New York: Harper & Row, 1962.

Miller, Roman J. *Around the World with the Battleships*. Chicago: A. C. McClurg & Co., 1909.

Millholland, Ray. *The Splinter Fleet of the Otranto Barrage*. New York: Bobbs-Merrill Co., 1936.

Neeser, Robert. *Landman's Log*. New Haven: Yale University Press, 1913.

______. *Our Many-sided Navy*. New Haven: Yale University Press, 1914.

______. *Our Navy and the Next War*. New York: Charles Scribner's Sons, 1915.

On the Pacific with Our Navy. Portland, Maine: L. H. Nelson Co., 1908.

Oswald, B. C. *Life and Humor in Our Navy*. Boston: Ball Publishing Co., 1919.

Pryor, James Chambers. *Naval Hygiene*. Philadelphia: P. Blakiston's Sons & Co., 1918.

Raff, L. Edison. *First Battalion Naval Militia, New York*. New York: Rudder Publishing Co., 1909.

Rodman, Hugh. *Yarns of a Kentucky Admiral*. Indianapolis: Bobbs-Merrill Co., 1928.

Sawyer, Frederick L. *Sons of Gunboats*. Annapolis, Md.: U.S. Naval Institute, 1946.

Schubert, Paul. *Come on "Texas."* New York: Jonathan Cape & Harrison Smith, 1930.

Selfridge, Thomas O., Jr. *Memoirs*. New York: G. P. Putnam's Sons, 1924.

Simpson, Edward. *Yarnlets: The Human Side of the Navy*. New York: G. P. Putnam's Sons, 1934.

Sims, William S. *The Victory at Sea*. Garden City, N.Y.: Doubleday, Page & Co., 1920.

Stirling, Yates. *Sea Duty: The Memoirs of a Fighting Admiral*. New York: G. P. Putnam's Sons, 1939.

Thebaud, L. H. *Naval Leadership with Some Hints to Junior Officers and Others*. Annapolis, Md.: U.S. Naval Institute, 1924.

Training Seamen, U.S. Navy. Washington: Navy Publishing Co., 1907.

Wiley, Henry A. *An Admiral from Texas*. Garden City, N.Y.: Doubleday, Doran & Co., 1934.

Willoughby, Malcolm F. *"Yankton": Yacht and Man-of-War*. Cambridge, Mass.: Crimson Printing Co., 1935.

Wilson, Joseph. *Naval Hygiene: Human Health and the Means of Preventing Disease.* Philadelphia: Lindsay & Blakiston, 1879.

Zumwalt, Elmo R., Jr. *On Watch: A Memoir*. New York: Quadrangle/New York Book Co., 1976.

10. ARTICLES

Allen, E. G. "Notes on Policy, Materiel, and Personnel." *USNIP* 41 (1915): 1489-98.

Allen, Walter H. "The Twelfth Regiment (Public Works) at Great Lakes." *USNIP* 47 (1921): 367-76.

Andrews, Adolphus. "Naval Personnel of Today." *USNIP* 62 (1936): 1402-7.

Andrews, Philip. "The Naval Training at San Francisco." *Overland*, 2d ser. 34 (December 1899): 549-55.

Baird, G. W. "The Ventilation of Ships." *USNIP* 6 (1880): 238-63.

Baker, E. R. "Detail and Duty in Guam." *Hospital Corps Quarterly* 14 (1929): 196-99.

Bakewell, Charles M. "Moral Training in Preparation for War." *USNIP* 40 (1914): 157-76.

"A Battleship That Will Never Sail the Seven Seas." *Scientific American* 116 (June 9, 1917): 569.

Beach, Edward L. "The Training Ship." *USNIP* 28 (1902): 21-38.

Bedford, S. R. "Making a Smart Ship." *USNIP* 55 (1929): 765-66.

Belknap, Reginald R. "A Captain to His Crew." *USNIP* 47 (1921): 1857-68.

Bieber, B. B. "A Proposed System of Punishment for Certain Offenses against Navy Regulations." *USNIP* 30 (1904): 201-2.

Blackmum, G. G. "Living Conditions in Guam." *Hospital Corps Quarterly* 11 (1927): 245-51.

Blue, Victor. "Converted Yachts or Small Gunboats for Training Landsmen." *USNIP* 28 (1902): 221-28.

Bonaparte, Charles J. "Experiences of a Cabinet Officer under Roosevelt." *Century* 79 (March 1910): 752-58.

Bowman, J. Beatrice. "Public Health Nursing in the Navy." *American Journal of Public Health* 17 (1927): 541-42.

Brandt, E. S. R. "A Four-to-Seven Year Enlistment." *USNIP* 50 (1924): 771-78.

Campbell, Nicholas H. "The Negro in the Navy." *Colored American Magazine* 6 (June 1903).

Carbaugh, H. C. "The Contract of Enlistment and Its Violation in the U.S. Army." *Army and Navy Life* 10 (1907): 177-95.

Chadwick, F. E. "Letter" and "Discussion" of letter. *USNIP* 27 (1901): 269-89, 749-50, and 28 (1902): 221-28.

Cleve, Joseph C. Van. "The Complete Recruiter." *USNIP* 58 (1932): 1627-30.

Connely, Willard. "Making Sailors without Ships." *Independent* 92 (November 10, 1917): 83-84, 299-300.

Coolidge, Julian Lowell. "Naval Training at Harvard." *Harvard Graduates' Magazine* 26 (1917): 202-8.

Corey, Herbert. "Across the Equator with the American Navy." *National Geographic Magazine* 39 (June 1921): 571-624.

Costello, Charles A. "The Principal Defects Found in Persons Examined for Service in the United States Navy." *American Journal of Public Health* 7 (1917): 489-92.

Cox, Leonard M. "The Enlisted Man's Annapolis." *USNIP* 43 (1917): 655-63.

Cramner, Gilbert. "The Making of a Man-o'-Warsman." *Ainslee's Magazine* 2 (September 1898): 101-7.

Crank, R. K. "The Navy as a Career." *Forum* 56 (November 1916): 629-32.

Cummings, D. E. "Enlisted Training in the Navy." *USNIP* 55 (1929): 878-86.
Cummings, Duncan. "Promotion in the U.S. Navy." *Chambers' Journal*, 6th ser. 75 (1898): 641.
Cunningham, A. C. "The Development of the Norfolk Navy Yard." *USNIP* 36 (1910): 221-37.
Daniels, Josephus. "Education of the Naval Life." *Journal of Education* 78 (1913): 260.
______. "A Message to the Boys of America." *St. Nicholas* 45 (July 1918): 785.
______. "Training Our Bluejackets for Peace." *Independent* 76 (December 11, 1913): 490-92.
______. "Venereal Disease in the Navy." *Social Hygiene* 1 (1915): 480-84.
Dawson, Dio L. "Battle Practice for the U.S. Fleet." *Overland Monthly*, n.s. 70 (September 1917): 269-78.
Decker, Benton C. "The Consolidated Mess of the Crew of the U.S.S. *Indiana*." *USNIP* 23 (1897): 463-67.
Delehanty, Daniel. "A Proposed System of Messing the Crews of Our Men-of-War." *USNIP* 14 (1888): 739-49.
Dillingham, Albert C. "How Shall We Induce Our Men to Continue in the Navy?" *USNIP* 35 (1909): 1919-28.
______. "Methods Employed at Training Stations for Training Apprentice Seamen for the Fleet." *USNIP* 33 (1907): 137-51.
______. "A Personnel Reserve for the Naval Service." *USNIP* 42 (1916): 1889-922.
______. "Training of the Personnel of the Fleet for Battle." *USNIP* 37 (1911): 209-15.
______. "U.S. Naval Training Service." *USNIP* 36 (1910): 343-74.
Dixon, B. F. "Excerpts from a Gunboat Cruise." *Hospital Corps Quarterly* 11 (1927): 1-28.
______. "The Romance of Enlisted Doctors." *Hospital Corps Quarterly* 9 (1925): 21-26.
______. "'Tin Cans.'" *Hospital Corps Quarterly* 12 (1928): 147-52.
Durr, Ernest. "The Training of Recruits." *USNIP* 43 (1917): 99-123.
Dyer, George P. "The Modern General Mess." *USNIP* 32 (1906): 621-43.
Eberle, E. W. "Discussion" of "The Training of Landsmen," by H. S. Knapp. *USNIP* 29 (1903): 230-33.
Exton, William, Jr. "Motion Picture Training Films in the Navy." *USNIP* 59 (1943): 933-38.
Farquhar, N. H. "Inducements for Retaining Trained Seamen in the Navy and Best System of Rewards for Long and Faithful Service." *USNIP* 11 (1885): 175-206.
Fenner, E. B. "Discipline." *USNIP* 47 (1921): 1371-85.
Flannery, V. L. "Pharmacist's Mate's School." *Hospital Corps Quarterly* 11 (1927): 32-34.
Folb, M. B. "Reminiscences of Isolated Duty at Cape Hatteras." *Hospital Corps Quarterly* 11 (1927): 257-63.
Foster, E. D. "Cafeteria Afloat." *USNIP* 63 (1937): 19-24.
Fullam, William F. "Absence Over Leave in the Fleet." *USNIP* 37 (1911): 1103-12.
______. "The Employment of Petty Officers in the Navy." *USNIP* 28 (1902): 467-73.
______. "The Organization, Training, and Discipline of the Navy Personnel as Viewed from the Ship." *USNIP* 22 (1896): 83-116.
______. "Street Riot Drill." *USNIP* 20 (1894): 169-76.
______. "The System of Naval Training and Discipline Required to Promote Efficiency and Attract Americans." *USNIP* 16 (1890): 473-536.
______. "The Training of Landsmen for the Navy." *USNIP* 28 (1902): 475-84.
Fullinwider, S. P. "The Fleet and Its Personnel." *USNIP* 30 (1904): 1-29.
Gallery, Philip D. "The Naval Academy Preparatory Class." *USNIP* 63 (1937): 276-79.
Gibbons, John H., and Barnard, Charles. "A School Afloat." *St Nicholas* 12 (July 1885): 678-85.
Gibson, William. "Life on Board a Man-of-War." *Harper's New Monthly Magazine* 46 (March 1873): 481-94.

Gilmer, F. H. "Psychology and the Navy." *USNIP* 47 (1921): 77-79.
Godfrey, Vincent H. "Permanency of Personnel: A Suggested Method of Approaching the Ideal." *USNIP* 61 (1935): 529-32.
Goodrich, Caspar F. "Desertion in the Navy." *USNIP* 31 (1905): 811-21.
______. "Naval Education." *USNIP* 5 (1879): 323-44.
Goodrich, Charles F. "Hygienic Notes on Ships' Bilges." *USNIP* 2 (1876): 93-99.
Gosnell, H. A. "World War Losses of the United States Navy." *USNIP* 63 (1937): 630-42.
Grimes, Will. "American Samoa." *Hospital Corps Quarterly* 12 (1928): 153-56.
Gulliver, L. J. "Better Iron Men for the Navy." *USNIP* 56 (1930): 527-30.
Haile, J. R. "One View of Our Enlisted Personnel Problem." *USNIP* 55 (1929): 284-88.
Hatch, Charles B. "The U.S. Naval Disciplinary Barracks, Port Royal, South Carolina." *USNIP* 38 (1912): 1379-84.
Heverly, J. B. "Survey Duty in the Tropics." *Hospital Corps Quarterly* 12 (1928): 17-21.
Hilton, Ordway. "The Navy Shore Patrol." *Journal of Criminal Law and Criminology* 34 (1943): 122-26.
Hoffman, J. Ogden. "The Job." *USNIP* 48 (1922): 1915-29.
______. "Recruiting Salesmanship." *USNIP* 47 (1921): 825-48.
Hood, John. "Desertion from the Navy." *USNIP* 31 (1905): 367-81.
Howland, Harold. "The Amateur Sea Dogs." *Independent* 88 (October 2, 1916): 18-20.
Hughes, James Perley. "Making Sailors." *Sunset* 59 (July 1927): 26-28, 68.
Hunt, Fred A. "Yerba Buena Island Naval Training Station." *Overland Monthly*, n.s. 62 (July 1913): 65-74.
Jackson, Orton P., and Evans, Frank E. "The Happy Ship." *St. Nicholas* 44 (August 1917): 918-23.
______. "The Training of a Man-o'-War's-Man." *St. Nicholas* 44 (July 1917): 833-37.
Johnston, Marbury. "Discipline in the Navy." *USNIP* 31 (1905): 367-81.
Johnston, R. Z. "Arms and the Man." *USNIP* 54 (1928): 26-30.
Joslin, Theodore G. "Another Adams Takes over the Helm." *World's Work* 58 (December 1929): 75-79.
Kerr, W. M. "Duties of Medical Officers and Hospital Corpsmen on Shore Patrol in a Foreign Country." *Hospital Corps Quarterly* 5 (1921): 29-34.
Kirwan, B. E. "A Cruise in Haiti, the Black Republic." *Hospital Corps Quarterly* 11 (1927): 175-82.
Knapp, Harry S. "The Training of Landsmen." *USNIP* 28 (1902): 895-909.
Krause, R. E. "Morale for Our 'New Navy.'" *USNIP* 47 (1921): 519-24.
Lane, Richard. "Recruits and Ratings." *USNIP* 61 (1935): 320-21.
Lankford, J. F., and Huntsinger, F. O. "Apprehending Repeaters." *Hospital Corps Quarterly* 5 (1921): 45-46.
Larsen, M. A. "Duty in American Samoa." *Hospital Corps Quarterly* 11 (1927): 183-85.
"The Laws of Hygiene as Applied to Berthing, Messing, Ventilation, and Interior Arrangements of Men-of-War." A discussion by the Naval Institute, Boston Branch, in *USNIP* 6 (1880): 349-54.
Leavitt, Julian. "The War Record of American Jews." *Sentinel* 3 (January 1919): 1-3.
Luce, Stephen B. "Manning of Our Navy and Mercantile Marine." *USNIP* 1 (1874): 17-37.
______. "Naval Training." *USNIP* 16 (1890): 367-96.
______. "Naval Training, II." *USNIP* 36 (1890): 102-3.
McCrackin, Alexander. "Desertion and the Bertillion System for Identification of Persons." *USNIP* 16 (1890): 361-66.
McEathron, E. D. "Selection of 'Strikers.'" *USNIP* 60 (1934): 655-56.
McIntosh, K. C. "Some Notes on Training Men for Clerical and Commissary Rates." *USNIP* 45 (1919): 223-32.

MacKaye, Milton. "The Modern Bluejacket." *Outlook and Independent* 152 (July 1929): 532-33, 558.

McNabb, George. "Reminiscences of an Influenza Epidemic." *Hospital Corps Quarterly* 12 (1928): 91-93.

Magruder, T. P. "The Enlisted Personnel." *USNIP* 36 (1910): 102-23.

Mann, W. L. "An Attempted Classification of the Personnel of the U.S. Naval Disciplinary Barracks, Port Royal, S.C." *USNIP* 39 (1913): 1085-95.

Marshall, Evard B. "The Life of a Naval Volunteer." *Scientific American* 115 (September 23, 1916): 279, 288-89.

Mayo, C. B. "The Sixth Division of the Bureau of Navigation." *Social Hygiene* 5 (1919): 461-72.

Moses, Stanford E. "Preventive Discipline." *USNIP* 49 (1923): 1442-46.

Munsterberg, Hugo. "Psychology and the Navy." *North American Review* 197 (1913): 159-80.

"The Navy as a Career for Young Men." *Scientific American* 115 (November 11, 1916): 432.

"Navy Pay and a Fifty-Cent Dollar." *Scientific American* 121 (November 8, 1919): 456.

Neeser, Robert W. "The American Fleet in Being: The Battleship as an Educational Institution." *Navy* 7 (September 1913): 357-63.

Newsom, Joel. "Results vs. Training." *USNIP* 65 (1939): 20-24.

Niblack, A. P. "The Enlistment, Training, and Organization of Crews for Our New Ships." *USNIP* 17 (1891): 3-49.

Norris, Walther B. "The Educational Development of the Navy." *Education* 35 (1915): 503-10.

Noyes, B. "The Training Ship *Minnesota*." *USNIP* 6 (1880): 98-108.

Palmer, Wayne Francis. "Men of the Navy." *New Outlook* 163 (January 1934): 34-39.

Parkes, W. M. "Training of Enlisted Men of the Engineer Force." *USNIP* 13 (1887): 341-44.

Phelps, W. W. "Naval Industrialism, Naval Commercialism, and Naval Discipline." *USNIP* 39 (1913): 509-50.

Potter, Frank H. "A Repair Shop for Men." *Outlook* 120 (December 4, 1918): 539-40.

______. "A School for Bluejackets: The Educational Work of the United States Navy." *Outlook* 104 (July 26, 1913): 694-705.

Pringle, Henry F. "Wilbur—Benevolent Blunderer." *Outlook* 148 (January 25, 1928): 123-26, 153.

Ray, H. J. "The Nation in Arms." *USNIP* 60 (1934): 205-12.

Reuterdahl, Henry. "How the American Artists Are Helping Their Navy." *Scientific American* 116 (June 2, 1917): 552, 556.

Riddle, Truman Post. "Recreational Camps for Enlisted Men." *USNIP* 63 (1937): 1765-76.

Rideing, William H. "Jack Ashore." *Harper's New Monthly Magazine* 47 (July 1873): 161-70.

Riggs, Charles E. "A Study of Venereal Prophylaxis in the Navy: An Analysis of Results Observed at the Naval Training Station, Norfolk, Virginia." *Social Hygiene* 3 (1917): 299-312.

Robinson, Helen Ring. "'Squads Right! Squads Left!' Making Sailors a Thousand Miles Inland." *Independent* 95 (July 1918): 120-21, 127.

Roden, E. K. "Our Navy as a Schoolhouse: Success of the New System in the First Year of Its Operation." *Scientific American* 114 (February 26, 1916): 218-19.

Roosevelt, Franklin D. "'The Naval Plattsburg': What the Navy Hopes to Obtain from Its First Civilian Training Cruise." *Outlook* 113 (June 28, 1916): 495-501.

Ruddock, Stella Beehler. "'Taggin' Ship.'" *Scribner's Magazine* 77 (February 1925): 193-99.

Satterlee, Herbert L. "Our Great National University." *North American Review* 195 (February 1912): 266-70.
Shockley, L. R. "Prophylactic Stations in China." *Hospital Corps Quarterly* 13 (1929): 119-22.
Shoemaker, W. R. "Some Personnel Accomplishments." *USNIP* 52 (1926): 1936-40.
Sigsbee, Mrs. Charles D. "Pets in the Navy." *St. Nicholas* 26 (November 1898): 61-64.
Skillman, J. H. "The Evolution of the Navy Ration." *USNIP* 60 (1934): 1678-81.
Slade, William Adams. "Books and Boys in Portsmouth Prison." *Survey* 43 (December 27, 1919): 309-10.
Spears, John R. "The Life of a Naval Apprentice." *Chatauguan* 13 (1891): 57-61.
Stapler, John. "Gunboats." *USNIP* 42 (1916): 861-72.
"State Medicine, Navy Style." *American Mercury* 43 (January 1939): 33-39.
Stevens, L. M. "An Angle of Recruiting." *USNIP* 55 (1929): 217-18.
Stevens, William O. "Sailor Life on a Man-of-War." *St. Nicholas* 34 (July 1907): 810-15.
Talbot, Melvin V. "The East through a Port Hole: Being Random Notes from the Log of a China Coast Cruiser." *North American Review* 229 (June 1930): 674-82.
Tardy, W. B. "The First Naval Training Cruise: Its Accomplishment and Portent." *USNIP* 43 (1917): 505-57.
Taylor, J. S. "The Social Status of the Sailor." *Social Hygiene* 4 (1918): 157-78.
Thom, J. C. "Rebuilding the Navy's Enlisted Personnel and Reestablishing Its Morale and Spirit." *USNIP* 46 (1920): 1627-36.
Thompson, John Donald. "Feeding the Crew of a Battleship." *Scientific American* 143 (December 1930): 443-45.
Tisdale, Ryland D. "Naval Apprentices, Inducements, Enlisting, and Training. The Seaman Branch of the Navy." *USNIP* 22 (1896): 265-95.
Todd, Forde A. "Present Vital Need of a Navy Personnel Policy." *USNIP* 45 (1919): 377-82.
Turnbull, Archibald Douglas. "Economy and Naval Personnel." *North American Review* 215 (April 1922): 459-63.
______. "Our Navy Divers." *St. Nicholas* 55 (June 1928): 638-40, 665-66.
Turpin, Walter S. "Training Our Gun Captains." *USNIP* 28 (1902): 885-94.
Vail, Stevens. "Making a Man of War's Man." *Junior Munsey* 11 (December 1901): 361-68.
Watts, Marion Brown. "The Service Wife." *American Mercury* 25 (February 1932): 160-66.
Wheelis, John M., Jr. "A Time Study of Morbidity and Mortality in the United States Navy." *American Journal of Public Health* 28 (1938): 1291-97.
Williams, Charles Richard. "On the History of Discipline in the Navy." *USNIP* 44 (1919): 355-76.
Williams, Roy F. "Lay Aft All Civilian Volunteers." *Scientific American* 115 (September 23, 1916): 278-79.
Wyckoft, A. B. "The United States Naval Apprentice System." *Scribner's Magazine* 10 (1891): 563-74.

SECONDARY WORKS

1. BOOKS

Albion, Robert G. *Naval and Maritime History: An Annotated Bibliography*. 3d ed. Mystic, Conn.: Munson Institute of American Maritime History, 1963.
Alden, John D. *Flush Decks and Four Pipes*. Annapolis, Md.: U.S. Naval Institute, 1965.

Bishop, Joseph Bucklin. *Charles Joseph Bonaparte: His Life and Public Services*. New York: Charles Scribner's Sons, 1922.

Daniels, Jonathan. *The End of Innocence*. Philadelphia: J. B. Lippincott Co., 1954.

Davis, Arthur Kyle, ed. *Virginia Communities in Wartime*. Publications of the Virginia War History Commission, vol 6. Richmond: Virginia War History Commission, 1926.

Dessez, Eunice C. *The First Enlisted Women, 1917-1918*. Philadelphia: Dorrance & Co., 1955.

Drury, Clifford M. *The History of the Chaplain Corps, United States Navy*. 6 vols. Washington: GPO, 1949-60.

Foner, Jack D. *Blacks and the Military in American History: A New Perspective*. New York: Praeger Publishers, 1974.

______. *The United States Soldier between Two Wars: Army Life and Reforms, 1865-1898*. New York: Humanities Press, 1970.

Freidel, Frank. *Franklin D. Roosevelt: The Apprenticeship*. Boston: Little Brown & Co., 1952.

______. *Franklin D. Roosevelt: The Ordeal*. Boston: Little Brown & Co., 1954.

Frothingham, Thomas G. *The Naval History of the World War: The United States Navy in the War, 1917-1918*. Cambridge: Harvard University Press, 1926.

Gleaves, Albert. *Life and Letters of Rear Admiral Stephen B. Luce*. New York: G. P. Putnam's Sons, 1925.

______, ed. *The Life of an American Sailor: Rear Admiral William Hemsley Emory, United States Navy, from His Letters and Memoirs*. New York: George H. Doran Co., 1923.

Hammond, Paul Y. *Organizing for Defense: The American Military in the Twentieth Century*. Princeton: Princeton University Press, 1961.

Hart, Robert A. *The Great White Fleet: Its Voyage around the World, 1907-1909*. Boston: Little, Brown & Co., 1965.

Healey, James C. *Foc's'le and Glory-Hole: A Study of the Merchant Seaman and His Occupation*. New York: Merchant Marine Publishers Association, 1936.

Henningsen, Henning. *Crossing the Equator: Sailors' Baptism and Other Initiation Rites*. Copenhagen, Denmark: Munksgaard, 1961.

Hohman, Elmo Paul. *History of American Merchant Seamen*. Hamden, Conn.: Shoe String Press, 1956.

Hopkins, C. Howard. *History of the Y.M.C.A. in North America*. New York: Association Press, 1951.

Howe, M. A. DeWolfe. *George von Lengerke Meyer: His Life and Public Services*. New York: Dodd, Mead & Co., 1919.

Johnson, Robert Erwin. *Thence round Cape Horn: The Story of United States Naval Forces on Pacific Station, 1818-1923*. Annapolis, Md.: U.S. Naval Institute, 1963.

Kaplan, Louis. *A Bibliography of American Autobiographies*. Madison: University of Wisconsin Press, 1961.

Karsten, Peter. *The Naval Aristocracy: The Golden Age of Annapolis and the Emergence of Modern American Navalism*. New York: Free Press, 1972.

Langley, Harold D. *Social Reform in the United States Navy, 1798-1862*. Urbana: University of Illinois Press, 1967.

Livermore, Seward W. *Politics Is Adjourned: Woodrow Wilson and the War Congress, 1916-18*. Middleton, Conn.: Wesleyan University Press, 1966.

Lloyd, Christopher. *The British Seaman, 1200-1860*. London: Collins, 1968.

Lockwood, Charles A., and Adamson, Hans Christian. *Tragedy at Honda*. Philadelphia: Chilton Co., 1960.

Lott, Arnold S. *Brave Ship, Brave Men*. Indianapolis: Bobbs-Merrill Co., 1964.

Merrill, James M., ed. *Quarter Deck and Fo'c'sle: The Exciting Story of the Navy*. Chicago: Rand McNally & Co., 1963.

Mitchell, Donald W. *History of the Modern American Navy from 1883 through Pearl Harbor*. New York: Alfred A. Knopf, 1946.

Morison, Elting E. *Admiral Sims and the Modern American Navy*. Boston: Houghton Mifflin Co., 1942.

Morrison, Joseph L. *Josephus Daniels: The Small-d Democrat*. Chapel Hill: University of North Carolina Press, 1966.

Moskos, Charles C., Jr. *The American Enlisted Man: The Rank and File in Today's Military*. New York: Russell Sage Foundation, 1970.

Nelson, Dennis D. *The Integration of the Negro into the U.S. Navy*. New York: Farrar, Straus & Young, 1951.

Paullin, Charles Oscar. *Paullin's History of Naval Administration, 1775-1911: A Collection of Articles from the U.S. Naval Institute "Proceedings."* Annapolis, Md.: U.S. Naval Institute, 1968.

Pennel, Grace F. *Monograph on Military Personnel and Related Records of the War Department, 1912-39*. St. Louis: National Personnel Records Center, Military Reference Branch, 1966.

Rickey, Don, Jr. *Forty Miles a Day on Beans and Hay: The Enlisted Soldier Fighting the Indian Wars*. Norman: University of Oklahoma Press, 1963.

Skallerup, Harry R. *Books Afloat and Ashore: A History of Books, Libraries, and Reading among Seamen during the Age of Sail*. Hamden, Conn.: Archon Books, 1974.

Smith, Richard K. *The Airships "Akron" and "Macon": Flying Aircraft Carriers of the United States Navy*. Annapolis, Md.: U.S. Naval Institute, 1965.

Sprout, Harold and Margaret. *The Rise of American Naval Power, 1776-1918*. Princeton: Princeton University Press, 1939.

Sweetman, Jack. *The Landing at Veracruz, 1914*. Annapolis, Md.: U.S. Naval Institute, 1968.

Tannenbaum, Frank. *Osborne of Sing Sing*. Chapel Hill: University of North Carolina Press, 1933.

Tolley, Kemp. *Yangtze Patrol: The U.S. Navy in China*. Annapolis, Md.: U.S. Naval Institute Press, 1971.

Turnbull, Archibald D., and Lord, Clifford L. *History of United States Naval Aviation*. New Haven: Yale University Press, 1949.

U. S. Navy Department, Office of Naval Operations. *United States Naval Aviation, 1910-1970*. Washington: GPO, 1970.

U.S. Navy Department, Office of the Chief of Naval Operations, Naval History Division. *Dictionary of American Naval Fighting Ships*. 6 vols. to date. Washington: GPO, 1959-.

______. *United States Naval History: A Bibliography*. 6th ed. Washington: GPO, 1972.

______. *U.S. Naval History Sources in the Washington Area and Suggested Research Topics*. 3d ed. Washington: GPO, 1970.

Wool, Harold. *The Military Specialist: Skilled Manpower for the Armed Forces*. Baltimore: Johns Hopkins Press, 1968.

Writers' Program, Ohio. *The Army and Navy Union, U.S.A.: A History of the Union and Its Auxiliary*. n.p.: Army and Navy Union, 1942.

2. ARTICLES

Aptheker, Herbert. "The Negro in the Union Navy." *Journal of Negro History* 32 (1947): 169-200.

Beers, Henry P. "The Bureau of Navigation, 1862-1942." *American Archivist* 6 (1943): 212-52.

Howard, Bill. "Two Centuries of Navy Jobs." *All Hands*, No. 585 (October 1965): 2-14.

Kevles, Daniels J. "Testing the Army's Intelligence: Psychologists and the Military in World War I." *Journal of American History* 55 (1968): 565-81.
Radom, Matthew. "The 'Americanization' of the U.S. Navy." *USNIP* 63 (1937): 231-34.
"Recruiting Posters, WW I." *USNIP* 98 (1972): 68-72.
Roloff, O. S. "One Hundred and Eighty Years of Naval Recruiting." *USNIP* 82 (1956): 1300-1308.

3. UNPUBLISHED STUDIES

Barboo, Samuel. "A Historical Review of the Hygiene of Shipboard Food Service in the United States Navy, 1775-1965." Ph.D. dissertation, University of California, Los Angeles, 1966.
Beers, Henry P. "Historical Sketch of the Bureau of Equipment, Navy Department." Typescript. National Archives Library, Washington, D. C., 1941.
Carter, Thomas Jerrell. "Injury Statistics, Enlisted Personnel, United States Navy, 1935-1936." Ph.D. dissertation, Johns Hopkins University, 1940.
Germain, Dom Aidan Henry. "Catholic Military and Naval Chaplains, 1776-1917." Ph.D. dissertation, Catholic University, 1929.
Jenkins, Innis LaRoche. "Josephus Daniels and the Navy Department, 1913-1916: A Study in Military Administration." Ph.D. dissertation, University of Maryland, 1960.
Lang, Frederick Robert. "A Ten Year Study of Gonorrhea in the United States Navy, 1929-1938, Inclusive." Ph.D. dissertation, Johns Hopkins University, 1941.
Mast, George Winfield. "A Ten Year Study of Syphilis in the United States Navy, 1929-1938, Inclusive." Ph.D. dissertation, University of Iowa, 1942.
U.S. Navy Department, Bureau of Naval Personnel, Enlisted Services and Records Division. "A Brief History of the Enlisted Service Number System." Typescript. Navy Department Library, Washington, D.C., 1953.
U.S. Navy Department, Bureau of Naval Personnel, Historical Section. "United States Naval Administration in World War II, Bureau of Naval Personnel: Enlisted Personnel." Typescript. Navy Department Library, Washington, D.C., 1945.
______. "United States Naval Administration in World War II, Bureau of Naval Personnel: Structure of the Bureau." Typescript. Navy Department Library, Washington, D.C., 1945.
U.S. Navy Department, Bureau of Naval Personnel, Recorder, Permanent Board for Control of the Enlisted Rating Structure. *Compilation of Enlisted Ratings and Apprenticeships, U.S. Navy, 1775 to the Present*. Mimeographed. Naval Academy Library, Annapolis, Md., September 1967.
Wheelis, John M., Jr. "Communicable Diseases in the United States Navy, 1935-1936; Incidence by Length of Service." Ph.D. Dissertation, Johns Hopkins University, 1940.
White, William Bruce. "The Military and the Melting Pot: The American Army and Minority Groups, 1865-1924." Ph.D. dissertation, University of Wisconsin, 1968.

Index

About the Author

Frederick S. Harrod, assistant professor of history at the U. S. Naval Academy, Annapolis, Maryland, specializes in American military and social history.